THE GLOBAL EXPERIENCE

Readings in World History to 1500

VOLUME I

Second Edition

THE GLOBAL EXPERIENCE

Readings in World History to 1500

VOLUME I

Edited by
PHILIP F. RILEY
FRANK A. GEROME
ROBERT L. LEMBRIGHT
HENRY A. MYERS
CHONG K. YOON
James Madison University

Special Contributor
MARY LOUISE LOE

Prentice Hall
Englewood Cliffs, New Jersey 07632

Library of Congress Cataloging-in-Publication Data

The Global experience / edited by Philip F. Riley ... [et al.] ;
  special contributor, Mary Louise Loe.
      p.   cm.
    Contents: v. 1. Readings in world history to 1500 — v.
2. Readings in world history since 1500.
    ISBN 0-13-356981-0 (v. 1). — ISBN 0-13-356999-3 (v. 2)
    1. World history. I. Riley, Philip F.
  D20.G56 1992
  909—dc20   91-22738
                                                       CIP

Acquisitions editor: *Steve Dalphin*
Production editor: *Linda B. Pawelchak*
Supervisory editor: *Joan L. Stone*
Copy editor: *Linda B. Pawelchak*
Cover design: *Ray Lundgren Graphics, Ltd.*
Prepress buyer: *Kelly Behr*
Manufacturing buyer: *Mary Ann Gloriande*
Editorial assistant: *Caffie Risher*

 © 1992, 1987 by Prentice Hall Career & Technology
Prentice-Hall, Inc.
A Paramount Communications Company
Englewood Cliffs. New Jersey 07632

Printed in the United States of America

10 9 8

ISBN 0-13-356981-0

Prentice-Hall International (UK) Limited, *London*
Prentice-Hall of Australia Pty. Limited, *Sydney*
Prentice-Hall Canada Inc., *Toronto*
Prentice-Hall Hispanoamericana, S.A., *Mexico*
Prentice-Hall of India Private Limited, *New Delhi*
Prentice-Hall of Japan, Inc., *Tokyo*
Simon & Schuster Asia Pte. Ltd., *Singapore*
Editora Prentice-Hall do Brasil, Ltda., *Rio de Janeiro*

For
Raymond C. Dingledine, Jr.
1919–1990
Teacher, Scholar, Friend

CONTENTS

Classical Civilizations   *61*

PREFACE

This anthology is a brief, balanced collection of primary materials, organized chronologically and focused on global themes.

In preparing this collection, we have been mindful of three concerns. First, any informed understanding of the world in the late twentieth century must begin with history. We believe the most useful mode of historical study — particularly for college students — is world history. Because men and women make history, the documents we have chosen depict the variety of their experiences over time on a global scale. To help students study and appreciate these experiences, we have selected excerpts from both classic texts and less familiar but equally important readings. This material illustrates patterns of global change and exchange, as well as the distinct achievements of the major civilizations.

Second, to encourage the comparative study of world history and to reinforce the underlying links between civilizations, we have organized the readings into chronological sections. By doing so we hope to underscore global patterns of development and, at the same time, permit our readers to study documents of special interest selectively.

Third, to help clarify our selections, particularly those readings that may be unfamiliar to students, we have included introductory comments as well as questions to consider. We hope this material will help students gain a better understanding of the text and connect their historical study to contemporary issues and problems.

Our students, particularly in their questions and criticisms, have shaped our work more than they know. Our colleagues at James Madison University have also helped immeasurably. Michael J. Galgano, Head, Department of History, has assisted us at every turn; he enthusiastically found us the means and time to complete this project. Martha B. Caldwell, William H. Ingham, Caroline Marshall, Daniel McFarland, and Jacqueline Walker provided insights and suggestions to make this a better book. Mary Louise Loe not only contributed the sections on Russian and Soviet history but helped us throughout our work.

Sheila Riley aided with the final editing. Debra Ryman and Gordon Miller skillfully assisted us in securing materials through interlibrary loan.

The second edition of *The Global Experience: Readings in World History* contains a number of new sections, new selections, and new translations, as well as changes in the selections published in our first edition. Among the new selections in Volume I are: A Japanese Creation Epic: *Nihongi*; A Mayan Creation Story: *Popol Vuh*; Papyrus Lansing: A Schoolbook; The Banquet of Ashurnasirpal; Widow Burning: Two Views of Sati; Guanyin: Compassion of the Bodhisattva; The Free Will: "The Burning House"; The Writings of St. Paul on Women; Tacitus, *The Annals*; Pliny the Younger, *Letters to Emperor Trajan*; M. Minucius Felix, *Octavius*; Commentaries on Islamic Law and Culture; Muslim Culture in Baghdad; The *Nibelungenlied*; Ibn Fadlan's Account of Vikings in Early Russia; Liutprand, Bishop of Cremona, *A Mission to Constantinople*; Memoirs of Usamah Ibn-Munqidh; The Rule of Saint Francis; A Father's Letter to His Sons Studying at Toulouse; Imperial Examination System; Emperor T'ai-tsung, "On the Art of Government"; Chinese Footbinding; John Pian del Carpini, *The Tartars*; Kuyuk Khan, Letter to Pope Innocent IV; The Yuan Code: Homicide; Tsunetomo Yamamoto, *Hagakure*; The Forty-Seven Ronin; Konstantin Mihailvic, *Memoirs of a Janissary*; Martin Luther at the Diet of Worms; Pero Vaz de Caminha and the Brazilian Indians; Antonio Pigafetta, *Magellan's Voyage*; and Bernal Díaz del Castillo, The Conquest of Mexico.

Among the new additions to Volume II are: Lady Mary Wortley Montague, Embassy to Constantinople; Anthony Monseratte, S.J., *Journey to the Court of Akbar*; Léonhard Euler, "Newton's Discovery of the Principle of Gravity"; Ceremonial for Visitors: Court Tribute; The Laws for the Military House (Buke Shohatto), 1615; Andrew Carnegie, *Triumphant Democracy*; "Women Miners in the English Coal Pits"; Robert Southey, "The Battle of Blenheim"; Heinrich von Treitschke, Conquest and National Greatness; Otto von Bismarck, Making German Patriotism Effective; Gandhi: Facing the British in India; First Japanese Embassy to the United States; Geisha: *Glimpse of Unfamiliar Japan*; "World War I: A Frenchman's Recollections"; Stalin, "Socialism in One Country"; Stalin *On the Draft Constitution of the U.S.S.R.*; Rudolf Hoess, "Eyewitness to Hitler's Genocide"; "Tojo Makes Plea of Self Defense"; Thomas and Margaret Melady, Statement of African Unity; Mikhail Gorbachev and *Perestroika*; Václav Havel, Address to Congress; Richard von Weizsäcker, "The Day of German Unity"; William F. Buckley, "Human Rights and American Foreign Policy"; Gustavo Gutiérrez, *A Theology of Liberation*; The Second "Maekawa" Report.

In making these revisions, we were guided by the advice and criticism of our colleagues, J. Chris Arndt, Gordon M. Fisher, Steven W. Guerrier, Raymond M. Hyser, and David Owusu-Ansah; as well as Robert C. Figueira, of Saint Mary's

College, Winona, Minnesota ; Donald C. Holsinger of Seattle Pacific University ; and John O. Hunwick of Northwestern University; and two reviewers—Norman R. Bennett, Boston University; and Charles Gruber, Marshall University. We are very grateful for all their criticism and we would appreciate your comments as well. Send your comments to Philip F. Riley, Department of History, James Madison University, Harrisonburg, VA 22807.

THE GLOBAL EXPERIENCE

Readings in World History to 1500

VOLUME I

EARLY CIVILIZATIONS

Global Conceptions of the Cosmos

When civilization developed, people sought to understand the physical universe and human existence through poetic myths and ritual dramas. These creation myths parallel the human experience of birth ; a god or gods rose out of a primordial ocean or void to create the physical universe. Humanity could be formed from tears, blood, or the earth itself with the duties of worship and obedience to the will of the god or gods. Once these myths had been created, they were celebrated at New Year's festivals, harvest festivals, or in funeral rites by religious leaders or monarchs whose right to govern was substantiated by these myths.

The most familiar Egyptian creation myth begins with the sun god Ra of Heliopolis, who created the world and other gods. Ra (also called Atum or Khepri) made a place for himself to stand while he created the physical universe, gods and goddesses, and finally humans. The Egyptians kings (pharaohs) of the Old Kingdom (2700–2200 B.C.) traced their right to rule and their funeral practices to Ra and his descendants.

Around 3100 B.C., the Sumerians of Mesopotamia created their own mythology of the universe. Their chief god was called An, the vault of heaven, who was pushed aside by his own son, the storm god Enlil, who actually created the universe. Yet, when the Semitic-speaking peoples of Babylonia arose, c. 2000 B.C., they replaced Enlil with their own chief god, Marduk, who became the hero of the *Enuma Elish*, or creation myth, which was celebrated each spring by the Babylonian kings during the New Year's festival.

The *Enuma Elish* begins with a watery void called Apsu (fresh water), into which many gods and goddesses are born. When Apsu was disturbed by their noisy clamor and decided to kill them, they decided to murder Apsu before he could destroy them. In response, Apsu's consort, Tiamat (Chaos or the sea), unleashed many terrible monsters against the murderers. The gods turned to Marduk who defeated Tiamat and her allies. Marduk then cut Tiamat in half and used her parts to create the earth and sky. He then ordered the lesser gods to create the universe — Mesopotamia — and finally humanity.

The best-known creation myth of the Hebrews, Genesis, developed between 1000–400 B.C. from oral and written traditions. Although the Hebrews were influenced by previous creation stories, they contributed the concept that there was only one creator god, who stood outside time and space, from whose thought or Word the universe began.

In the Hebrew account, God made a conscious decision to create human beings who were placed in the Garden of Eden. Evil came to this idyllic paradise when a snake persuaded Adam and Eve to disobey God's law and to eat of the Tree of Knowledge. For their original sin, or willful disobedience, humans were forever driven from Paradise.

In the East, the Japanese creation myth *Nihongi* (A.D. 712) contains similar elements to those of the Mediterranean world. Before the separation of earth and heaven, there was a chaotic egg-like mass until the divine couple Izanagi and Izanami, male and female, created the islands of Japan. Once this had been accomplished, the divine pair made their beautiful daughter, the Sun-Goddess, ruler of Heaven. Her authority was soon challenged by her wicked and rude brother, Mikoto, whose actions so disturbed the Sun-Goddess that she retired into a cave, turning day into night until she was tricked into returning. Eventually, the Sun-Goddess's descendants ruled the earth as the emperors.

From the Americas, the Quiché tribe, a part of the Mayan civilization, had their own cosmic myth called the *Popol Vuh* (A.D. 300–1000?). This account begins in the primordial waters where a group of gods, called the Forefathers, planned and created the universe and humans, who had been made out of wood, not flesh. Soon however, the gods decided to destroy these people because they did not honor nor think of their creators. The gods then created true humans; yet some of the predecessors survived as the human-faced monkeys in the forests.

1

An Egyptian Creation Story: The Creation According to Ra

The Egyptian religion developed during the Old Kingdom (3100–2200 B.C.). The following selection was created by the priests of Ra whose central sanctuary was located in Heliopolis, near the city of Memphis. In this account, the great god Ra emerges from the waters of Nun and through an act of will or masturbation creates the Egyptian universe.

QUESTIONS TO CONSIDER

1. What are the similarities and differences in the Egyptian creation myth as compared to those of the Babylonians (see Reading 2), the Hebrews (see Reading 3), the Japanese (see Reading 4), and the Mayans (see Reading 5)?
2. Compare the role or duties of humans in Egypt with those in the other creation accounts. Are there any similarities?
3. How did these myths support governmental authority?

The Book of Knowing the Creations of Ra and of Smiting Down Apophis.[1] The words to be spoken:

Thus said the Universal Lord after he had come into being: I am the one who came into being as Khepri.[2] When I came into being, being [itself] came into being. All beings came into being after I came into being. Manifold were the beings from that which came forth from my mouth. Not yet had the heaven come into being; not yet had the earth come into being; not yet had the ground been created or creeping things in this place. I raised some creatures in the Primordial Waters as [still] inert things, when I had not yet found a place upon which I could stand.[3] I found it favorable in my heart, I conceived with my sight. I made all forms, I being all alone. Not yet had I spat out what was Shu,[4] not yet had I emitted what was Tefnut,[5] not yet had there come into being one who could act together with me.

I conceived in my own heart; there came into being a vast number of forms of divine beings, as forms of children and forms of their children.[6]

I it was who aroused desire with my fist; I masturbated with my hand, and I spat it from my own mouth. I spat it out as Shu; I spewed it out as Tefnut. By my father Nun, the Primordial Waters, were they brought up, my Eye[7] watching after them since the aeons when they were distant from me.

After I had come into being as the only god, there were three gods aside from me.[8] I came into being in this earth, but Shu and Tefnut rejoiced in Nun, the Primordial Waters, in which they existed. They brought back to me my Eye which had followed after them. After I had united my members, I wept over them, and that was the coming into being of mankind, from the tears which came forth from my Eye.[9] . . . And so I advanced its place onto my brow, and when it was exercising rule over this entire land, its wrath fell away completely, for I had replaced that which had been taken from it.

Joseph Kaster, trans. and ed., "The Creation According to Ra," in *Wings of the Falcon: Life and Thought of Ancient Egypt* (New York: Holt, Rinehart and Winston, 1968), pp. 54–57. Copyright © 1968 by Joseph Kaster. Reprinted by permission of Henry Holt and Company, Inc. This Egyptian account of creation was taken from the third book, called *The Book of Smiting Down Apophis,* of the Bremner-Rhind Papyrus in the British Museum.

1. Each night as Ra, the sun, set in the west, he passed beneath the earth and was opposed by a huge serpent called Apophis. Ra defeated Apophis daily and emerged in the eastern horizon.

2. Throughout this text, there is a continual play on the verb *kheper,* "come, or bring into being," and *Khepri-Kheprer,* "he who comes into being, or brings into being." *Khepri* is depicted as a scarab beetle in Egyptian art.

3. Before he had created the mound of earth called the Primeval Hill or *benben.*

4. Male god of air and light.

5. Goddess of moisture and wife of Shu.

6. Note here the theme of creation by the intellectual conception from the mind of Ra.

7. Ra sent his first Eye to look after his children and replaced it with another eye. When the original Eye returned, it was angry but Ra pacified his Eye by transforming it into the uraeus-serpent, a cobra which he placed on his brow.

8. Nun, Shu, and Tefnut.

9. The Egyptians loved puns. The word for "mankind" is *remet,* and the word for "tears" is *remyt.*

I came forth from among the roots,[10] and I created all creeping things, and all that exists among them. Then by Shu and Tefnut were Geb and Nut[11] begotten, and by Geb and Nut were begotten Osiris, Horus, Set, Isis, and Nephthys[12] from the womb, one after the other, and they begot their multitudes in this land.

2

A Babylonian Creation Epic: *Enuma Elish*

This epic of creation is thought to have been created sometime during the second millenium B.C., in the Old Babylonian Period. After recounting the struggle of Marduk against the forces of chaos, it describes the creation of the physical universe.

QUESTIONS TO CONSIDER

1. What comparisons can you make between the *Enuma Elish* and the other creation myths?
2. What does Tiamat represent and why did she wish revenge?
3. Who actually created world order in this myth?

When on high the heaven had not been named,
Firm ground below had not been called by name,
Naught but primordial Apsu, their begetter,
(And) Mummu-Tiamat, she who bore them all,
Their[1] waters commingling as a single body;
No reed hut had been matted, no marsh land had appeared,
When no gods whatever had been brought into being,

From "The Creation Epic," trans. E. A. Speiser, in *Ancient Near Eastern Texts Relating to the Old Testament,* 3rd ed. with Supplement, ed. James B. Pritchard (Princeton: Princeton University Press, 1969), pp. 60–64, 66–68, 72. Copyright © 1969 by Princeton University Press. Reprinted by permission of Princeton University Press.

10. This refers to the creation of vegetation.
11. Geb is the earth and is married to his sister, Nut, who is heaven.
12. Osiris was the god of agriculture and ruler of the Land of the Dead. He married his sister Isis, a mother-goddess, who resurrected Osiris after he had been murdered. Horus, son of Osiris and Isis, succeeded his father as ruler of Egypt and all living Egyptian pharaohs were identified as the living Horus. Set was the brother to Osiris and Isis. He was the god of the desert who murdered Osiris in order to rule Egypt. His sister-wife is Nephthys, who is a protector-goddess of the dead.

1. The fresh waters of Apsu and the marine waters of Tiamat, "the sea."

Uncalled by name, their destinies undetermined —
Then it was that the gods were formed within them.[2] . . .

The divine brothers banded together,
They disturbed Tiamat *as they surged back and forth,*
Yea, they troubled the mood of Tiamat
By their *hilarity* in the Abode of Heaven.
Apsu could not lessen their clamor
And Tiamat was speechless at their [*ways*].
Their doings were loathsome unto [. . .].
Unsavory were their ways; they were *overbearing.*
Then Apsu, the begetter of the great gods,
Cried out, addressing Mummu, his vizier:
"O Mummu, my vizier, who rejoicest my spirit,
Come hither and let us go to Tiamat!"
They went and sat down before Tiamat,
Exchanging counsel about the gods, their first-born.
Apsu, opening his mouth,
Said unto *resplendent* Tiamat:
"Their ways are verily loathsome unto me.
By day I find no relief, nor repose by night.
I will destroy, I will wreck their ways,
That quiet may be restored. Let us have rest!" . . .

(Now) whatever they had plotted between them,
Was repeated unto the gods, their first-born.
When the gods heard (this), they were astir,
(Then) lapsed into silence and remained speechless.
Surpassing in wisdom, accomplished, resourceful,
Ea, the all-wise, saw through their scheme.
A master design against it he devised and set up,
Made artful his spell against it, surpassing and holy.
He recited it and made it subsist in the deep,
As he poured sleep upon him. Sound asleep he lay.
When Apsu he had made prone, drenched with sleep,
Mummu, the adviser, was powerless to stir
He loosened his band, tore off his tiara,
Removed his halo (and) put it on himself.
Having fettered Apsu, he slew him.
Mummu he bound and left behind lock.
Having thus upon Apsu established his dwelling,
He laid hold on Mummu, holding him by the nose-rope.

In the chamber of fates, the abode of destinies,
A god was engendered, most able and wisest of gods.[3]

2. The waters of Apsu and Tiamat.
3. "The Deep."

In the heart of Apsu was Marduk created,
In the heart of holy Apsu was Marduk created.
He who begot him was Ea, his father ;
She who bore him was Damkina, his mother.
The breast of goddesses he did suck.
The nurse that nursed him filled him with awesomeness.
Alluring was his figure, sparkling the lift of his eyes.
Lordly was his gait, commanding from of old.
When Ea saw him, the father who begot him,
He exulted and glowed, his heart filled with gladness.
He rendered him perfect and endowed him with a double godhead.
Greatly exalted was he above them, exceeding throughout.
Perfect were his members beyond comprehension,
Unsuited for understanding, difficult to perceive.
Four were his eyes, four were his ears ;
When he moved his lips, fire blazed forth.
Large were all four hearing organs,
And the eyes, in like number, scanned all things.
He was the loftiest of the gods, surpassing was his stature ;
His members were enormous, he was exceeding tall.
"My little son, my little son!
My son, the Sun! Sun of the heavens!"
Clothed with the halo of ten gods, he was strong to the utmost,
As their awesome flashes were heaped upon him.
Anu brought forth and begot the fourfold wind
Consigning to its power the *leader of the host.*
       He fashioned . . . , *station[ed]* the whirlwind,
He produced streams to disturb Tiamat.
The gods, given no rest, *suffer* in the storm.
Their heart(s) having plotted evil,
To Tiamat, their mother, said :
"When they slew Apsu, thy consort,
Thou didst not aid him but remainedst still.
When the dread fourfold wind he created,
Thy vitals were diluted and so we can have no rest.
Let Apsu, thy consort, be in thy mind
And Mummu, who has been vanquished! Thou art left alone!...

[When] Tiamat [heard] (these) words, she was pleased :
They thronged and marched at the side of Tiamat.
Enraged, they plot without cease night and day,
They are set for combat, growling, raging,
They form a council to prepare for the fight....

Lord Anshar, father of the gods, [rose up] in grandeur,
And having pondered in his heart, he [said to the Anunnaki][4]

4. The gods.

"He whose [strength] is potent shall be [our] avenger,
He who is *keen* in battle, Marduk, the hero!"
Ea called [Marduk] to his place of seclusion.
[Giv]ing counsel, he told him what was in his heart:
"O Marduk, consider my advice. Hearken to thy father,
For thou art my son who comforts his heart.
When facing Anshar, approach as though in combat;
Stand up as thou speakest; seeing thee, he will grow restful."
The lord rejoiced at the word of his father;
He approached and stood up facing Anshar.
When Anshar saw him, his heart filled with joy.
He kissed his lips, his (own) gloom dispelled.
"[Anshar], be not muted; open wide thy lips.
I will go and attain thy heart's desire.
[Anshar], be not muted; open wide thy lips.
I will go and attain thy heart's desire!
What male is it who has pressed his fight against thee?
[*It is but*] Tiamat, a woman, that flies at thee with weapons!
[O my father-]creator, be glad and rejoice;
The neck of Tiamat thou shalt soon tread upon!...

If I indeed, as your avenger,
Am to vanquish Tiamat and save your lives,
Set up the Assembly, proclaim supreme my destiny!
When jointly in Ubshukinna[5] you have sat down rejoicing,
Let my word, instead of you, determine the fates.
Unalterable shall be what I may bring into being;
Neither recalled nor changed shall be the command of my lips."...

They erected for him a princely throne.
Facing his fathers, he sat down, presiding.
"Thou art the most honored of the great gods,
Thy decree is unrivaled, thy command is Anu.
Thou, Marduk, art the most honored of the great gods,
Thy decree is unrivaled, thy word is Anu.
From this day unchangeable shall be thy pronouncement.
To raise or bring low — these shall be (in) thy hand.
Thy utterance shall be true, thy command shall be unimpeachable.
No one among the gods shall transgress thy bounds!
Adornment being wanted for the seats of the gods,
Let the place of their shrines ever be in thy place.
O Marduk, thou art indeed our avenger.
We have granted thee kingship over the universe entire.
When in Assembly thou sittest, thy word shall be supreme.
Thy weapons shall not fail; they shall smash thy foes!
O lord, spare the life of him who trusts thee,

5. The Assembly Hall.

But pour out the life of the god who seized evil."
Having placed in their midst the Images,
They addressed themselves to Marduk, their first-born :
"Lord, truly thy decree is first among gods.
Say but to wreck or create ; it shall be.
Open thy mouth : the Images will vanish!
Speak again, and the Images shall be whole!"
At the word of his mouth the Images vanished.
He spoke again, and the Images were restored.
When the gods, his fathers, saw the fruit of his word,
Joyfully they did homage : "Marduk is king!"
They conferred on him scepter, throne, and *vestment*;
They gave him matchless weapons that ward off the foes :
"Go and cut off the life of Tiamat.
May the winds bear her blood to places undisclosed." ...

"Stand thou up, that I and thou meet in single combat!"
When Tiamat heard this,
She was like one possessed ; she took leave of her senses.
In fury Tiamat cried out aloud.
To the roots her legs shook both together.
She recites a charm, keeps casting her spell,
While the gods of battle sharpen their weapons.
Then joined issue Tiamat and Marduk, wisest of gods.
They strove in single combat, locked in battle.
The lord spread out his net to enfold her,
The Evil Wind, which followed behind, he let loose in her face.
When Tiamat opened her mouth to consume him,
He drove in the Evil Wind that she close not her lips.
As the fierce winds charged her belly,
Her body was distended and her mouth was wide open.
He released the arrow, it tore her belly,
It cut through her insides, splitting the heart.
Having thus subdued her, he extinguished her life.
He cast down her carcass to stand upon it.
After he had slain Tiamat, the leader,
Her band was shattered, her troupe broken up ;
And the gods, her helpers who marched at her side,
Trembling with terror, turned their backs about,
In order to save and preserve their lives.
Tightly encircled, they could not escape.
He made them captives and he smashed their weapons.
Thrown into the net, they found themselves ensnared ;
Placed in cells, they were filled with wailing ;
Bearing his wrath, they were held imprisoned. . . .

And turned back to Tiamat whom he had bound.
The lord trod on the legs of Tiamat,

With his unsparing mace he crushed her skull.
When the arteries of her blood he had severed,
The North Wind bore (it) to places undisclosed.
On seeing this, his fathers were joyful and jubilant,
They brought gifts of homage, they to him.
Then the lord paused to view her dead body,
That he might divide the monster and do artful works.
He split her like a shellfish into two parts :
Half of her he set up and ceiled it as sky,
Pulled down the bar and posted guards.
He bade them to allow not her waters to escape.
He crossed the heavens and surveyed the regions. . . .

He constructed stations for the great gods,
Fixing their astral likenesses as the Images.
He determined the year by designating the zones :
He set up three constellations for each of the twelve months.
After defining the days of the year [by means] of (heavenly) figures,
He founded the station of Nebiru[6] to determine their (heavenly) bands,
That none might transgress or fall short. . . .

The Moon he caused to shine, the night (to him) entrusting.
He appointed him a creature of the night to signify the days :
"Monthly, without cease, form designs with a crown.
At the month's very start, rising over the land,
Thou shalt have luminous horns to signify six days,
On the seventh day reaching a [half]-crown. . . .

When Marduk hears the words of the gods,
His heart prompts (him) to fashion artful works.
Opening his mouth, he addresses Ea
To impart the plan he had conceived in his heart :
"Blood I will mass and cause bones to be.
I will establish a savage, 'man' shall be his name.
Verily, savage-man I will create.
He shall be charged with the service of the gods that they might be at ease ! . . .

After Ea, the wise, had created mankind,
Had imposed upon it the service of the gods —
That work was beyond comprehension ;
As artfully planned by Marduk, did Nudimmud create it —
Marduk, the king of the gods divided
All the Anunnaki above and below.
He assigned (them) to Anu to guard his instructions.
Three hundred in the heavens he stationed as a guard.
In like manner the ways of the earth he defined.

6. Jupiter.

In heaven and on earth six hundred (thus) he settled.
After he had ordered all the instructions,
To the Anunnaki of heaven and earth had allotted their portions,
The Anunnaki opened their mouths
And said to Marduk, their lord:
"Now, O lord, thou who hast caused our deliverance,
What shall be our homage to thee?
Let us build a shrine whose name shall be called
'Lo, a chamber for our nightly rest'; let us repose in it!
Let us build a throne, a recess for his abode!
On the day that we arrive we shall repose in it."
When Marduk heard this,
Brightly glowed his features, like the day:
"Construct Babylon, whose building you have requested,
Let its brickwork be fashioned. You shall name it 'The Sanctuary.'"

3

A Hebrew Creation Story: Genesis

A third and later (1000–400 B.C.) creation account is that of the Hebrews. In this account, God creates the world in six days. He gives Adam and Eve the Garden of Eden as their home until they commit the "Original Sin."

QUESTIONS TO CONSIDER

1. Discuss the differences or similarities of *Genesis* to the other creation stories.
2. Why might one say that the Hebrew account is more sophisticated or refined than the others?
3. How does the role of human beings in *Genesis* compare with that found among the Babylonians (see Reading 2), the Japanese (see Reading 4), or the Mayans (see Reading 5)?
4. There are two creation accounts of men and women in *Genesis*. What are the political and social implications of these differing accounts?

Chapter 1

In the beginning God created the heaven and the earth.

And the earth was without form, and void; and darkness was upon the face of the deep. And the Spirit of God moved upon the face of the waters.

From Genesis, 1–3 (King James Version); slightly modernized.

And God said, Let there be light : and there was light.

And God saw the light, that it was good : and God divided the light from the darkness.

And God called the light Day, and the darkness he called Night. And the evening and the morning were the first day.

And God said, Let there be a firmament in the midst of the waters, and let it divide the waters from the waters.

And God made the firmament, and divided the waters which were under the firmament from the waters which were above the firmament : and it was so.

And God called the firmament Heaven. And the evening and the morning were the second day.

And God said, Let the waters under the heaven be gathered together unto one place, and let the dry land appear : and it was so.

And God called the dry land Earth ; and the gathering together of the waters called he Seas : and God saw that it was good.

And God said, Let the earth bring forth grass, the herb yielding seed, and the fruit tree yielding fruit after his kind, whose seed is in itself, upon the earth : and it was so.

And the earth brought forth grass, and herb yielding seed after his kind, and the tree yielding fruit, whose seed was in itself, after his kind : and God saw that it was good.

And the evening and the morning were the third day.

And God said, Let there be lights in the firmament of the heaven to divide the day from the night ; and let them be for signs, and for seasons, and for days, and years :

And let them be for lights in the firmament of the heaven to give light upon the earth : and it was so.

And God made two great lights ; the greater light to rule the day, and the lesser light to rule the night : he made the stars also.

And God set them in the firmament of the heaven to give light upon the earth,

And to rule over the day and over the night, and to divide the light from the darkness : and God saw that it was good.

And the evening and the morning were the fourth day.

And God said, Let the waters bring forth abundantly the moving creature that hath life, and fowl that may fly above the earth in the open firmament of heaven.

And God created great whales, and every living creature that moveth, which the waters brought forth abundantly, after their kind, and every winged fowl after his kind : and God saw that it was good.

And God blessed them, saying, Be fruitful, and multiply, and fill the waters in the seas, and let fowl multiply in the earth.

And the evening and the morning were the fifth day.

And God said, Let the earth bring forth the living creature after his kind, cattle, and creeping thing, and beast of the earth after his kind : and it was so.

And God made the beast of the earth after his kind, and cattle after their kind, and every thing that creepeth upon the earth after his kind : and God saw that it was good.

And God said, Let us make man in our image, after our likeness : and let them have dominion over the fish of the sea, and over the fowl of the air, and over the cattle, and over all the earth, and over every creeping thing that creepeth upon the earth.

So God created man in his own image, in the image of God created he him ; male and female created he them.

And God blessed them, and God said unto them, Be fruitful, and multiply, and replenish the earth, and subdue it : and have dominion over the fish of the sea, and over the fowl of the air, and over every living thing that moveth upon the earth.

And God said, Behold, I have given you every herb bearing seed, which is upon the face of all the earth, and every tree in the which is the fruit of a tree yielding seed ; to you it shall be for meat.

And to every beast of the earth, and to every fowl of the air, and to every thing that creepeth upon the earth, wherein there is life, I have given every green herb for meat : and it was so.

And God saw everything that he had made, and, behold, it was very good. And the evening and the morning were the sixth day.

Chapter 2

Thus the heavens and the earth were finished, and all the host of them.

And on the seventh day God ended his work which he had made ; and he rested on the seventh day from all his work which he had made.

And God blessed the seventh day and sanctified it : because that in it he had rested from all his work which God created and made.

These are the generations of the heavens and of the earth when they were created, in the day that the Lord God made the earth and the heavens,

And every plant of the field before it was in the earth, and every herb of the field before it grew : for the Lord God had not caused it to rain upon the earth, and there was not a man to till the ground.

But there went up a mist from the earth, and watered the whole face of the ground.

And the Lord God formed man of the dust of the ground, and breathed into his nostrils the breath of life ; and man became a living soul.

And the Lord God planted a garden eastward in Eden ; and there he put the man whom he had formed.

And out of the ground made the Lord God to grow every tree that is pleasant to the sight, and good for food ; the tree of life also in the midst of the garden, and the tree of knowledge of good and evil.

And a river went out of Eden to water the garden ; and from thence it was parted and became into four heads.

The name of the first is Pishon : that is it which compasseth the whole land of Havilah, where there is gold ;

And the gold of that land is good : there is bdellium and the onyx stone.

And the name of the second river is Gihon : the same is it that compasseth the whole land of Ethiopia.

And the name of the third river is Haddekel : that is it which goeth toward the east of Assyria. And the fourth river is Euphrates.

And the Lord God took the man, and put him into the garden of Eden to dress it and to keep it.

And the Lord God commanded the man, saying, Of every tree of the garden thou mayest freely eat :

But of the tree of knowledge of good and evil, thou shall not eat of it : for in the day that thou eatest thereof thou shalt surely die.

And the Lord God said, It is not good that the man should be alone ; I will make him an help mate for him.

And out of the ground the Lord God formed every beast of the field, and every fowl of the air ; and brought them unto Adam to see what he would call them : and whatsoever Adam called every living creature, that was the name thereof.

And Adam gave names to all cattle, and to the fowl of the air, and to every beast of the field ; but for Adam there was not found an help mate for him.

And the Lord God caused a deep sleep to fall upon Adam, and he slept : and he took one of his ribs, and closed up the flesh instead thereof ;

And the rib, which the Lord God had taken from man, made he a woman, and brought her unto the man.

And Adam said, This is now bone of my bones, and flesh of my flesh : she shall be called Woman, because she was taken out of Man.

Therefore shall a man leave his father and his mother, and shall cleave unto his wife : and they shall be one flesh.

And they were both naked, the man and his wife, and were not ashamed.

Chapter 3

Now the serpent was more subtil than any beast of the field which the Lord God had made. And he said unto the woman, Yea, hath God said, Ye shall not eat of every tree of the garden ?

And the woman said unto the serpent, We may eat of the fruit of the trees of the garden :

But of the fruit of the tree which is in the midst of the garden, God hath said, Ye shall not eat of it, neither shall ye touch it, lest ye die.

And the serpent said unto the woman, ye shall not surely die :

For God doth know that in the day ye eat thereof, then your eyes shall be opened, and ye shall be as gods, knowing good and evil.

And when the woman saw that the tree was good for food, and that it was pleasant to the eyes, and a tree to be desired to make one wise, she took of the fruit thereof, and did eat, and gave also unto her husband with her; and he did eat.

And the eyes of them both were opened, and they knew that they were naked; and they sewed fig leaves together, and made themselves aprons.

And they heard the voice of the Lord God walking in the garden in the cool of the day: and Adam and his wife hid themselves from the presence of the Lord God amongst the trees of the garden.

And the Lord God called unto Adam, and said unto him, Where art thou?

And he said, I heard thy voice in the garden, and I was afraid, because I was naked; and I hid myself.

And he said, Who told thee that thou wast naked? Hast thou eaten of the tree, whereof I commanded thee that thou shouldest not eat?

And the man said, The woman whom thou gavest to be with me, she gave me of the tree, and I did eat.

And the Lord God said unto the woman, What is this that thou hast done? And the woman said, The serpent beguiled me, and I did eat.

And the Lord God said unto the serpent, Because thou hast done this, thou art cursed above all cattle, and above every beast of the field; upon thy belly shalt thou go, and dust shalt thou eat all the days of thy life:

And I will put enmity between thee and the woman, and between thy seed and her seed; it shall bruise thy head, and thou shalt bruise his heel.

Unto the woman he said, I will greatly multiply thy sorrow and thy conception; in sorrow thou shalt bring forth children; and thy desire shall be to thy husband, and he shall rule over thee.

And unto Adam he said, Because thou has hearkened unto the voice of thy wife, and hast eaten of the tree, of which I commanded thee, saying, Thou shalt not eat of it: cursed is the ground for thy sake; in sorrow shalt thou eat of it all the days of thy life;

Thorns also and thistles shall it bring forth to thee; and thou shalt eat the herb of the field:

In the sweat of thy face shalt thou eat bread, till thou return unto the ground; for out of it wast thou taken: for dust thou art, and unto dust shalt thou return.

And Adam called his wife's name Eve; because she was the mother of all living.

Unto Adam also and to his wife did the Lord God make coats of skins, and clothed them.

And the Lord God said, Behold, the man is become as one of us, to know good and evil: and now, lest he put forth his hand, and take also of the tree of life, and eat, and live for ever:

Therefore the Lord God sent him forth from the garden of Eden, to till the ground from whence he was taken.

So he drove out the man; and he placed at the east of the garden of Eden Cherubims, and a flaming sword which turned every way, to keep the way of the tree of life.

4

A Japanese Creation Epic: *Nihongi*

The two oldest sources on Japanese mythology and history, *Kojiki* (*Record of Ancient Matters*) and *Nihongi* (*Chronicle of Japan*), completed in A.D. 712 and A.D. 720 respectively, tell about the creation of heaven and earth and the divine origins of the land of Japan and its reigning family. According to the *Nihongi*, Amaterasu-o-Mikami, the Sun-Goddess and progenitrix of the Japanese imperial line, was chosen by her divine parents, Izanagi-no-Mikoto and Izanami-no-Mikoto, to rule the plain of High Heaven (Takama-no-hara). The grandson of the Sun-Goddess, Ninigi-no-Mikoto, descended on Taka-chiho-no-mine, a sacred mountain top in modern Kyushu, and his grandson, Jimmu, finally established his rule as the first emperor of Japan in 660 B.C. Akihito (r. 1989–   ), the reigning monarch of Japan today, is regarded as the 125th direct descendant of Emperor Jimmu. The following selection is an excerpt from *Nihongi*.

QUESTIONS TO CONSIDER

1. Compare and contrast the creation epic of Japan with the creation stories of ancient Babylonia (Reading 2) and Genesis (Reading 3).
2. How do you compare Amaterasu-o-Mikami, the Sun-Goddess of Japan, with the sun god Ra of Heliopolis (Reading 1)?

Of old, Heaven and Earth were not yet separated, and the In and Yo[1] not yet divided. They formed a chaotic mass like an egg which was of obscurely defined limits and contained germs.

The purer and clearer part was thinly drawn out, and formed Heaven, while the heavier and grosser element settled down and became Earth. . . .

Thereafter Divine Beings were produced between them.

Hence, it is said that when the world began to be created, the soil of which lands were composed floated about in a manner which might be compared to the floating of a fish sporting on the surface of the water.

At this time a certain thing was produced between Heaven and Earth. It was in form like a reed-shoot. Now this became transformed into a God, and was called

W. G. Aston, trans., *Nihongi, Chronicles of Japan from the Earliest Times to A.D. 607*, Transactions and Proceedings of The Japan Society, Supplement I (London : Kegan, Paul, Trench, Trubner & Co., 1896), pp. 1–45.

1. The basic dualism of nature in Chinese philosophy. Yo or Yang in Chinese represents male : light, hot, and positive, and In or Yin in Chinese is female : dark, cold, and negative.

Kuni-toko-tachi-no-Mikoto. . . . [and seven other deities including Izanagi-no-Mikoto and Iznami-no-Mikoto]. . . .

Being formed by the mutual action of Heavenly and Earthly principles, they were made male and female. From Kuni-no-toko-tachi-no-Mikoto to Izanagi-no-Mikoto and Izanami-no-Mikoto are called the seven generations of the age of the Gods.

Izanagi-no-Mikoto and Izanami-no-Mikoto stood on the floating bridge of Heaven, and held counsel together, saying: "Is there not a country beneath?" Thereupon they thrust down the jewel-spear of Heaven and groping about therewith found the Ocean. The brine which dripped from the point of the spear coagulated and became an island which received the name of Ono-goro-jima.[2]

The two Deities thereupon descended and dwelt in this island. Accordingly they wished to become husband and wife together, and to produce countries.

So they made Ono-goro-jima the pillar of the center of the land.

Now the male deity turning by the left, and the female deity by the right, they went around the pillar of the land separately. When they met together on one side, the female deity spoke first and said: "How delightful! I have met with a lovely youth." The male deity was displeased, and said: "I am a man, and by right should have spoken first. How is it that on the contrary thou, a woman, shouldst have been the first to speak? This was unlucky. Let us go round again." Upon this the two deities went back, and having met anew, this time the male deity spoke first, and said: "How delightful! I have met a lovely maiden."

Then he inquired of the female deity, saying: "In thy body, is there aught formed?" She answered, and said: "In my body there is a place which is the source of femininity." The male deity said: "In my body again there is place which is the source of masculinity. I wish to unite this source-place of my body to the source-place of thy body." Hereupon the male and female first became united as husband and wife.

Now when the time of birth arrived [they gave birth to one island after another in all eight islands which were known as Oho-ya-shima country][3] . . .

They next produced the sea, then the rivers, and then the mountains. Then produced Ku-ku-no-chi, the ancestor of the trees, and next the ancestor of herbs, Kaya-no-hime.

After this Izanagi-no-Mikoto and Izanami-no-Mikoto consulted together, saying: "We have now produced the Great-eight-island country, with the mountains, rivers, herbs, and trees. Why should we not produce someone who shall be lord of the universe? They then together produced the Sun-Goddess, who was called [Amaterasu-o-Mikami].

The resplendent luster of this child shone throughout all the six quarters. Therefore the two Deities rejoiced, saying: "We have had many children, but none of them have been equal to this wondrous infant. She ought not to be kept long in this land, but we ought of our own accord to send her at once to Heaven, and entrust to her the affairs of Heaven."

2. The islets off the coast of the larger island of Ahaji in western Japan.
3. Land-of-the-Eight-Great-Islands, old name for Japan.

At this time Heaven and Earth were still not far separated, and therefore they sent her up to Heaven by the ladder of Heaven.

They next produced the Moon God.

His radiance was next to that of the Sun in splendor. This God was to be the consort of the Sun-Goddess, and to share in her government. They therefore sent him also to Heaven. . . .

Their next child was Sosano-wo-no-Mikoto.

This God had a fierce temper and was given to cruel acts. Moreover he made a practice of continually weeping and wailing. So he brought many of the people of the land to an untimely end. Again he caused green mountains to become withered. Therefore the two Gods, his parents, addressed Sosa-no-wo-no-Mikoto, saying : "Thou art exceedingly wicked, and it is not meet that thou shouldst reign over the world. Certainly thou must depart far away to the Nether-Land." So they at length expelled him. . . .

Upon this Sosa-no-wo-no-Mikoto made petition, saying : "I will now obey thy instructions and proceed to the Nether-Land. Therefore I wish for a short time to go to the Plain of High Heaven and meet with my elder sister, after which I will go away for ever." Permission was granted him, and he therefore ascended to Heaven. . . .

Now at first when Sosa-no-wo-no-Mikoto went up to Heaven, by reason of the fierceness of his divine nature there was a commotion in the sea and the hills and mountains groaned aloud. [The Sun Goddess], knowing the violence and wickedness of this Deity, was startled and changed countenance, when she heard the manner of his coming. She said [to herself] : "Is my younger brother coming with good intentions ? I think it must be his purpose to rob me of my kingdom. . . .

After this Sosa-no-wo-no-Mikoto's behavior was exceedingly rude. In what way ? The [Sun-Goddess] had made august rice fields of Heavenly narrow rice fields and Heavenly long rice fields. The Sosa-no-wo-no-Mikoto, when the seed was sown in spring, broke down the divisions between the plots of rice, and in autumn let loose the Heavenly piebald colts,[4] and made them lie down in the midst of rice fields. Again, when he saw that the [Sun-Goddess] was about to celebrate the feast of first fruits, he secretly voided excrement in the New Place. Moreover, when he saw that the [Sun-Goddess] was in her sacred weaving hall, engaged in weaving the garments of the Gods, he flayed the piebald colt of Heaven, and breaking a hole in the roof-tiles of the hall, flung it in. Then, the [Sun-Goddess] startled with alarm, and wounded herself with the shuttle. Indignant at this, she straightway entered the Rock-cave of Heaven, and having fastened the Rock-door, dwelt there in seclusion. Therefore, constant darkness prevailed on all sides, and the alternation of night and day was unknown.

Then the eighty myriads of Gods met on the bank of the Tranquil River of Heaven, and considered in what manner they should supplicate her. Accordingly, [a deity][5] with profound device and far-reaching thought, at length gathered long-

---

4. Indian myth has a piebald or spotted deer or cow among celestial objects ; a mythological colt.

5. A god named Omoho-kane-no-Kami.

singing birds of Eternal Land and made them utter their prolonged cry to one another. Moreover, he made [a powerful deity][6] to stand beside the Rock-door. Then
[two other deities] dug up a five hundred branched True Sakaki tree[7] of the Heavenly Mt. Kagu.[8] On its upper branches they hung an august five-hundred string of
Yasaka jewels.[9] On the middle branches they hung an eight-hand mirror.[10] . . .
Then they recited their liturgy together.

Moreover, [another deity][11] took in her hand a spear with Eulalia grass,[12]
and standing before the door of the Rock-cave of Heaven, skillfully performed a
mimic dance. She took moreover, the true Sakaki tree of the Heavenly Mount
Kagu, and made of it a head-dress, she took club moss and made of it braces, she
kindled fires, she placed a tub bottom upwards, and gave forth a divinely-inspired
utterance.

Now the [Sun-Goddess] heard this, and said : "Since I have shut myself up in
the Rock-cave, there ought surely to be continual night in the Central Land of fer-
tile reed plains. How then can [this deity] be so jolly?" So with her august hand,
she opened for a narrow space the Rock-door and peeped out. Then the [awaiting
powerful deity] forthwith took the [Sun-Goddess] by the hand, and led her out
[. . . and the radiance of the Sun-Goddess filled the universe].

5

A Mayan Creation Story: *Popol Vuh*

Indians in the Americas also had their versions of human origins. The Quiché
of Guatemala, a branch of the Mayan civilization, developed one of the most
famous accounts in a sacred book, the *Popol Vuh*, which also contained information about Mayan customs, religion, and history. This account was the
most important surviving document of the pre-Columbian era and was first
published in Spanish in 1857.

QUESTIONS TO CONSIDER

1. What were some of the characteristics of the first men created according to
this Mayan legend?

6. A god named Ta-jikara-wo-no-Kami.
7. The Sakaki, or cleyera Japonica, is the sacred tree of the Shinto religion of Japan. It is used
in Shinto religious ceremonies.
8. A mountain in Yamato. Heaven is supposed to have a counterpart.
9. An eight-feet–long sacred curved jewel, which is one of the three Imperial Regalia.
10. A large size mirror.
11. A terrible female of Heaven named Ama-no-uzume-no Mikoto.
12. Eulalia japonica, a kind of grass.

2. Why were the first people who looked and talked like men destroyed by a flood? In what key ways did their successors, the "true humans," differ?
3. Compare and contrast this Mayan version of creation with the others in this section. Are there similarities and/or differences?

And instantly the figures were made of wood. They looked like men, talked like men, and populated the surface of the earth.

They existed and multiplied; they had daughters, they had sons, these wooden figures; but they did not have souls, nor minds, they did not remember their Creator, their Maker; they walked on all fours, aimlessly.

They no longer remembered the Heart of Heaven and therefore they fell out of favor. It was merely a trial, an attempt at man. At first they spoke, but their face was without expression; their feet and hands had no strength; they had no blood, nor substance, nor moisture, nor flesh; their cheeks were dry, their feet and hands were dry, and their flesh was yellow.

Therefore, they no longer thought of their Creator nor their Maker, nor of those who made them and cared for them.

These were the first men who existed in great numbers on the face of the earth. . . .

Immediately the wooden figures were annihilated, destroyed, broken up, and killed.

A flood was brought about by the Heart of Heaven; a great flood was formed which fell on the heads of the wooden creatures.

Of Tzite [wood], the flesh of man was made, but when woman was fashioned by the Creator and the Maker, her flesh was made of rushes. These were the materials the Creator and the Maker wanted to use in making them.

But those that they had made, that they had created, did not think, did not speak with their Creator, their Maker. And for this reason they were killed, they were deluged. A heavy resin fell from the sky. . . .

This was to punish them because they had not thought of their mother, nor their father, the Heart of Heaven, called Hurac'an. And for this reason the face of the earth was darkened and a black rain began to fall, by day and by night.

Then came the small animals and the large animals, and sticks and stones struck their faces. And all began to speak: their earthen jars, their griddles, their plates, their pots, their grinding stones, all rose up and struck their faces.

"You have done us much harm; you ate us, and now we shall kill you," said their dogs and birds of the barnyard.

And the grinding stones said: "We were tormented by you; every day, every day, at night, at dawn, all the time our faces went *holi, holi, huqui, huqui*, because of you. This was the tribute we paid you. But now that you are no longer men, you shall feel our strength. We shall grind and tear your flesh to pieces," said their grinding stones.

From *Popol Vuh: The Sacred Book of the Ancient Quiché Maya,* from the translation of Adrián Recinos. (Norman, OK: University of Oklahoma Press, 1952), pp. 89–93, passim. Copyright © by the University of Oklahoma Press.

And then their dogs spoke and said: "Why did you give us nothing to eat? You scarcely looked at us, but you chased us and threw us out. You always had a stick ready to strike us while you were eating.

"Thus it was that you treated us. You did not speak to us. Perhaps we shall not kill you now; but why did you not look ahead, why did you not think about yourselves? Now we shall destroy you, now you shall feel the teeth of our mouths; we shall devour you," said the dogs, and then they destroyed their faces.

And at the same time, their griddles and pots spoke: "Pain and suffering you have caused us. Our mouths and our faces were blackened with soot; we were always put on the fire and you burned us as though we felt no pain. Now you shall feel it, we shall burn you," said their pots, and they all destroyed their [the wooden men's] faces. The stones of the hearth, which were heaped together, hurled themselves straight from the fire against their heads, causing them pain.

The desperate ones [the men of wood] ran as quickly as they could; they wanted to climb to the tops of the houses, and the houses fell down and threw them to the ground; they wanted to climb to the treetops, and the trees cast them far away; they wanted to enter the caverns, and the caverns repelled them.

So was the ruin of the men who had been created and formed, the men made to be destroyed and annihilated; the mouths and faces of all of them were mangled.

And it is said that their descendants are the monkeys which now live in the forests; these are all that remain of them because their flesh was made only of wood by the Creator and the Maker.

And therefore the monkey looks like man, and is an example of a generation of men which were created and made but were only wooden figures.

A Sumerian Heroic Legend

6

The Epic of Gilgamesh

Gilgamesh, the semi-legendary Sumerian king who ruled the city of Uruk around 2700 B.C., is the subject of the world's first great epic poem. Gilgamesh was a roguish king whose lusty appetites were resented by his subjects, who prayed for a deliverer. To punish Gilgamesh for his sins, the gods created the uncivilized Enkidu and sent him to chastise Gilgamesh and spare Uruk further harm. But instead of becoming mortal enemies, Gilgamesh and Enkidu became fast friends and set off together on a series of adventures, detailed in the first half of this epic.

Their first adventure is to secure timber from the distant Cedar Forest, which is guarded by the ogre, Humbaba, whom they must kill. Upon their return to Uruk, the fierce Ishtar, goddess of love, tries to entice Gilgamesh into marriage; however, because Gilgamesh and Enkidu spurn Ishtar she sends down the Bull of Heaven to punish them. Gilgamesh and Enkidu kill this creature, thereby angering the powerful Enlil, king of the gods, who takes his revenge by killing Enkidu. King Gilgamesh is devastated by his friend's death and laments humanity's fate.

The second half of the epic is devoted to Gilgamesh's quest for the secret of life. He descends into the Netherworld in search of Utnapishtim, to whom the gods had granted immortality and from whom he hopes to learn the key to life. When the two meet, Utnapishtim introduces Gilgamesh to the story of the Great Flood, which had killed all life save for Utnapishtim, his family, and the animals he had placed in his great ship. At the end of the Flood tale, Utnapishtim tells Gilgamesh of a certain Plant of Life that can give immortality. Gilgamesh is able to retrieve this plant and bring it back to the living; yet his hopes are dashed when it is eaten by a snake. At the end of the poem, Gilgamesh can only lament the human fate, old age and death.

QUESTIONS TO CONSIDER

1. What elements of this epic do you also find in Homer's *Odyssey* (see Reading 18)?
2. Why was Enkidu created and how was he changed?
3. In the second half of the epic, what is Gilgamesh seeking? Does he succeed in this quest?
4. What part of the epic is the most familiar to you?

I will proclaim to the world the deeds of Gilgamesh. This was the man to whom all things were known; this was the king who knew the countries of the world. He was wise, he saw mysteries and knew secret things, he brought us a tale of the days before the flood. He went on a long journey, was weary, wornout with labour, returning he rested, he engraved on a stone the whole story.

When the gods created Gilgamesh they gave him a perfect body. Shamash the glorious sun endowed him with beauty, Adad the god of the storm endowed him with courage, the great gods made his beauty perfect, surpassing all others, terrifying like a great wild bull. Two thirds they made him god and one third man.

In Uruk he built walls, a great rampart, and the temple of blessed Eanna for the god of the firmament Anu, and for Ishtar the goddess of love. . . .

The Coming of Enkidu

Gilgamesh went abroad in the world, but he met with none who could withstand his arms till he came to Uruk. But the men of Uruk muttered in their houses, 'Gilgamesh sounds the tocsin for his amusement, his arrogance has no bounds by

From *The Epic of Gilgamesh*, introduction and translation by N. K. Sandars (New York: Penguin Books, 1972), pp. 61–65, 67–69, 85–86, 89, 108–111, 116–117. Copyright © N. K. Sandars, 1960, 1964, 1970. Reproduced by permission of Penguin Books Ltd.

day or night. No son is left with his father, for Gilgamesh takes them all, even the children ; yet the king should be a shepherd to his people. His lust leaves no virgin to her lover, neither the warrior's daughter nor the wife of the noble ; yet this is the shepherd of the city, wise, comely, and resolute.'

The gods heard their lament, the gods of heaven cried to the Lord of Uruk, to Anu the god of Uruk. . . . When Anu had heard their lamentation the gods cried to Aruru, the goddess of creation, 'You made him, O Aruru, now create his equal ; let it be as like him as his own reflection, his second self, stormy heart for stormy heart. Let them contend together and leave Uruk in quiet.'

So the goddess conceived an image in her mind, and it was of the stuff of Anu of the firmament. She dipped her hands in water and pinched off clay, she let it fall in the wilderness, and noble Enkidu was created. There was virtue in him of the god of war, of Ninurta himself. His body was rough, he had long hair like a woman's ; it waved like the hair of Nisaba, the goddess of corn. His body was covered with matted hair like Samuqan's, the god of cattle. He was innocent of mankind ; he knew nothing of the cultivated land.

Enkidu ate grass in the hills with the gazelle and lurked with wild beasts at the water-holes ; he had joy of the water with the herds of wild game. But there was a trapper who met him one day face to face at the drinking-hole, for the wild game had entered his territory. On three days he met him face to face, and the trapper was frozen with fear. He went back to his house with the game that he had caught, and he was dumb, benumbed with terror. His face was altered like that of one who has made a long journey. . . .

So the trapper set out on his journey to Uruk and addressed himself to Gilgamesh saying, 'A man unlike any other is roaming now in the pastures ; he is as strong as a star from heaven and I am afraid to approach him. He helps the wild game to escape ; he fills in my pits and pulls up my traps.' Gilgamesh said, 'Trapper, go back, take with you a harlot, a child of pleasure. At the drinking-hole she will strip, and when he sees her beckoning he will embrace her and the game of the wilderness will surely reject him.'

Now the trapper returned, taking the harlot with him. After a three days' journey they came to the drinking-hole, and there they sat down ; the harlot and the trapper sat facing one another and waited for the game to come. For the first day and for the second day the two sat waiting, but on the third day the herds came ; they came down to drink and Enkidu was with them. The small wild creatures of the plains were glad of the water, and Enkidu with them, who ate grass with the gazelle and was born in the hills ; and she saw him, the savage man, come from far-off in the hills. The trapper spoke to her : 'There he is. Now, woman, make your breasts bare, have no shame, do not delay but welcome his love. Let him see you naked, let him possess your body. When he comes near uncover yourself and lie with him ; teach him, the savage man, your woman's art, for when he murmurs love to you the wild beasts that shared his life in the hills will reject him.'

She was not ashamed to take him, she made herself naked and welcomed his eagerness ; as he lay on her murmuring love she taught him the woman's art. For six days and seven nights they lay together, for Enkidu had forgotten his home in the hills ; but when he was satisfied he went back to the wild beasts. Then, when the gazelle saw him, they bolted away ; when the wild creatures saw him they fled. Enkidu would have followed, but his body was bound as though with a cord, his knees gave way when he started to run, his swiftness was gone. And now the wild creatures had all fled away; Enkidu was grown weak, for wisdom was in him, and the thoughts of a man were in his heart. So he returned and sat down at the woman's feet, and listened intently to what she said, 'You are wise, Enkidu, and now you have become like a god. Why do you want to run wild with the beasts in the hills? Come with me. I will take you to strong-walled Uruk, to the blessed temple of Ishtar and of Anu, of love and of heaven: there Gilgamesh lives, who is very strong, and like a wild bull he lords it over men.'...

And now she said to Enkidu, 'When I look at you you have become like a god. Why do you yearn to run wild again with the beasts in the hills? Get up from the ground, the bed of a shepherd.' He listened to her words with care. It was good advice that she gave. She divided her clothing in two and with the one half she clothed him and with the other herself; and holding his hand she led him like a child to the sheepfolds, into the shepherds' tents. There all the shepherds crowded round to see him, they put down bread in front of him, but Enkidu could only suck the milk of wild animals. He fumbled and gaped, at a loss what to do or how he should eat the bread and drink the strong wine. Then the woman said, 'Enkidu, eat bread, it is the staff of life; drink the wine, it is the custom of the land.' So he ate till he was full and drank strong wine, seven goblets. He became merry, his heart exulted and his face shone. He rubbed down the matted hair of his body and anointed himself with oil. Enkidu had become a man; but when he had put on man's clothing he appeared like a bridegroom.

Now Enkidu strode in front and the woman followed behind. He entered Uruk, that great market, and all the folk thronged round him where he stood in the street in strong-walled Uruk. The people jostled; speaking of him they said, 'He is the spit of Gilgamesh.' 'He is shorter.' 'He is bigger of bone.' 'This is the one who was reared on the milk of wild beasts. His is the greatest strength.' The men rejoiced: 'Now Gilgamesh has met his match. This great one, this hero whose beauty is like a god, he is a match even for Gilgamesh.'

In Uruk the bridal bed was made, fit for the goddess of love. The bride waited for the bridegroom, but in the night Gilgamesh got up and came to the house. Then Enkidu stepped out, he stood in the street and blocked the way. Mighty Gilgamesh came on and Enkidu met him at the gate. He put out his foot and prevented Gilgamesh from entering the house, so they grappled, holding each other like bulls. They broke the doorposts and the walls shook, they snorted like bulls locked together. They shattered the doorposts and the walls shook. Gilgamesh bent his knee with his foot planted on the ground and with a turn Enkidu was thrown. Then immediately his fury died. When Enkidu was thrown he said to Gilgamesh, 'There is not another like you in the world. Ninsun, who is as strong as a wild ox in the byre, she was the mother who bore you, and now you are raised above all men, and Enlil has given you the kingship, for your strength surpasses the strength of men.' So Enkidu and Gilgamesh embraced and their friendship was sealed. . . .

After they had become good friends, Gilgamesh and Enkidu set out for the Cedar Forest (possibly southern Turkey or Phoenicia) in order to secure wood for the city. However, before they got the wood they had to kill a fire-breathing ogre called Humbaba. Succeeding in this mission, they returned to Uruk, where Gilgamesh was offered marriage by the goddess of love, Ishtar (or Inanna).

Gilgamesh opened his mouth and answered glorious Ishtar, 'If I take you in marriage, what gifts can I give in return? What ointments and clothing for your body? I would gladly give you bread and all sorts of food fit for a god. I would give you wine to drink fit for a queen. I would pour out barley to stuff your granary; but as for making you my wife — that I will not. How would it go with me? Your lovers have found you like a brazier which smoulders in the cold, a backdoor which keeps out neither squall of wind nor storm, a castle which crushes the garrison, pitch that blackens the bearer, a water-skin that chafes the carrier, a stone which falls from the parapet, a battering-ram turned back from the enemy, a sandal that trips the wearer. Which of your lovers did you ever love for ever? What shepherd of yours has pleased you for all time?' . . .

Gravely insulted by the king's words, Ishtar asked her father, Anu, to punish Gilgamesh by sending the Bull of Heaven to ravage the land. Gilgamesh and Enkidu managed to kill the bull, whose hind leg Enkidu tore off and flung at the goddess. Such a serious offense against the gods demanded immediate punishment; thus did Enkidu fall ill and die.

So Enkidu lay stretched out before Gilgamesh; his tears ran down in streams and he said to Gilgamesh, 'O my brother, so dear as you are to me, brother, yet they will take me from you.' Again he said, 'I must sit down on the threshold of the dead and never again will I see my dear brother with my eyes.' . . .

Gilgamesh was unreconciled to the death of his beloved friend Enkidu. He decided to make a long and difficult journey to the Netherworld in order to search for the secret of immortality. There he encountered the Sumerian Akkadian Noah called Utnapishtim (or Ziusudra). Utnapishtim tells Gilgamesh of a Flood that had been sent by the gods to destroy all life except for Utnapishtim and his family.

'In those days the world teemed, the people multiplied, the world bellowed like a wild bull, and the great god was aroused by the clamour. Enlil heard the clamour and he said to the gods in council, "The uproar of mankind is intolerable and sleep is no longer possible by reason of the babel." So the gods agreed to exterminate mankind. Enlil did this, but Ea because of his oath warned me in a dream. He whispered their words to my house of reeds, "Reed-house, reed-house! Wall, O wall, hearken reed-house, wall reflect; O man of Shurrupak, son of Ubara-Tutu; tear down your house and build a boat, abandon possessions and look for life, despise worldly goods and save your soul alive. Tear down your house, I say, and build a boat. These are the measurements of the barque as you shall build her: let her beam equal her length, let her deck be roofed like the vault that covers the abyss; then take up into the boat the seed of all living creatures."
'In the first light of dawn all my household gathered round me, the children brought pitch and the men whatever was necessary. On the fifth day I laid the keel and the ribs, then I made fast the planking. The ground-space was one acre, each

side of the deck measured one hundred and twenty cubits, making a square. I built six decks below, seven in all, I divided them into nine sections with bulkheads between. I drove in wedges where needed, I saw to the punt-poles, and laid in supplies. The carriers brought oil in baskets, I poured pitch into the furnace and asphalt and oil; more oil was consumed in caulking, and more again the master of the boat took into his stores. I slaughtered bullocks for the people and every day I killed sheep. I gave the shipwrights wine to drink as though it were river water, raw wine and red wine and oil and white wine. There was feasting then as there is at the time of the New Year's festival; I myself anointed my head. On the seventh day the boat was complete.

'Then was the launching full of difficulty; there was shifting of ballast above and below till two thirds was submerged. I loaded into her all that I had of gold and of living things, my family, my kin, the beast of the field both wild and tame, and all the craftsmen. I sent them on board, for the time that Shamash had ordained was already fulfilled when he said, "In the evening, when the rider of the storm sends down the destroying rain, enter the boat and batten her down." The time was fulfilled, the evening came, the rider of the storm sent down the rain. I looked out at the weather and it was terrible, so I too boarded the boat and battened her down. All was now complete, the battening and the caulking; so I handed the tiller to Puzur-Amurri the steersman, with the navigation and the care of the whole boat. . . .

'For six days and six nights the winds blew, torrent and tempest and flood overwhelmed the world, tempest and flood raged together like warring hosts. When the seventh day dawned the storm from the south subsided, the sea grew calm, the flood was stilled; I looked at the face of the world and there was silence, all mankind was turned to clay. The surface of the sea stretched as flat as a rooftop; I opened a hatch and the light fell on my face. Then I bowed low, I sat down and I wept, the tears streamed down my face, for on every side was the waste of water. I looked for land in vain, but fourteen leagues distant there appeared a mountain, and there the boat grounded; on the mountain of Nisir the boat held fast, she held fast and did not budge. One day she held, and a second day on the mountain of Nisir she held fast and did not budge. A third day, and a fourth day she held fast on the mountain and did not budge; a fifth day and a sixth day she held fast on the mountain. When the seventh day dawned I loosed a dove and let her go. She flew away, but finding no resting-place she returned. Then I loosed a swallow, and she flew away but finding no resting-place she returned. I loosed a raven, she saw that the waters had retreated, she ate, she flew around, she cawed, and she did not come back. Then I threw everything open to the four winds, I made a sacrifice and poured out a libation on the mountain top. Seven and again seven cauldrons I set up on their stands, I heaped up wood and cane and cedar and myrtle. When the gods smelled the sweet savour, they gathered like flies over the sacrifice.'

Utnapishtim then revealed to Gilgamesh the secret of immortality. With the aid of his ferryman, Urshanabi, King Gilgamesh secured this mysterious prickly plant, but his hopes for future rejuvenation were not to be.

'Gilgamesh, I shall reveal a secret thing, it is a mystery of the gods that I am telling you. There is a plant that grows under the water, it has a prickle like a thorn, like a rose; it will wound your hands, but if you succeed in taking it, then your hands will hold that which restores his lost youth to a man.'

When Gilgamesh heard this he opened the sluices so that a sweet-water current might carry him out to the deepest channel; he tied heavy stones to his feet and they dragged him down to the water-bed. There he saw the plant growing; although it pricked him he took it in his hands; then he cut the heavy stones from his feet, and the sea carried him and threw him on to the shore. Gilgamesh said to Urshanabi the ferryman, 'Come here, and see this marvellous plant. By its virtue a man may win back all his former strength. I will take it to Uruk of the strong walls; there I will give it to the old men to eat. Its name shall be "The Old Men Are Young Again"; and at last I shall eat it myself and have back all my lost youth.' So Gilgamesh returned by the gate through which he had come, Gilgamesh and Urshanabi went together. They travelled their twenty leagues and then they broke their fast; after thirty leagues they stopped for the night.

Gilgamesh saw a well of cool water and he went down and bathed; but deep in the pool there was lying a serpent, and the serpent sensed the sweetness of the flower. It rose out of the water and snatched it away, and immediately it sloughed its skin and returned to the well. Then Gilgamesh sat down and wept, the tears ran down his face, and he took the hand of Urshanabi; 'O Urshanabi, was it for this that I toiled with my hands, is it for this I have wrung out my heart's blood? For myself I have gained nothing; not I, but the beast of the earth has joy of it now. Already the stream has carried it twenty leagues back to the channels where I found it. I found a sign and now I have lost it. Let us leave the boat on the bank and go.'

After twenty leagues they broke their fast, after thirty leagues they stopped for the night; in three days they had walked as much as a journey of a month and fifteen days. When the journey was accomplished they arrived at Uruk, the strong-walled city. Gilgamesh spoke to him, to Urshanabi the ferryman, 'Urshanabi, climb up on to the wall of Uruk, inspect its foundation terrace, and examine well the brickwork; see if it is not of burnt bricks; and did not the seven wise men lay these foundations? One third of the whole is city, one third is garden, and one third is field, with the precinct of the goddess Ishtar. These parts and the precinct are all Uruk.'

This too was the work of Gilgamesh, the king, who knew the countries of the world. He was wise, he saw mysteries and knew secret things, he brought us a tale of the days before the flood. He went a long journey, was weary, worn out with labour, and returning engraved on a stone the whole story.

The Babylonian Code of Law

Hammurabi (c. 1792–1750 B.C.) was the sixth Amoritic king of Babylon. The people of Babylon were a Western–Semitic-speaking group who had drifted into Mesopotamia during the third Sumerian Dynasty of Ur. As these Amorites invaded the area, the region had deteriorated into several petty city-states, each trying through either diplomacy or swift attacks to maintain its precarious existence.

Inheriting a rather small area (50 × 30 miles) from his father, King Hammurabi began to enlarge his domain in his twenty-ninth year. He moved against one Sumerian city after another until he had conquered the entire southern region. Then from his thirty-second through thirty-eighth years, he was finally able to consolidate his hold upon Assyria and Northern Syria.

In the second year of his reign, Hammurabi had the Babylonian Code of Law carved on an eight-foot block of black basalt. The text consists of a prologue, epilogue, and 282 laws. The cases deal with court procedures, thefts, slaves, crafts, land tenure, farming, domestic life, trade, and consumer protection. The copy we possess comes from late in the reign and was discovered in the Elamite city of Susa, where it had been taken by invaders.

7

The Laws of Hammurabi

QUESTIONS TO CONSIDER

1. Was there legal equality among the Babylonians?
2. What legal rights did women have? How do those rights compare with those of men?
3. What legal similarities can you find in the Hebrew laws (see Reading 12)?
4. How did the Babylonian laws aid consumers?

1. If a man accuse a man, and charge him with murder, but cannot convict him, the accuser shall be put to death.

2. If a man charge a man with sorcery, but cannot convict him, he who is charged with sorcery shall go to the sacred river, and he shall throw himself into the river; if the river overcome him, his prosecutor shall take to himself his house. If the river show that man to be innocent and he come forth unharmed, he that charged him with sorcery shall be put to death. He who threw himself into the river shall take to himself the house of his accuser.

3. If a man, in a case (before the court), offer testimony concerning deeds of violence, and do not establish the testimony that he has given — if that case be a case involving life, that man shall be put to death. . . .

14. If a man steal a man's son who is a minor, he shall be put to death. . . .

16. If a man harbor in his house a runaway male or female slave of the palace or of a common man and do not bring him forth at the call of the commandant, the owner of the house shall be put to death.

From D. D. Luckenbill, trans., and Edward Chiera, ed., "The Code of Hammurabi," in J. M. Powis Smith, *The Origin and History of Hebrew Law* (Chicago: University of Chicago Press, 1960), pp. 183, 185–186, 189, 191, 195–196, 199–202, 204–205, 209–210, 212–213, 218. Copyright © 1931 by The University of Chicago. Reprinted by permission.

17. If a man catch a runaway male or female slave, in the country, and bring him back to the owner, the owner of the slave shall pay him two shekels of silver. . . .

21. If a man make a breach in a house, they shall put him to death in front of that breach, and they shall bury him there.

22. If a man practice brigandage and be captured, that man shall be put to death.

23. If the brigand be not captured, the man who has been robbed shall establish the amount of his loss before the god, and the city and the governor, in whose land or border the robbery was committed, shall compensate him for whatsoever was lost.

24. If there were loss of life, the city and governor shall pay one mana of silver to his heirs. . . .

42. If a man rent a field for cultivation and do not produce any grain in the field, because he has not performed the necessary work on the field they shall convict him, and he shall give to the owner of the field grain on the basis of the adjacent (fields). . . .

55. If a man open his canal for irrigation and neglect it and he let the water carry away an adjacent field, he shall measure out grain on the basis of the adjacent fields. . . .

98. If a man give silver to a man for a partnership, they shall divide equally before God the profit and the loss, whatever there is (of either). . . .

100. If he (the peddler) made money (*lit.*, saw profit) where he went, he shall write down the interest on all the money he received, and he shall count up his days, and make his return to the merchant.

101. If he made no money where he went, the agent shall double the amount of money obtained and he shall pay it to the merchant. . . .

103. If, when he goes on a journey, an enemy rob him of anything he was carrying, the agent shall take an oath in the name of God and go free. . . .

108. If a barmaid do not take grain in payment of drink, but if she take money by the great stone, or make the measure of drink smaller than the measure of grain, they shall prosecute that barmaid, and they shall throw her into the water.

109. If outlaws hatch a conspiracy in the house of a wine-seller, and she do not arrest these outlaws and bring them to the palace, that wine-seller shall be put to death.

110. If a priestess or a nun who is not resident in a convent open a wineshop or enter a wineshop for a drink, they shall burn that woman. . . .

129. If the wife of a man be taken in lying with another man, they shall bind them and throw them into the water. If the husband of the woman spare the life of his wife, the king shall spare the life of his servant (i.e., subject). . . .

131. If a man accuse his wife and she have not been taken in lying with another man, she shall take an oath in the name of God and she shall return to her house. . . .

137. If a man set his face to put away a concubine who has borne him children or a wife who has presented him with children, they shall return to that woman her dowry and shall give to her part of field, garden, and goods, and she

shall bring up her children ; from the time that her children are grown up, from whatever is given to her children they shall give to her a portion corresponding to that of a son and the man of her choice may marry her.

138. If a man put away his wife who has not borne him children, he shall give her money to the amount of her marriage settlement and he shall make good to her the dowry which she brought from her father's house and then he may put her away. . . .

142. If a woman hate her husband and say, "Thou shalt not have me," her past shall be inquired into for any deficiency of hers ; and if she have been careful and be without past sin and her husband have been going out and greatly belittling her, that woman has no blame. She shall take her dowry and go to her father's house.

143. If she have not been careful, have been going out, ruining her house and belittling her husband, they shall throw that woman into the water. . . .

145. If a man take a wife and she do not present him with children, and he set his face to take a concubine, that man may take a concubine and bring her into his house. That concubine shall not take precedence of his wife. . . .

153. If the wife of a man bring about the death of her husband because of another man, they shall impale that woman. . . .

162. If a man take a wife and she bear him children and that woman die, her father may not lay claim to her dowry. Her dowry belongs to her children. . . .

169. If he have committed a crime against his father sufficiently grave to cut him off from sonship, they shall condone his first (offense). If he commit a grave crime a second time, the father may cut off his son from sonship. . . .

195. If a man strike his father, they shall cut off his hand.

196. If a man destroy the eye of another man, they shall destroy his eye.

197. If he break a man's bone, they shall break his bone.

198. If he destroy the eye of a common man or break a bone of a common man, he shall pay one mana of silver.

199. If he destroy the eye of a man's slave or break a bone of a man's slave, he shall pay one-half his price.

200. If a man knock out a tooth of a man of his own rank, they shall knock out his tooth.

201. If he knock out a tooth of a common man, he shall pay one-third mana of silver.

202. If a man smite on the cheek a man who is his superior, he shall receive sixty strokes with an oxtail whip in public. . . .

215. If a physician make a deep incision upon a man (i.e., perform a major operation) with his bronze lancet and save the man's life ; or if he operate on the eye socket of a man with his bronze lancet and save that man's eye, he shall receive ten shekels of silver. . . .

218. If a physician make a deep incision upon a man with his bronze lancet and cause the man's death, or operate on the eye socket of a man with his bronze lancet and destroy the man's eye, they shall cut off his hand. . . .

226. If a barber without (the consent of) the owner of the slave cut the hair of the forehead of a slave (making him) unrecognizable, they shall cut off the hand of that barber. . . .

229. If a builder erect a house for a man and do not make its construction firm, and the house which he built collapse and cause the death of the owner of the house, that builder shall be put to death.

230. If it cause the death of a son of the owner of the house, they shall put to death a son of that builder.

231. If it cause the death of a slave of the owner of the house, he shall give to the owner of the house slave for slave. . . .

278. If a man buy a male or female slave, and the slave have not completed his month when epilepsy attacks him, the buyer shall return him to the seller and shall receive the money which he paid.

279. If a man buy a male or female slave of a man in a foreign country, and there be a claim against him, the seller shall be responsible for the claim.

280. If a man buy a male or female slave of a man in a foreign country, and if when he comes back to his own land the (former) owner of the male or female slave recognize his male or female slave, if the male or female slave be natives of the land, their freedom shall be granted without money.

281. If they be natives of another land, the buyer shall declare before God the money which he paid (for them), and the owner of the male or female slave shall give to the merchant the money which he paid out, and shall (thus) redeem his male or female slave.

282. If a male slave say to his master, "Thou art not my master," his master shall prove him to be his slave and shall cut off his ear.

The Start of Chinese Writing

In the late nineteenth century, Chinese farmers near Anyang, an ancient capital of the Shang dynasty (c. 1766–1027 B.C. or 1523–1122 B.C.), discovered curious pieces of bone in their fields. Since then, some one hundred thousand pieces of such bone have been dug up at that site. These so-called "dragon bones," often sold as medicine, were actually the undershells of tortoises, the shoulder blades of cattle, and other flat bones. In 1899, Chinese scholars in Peking noticed inscriptions on the dragon bones. This occurrence led to two important historic discoveries: the discovery of the archaeological sites in Anyang, where excavations began in 1928; and the discovery that the inscriptions were a very ancient form of Chinese writing. The bones were dated from the middle of the second millennium B.C.

These inscriptions, however, are not the only evidence of the development of early Chinese writing. Neolithic potsherds (fragments of broken earthen pots) dating from the fifth millennium B.C. also have inscriptions, although these await further study. Certainly the inscribed bones and shells provide a link between the archaic signs and present-day Chinese characters. About 5000 signs scratched on the bones and shells have been recognized. These inscriptions have shed light on the life, thought, religion, and government of Shang China. Because these bones and shells were used in a method of divination, they are now called "oracle bones."

8

The Oracle Bones of Shang

In Shang China, the oracle bones were the most important means of communication between humans and the gods. Shang rulers, as well as the people, never made any important decisions without first consulting the Supreme God. Shang diviners inscribed questions on the bones and then heated them with a red-hot bronze rod or live coal. The questions asked included such subjects as the efficacy of sacrifices; the best times for planting, hunting, fishing, and war; the weather; illness; and travel directions and timing. The reply of the Supreme God to these questions was revealed through the shape or direction of the cracks resulting from the heat. Diviners interpreted the meanings of the cracks, and generally replies were either "yes," "no," "lucky," or "unlucky." The answers were inscribed in the bone or shell for a permanent record. Each inscription generally consisted of approximately 12 characters, although some have had as many as 60 characters.

The characters that were used on the oracle bones were basically pictographs, which represented animals, plants, the sun, the moon, water, fire, houses, spears, and human beings. A circle with a dot in the center represented the sun. A crescent represented the moon. Three peaks represented a mountain. A vertical line with two spreading strokes at the bottom and two others at the top stood for a tree.

Because abstract ideas could not be pictured, ideographs were created. For example, one, two, and three were represented by one, two, and three horizontal strokes, respectively. Two trees standing side by side represented a forest. A woman holding a child meant "good." Two women suggested "quarrel." A woman with a broom meant "wife." An ear between the two panels of a door meant to "hear."

The following material illustrates the development of Chinese writing. Table 1 compares Sumerian words with Chinese oracle characters, and Table 2 displays the evolution of Chinese script. Figure 1 is a photograph of a Shang oracle shell.

QUESTIONS TO CONSIDER

1. How do the oracle bones as writing media compare with those used by the ancient Sumerians and the Egyptians?
2. What principles contributed to the original construction of Chinese characters?

Table 1   *A Comparison of Sumerian Words with Chinese Oracle-Bone Characters*

	Sumerian		Shang oracle inscription		Modern Chinese
1. *a.* heaven	*an*	✳	*t'ien*		天
b. god	*dingir*		*ti*		帝
2. earth	*ki*		*t'u*		土
3. man	*lu*		*jen*		人
4. woman	*munus*	▽	*nü*		女
5. mountain	*kur*		*shan*		山
6. slave-girl	*geme*		*pei*		婢
7. head	*sag*		*shou*		首
8. *a.* mouth	*ka*		*k'ou*		口
b. speak	*dug*		*yüeh*		曰
9. food	*ninda*	▽	*shih*		食
			ssu		飤
10. eat	*ku*		*shih*	(same as in no. 9)	食
			hsiang		饗
11. water	*a*	≈	*shui*		水
12. drink	*nag*		*yin*		飲
13. *a.* to go	*du*		*chih*		之
			wang		往
b. to stand	*gub*		*li*		立
14. bird	***mushen***		*chui*		佳
			niao		鳥
15. fish	*ha*		*yü*		魚
16. ox	*gud*		*mou*		牡
17. cow	*ab*		*p'in*		牝
18. barley	*she*		*mou*		牟、麰
wheat			*lai*		來
			mai		麥

Source: Ping-ti Ho, *The Cradle of the East* (Hong Kong: The Chinese University of Hong Kong; Chicago: The University of Chicago Press, 1975), pp. 247–248. Copyright © 1975 by The Chinese University of Hong Kong. Reprinted with permission of The University of Chicago Press.

Table 2 *The Development of Chinese Script*

PICTOGRAPHS					
Archaic script	Small seal	Modern script	Forms in writing	Meaning	Rad. no.
(archaic glyphs)	*(small seal glyphs)*	人 儿 虎 厇 羊 象 鳥 魚 壺 車 月 山	*(writing form glyphs)*	*jên,* man	9
				hu, tiger	141
				yang, sheep	123
				hsiang, elephant	—
				niao, bird	196
				yü, fish	195
				hu, wine-vessel	—
				chhê, chariot, car	159
				yüeh, moon	74
				shan, mountain	46

INDIRECT SYMBOLS

射 *shê*, to shoot with a bow; 伐 *fa*, to attack (man being decapitated); 為 *wei*, lead, manage, do (hand leading an elephant by the trunk); 立 *li*, to stand (a man standing); 降 *chiang*, descend (hill and two footprints pointing downwards); 陟 *chih*, to mount (footprints upwards); 至 *chih*, arrive at (arrow hitting target); 回 *hui*, revolve (meander); 曰 *yüeh*, speak (mouth and breath); 甘 *kan*, sweet (mouth and something in it); 高 *kao*, high (picture of a high building); 長 *chang*, senior, grown up, *chhang*, extended (long-haired man walking on stick); 力 *li*, strength(ard or plough); 富 *fu*, blest (picture of a jar); 酉 *yu*, wine-must (jar and liquid inside).

ASSOCIATIVE COMPOUNDS

父 *fu*, father (hand and stick); 婦 *fu*, wife (女 woman and 帚 broom); 好 *hao*, to love, *hao*, good (woman and 子 child); 奻 *wan*, to quarrel (two women); 林 *lin*, forest (two 木 trees); 森 *sên*, umbrageous (three trees); 析 *hsi*, split (tree and 斤 axe); 牧 *mu*, tend cattle (ox and hand wielding whip); 鳴 *ming*, sing (鳥 bird and 口 mouth); 男 *nan*, male, man (employ 力 strength in the 田 fields).

DETERMINATIVE-PHONETIC CHARACTERS

耳 *êrh*, ear, is PHONETIC in: 珥 *êrh*, ear-pendant (determinative 玉 jade, precious stone; word cognate to 耳); 餌 *êrh*, cake (det. 食 food or 鬲 cauldron); 耴 *êrh*, plume (det. 毛 hair); 佴 *êrh*, assistant (det. 亻人 man); 蛋 *êrh*, bait (det. 虫 worm); 衈 *êrh*, a sacrifice (det. 血 blood; 恥 *chhih*, shame (det. 心 heart); 弭 *mi*, repress, ends of a bow (det. 弓 bow); DETERMINATIVE in: 聞 *wên*, to hear (phonetic 門 *mên*); 聆 *ling*, listen to, apprehend (phon. 令 *ling*); 聾 *lung*, deaf (phon. 龍 *lung*); 聰 *tshung*, acute of hearing, clever (phon. 悤 *tshung*); 聳 *sung*, alarm, excite (phon. 從 *tshung*).
立 *li*, to stand, is PHONETIC in: 笠 *li*, conical hat (det. 竹 bamboo); 粒 *li*, grain of rice (det. 米 rice or 食 food); 苙 *li*, pen for animals, *chi*, hyacinth (det. 艸 herb, plant); 泣 *chhi*, to weep (det. 氵水 water); 拉 *la*, to pull, break (det. 扌手 hand); 翋 *la*, to fly (det. 羽 wings); 霕 *li,chhih*, heavy rain (det. 雨 rain); 颯 飂 *sa*, storm (det. 風 wind); DETERMINATIVE in: 站 *chan*, to stop (phon. 占 *chan*); 竚 *chu*, to wait for (phon. 宁 *chu*); 竣 *chün, tsun*, stop work (phon. 夋 *chün*); 靖 *ching*, quiet (phon. 青 *chhing*); 端 *tuan*, extremity, origin, end, principle (phon. 耑 *chuan*); 竭 *chieh*, exhausted (phon. 曷 *ho*).

Source: Joseph Needham, *Science and Civilisation in China,* vol. 1 (New York: Cambridge University Press, 1954), p. 29. Reprinted with permission.

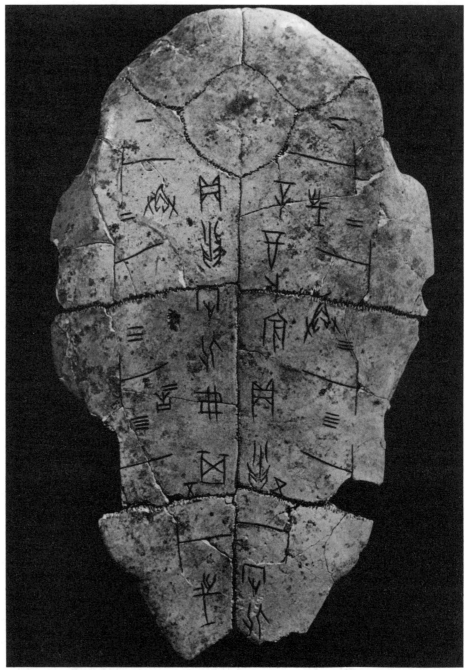

Figure 1   *Oracle shell from the Shang dynasty. The inscribed characters indicate questions being posed to the Supreme God; the heat-induced cracks were interpreted as answers. (Photograph by Wan-go Weng / Collection Academia Sinica, Taipei.)*

Religious Reform in Egypt

The Egyptian pharaoh Amenhotep IV (c. 1367 B.C.) and his wife Nefertiti attempted to break completely with traditional Egyptian religion. They substituted the worship of the sun disk, Aton, in place of the hundreds of older gods. This radical change caused a revolution in both literary and artistic styles; intimate family scenes now portrayed the pharaoh as a loving father and husband, while hymns and funeral inscriptions prayed to and through him to reach the new cosmic god.

Evidently, priests opposed the pharaoh's new ideas. In his fifth regnal year, Amenhotep and his family left the capital of Thebes for a new city, which the pharaoh called Akhetaton (meaning the gleaming horizon of Aton). Not content with just changing his residence, the pharaoh also changed his name to Akhenaton (meaning one who is serviceable to Aton) as well as all the names and titles of his family. Orders were given to destroy the old gods' names on the temples and tombs, including those of his father, Amenhotep III.

Once the political and religious changes occurred, knowledge about the royal family — especially Nefertiti — became clouded. The queen disappeared from public view and was, perhaps, replaced in the affections of the pharaoh by a man called Smenkhkare, who may have been Akhenaton's son. Although the pharaoh continued his religious reform unabated, the Egyptian Empire began to disintegrate because of attacks from the Hittite Empire or its client states.

The following Hymn to Aton reflects Akhenaton's belief in the universality and, at the same time, the uniqueness of Aton. It often has been compared with Psalm 104. This selection juxtaposes corresponding passages of the Hymn to Aton (*left column*) and Psalm 104 of the Old Testament (*right column*).

9

The Hymn to Aton and Psalm 104

QUESTIONS TO CONSIDER

1. Why was the Aton worship such a dramatic change in Egyptian history?
2. What was the relationship and role of the pharaoh to Aton?
3. Compare the ethical principles of the Hebrews (see Readings 11–15) and this hymn. What is missing from the *Hymn to Aton*?

Praise of Re Har-akhti, Rejoicing on the Horizon, in his name as Shu Who Is in the Aton-disc,[1] living forever and ever; the living great Aton who is in jubilee, lord of all that the Aton encircles, lord of heaven, lord of earth, lord of the House of Aton in Akhet-Aton;[2] (and praise of) the King of Upper and Lower Egypt, who lives on truth, the Lord of the Two Lands: Nefer-kheperu-Re Wa-en-Re; the Son of Re, who lives on truth, the Lord of Diadems: Akh-en-Aton, long in his lifetime; (and praise of) the Chief Wife of the King, his beloved, the Lady of the Two Lands: Nefer-neferu-Aton Nefert-iti, living, healthy, and youthful forever and ever; (by) the Fan-bearer on the Right Hand of the King . . . Eye. He says:

Thou appearest beautifully on the
    horizon of heaven,
Thou living Aton, the beginning of
    life!
When thou art risen on the eastern
    horizon,
Thou hast filled every land with thy
    beauty.
Thou art gracious, great, glistening,
    and high over every land;
Thy rays encompass the lands to the
    limit of all that thou hast made:
As thou art Re, thou reaches to the
    end of them;[3]
(Thou) subduest them (for) thy
    beloved son.[4]

From "The Hymn to the Aton," trans. John A. Wilson, in *Ancient Near Eastern Texts Relating to the Old Testament,* 3rd ed. with Supplement, ed. James B. Pritchard (Princeton : Princeton University Press, 1969), pp. 369–371. Copyright © 1969 by Princeton University Press. Reprinted with permission of Princeton University Press. Psalm 104 is from the King James Version.

1. The Aton had a dogmatic name written within a royal cartouche and including the three old solar deities, Re, Har-of-the-Horizon, and Shu.
2. Akhet-Aton was the name of the capital at Tell el-Amarna.
3. Pun : *Ra* "Re," and *er-ra* "to the end."
4. Akh-en-Aton.

Though thou art far away, thy rays
   are on earth;
Though thou art in *their* faces, *no
   one knows thy* going.

When thou settest in the western
   horizon,
The land is in darkness, in the
   manner of death.
They sleep in a room, with heads
   wrapped up,
Nor sees one eye the other.
All their goods which are under
   their heads might be stolen,
(But) they would not perceive (it).
Every lion is come forth from his
   den;
All creeping things, they sting.
Darkness *is a shroud,* and the earth
   is in stillness,
For he who made them rests in his
   horizon.

At daybreak, when thou arisest on
   the horizon,
When thou shinest as the Aton by
   day,
Thou drivest away the darkness and
   givest thy rays.
The Two Lands are in festivity *every
   day,*
Awake and standing upon (their)
   feet,
For thou hast raised them up.
Washing their bodies, taking (their)
   clothing,
Their arms are (raised) in praise at
   thy appearance.
All the world, they do their work.
All beasts are content with their
   pasturage;
Trees and plants are flourishing.
The birds which fly from their
   nests,
Their wings are (stretched out) in
   praise to thy *Ra.*
All beasts spring upon (their) feet.
Whatever flies and alights,

Thou makest darkness, and it is
night: wherein all the beasts of the
forest do creep *forth.*
   The young lions roar after their
prey, and seek their meat from God.

The sun ariseth, they gather themselves together, and lay them down in
their dens.
   Man goeth forth unto his work
and to his labour until the evening.
   They give drink to every beast of
the field: the wild asses quench their
thirst.
   By them shall the fowls of the
heaven have their habitation, *which*
sing among the branches.
   He watereth the hills from his
chambers: the earth is satisfied with
the fruit of thy works.

They live when thou hast risen (for)
  them.
The ships are sailing north and
  south as well,
For every way is open at thy
  appearance.
The fish in the river dart before thy
  face;
Thy rays are in the midst of the
  great green sea.

Creator of seed in women,
Thou who makest fluid into man,
Who maintainest the son in the
  womb of his mother,
Who soothest him with that which
  stills his weeping,
Thou nurse (even) in the womb,
Who givest breath to sustain all that
  he has made!
When he descends from the womb
  to *breathe*
On the day when he is born,
Thou openest his mouth
  completely,
Thou suppliest his necessities.
When the chick in the egg speaks
  within the shell,
Thou givest him breath within it to
  maintain him.
When thou hast made him his
  fulfillment within the egg, to
  break it,
He comes forth from the egg to
  speak at his completed (time);
He walks upon his legs when he
  comes forth from it.

How manifold it is, what thou hast
  made!
They are hidden from the face (of
  man).
O sole god, like whom there is no
  other!
Thou didst create the world
  according to thy desire,

He causeth the grass to grow for
the cattle, and herb for the service of
man: that he may bring forth food
out of the earth;

So is this great and wide sea,
wherein *are* things creeping
innumerable, both small and great
beasts.
  There go the ships: *there is* that
leviathan, *whom* thou hast made to
play therein.

O LORD, how manifold are thy
works! in wisdom hast thou made

Whilst thou wert alone : All men,
cattle, and wild beasts,

Whatever is on earth, going upon
(its) feet,
And what is on high, flying with its
wings.
The countries of Syria and Nubia,
the *land* of Egypt,
Thou settest every man in his place,
Thou suppliest their necessities :
Everyone has his food, and his time
of life is reckoned.
Their tongues are separate in
speech,
And their natures as well ;
Their skins are distinguished,
As thou distinguishest the foreign
peoples.
Thou makest a Nile in the
underworld,
Thou bringest it forth as thou
desirest
To maintain the people (of Egypt)[5]
According as thou madest them for
thyself,
The lord of all of them, wearying
(himself) with them,
The lord of every land, rising for
them,
The Aton of the day, great of
majesty.
All distant foreign countries, thou
makest their life (also),
For thou hast set a Nile in heaven,
That it may descend for them and
make waves upon the mountains,
Like the great green sea,
To water their fields in their towns.[6]
How effective they are, thy plans, O
lord of eternity !
The Nile in heaven, it is for the
foreign peoples

them all : the earth is full of thy
riches.

These wait all upon thee ; that
thou mayest give *them* their meat in
due season.

He sendeth the springs into the
valleys, *which* run among the hills.

5. The Egyptian believed that their Nile came from the waters under the earth, called by
them Nun.
6. The rain of foreign countries is like the Nile of rainless Egypt.

And for the beasts of every desert
    that go upon (their) feet;
(While the true) Nile comes from
    the underworld for Egypt.

Thy rays suckle every meadow.
When thou risest, they live, they
    grow for thee.
Thou makest the seasons in order
    to rear all that thou hast made,
The winter to cool them,
And the heat that *they* may taste
    thee.
Thou hast made the distant sky in
    order to rise therein,
In order to see all that thou dost
    make.
Whilst thou wert alone,
Rising in thy form as the living
    Aton,
Appearing, shining, *withdrawing or
approaching,*
Thou madest millions of forms of
    thyself alone.
Cities, towns, fields, road, and
    river —
Every eye beholds thee over against
    them,
For thou art the Aton of the day
    over *the earth.* . . .

Thou art in my heart,
And there is no other that knows
    thee
Save thy son Nefer-kheperu-Re Wa-
    en-Re,[7]
For thou hast made him well-versed
    in thy plans and in thy strength.[8]
The world came into being by thy
    hand,
According as thou hast made them.
When thou hast risen they live,

    7. Even though the hymn was recited by the official Eye, he states that Akh-en-Aton alone knows the Aton.
    8. Pharaoh was the official intermediary between the Egyptians and their gods. The Amarna religion did not change this dogma.

When thou settest they die.
Thou art lifetime thy own self,
For one lives (only) through thee.
Eyes are (fixed) on beauty until
  thou settest.
All work is laid aside when thou
  settest in the west.
(But) when (thou) risest (again),
[*Everything is*] made to flourish for
  the king, . . .
Since thou didst found the earth
And raise them up for thy son,
Who came forth from thy body :
  the king of Upper and Lower
  Egypt, . . . Akh-en-Aton, . . . and
  the Chief Wife of the King . . .
  Nefert-iti, living and youthful
  forever and ever.

Education in Egypt

The ancient Egyptians had a high regard for education, which meant learning the complicated hieroglyphic writing. Thousands of papyri, writing tablets, and shards of pottery have been preserved. These were covered with exercises which young boys had to reproduce in order to learn the scribal art.

Writing was taught in the "House of Life" by having the students copy ancient texts such as "Instructions," maxims, prayers, business letters, legal documents, hymns and religious texts, while their teachers made corrections. As the student copied down these texts, they learned spelling, grammar, and practical or moral ideas contained within them.

It is thought that the scribal profession was open to any male in Egypt. Once a boy had learned how to read and write, he could enter the "House of Life" as a teacher. If the student really applied himself, other positions in the civil service, even that of governor or vizir, or service in the temples might provide employment opportunities. Some of the letters suggest that senior officials wrote instructive letters or literature in order to help a young man advance in his career.

The following selection is from a book called the *Papyrus Lansing* and is dated to the late New Kingdom period (after 1200 B.C.). A royal scribe urges his apprentice to work hard as the scribal profession is the best when compared to any other. His apprentice responds with appreciation for his mentor's advice.

10

Papyrus Lansing: A Schoolbook

QUESTIONS TO CONSIDER

1. Why was the scribe unhappy with his apprentice?
2. Why is the scribal profession the best of all?
3. How does the apprentice show his appreciation for his teacher?

Title

[Beginning of the instruction in letter-writing made by the royal scribe and chief overseer of the cattle of Amen-Re, King of Gods, Nebmare-nakht] for his apprentice, the scribe Wenemdiamun.

Praise of the Scribe's Profession

[The royal scribe] and chief overseer of the cattle of Amen-[Re, King of Gods, Nebmare-nakht speaks to the scribe Wenemdiamun]. [Apply yourself to this] noble profession. . . . You will find it useful. . . . You will be advanced by your superiors. You will be sent on a mission. . . . Love writing, shun dancing; then you become a worthy official. Do not long for the marsh thicket. Turn your back on throw stick and chase. By day write with your fingers; recite by night. Befriend the scroll, the palette. It pleases more than wine. Writing for him who knows it is better than all other professions. It pleases more than bread and beer, more than clothing and ointment. It is worth more than an inheritance in Egypt, than a tomb in the west.

Advice to the Unwilling Pupil

Young fellow, how conceited you are! You do not listen when I speak. Your heart is denser than a great obelisk, a hundred cubits high, ten cubits thick. When it is finished and ready for loading, many work gangs draw it. It hears the words of men; it is loaded on a barge. Departing from Yebu it is conveyed, until it comes to rest on its place in Thebes.

So also a cow is bought this year, and it plows the following year. It learns to listen to the herdsman; it only lacks words. Horses brought from the field, they forget their mothers. Yoked they go up and down on all his majesty's errands.

Miriam Lichtheim, *Ancient Egyptian Literature. Three Volumes,* pages 168–173 (Berkeley : University of California Press, 1976). Copyright © 1973–1980 Regents.

They become like those that bore them, that stand in the stable. They do their utmost for fear of a beating.

But though I beat you with every kind of stick, you do not listen. If I knew another way of doing it, I would do it for you, that you might listen. You are a person fit for writing, though you have not yet known a woman. Your heart discerns, your fingers are skilled, your mouth is apt for reciting.

Writing is more enjoyable than enjoying a basket of . . . and beans ; more enjoyable than a mother's giving birth, when her heart knows no distaste. She is constant in nursing her son ; her breast is in his mouth every day. Happy is the heart <of>[1] him who writes ; he is young each day.

The Idle Scribe Is Worthless

The royal scribe and chief overseer of the cattle of Amen-Re, King of Gods, Nebmare-nakht, speaks to the scribe Wenemdiamun, as follows. You are busy coming and going, and don't think of writing. You resist listening to me ; you neglect my teachings.

You are worse than the goose of the shore, that is busy with mischief. It spends the summer destroying the dates, the winter destroying the seed-grain. It spends the balance of the year in pursuit of the cultivators. It does not let seed be cast to the ground without snatching it ? in its fall. ? One cannot catch it by snaring. One does not offer it in the temple. The evil, sharpeyed bird that does no work !

You are worse than the desert antelope that lives by running. It spends no day in plowing. Never at all does it tread on the threshing-floor. It lives on the oxen's labor, without entering among them. But though I spend the day telling you "Write," it seems like a plague to you. Writing is very pleasant ! . . .

All Occupations Are Bad Except That of the Scribe

See for yourself with your own eye. The occupations lie before you.

The washerman's day is going up, going down. All his limbs are weak, <from> whitening his neighbors' clothes every day, from washing their linen.

The maker of pots is smeared with soil, like one whose relations have died. His hands, his feet are full of clay ; he is like one who lives in the bog.

The cobbler mingles with vats. His odor is penetrating. His hands are red with madder, like one who is smeared with blood. He looks behind him for the kite, like one whose flesh is exposed.

The watchman prepares garlands and polishes vase-stands. He spends a night of toil just as one on whom the sun shines.

The merchants travel downstream and upstream. They are as busy as can be, carrying goods from one town to another. They supply him who has wants. But the tax collectors carry off the gold, that most precious of metals.

1. Words omitted by scribes are represented by the symbols < / >.

The ships' crews from every house (of commerce), they receive their loads. They depart from Egypt for Syria, and each man's god is with him. (But) not one of them says: "We shall see Egypt again!"

The carpenter who is in the shipyard carries the timber and stacks it. If he gives today the output of yesterday, woe to his limbs! The shipwright stands behind him to tell him evil things.

His outworker who is in the fields, his is the toughest of all the jobs. He spends the day loaded with his tools, tied to his tool-box. When he returns home at night, he is loaded with the tool-box and the timbers, his drinking mug, and his whetstones.

The scribe, he alone, records the output of all of them. Take note of it!

The Misfortunes of the Peasant

Let me also expound to you the situation of the peasant, that other tough occupation. [Comes] the inundation and soaks him . . . , he attends to his equipment. By day he cuts his farming tools; by night he twists rope. Even his midday hour he spends on farm labor. He equips himself to go to the field as if he were a warrior. The dried field lies before him; he goes out to get his team. When he has been after the herdsman for many days, he gets his team and comes back with it. He makes for it a place in the field. Comes dawn, he goes to make a start and does not find it in its place. He spends three days searching for it; he finds it in the bog. He finds no hides on them; the jackals have chewed them. He comes out, his garment in his hand, to beg for himself a team.

When he reaches his field he finds <it> ? broken up ?. He spends time cultivating, and the snake is after him. It finishes off the seed as it is cast to the ground. He does not see a green blade. He does three plowings with borrowed grain. His wife has gone down to the merchants and found nothing for ? barter. ? Now the scribe lands on the shore. He surveys the harvest. Attendants are behind him with staffs, Nubians[2] with clubs. One says (to him): "Give grain." "There is none." He is beaten savagely. He is bound, thrown in the well, submerged head down. His wife is bound in his presence. His children are in fetters. His neighbors abandon them and flee. When it's over, there's no grain.

If you have any sense, be a scribe. If you have learned about the peasant, you will not be able to be one. Take note of it! . . .

The Scribe Does Not Suffer Like the Soldier

Furthermore. Look, I instruct you to make you sound; to make you hold the palette freely. To make you become one whom the king trusts; to make you gain entrance to treasury and granary. To make you receive the ship-load at the gate of the granary. To make you issue the offerings on feast days. You are dressed in fine clothes; you own horses. Your boat is on the river; you are supplied with atten-

---

2. The southern border of ancient Egypt stopped at the First Cataract, near present day Aswan. This area was known as Nubia to which the Egyptians traveled for trade in oils, spices, and gold during the Old Kingdom. Later, during the Middle and New Kingdom, the Egyptians ruled Nubia as a province.

dants. You stride about inspecting. A mansion is built in your town. You have a powerful office, given you by the king. Male and female slaves are about you. Those who are in the fields grasp your hand, on plots that you have made. Look, I make you into a staff of life! Put the writings in your heart, and you will be protected from all kinds of toil. You will become a worthy official.

Do you not recall the (fate of) the unskilled man? His name is not known. He is ever burdened <like an ass carrying> in front of the scribe who knows what he is about.

Come, <let me tell> you the woes of the soldier, and how many are his superiors: the general, the troop-commander, the officer who leads, the standard-bearer, the lieutenant, the scribe, the commander of fifty, and the garrison-captain. They go in and out in the halls of the palace, saying: "Get laborers!" He is awakened at any hour. One is after him as (after) a donkey. He toils until the Aten (sun) sets in his darkness of night. He is hungry, his belly hurts; he is dead while yet alive. When he receives the grain-ration, having been released from duty, it is not good for grinding.

He is called up for Syria. He may not rest. There are no clothes, no sandals. The weapons of war are assembled at the fortress of Sile. His march is uphill through mountains. He drinks water every third day; it is smelly and tastes of salt. His body is ravaged by illness. The enemy comes, surrounds him with missiles, and life recedes from him. He is told: "Quick, forward, valiant soldier! Win for yourself a good name!" He does not know what he is about. His body is weak, his legs fail him. When victory is won, the captives are handed over to his majesty, to be taken to Egypt. The foreign woman faints on the march; she hangs herself <on> the soldier's neck. His knapsack drops, another grabs it while he is burdened with the woman. His wife and children are in their village; he dies and does not reach it. If he comes out alive, he is worn out from marching. Be he at large, be he detained, the soldier suffers. If he leaps and joins the deserters, all his people are imprisoned. He dies on the edge of the desert, and there is none to perpetuate his name. He suffers in death as in life. A big sack is brought for him; he does not know his resting place.

Be a scribe, and be spared from soldiering! You call and one says: "Here I am." You are safe from torments. Every man seeks to raise himself up. Take note of it!

The Pupil Wishes to Build a Mansion for His Teacher

Furthermore. (To) the royal scribe and chief overseer of the cattle of Amen-Re, King of Gods, Nebmare-nakht. The scribe Wenemdiamun greets his lord: In life, prosperity, and health! This letter is to inform my lord. Another message to my lord. I grew into a youth at your side. You beat my back; your teaching entered my ear. I am like a pawing horse. Sleep does not enter my heart by day; nor is it upon me at night. (For I say): I will serve my lord just as a slave serves his master.

I shall build a new mansion for you <on> the ground of your town, with trees (planted) on all its sides. There are stables within it. Its barns are full of barley and emmer, wheat,? cumin,? dates, . . . beans, lentils, coriander, peas, seed-grain, . . . flax, herbs, reeds, rushes, . . . dung for the winter, alfa grass, reeds, . . .

grass, produced by the basketful. Your herds abound in draft animals, your cows are pregnant. I will make for you five aruras of cucumber beds to the south.

Moses and the Law

According to the Bible, Moses (after 1300 B.C.) was born to Hebrew parents during the time when Israelites were persecuted by Egyptians and treated as slaves. As a grown man, Moses fled into the desert to escape punishment by the pharaoh for killing an Egyptian. Upon God's command, he led the Hebrew people on an exodus out of Egypt to the promised land of Canaan.

During the 40-year exodus, Moses was led, by God, into the mountains of Mount Sinai and given the Ten Commandments and the Laws, which formed the basis of formal Hebrew religion. If the Israelites followed these laws, God would guide, protect, and lead the people to the Promised Land of Canaan.

Although tradition ascribed the writing of the first five books of the Bible (the Torah or Pentateuch) to the period of Moses, biblical scholars have shown that, in truth, the various parts of the Torah must have been created over many centuries. Some sections of the Torah reveal a wandering, pastoral people, while others describe a settled, highly organized group.

The greatest problem for Moses and his successors was to keep the Hebrew religion untainted by Canaanite practices. These included polytheism, ritual prostitution, image making, and child sacrifices, to name but a few.

In the following passages from Exodus, God makes a Covenant with the Hebrews, choosing them for a holy mission to show that the whole earth belonged to Him. The terms of the Covenant, embodied in the Ten Commandments, are the moral and ethical laws and religious duties by which the Hebrews were expected to live. If they abided by these commandments, God promised that an angel would guide them into Canaan ; those who disobeyed would be destroyed. Yet it can be seen how easily the Hebrews could fall into Canaanite ways — even while Moses was receiving the Covenant.

11

The Ten Commandments

Leading the Hebrews on the Exodus out of Egypt, Moses ascends Mount Sinai, where he receives the Ten Commandments. These commandments are the terms of the agreement or Covenant between God and the Hebrews.

QUESTIONS TO CONSIDER

1. What elements of the Ten Commandments show a refined moral concern?
2. What things are permitted or denied in the Hebrew religion?
3. What teachings were transmitted to other Near Eastern religions?
4. Are there any similar ethical principles in the Hindu religion (see Readings 21–24), the Buddhist religion (see Readings 27–28), or Chinese philosophy (see Reading 32)?

And God spoke all these words, saying,

I am the Lord thy God, which have brought thee out of the land of Egypt, out of the house of bondage.

Thou shalt have no other gods before me.

Thou shalt not make unto thee any graven image, or any likeness of any thing that is in heaven above, or that is in the earth beneath, or that is in the water under the earth:

Thou shalt not bow down thyself to them, nor serve them: for I the Lord thy God am a jealous God, visiting the iniquity of the fathers upon the children unto the third and fourth generation of them that hate me;

And showing mercy unto thousands of them that love me, and keep my commandments.

Thou shalt not take the name of the Lord thy God in vain; for the Lord will not hold him guiltless that taketh his name in vain.

Remember the sabbath day, to keep it holy.

Six days shalt thou labour, and do all thy work:

But the seventh day is the sabbath of the Lord thy God: in it thou shalt not do any work, thou, nor thy son, nor thy daughter, thy manservant, nor thy maidservant, nor thy cattle, nor thy stranger that is within thy gates:

For in six days the Lord made heaven and earth, the sea and all that in them is, and rested the seventh day: wherefore the Lord blessed the sabbath day, and hallowed it.

Honour thy father and thy mother: that thy days may be long upon the land which the Lord thy God giveth thee.

Thou shalt not kill.

Thou shalt not commit adultery.

Thou shalt not steal.

Thou shalt not bear false witness against thy neighbour.

Thou shalt not covet thy neighbour's house, thou shalt not covet thy neighbour's wife, nor his manservant, nor his maidservant, nor his ox, nor his ass, nor any thing that is thy neighbour's.

And all the people saw the thunderings, and the lightnings, and the noise of the trumpet, and the mountain smoking: and when the people saw it, they removed, and stood afar off.

And they said unto Moses, Speak thou with us, and we will hear: but let not God speak with us, lest we die.

And Moses said unto the people, Fear not: for God is come to prove you, and that his fear may be before your faces, that ye sin not.

From Exodus, 20:1–26 (King James Version); slightly modernized.

And the people stood afar off, and Moses drew near unto the thick darkness where God was.

And the Lord said unto Moses, Thus thou shalt say unto the children of Israel, Ye have seen that I have talked with you from heaven.

Ye shall not make with me gods of silver, neither shall ye make unto you gods of gold.

An altar of earth thou shalt make unto me, and shalt sacrifice thereon thy burnt offerings, and thy peace offerings, thy sheep, and thine oxen : in all places where I record my name I will come unto thee, and I will bless thee.

And if thou wilt make me an altar of stone, thou shalt not build it of hewn stone : for if thou lift up thy tool upon it, thou hast polluted it.

Neither shalt thou go up by steps unto mine altar, that thy nakedness be not discovered thereon.

12

Laws and Ordinances

These passages from the Book of the Covenant (Exodus) reveal a very strict code of punishment. Many of these laws seem to parallel the Laws of Hammurabi.

QUESTION TO CONSIDER

1. What are the similarities between these laws and those of Hammurabi (see Reading 7)?

Now these are the judgments which thou shalt set before them.

If thou buy an Hebrew servant, six years he shall serve : and in the seventh he shall go out free for nothing.

If he came in by himself, he shall go out by himself : if he were married, then his wife shall go out with him.

If his master have given him a wife, and she have born him sons or daughters ; the wife and her children shall be her master's, and he shall go out by himself.

And if the servant shall plainly say, I love my master, my wife, and my children ; I will not go out free :

Then his master shall bring him unto the judges ; he shall also bring him to the door, or unto the door post ; and his master shall bore his ear through with an aul ; and he shall serve him for ever.

From Exodus, 21 :1–36 (King James Version) ; slightly modernized.

And if a man sell his daughter to be a maidservant, she shall not go out as the menservants do.

If she please not her master, who hath betrothed her to himself, then shall he let her be redeemed : to sell her unto a strange nation he shall have no power, seeing he hath dealt deceitfully with her.

And if he have betrothed her unto his son, he shall deal with her after the manner of daughters.

If he take him another wife ; her food, her raiment, her duty of marriage, shall he not diminish.

And if he do not these three unto her, then shall she go out free without money.

He that smiteth a man, so that he die, shall be surely put to death.

And if a man lie not in wait, but God deliver him into his hand ; then I will appoint thee a place whither he shall flee.

But if a man come presumptuously upon his neighbour, to slay him with guile ; thou shalt take him from mine altar, that he may die.

And he that smiteth his father, or his mother, shall be surely put to death.

And he that stealeth a man, and selleth him, or if he be found in his hand, he shall surely be put to death.

And he that curseth his father, or his mother, shall surely be put to death.

And if men strive together, and one smite another with a stone, or with his fist, and he die not, but keepeth his bed :

If he rise again, and walk abroad upon his staff, then shall he that smote him be quit : only he shall pay for the loss of his time, and shall cause him to be thoroughly healed.

And if a man smite his servant, or his maid, with a rod, and he die under his hand ; he shall be surely punished.

Notwithstanding, if he continue a day or two, he shall not be punished : for he is his money.

If men strive, and hurt a woman with child, so that her fruit depart from her, and yet no mischief follow : he shall be surely punished, according as the woman's husband will lay upon him ; and he shall pay as the judges determine.

And if any mischief follow, then thou shalt give life for life,

Eye for eye, tooth for tooth, hand for hand, foot for foot,

Burning for burning, wound for wound, stripe for stripe.

And if a man smite the eye of his servant, or the eye of his maid, that it perish ; he shall let him go free for his eye's sake.

And if he smite out his manservant's tooth, or his maidservant's tooth ; he shall let him go free for his tooth's sake.

If an ox gore a man or a woman that they die : then the ox shall be surely stoned, and his flesh shall not be eaten ; but the owner of the ox shall be quit.

But if the ox were wont to push with horn in time past, and it hath been testified to his owner, and he hath not kept him in, but that he hath killed a man or a woman ; the ox shall be stoned, and his owner shall also be put to death.

If there be laid on him a sum of money, then he shall give for the ransom of his life whatsoever is laid upon him.

Whether he have gored a son, or have gored a daughter, according to this judgment shall it be done unto him.

If the ox shall push a manservant or a maidservant; he shall give unto their master thirty shekels of silver, and the ox shall be stoned.

And if a man shall open a pit, or if a man shall dig a pit, and not cover it, and an ox or an ass fall therein;

The owner of the pit shall make it good, and give money unto the owner of them; and the dead beast shall be his.

And if one man's ox hurt another's, that he die; then they shall sell the live ox, and divide the money of it; and the dead ox also they shall divide.

Or if it be known that the ox hath used to push in time past, and his owner hath not kept him in; he shall surely pay ox for ox; and the dead shall be his own.

13

Cult and Covenant

This section describes the festivals of the Hebrews and the sacrifices that were to be made to God. If the Hebrews obeyed the laws of the Covenant, they would prosper; if they did not, God vowed to destroy them.

QUESTIONS TO CONSIDER

1. What is a covenant?
2. What were the obligations of the Hebrews to their God?
3. What results did God promise the Hebrews?

And six years thou shalt sow thy land, and shalt gather in the fruits thereof:

But the seventh year thou shalt let it rest and lie still; that the poor of thy people may eat: and what they leave the beasts of the field shall eat. In like manner thou shalt deal with thy vineyard, and with thy oliveyard.

Six days thou shalt do thy work, and on the seventh day thou shalt rest: that thine ox and thine ass may rest, and the son of thy handmaid, and the stranger, may be refreshed.

And in all things that I have said unto you be circumspect: and make no mention of the name of other gods, neither let it be heard out of thy mouth.

Three times thou shalt keep a feast unto me in the year.

Thou shalt keep the feast of unleavened bread: (thou shalt eat unleavened seven days, as I commanded thee in the time appointed of the month Abib; for in it thou camest out from Egypt: and none shall appear before me empty:)

From Exodus, 23:10–33 (King James Version); slightly modernized.

And the feast of harvest, the firstfruits of thy labours, which thou hast sown in the field : and the feast of in-gathering, which is in the end of the year, when thou hast gathered in thy labours out of the field.

Three times in the year all thy males shall appear before the Lord God.

Thou shalt not offer the blood of my sacrifice with leavened bread ; neither shall the fat of my sacrifice remain until the morning.

The first of the firstfruits of thy land thou shalt bring into the house of the Lord thy God. Thou shalt not boil a kid in his mother's milk.

Behold, I send an Angel before thee, to keep thee in the way, and to bring thee into the place which I have prepared.

Beware of him, and obey his voice, provoke him not ; for he will not pardon your transgressions : for my name is in him.

But if thou shalt indeed obey his voice, and do all that I speak ; then I will be an enemy unto thine enemies, and an adversary unto thine adversaries.

For mine Angel shall go before thee, and bring thee in unto the Amorites, and the Hittites, and the Perizzites, and the Canaanites, and the Hivites and the Jebusites ; and I will cut them off.

Thou shalt not bow down to their gods, nor serve them, nor do after their works : but thou shalt utterly overthrow them, and quite breakdown their images.

And ye shall serve the Lord your God, and he shall bless thy bread, and thy water ; and I will take sickness away from the midst of thee.

There shall nothing cast their young, nor be barren, in thy land : the number of thy days I will fulfill.

I will send my fear before thee, and will destroy all the people to whom thou shalt come, and I will make all thine enemies turn their backs unto thee.

And I will send hornets before thee, which shall drive out the Hivite, the Canaanite, and the Hittite, from before thee.

I will not drive them out from before thee in one year ; lest the land become desolate, and the beast of the field multiply against thee.

By little and little I will drive them out from before thee, until thou be increased, and inherit the land.

And I will set thy bounds from the Red sea even unto the sea of the Philistines, and from the desert unto the river : for I will deliver the inhabitants of the land into your hand ; and thou shalt drive them out before thee.

Thou shalt make no covenant with them, nor with their gods.

They shall not dwell in thy land, lest they make thee sin against me : for if thou serve their gods, it will surely be a snare unto thee.

14

Sin

While Moses was receiving the Ten Commandments, the Hebrews broke God's commandments.

QUESTIONS TO CONSIDER

1. What sin did the Hebrews commit that angered their God?
2. Why would other religions have accepted the Hebrew's act of worship?

And when the people saw that Moses delayed to come down out of the mount, the people gathered themselves together unto Aaron, and said unto him, Up, make us gods, which shall go before us ; for as for this Moses, the man that brought us up out of the land of Egypt, we know not what is become of him.

And Aaron said unto them, Break off the golden earrings, which are in the ears of your wives, of your sons, and of your daughters, and bring them to me.

And all the people broke off the golden earrings which were in their ears, and brought them unto Aaron.

And he received them at their hand, and fashioned it with a graving tool, after he made it a molten calf : and they said, These be thy gods, O Israel, which brought thee up out of the land of Egypt.

And when Aaron saw it, he built an altar before it ; and Aaron made proclamation, and said, Tomorrow is a feast to the Lord.

And they rose up early on the morrow, and offered burnt offerings, and brought peace offerings ; and the people sat down to eat and to drink, and rose up to play.

And the Lord said unto Moses, Go, get thee down ; for thy people, which thou broughtest out of the land of Egypt, have corrupted themselves :

They turned aside quickly out of the way which I commanded them : they have made them a molten calf, and have worshipped it, and have sacrificed thereunto, and said, These be thy gods, O Israel, which have brought thee up out of the land of Egypt.

And the Lord said unto Moses, I have seen this people, and, behold, it is a stiffnecked people :

Now therefore let me alone, that my wrath may wax hot against them, and that I may consume them : and I will make of thee a great nation.

And Moses besought the Lord his God, and said, Lord, why doth thy wrath wax hot against thy people, which thou hast brought forth out of the land of Egypt with great power, and with a mighty hand?

Wherefore should the Egyptians speak, and say, For mischief did he bring them out, to slay them in the mountains, and to consume them from the face of the earth ? Turn from thy fierce wrath, and repent of this evil against thy people.

Remember Abraham, Isaac, and Israel, thy servants, to whom thou swarest by thine own self, and saidst unto them, I will multiply your seed as the stars of heaven, and all this land that I have spoken of will I give unto your seed, and they shall inherit it for ever.

And the Lord repented of the evil which he thought to do unto his people.

And Moses turned, and went down from the mount, and the two tables of the testimony were in his hand : the tables were written on both their sides ; on the one side and on the other were they written.

And the tables were the work of God, and the writing was the writing of God, graven upon the tables.

From Exodus, 32 :1–35 (King James Version) ; slightly modernized.

And when Joshua heard the noise of the people as they shouted, he said unto Moses, There is a noise of war in the camp.

And he said, It is not the voice of them that shout for mastery, neither is it the voice of them that cry for being overcome : but the noise of them that sing do I hear.

And it came to pass, as soon as he came nigh unto the camp, that he saw the calf, and the dancing : and Moses' anger was waxed hot, and he cast the tables out of his hands, and broke them beneath the mount.

And he took the calf which they had made, and burnt it in the fire, and ground it to powder, and threw it upon the water, and made the children of Israel drink of it.

And Moses said unto Aaron, What did this people unto thee, that thou hast brought so great a sin upon them ?

And Aaron said, Let not the anger of my lord wax hot : thou knowest the people, that they are set on mischief.

For they said unto me, Make us gods, which shall go before us : for as for this Moses, the man that brought us up out of the land of Egypt, we know not what is become of him.

And I said unto them, Whosoever hath any gold, let them break it off. So they gave it me : then I cast it into the fire, and there came out this calf.

And when Moses saw that the people were naked ; (for Aaron had made them naked unto their shame among their enemies :)

Then Moses stood in the gate of the camp, and said, Who is on the Lord's side ? let him come unto me. And all the sons of Levi gathered themselves together unto him.

And he said unto them, Thus saith the Lord God of Israel, Put every man his sword by his side, and go in and out from gate to gate throughout the camp, and slay every man his brother, and every man his companion, and every man his neighbour.

And the children of Levi did according to the word of Moses : and there fell of the people that day about three thousand men.

For Moses had said, Consecrate yourselves to day to the Lord, even every man upon his son, and upon his brother ; that he may bestow upon you a blessing this day.

And it came to pass on the morrow, that Moses said unto the people, Ye have sinned a great sin : and now I will go up unto the Lord ; perhaps I shall make an atonement for your sin.

And Moses returned unto the Lord, and said, Oh, this people have sinned a great sin, and have made them gods of gold.

Yet now, if thou wilt forgive their sin — ; and if not, blot me, I pray thee, out of thy book which thou hast written.

And the Lord said unto Moses, Whosoever hath sinned against me, him will I blot out of my book.

Therefore now go, lead the people unto the place of which I have spoken unto thee : behold, mine Angel shall go before thee : nevertheless in the day when I visit I will visit their sin upon them.

And the Lord plagued the people, because they made the calf, which Aaron made.

15

Atonement

Before God would lead the Hebrews to the Promised Land, they had to demonstrate their repentance. Moses' pleas of forgiveness were ultimately accepted by God.

QUESTIONS TO CONSIDER

1. How was God to punish the Hebrews for their sins?
2. How did Moses atone for these sins?

And the Lord said unto Moses, Depart, and go up hence, thou and the people which thou hast brought up out of the land of Egypt, unto the land which I swore unto Abraham, to Isaac, and to Jacob, saying, Unto thy seed will I give it:

And I will send an angel before thee; and I will drive out the Canaanite, the Amorite, and the Hittite, and the Perizzite, the Hivite, and the Jebusite:

Unto a land flowing with milk and honey: for I will not go up in the midst of thee; for thou art a stiffnecked people: lest I consume thee in the way.

And when the people heard these evil tidings, they mourned: and no man did put on him his ornaments.

For the Lord had said unto Moses, Say unto the children of Israel, ye are a stiffnecked people: I will come up into the midst of thee in a moment, and consume thee: therefore now put off thy ornaments from thee, that I may know what to do unto thee.

And the children of Israel stripped themselves of their ornaments by the mount Horeb.

And Moses took the tabernacle, and pitched it without the camp, afar off from the camp, and called it the Tabernacle of the congregation. And it came to pass, that every one which sought the Lord went out unto the tabernacle of the congregation, which was without the camp.

And it came to pass, when Moses went out unto the tabernacle, that all the people rose up, and stood every man at his tent door, and looked after Moses until he was gone into the tabernacle.

And it came to pass, as Moses entered into the tabernacle, the cloudy pillar descended, and stood at the door of the tabernacle, and the LORD talked with Moses.

From Exodus, 33:1–17 (King James Version); slightly modernized.

And all the people saw the cloudy pillar stand at the tabernacle door : and all the people rose up and worshipped, every man in his tent door.

And the Lord spake unto Moses face to face, as a man speaketh unto his friend. And he turned again into the camp : but his servant Joshua, the son of Nun, a young man, departed not out of the tabernacle.

And Moses said unto the Lord, See, thou sayest unto me, Bring up this people : and thou hast not let me know whom thou wilt sent with me. Yet thou hast said, I know thee by name, and thou hast also found grace in my sight.

Now therefore, I pray thee, if I have found grace in thy sight, show me now thy way, that I may know thee, that I may find grace in thy sight : and consider that this nation is thy people.

And he said, My presence shall go with thee, and I will give thee rest.

And he said unto him, If thy presence go not with me, carry us not up hence.

For wherein shall it be known here that I and thy people have found grace in thy sight ? Is it not in that thou goest with us ? so shall we be separated, I and thy people, from all the people that are upon the face of the earth.

And the Lord said unto Moses, I will do this thing also that thou hast spoken : for thou hast found grace in my sight, and I know thee by name.

The Assyrian Empire

Situated in the rolling hills north of Babylonia, Assyria was never a major empire until the late tenth century B.C. The land had been invaded time and again by the Akkadians, Babylonians, Kassites, and, finally, the Arameans. In 911 B.C., the Assyrian kings finally confronted the threat posed by the Arameans and expelled them. Thereafter, year by year, the kings went to war and conquered most of the ancient Near East.

The success achieved by Assyria resulted from studying war techniques as a science. The army was divided into light and heavy infantry as well as chariotry, which was supplemented by rolling siege engines. Special schools were set up to teach the techniques of sapping and mining city walls. Conquered areas were welded together through a great system of roads and were controlled by royal governors, supported by garrisons of soldiers. These newly conquered areas saw their populations dispersed or transported throughout Assyria. Booty and tribute kept Assyria constantly expanding. If any city tried to revolt, it could expect swift and severe punishment. Yet the Assyrian empire fell in 612 B.C. when it was attacked by a triple alliance of the Babylonians, Medes, and Scythians.

A typical example of an Assyrian king is Ashurnasirpal (884–859 B.C.). He was at war for most of his reign, attacking northwestern Mesopotamia, Anatolia, Syria, and Phoenicia both for booty and for enlargement of his empire. Nonetheless, he found time to construct a new, six-acre palace at Calah (modern Nimrud) on the Upper Zab, west of the Tigris River — a palace that was very well built and beautifully decorated.

The following selection comes from the Assyrian royal archives and describes King Ashurnasirpal's ferocious treatment of rebels.

16

Assyrian War Tactics

QUESTIONS TO CONSIDER

1. Why do you suppose that the Assyrian king resorted to such harshness in dealing with rebels?
2. Why would the subjects of Assyria rebel even though they were aware of the consequences?
3. Do you know of a kingdom and peoples who disappeared from history due to Assyrian destruction?

While I was staying in the land of Kutmuhi, they brought me the word: "The city of Sûru of Bît-Halupê has revolted, they have slain Hamatai, their governor, and Ahiababa, the son of a nobody, whom they brought from Bît-Adini, they have set up as king over them." With the help of Adad and the great gods who have made great my kingdom, I mobilized (my) chariots and armies and marched along the bank of the Habur. During my advance I received much tribute from Shulmanu-haman-ilâni of the city of Gardiganni, from Ilu-Adad of the city of Katna, — silver, gold, lead, vessels of copper, and garments of brightly colored wool, and garments of linen. To the city of Sûru of Bît-Halupê I drew near, and the terror of the splendor of Assur, my lord, overwhelmed them. The chief men and the elders of the city, to save their lives, came forth into my presence and embraced my feet, saying: "If it is thy pleasure, slay! If it is thy pleasure, let live! That which thy heart desireth, do!" Ahiababa, the son of nobody, whom they had brought from Bît-Adini, I took captive. In the valor of my heart and with the fury of my weapons I stormed the city. All the rebels they seized and delivered them up. My officers I caused to enter into his palace and his temples. His silver, his gold, his goods and his possessions, copper, iron, lead, vessels of copper, cups of copper, dishes of copper, a great hoard of copper, alabaster, tables with inlay, the women of his palaces, his daughters, the captive rebels together with their possessions, the gods together with their possessions, precious stone from the mountains, his chariot with equipment, his horses, broken to the yoke, trappings of men and trappings of horses, garments of brightly colored wool and garments of linen, goodly oil, cedar, and fine sweet-scented herbs, panels(?) of cedar, purple and crimson wool, his wagons, his cattle, his sheep, his heavy spoil, which like the stars of heaven could not be counted, I carried off. Azi-ilu I set over them as my own governor. I built a pillar over against his city gate, and I flayed all the chief men who had revolted, and I covered the pillar with their skins; some I walled up within the pillar, some I impaled upon the pillar on stakes, and others I bound to stakes round about the pillar; many within the border of my own land I flayed, and I spread their skins upon

From Daniel David Luckenbill, ed., *Ancient Records of Assyria and Babylonia,* vol. 1 (New York: Greenwood Press, 1968), pp. 144–145.

the walls ; and I cut off the limbs of the officers, of the royal officers who had re-
belled. Ahiababa I took to Nineveh, I flayed him, I spread his skin upon the wall of
Nineveh. My power and might I established over the land of Lakê. While I was
staying in the city of Sûru, (I received) tribute from all the kings of the land of
Lakê, — silver, gold, lead, copper, vessels of copper, cattle, sheep, garments of
brightly colored wool, and garments of linen, and I increased the tribute and taxes
and imposed them upon them. At that time, the tribute of Haiâni of the city of
Hindani, — silver, gold, lead, copper, *umu*-stone, alabaster, purple wool, and
(Bactrian) camels I received from him as tribute. At that time I fashioned a heroic
image of my royal self, my power and my glory I inscribed thereon, in the midst of
his palace I set it up. I fashioned memorial steles and inscribed thereon my glory
and my prowess, and I set them up by his city gate.

17

The Banquet of Ashurnasirpal

This selection demonstrates Ashurnasirpal's lavish decoration and munifi-
cence at the inauguration of his new palace in his capital city of Calah.

QUESTIONS TO CONSIDER

1. What does the passage on Calah reveal about the personality of the Assyrian
   king?
2. What other monarchs were known for their building activities?

(This is) the palace of Ashurnasirpal, the high priest of Ashur, . . . — the legitimate king, the king of the world, the king of Assyria, . . . — the heroic warrior
who always acts upon trust-inspiring signs given by his lord Ashur and (therefore)
has no rival among the rulers of the four quarters (of the world) ; the shepherd of
all mortals, not afraid of battle (but) an onrushing flood which brooks no resistance ; the king who subdues the unsubmissive (and) rules over all mankind ; the
king who always acts upon trust-inspiring signs given by his lords, the great gods,
and therefore has personally conquered all countries ; who has acquired dominion
over the mountain regions and received their tribute ; he takes hostages, triumphs
over all the countries from beyond the Tigris to the Lebanon and the Great Sea,
he has brought into submission the entire country of Laqe and the region of Suhu

From "The Banquet of Ashurnasirpal II," trans. A. Leo Oppenhein, in *Ancient Near Eastern Texts Relating to the Old Testament,* 3rd ed. with Supplement, ed. James B. Pritchard (Princeton : Princeton
University Press, 1969), pp. 558–561. Copyright © 1969 by Princeton University Press. Reprinted
with permission of Princeton University Press.

as far as the town of Rapiqu; personally he conquered (the region) from the source of the Subnat River to Urartu....

I took over again the city of Calah in that wisdom of mine, the knowledge which Ea, the king of the subterranean waters, has bestowed upon me, I removed the old hill of rubble: I dug down to the water level; I heaped up a (new) terrace (measuring) from the water level to the upper edge 120 layers of bricks; upon that I erected as my royal seat and for my personal enjoyment 7 (text: 8) beautiful halls (roofed with) boxwood, *Magan-ash*, cedar, cypress, terebinth, *tarpi'u* and *meḫru* (beams); I sheathed doors made of cedar, cypress, juniper, boxwood and *Magan-ash* with bands of bronze; I hung them in their doorways; I surrounded them (the doors) with decorative bronze bolts; to proclaim my heroic deeds I painted on their (the palaces') walls with vivid blue paint how I have marched across the mountain ranges, the foreign countries and the seas, my conquests in all countries;[1] I had lapis lazuli colored glazed bricks made and set (them in the wall) above their gates. I brought in people from the countries over which I rule, those who were conquered by me personally, (that is) from the country Suhi (those of) the town Great [. . .], from the entire land of Zamua, the countries Bit-Zamani and [Kir]rure, the town of Sirqu which is across the Euphrates, and many inhabitants of Laqe, of Syria and (who are subjects) of Lubarna, the ruler of Hattina; I settled them therein (the city of Calah).

I dug a canal from the Upper Zab River; I cut (for this purpose) straight through the mountain(s); I called it Patti-hegalli ("Channel-of-Abundance"); I provided the lowlands along the Tigris with irrigation; I planted orchards at its (the city's) outskirts, with all sorts of fruit trees.

I pressed the grapes and offered (them) as first fruits in a libation to my lord Ashur and to all the sanctuaries of my country. I (then) dedicated that city to my lord Ashur.

[I collected and planted in my garden] from the countries through which I marched and the mountains which I crossed, the trees (and plants raised from) seeds from wherever I discovered (them, such as): cedars, cypress, *šimmešallu*-perfume trees, *burāšu*-junipers, myrrh-producing trees, *daprānu*-junipers, nut-bearing trees, date palms, ebony, *Magan-ash*, olive trees, *tamarind*, oaks, *tarpi'u*-terebinth trees, *luddu*-nut-bearing trees, pistachio and *cornel*-trees, *meḫru*-trees, ŠE.MUR-trees, *tijatu*-trees, Kanish oaks, willows, *ṣadānu*-trees, pomegranates, plum trees, fir trees, *ingirašu*-trees, *kamešseru*-pear trees, *supurgillu*-bearing trees, fig trees, grape vines, *angašu*-pear trees, aromatic *ṣumlalu*-trees, *titip*-trees, *ḫip / būtu*-trees, *zanzaliqqu*-trees, "swamp-apple" trees, *ḫambuqūqu*-trees, *nuḫurtu*-trees, *urzīnu*-trees, resinous *kanaktu*-trees [. . .]. In the gardens in [Calah] they vied with each other in fragrance; the paths i[n the gardens were well *kept*], the irrigation weirs [distributed the water *evenly*]; its pomegranates glow in the pleasure garden like the stars in the sky, they are interwoven like grapes on the vine; . . . in the pleasure garden [. . .] in the garden of happiness flourished like ce[dar trees] (break).

---

1. This refers to murals executed in blue paint.

(ii)

I erected in Calah, the center of my overlordship, temples such as those of Enlil and Ninurta which did not exist there before; I rebuilt in it the (following) temples of the great gods. . . . In them I established the (sacred) pedestals of the(se), my divine lords. I decorated them splendidly; I roofed them with cedar beams, made large cedar doors, sheathed them with bands of bronze, placed them in their doorways. I placed figural representations made of shining bronze in their doorways. I made (the images of) their great godheads sumptuous with red gold and shining stones. I presented them with golden jewelry and many other precious objects which I had won as booty. . . .

I organized the abandoned towns which during the rule of my fathers had become hills of rubble, and had many people settle therein; I rebuilt the old palaces across my entire country in due splendor; I stored in them barley and straw. . . .

When Ashurnasirpal, king of Assyria, inaugurated the palace in Calah, a palace of joy and (erected with) great ingenuity, he invited into it Ashur, the great lord and the gods of his entire country, (he prepared a banquet[2] of) 1,000 fattened head of cattle, 1,000 calves, *10,000* stable sheep, 15,000 lambs — for my lady Ishtar (alone) 200 head of cattle (and) 1,000 *sihhu*-sheep — 1,000 spring lambs, 500 stags, 500 gazelles, 1,000 *ducks,* 500 *geese,* 500 *kurkû*-geese, 1,000 *mesuku*-birds, 1,000 *qāribu*-birds, 10,000 doves, 10,000 *sukanūnu*-doves, 10,000 other (assorted) small birds, 10,000 (assorted) fish, 10,000 jerboa, 10,000 (assorted) eggs; 10,000 loaves of bread, 10,000 (jars of) beer, 10,000 skins with wine, 10,000 pointed bottom vessels with *šu'u*-seeds in sesame oil, 10,000 small pots with *ṣarhu*-condiment, 1,000 wooden crates with vegetables, 300 (containers with) oil, 300 (containers with) salted *seeds,* 300 (containers with) mixed *raqqūte*-plants, 100 with *kudimmu*-spice, 100 (containers with) . . . , 100 (containers with) parched barley, 100 (containers with) green *abahšinnu*-stalks, 100 (containers with) fine mixed beer, 100 pomegranates, 100 bunches of grapes, 100 mixed *zamru*-fruits, 100 pistachio cones, 100 with the fruits of the *šūši*-tree, 100 with garlic, 100 with onions, 100 with *kuniphu* (seeds), 100 with the . . . of turnips, 100 with *hinhinnu*-spice, 100 with *budû*-spice, 100 with honey, 100 with rendered butter, 100 with roasted . . . barley, 100 with roasted *šu'u*-seeds, 100 with *karkartu*-plants, 100 with fruits of the *ti'atu*-tree, 100 with *kasû*-plants, 100 with milk, 100 with cheese, 100 jars with "mixture," 100 with pickled *arsuppu*-grain, ten homer of shelled *luddu*-nuts, ten homer of shelled pistachio nuts, ten homer of fruits of

2. The Gargantuan bill of fare given here provides us in spite of all its lexical difficulties with the basic features of a banquet menu. The list is structured as follows: (1) meat dishes (sheep, cattle, with some game; fowl consisting mostly of small birds with aquatic birds in the second place) and equal amounts of fish and jerboa with assorted eggs in large number; (2) bread; (3) beer and wine in equal amounts; (4) side dishes consisting mainly of pickled and spiced fruit, and seeds of a wide variety, also onion; (5) dessert (sweet fruits, nuts, honey, cheese) and savories, most of which cannot be identified yet. At the end, the list mentions perfumed oil and sweet smelling substances.

the *šūšu*-tree, ten homer of fruits of the *ḫabbaqūqu*-tree, ten homer of dates, ten homer of the fruits of the *titip*-tree, ten homer of *cumin*, ten homer of *saḫḫunu*, ten homer of *uriānu*, ten homer of *andaḫšu*-bulbs, ten homer of *šišanibbe*-plants, (iv) ten homer of the fruits of the *simbūru*-tree, ten homer of thyme, ten homer of perfumed oil, ten homer of sweet smelling matters, ten homer of . . . , ten homer of the fruits of the *naṣubu*-tree, ten homer of *zimzimmu*-onions, ten homer of olives.

When I inaugurated the palace at Calah I treated for ten days with food and drink 47,074 persons, men and women, who were bid to come from across my entire country, (also) 5,000 important persons, delegates from the country Suhu, from Hindana, Hattina, Hatti, Tyre, Sidon, Gurguma, Malida, Hubushka, Gilzana, Kuma (and) Musasir, (also) 16,000 inhabitants of Calah from all ways of life, 1,500 officials of all my palaces, altogether 69,574 invited guests from all the (mentioned) countries including the people of Calah; I (furthermore) provided them with the means to clean and anoint themselves. I did them due honors and sent them back, healthy and happy, to their own countries.

CLASSICAL CIVILIZATIONS

Early Greeks and Their Gods

Greeks differed from other peoples of the ancient Near East in many ways. One difference involved their reducing the conceptual distance between gods and people. Greek gods had human failings on a larger-than-life scale as well as superhuman powers. In the earliest surviving Greek literary works of any importance, we find the poet Homer narrating exciting adventures in which the gods side with humans or against them, but mortal beings are always the focal point. Homer's gods are intent on avenging offenses or insults to themselves, their priests, any semi-divine offspring, and their "special interests." For example, Artemis, goddess of the chase, avenges wanton destruction of wild animals, and Hera, goddess of marriage, gets even with home-wreckers. Somewhat less frequently, Homer's gods reward those who serve them well.

Homer lived and wrote his epics sometime around 800 B.C., during the period of the "Greek Dark Ages," which followed the fall of Mycenaean civilization. Still, he wrote about the earlier Mycenaean-age Greeks, whom he called "Achaeans" or "Danaans," in what for him was the glorious, heroic time of the Trojan War. According to Homer, the war began when a Trojan prince stole away Helen of Troy, the wife of Menelaus, who was King of Sparta. This incident angered the goddess Hera and led King Agamemnon of Mycenae (brother of Menelaus) to gather an all-Achaean expedition for the destruction of Troy.

Homer probably composed his epics to be sung before warriors in banquet halls and incorporated some material from earlier poets. A large part of Homer's appeal, however, has always focused on his highly developed and consistent characters. Over the centuries, these figures have remained quite believable, even in their confrontations with gods and monsters.

Two works are attributed to Homer: *The Iliad* (from "Ilion" or "Ilium," the ancient names for Troy), which describes the Achaean siege of Troy; and *The Odyssey*, from which the following selection is taken. This latter work deals with the return from Troy of Odysseus, the wily Achaean who designed the "Trojan horse," which brought victory to the Achaeans. In the course of their long and arduous sea voyage, Odysseus and his men come to the land of the Cyclopes, savage one-eyed giants; in the passage excerpted here, Odysseus tells of his encounter with one of these giants, Polyphemus. Afterwards, mounting catastrophes overtake the men, as the curse of Polyphemus is carried out by his father, Poseidon. But the ending is a happy one : Odysseus safely reaches his kingdom of Ithaca, where his faithful wife, Penelope, has waited for many years, resisting the advances of many suitors. Odysseus then kills the suitors in a final glorious battle in the halls of his home.

18

Homer, *The Odyssey*

QUESTIONS TO CONSIDER

1. What does Odysseus find striking about the land of the Cyclopes?
2. How do Odysseus and the men with him become captives in the cave of Polyphemus?
3. When Polyphemus is injured, why do the other Cyclopes show indifference to his fate?

"We left (the land of the Lotus-eaters) and sailed on. . . . And we came to the land of the Cyclopes, a fierce, uncivilized people who never lift a hand to plant or plough but put their trust in Providence. All the crops they require spring up unsown and untilled, wheat and barley and the vines whose generous clusters give them wine when ripened for them by the timely rains. The Cyclopes have no assemblies for the making of laws, nor any settled customs, but live in hollow caverns in the mountain heights, where each man is lawgiver to his children and his wives, and nobody cares a jot for his neighbours.

"Not very far from the harbour on their coast, and not so near either, there lies a luxuriant island, covered with woods, which is the home of innumerable goats. The goats are wild, for man has made no pathways that might frighten them off, nor do hunters visit the island with their hounds to rough it in the forests and to range the mountain-tops. Used neither for grazing nor for ploughing, it lies for ever unsown and untilled; and this land where no man goes makes a happy pasture for the bleating goats. I must explain that the Cyclopes have nothing like our ships with their crimson prows; nor have they any shipwrights to build merchantmen that could serve their needs by plying to foreign ports in the course of that overseas traffic which ships have established between the nations. Such craftsmen would have turned the island into a fine colony for the Cyclopes. For it is by no means a poor country, but capable of yielding any crop in due season. Along the shore of the grey sea there are soft water-meadows where the vine would never wither; and there is plenty of land level enough for the plough, where they could count on cutting a deep crop at every harvest-time, for the soil

From Homer, *The Odyssey,* Book IX, trans. E. V. Rieu (Baltimore : Penguin, 1946, 1962), pp. 142–154. Copyright © E. V. Rieu, 1946. Reproduced by permission of Penguin Books Ltd.

below the surface is exceedingly rich. Also, it has a safe harbour, in which there is no occasion to tie up at all. You need neither cast anchor nor make fast with hawsers : all your crew have to do is to beach their boat and wait till the spirit moves them and the right wind blows. Finally, at the head of the harbour there is a stream of fresh water, running out of a cave in a grove of poplar-trees.

"This is where we came to land. Some god must have guided us through the murky night, for it was impossible to see ahead. The ships were in a thick fog, and overhead not a gleam of light came through from the moon, which was obscured by clouds. In these circumstances not a man among us caught sight of the island nor did we even see the long rollers beating up to the coast, before our good ships ran aground. It was not till they were beached that we lowered sail. We then jumped out on the shore, fell asleep where we were and so waited for the blessed light of day.

"When the fresh Dawn came and with her crimson streamers lit the sky, we were delighted with what we saw of the island and set out to explore it. Presently, in order that my company might have something to eat, the Nymphs, those Children of Zeus, set the mountain goats on the move. Directly we saw them we fetched our curved bows and our long spears from the ships, separated into three parties, and let fly at the game ; and in a short time Providence had sent us a satisfactory bag. There were twelve ships in my squadron : nine goats fell to each, while to me they made a special allotment of ten. So the whole day long till the sun set we sat and enjoyed this rich supply of meat, which we washed down by mellow wine, since the ships had not yet run dry of our red vintage. There was still some in the holds, for when we took the sacred citadel of the Cicones, every member of the company had drawn off a generous supply in jars. There we sat, and as we looked across at the neighbouring land of the Cyclopes, we could not only see the smoke from their fires but hear their voices and the bleating of their sheep and goats. The sun went down, night fell, and we slept on the sea-shore.

"With the first rosy light of Dawn, I assembled my company and gave them their orders. 'My good friends', I said, 'for the time being I want you to stay here, while I go in my own ship with my own crew to find out what kind of men are over there, and whether they are brutal and lawless savages or hospitable and god-fearing people.'

"Then I climbed into my ship and told my men to follow me and loose the hawsers. They came on board at once, went to the benches, sat down in their places and churned the grey water with their oars. It was no great distance to the mainland coast. As we approached its nearest point, we made out a cave there, close to the sea, with a high entrance overhung by laurels. Here large flocks of sheep and goats were penned at night, and round the mouth a yard had been built with a great wall of stones bedded deep between tall pines and high-branched oaks. It was the den of a giant, the lonely shepherd of sequestered flocks, who had no truck with others of his kind but lived aloof in his own lawless way. And what a formidable monster he was! No one would have taken him for a man who ate bread like ourselves ; he reminded one rather of some wooded peak in the high hills, lifting itself in solitary state.

"At this point, I told the rest of my loyal following to stay there on guard by the ship while I myself picked out the twelve best men in the company and advanced. I took with me in a goatskin some dark and mellow wine which had been given to me by Maron son of Euanthes, the priest of Apollo (who was patron-deity of Ismarus), because we had protected him and his child and wife out of respect for his office, when we came upon his home in a grove of trees sacred to Phoebus Apollo. This man made me some fine presents: he gave me seven talents of wrought gold, with a mixing-bowl of solid silver, and he drew off for me as well a full dozen jars of mellow unmixed wine. And a wonderful drink it was. It had been kept secret from all his serving-men and maids, in fact from everyone in the house but himself, his good wife, and a single stewardess. When they drank this red and honeyed vintage, he used to pour one cupful of wine into twenty of water, and the sweet fumes that came up from the bowl were irresistible — those were occasions when abstinence could have no charms.

"Well, I filled a big bottle with this wine and took some food in a wallet along with me also; for I had an instant foreboding, though I am no coward, that we were going to find ourselves face to face with some being of colossal strength and ferocity, to whom the law of man and god meant nothing. It took us very little time to reach the cave, but we did not find its owner at home: he was tending his fat sheep in the pastures. So we went inside and had a good look round. There were baskets laden with cheeses, and the folds were thronged with lambs and kids, each class, the firstlings, the summer lambs, and the little ones, being separately penned. All his well-made vessels, the pails and bowls he used for milking, were swimming with whey.

"Now my men's idea was first to make off with some of the cheeses, then come back, drive the kids and lambs quickly out of the pens down to the good ship, and so set sail across the salt water. They pleaded with me; but though it would have been far better so, I was not to be persuaded. I wished to see the owner of the cave and had hopes of some friendly gifts from my host. As things fell out, my company were to have an unpleasant surprise when he did put in an appearance.

"We lit a fire, killed a beast and made offerings, took some cheeses just for ourselves, and when we had eaten, sat down in the cave to await his arrival. At last he came up, shepherding his flocks and carrying a huge bundle of dry wood to burn at supper-time. With a great din he cast this down inside the cavern, giving us such a fright that we hastily retreated to an inner recess. Meanwhile he drove his fat sheep into the wider part of the cave — I mean all the ewes that he milked: the rams and he-goats he left out of doors in the walled yard. He then picked up a huge stone, with which he closed the entrance. It was a mighty slab, such as you couldn't have budged from the ground, not with a score of heavy four-wheeled waggons to help you. That will give you some idea of the monstrous size of the rock with which he closed the cave. Next he sat down to milk his ewes and bleating goats, which he did methodically, putting her young to each mother as he finished. He then curdled half the white milk, gathered it all up, and stored it in wicker baskets; the remainder he left standing in pails, so that it would be handy at suppertime and when he wanted a drink. When he had done with his business and finished all his jobs, he lit up the fire, spied us, and began asking questions.

"'Strangers!' he said. 'And who may you be? Where do you hail from over the highways of the sea? Is yours a trading venture; or are you cruising the main on chance, like roving pirates, who risk their lives to ruin other people?'

"Our hearts sank within us. The booming voice and the very sight of the monster filled us with panic. Still, I managed to find words to answer him.

"'We are Achaeans,' I said, 'on our way back from Troy, driven astray by contrary winds across a vast expanse of sea. Far from planning to come here, we meant to sail straight home; but we lost our bearings, as Zeus, I suppose, intended that we should. We are proud to belong to the forces of Agamemnon, Atreus' son, who by sacking the great city of Ilium and destroying all its armies has made himself the most famous man in the world today. We, less fortunate, are visiting you here as suppliants, in the hope that you may give us friendly entertainment or even go further in your generosity. You know the laws of hospitality: I beseech you, good sir, to remember your duty to the gods. For we throw ourselves on your mercy; and Zeus is there to avenge the suppliant and the guest. He is the travellers' god: he guards their steps and he invests them with their rights.'

"So said I, and promptly he answered me out of his pitiless heart: 'Stranger, you must be a fool, or must have come from very far afield, to preach to me of fear or reverence for the gods. We Cyclopes care not a jot for Zeus with his aegis, nor for the rest of the blessed gods, since we are much stronger than they. It would never occur to me to spare you or your men against my will for fear of trouble from Zeus. But tell me where you moored your good ship when you came. Was it somewhere up the coast, or nearby? I should like to see her.'

"He was trying to get the better of me, but I knew enough of the world to see through him and I met him with deceit.

"'As for my ship,' I answered, 'it was wrecked by the Earthshaker Poseidon on the confines of your land. The wind had carried us onto a lee shore. He drove the ship up to a headland and gurtled it on the rocks. But I and my friends here managed to escape with our lives.'

"To this the cruel brute made no reply. Instead, he jumped up, and reaching out towards my men, seized a couple and dashed their heads against the floor as though they had been puppies. Their brains ran out on the ground and soaked the earth. Limb by limb he tore them to pieces to make his meal, which he devoured like a mountain lion, never pausing till entrails and flesh, marrow and bones, were all consumed, while we could do nothing but weep and lift up our hands to Zeus in horror at the ghastly sight, paralysed by our sense of utter helplessness. When the Cyclops had filled his great belly with this meal of human flesh, which he washed down with unwatered milk, he stretched himself out for sleep among his flocks inside the cave. And now my manhood prompted me to action: I thought I would draw my sharp sword from the scabbard at my side, creep up to him, feel for the right place with my hand and stab him in the breast where the liver is supported by the midriff. But on second thoughts I refrained, realizing that we should have perished there as surely as the Cyclops, for we should have found it impossible with our unaided hands to push aside the huge rock with which he had closed the great mouth of the cave. So for the time being we just sat groaning there and waited for the blessed light of day.

"No sooner had the tender Dawn shown her roses in the East, than the Cyclops lit up the fire and milked his splendid ewes, all in their proper order, putting her young to each. This business over and his morning labours done, he once more snatched up a couple of my men and prepared his meal. When he had eaten, he turned his fatted sheep out of the cave, removing the great doorstone without an effort. But he replaced it immediately, as easily as though he were putting the lid on a quiver. Then, with many a whistle, he drove his rich flocks off towards the high pasture, while I was left, with murder in my heart, beating about for some scheme by which I might pay him back if only Athena would grant me my prayer. The best plan I could think of was this. Lying by the pen, the Cyclops had a huge staff of green olive-wood, which he had cut to carry in his hand when it was seasoned. To us it looked more like the mast of some black ship of twenty oars, a broad-bottomed freighter such as they use for long sea voyages. That was the impression which its length and thickness made on us. On this piece of timber I set to work and cut off a fathom's length, which I handed over to my men and told them to smooth down. When they had dressed it, I took a hand and sharpened it to a point. Then I poked it into the blazing fire to make it hard, and finally I laid it carefully by, hiding it under the dung, of which there were heaps scattered in profusion throughout the cave. I then told my company to casts lots among themselves for the dangerous task of helping me to lift the pole and twist it in the Cyclops' eye when he was sound asleep. The lot fell on the very men that I myself should have chosen, four of them, so that counting myself we made a party of five.

"Evening came, and with it the Cyclops, shepherding his woolly sheep, every one of which he herded into the broad part of the cave, leaving none out in the walled yard, either because he suspected something or because a god had warned him. He raised the great doorstone, set it in its place, and then sat down to milk his ewes and bleating goats, which he did in an orderly way, giving each mother its young one in due course. When this business was over and his work finished, he once more seized upon two of us and prepared his supper. Then came my chance. With an ivy-wood bowl of my dark wine in my hands, I went up to him and said : 'Here, Cyclops, have some wine to wash down that meal of human flesh, and find out for yourself what kind of vintage was stored away in our ship's hold. I brought it for you by way of an offering in the hope that you would be charitable and help me on my homeward way. But your savagery is more than we can bear. Cruel monster, how can you expect ever to have a visitor again from the world of men, after such deeds as you have done ?'

"The Cyclops took the wine and drank it up. And the delicious draught gave him such exquisite pleasure that he asked me for another bowlful.

"'Be good enough,' he said, 'to let me have some more ; and tell me your name, here and now, so that I may make you a gift that you will value. We Cyclopes have wine of our own made from the grapes that our rich soil and timely rains produce. But this vintage of yours is nectar and ambrosia distilled.'

"So said the Cyclops, and I handed him another bowlful of the ruddy wine. Three times I filled up for him ; and three times the fool drained the bowl to the dregs. At last, when the wine had fuddled his wits, I addressed him with disarming suavity.

"'Cyclops,' I said, 'you wish to know the name I bear. I'll tell it to you ; and in return I should like to have the gift you promised me. My name is Nobody. That is what I am called by my mother and father and by all my friends.'

"The Cyclops answered me with a cruel jest. 'Of all his company I will eat Nobody last, and the rest before him. That shall be your gift.'

"He had hardly spoken before he toppled over and fell face upwards on the floor, where he lay with his great neck twisted to one side, conquered, as all men are, by sleep. His drunkenness made him vomit, and a stream of wine mixed with morsels of men's flesh poured from his throat. I went at once and thrust our pole deep under the ashes of the fire to make it hot, and meanwhile gave a word of encouragement to all my men, to make sure that no one should play the coward and leave me in the lurch. When the fierce glow from the olive stake warned me that it was about to catch alight in the flames, green as it was, I withdrew it from the fire and brought it over to the spot where my men were standing ready. Heaven now inspired them with a reckless courage. Seizing the olive pole, they drove its sharpened end into the Cyclops' eye, while I used my weight from above to twist it home, like a man boring a ship's timber with a drill which his mates below him twirl with a strap they hold at either end, so that it spins continuously. In much the same way we handled our pole with its red-hot point and twisted it in his eye till the blood boiled up round the burning wood. The fiery smoke from the blazing eyeball singed his lids and brow all round, and the very roots of his eye crackled in the heat. I was reminded of the loud hiss that comes from a great axe or adze when a smith plunges it into the cold water — to temper it and give strength to the iron. That is how the Cyclops' eye hissed round the olive stake. He gave a dreadful shriek, which echoed round the rocky walls, and we backed away from him in terror, while he pulled the stake from his eye, streaming with blood. Then he hurled it away from him with frenzied hands and raised a great shout for the other Cyclopes who lived in neighbouring caves along the windy heights. These, hearing his screams, came up from every quarter and gathering outside the cave asked him what ailed him:

"'What on earth is wrong with you, Polyphemus? Why must you disturb the peaceful night and spoil our sleep with all this shouting? Is a robber driving off your sheep, or is somebody trying by treachery or violence to kill you?'

"Out of the cave came Polyphemus' great voice in reply: 'O my friends, it's Nobody's treachery, no violence, that is doing me to death.'

"'Well then,' they answered, in a way that settled the matter, 'if nobody is assaulting you in your solitude, you must be sick. Sickness comes from almighty Zeus and cannot be helped. All you can do is pray to your father, the Lord Poseidon.'

"And off they went, while I chuckled to myself at the way in which my happy notion of a false name had taken them in. The Cyclops, still moaning in agonies of pain, groped about with his hands and pushed the rock away from the mouth of the cave. But then he sat himself down in the doorway and stretched out both arms in the hope of catching us in the act of slipping out among the sheep. What a fool he must have thought me! Meanwhile I was cudgelling my brains for the best possible course, trying to hit on some way of saving my friends as well as my own skin. Plan after plan, dodge after dodge, passed through my mind. It was a matter of life or death: we were in mortal peril. And this was the scheme I eventually chose. There were in the flock some well-bred, thick-fleeced rams, fine, big animals in their coats of black wool. These I quietly lashed together, with the plaited withes which the savage monster used for his bed. I took them in threes. The middle one in each case was to carry one of my followers, while its fellows went on either side to protect him. Each of my men thus had three sheep to bear him. But for myself I chose a full-grown ram who was the pick of the whole flock. Seizing him by the back, I curled myself up under his shaggy belly and lay there upside down, with a firm grip on his wonderful fleece and with patience in my heart. Thus in fear and trembling we waited for the blessed Dawn.

"As soon as she arrived and flecked the East with red, the rams of the flock began to scramble out and make for the pastures, but the ewes, unmilked as they were and with udders full to bursting, stood bleating by the pens. Their master, though he was worn out by the agonies he had gone through, passed his hand along the backs of all the animals as they came to a stand before him ; but the idiot never noticed that my men were tied up under the breasts of his own woolly sheep. The last of the flock to come up to the doorway was the big ram, burdened by his own fleece and by me with my teeming brain. As he felt him with his big hands the great Polyphemus broke into speech :

"'Sweet ram,' he said, 'what does this mean ? Why are you the last of the flock to pass out of the cave, you who have never lagged behind the sheep, you who always step so proudly out and are the first of them to crop the lush shoots of the grass, first to make your way to the flowing stream, and first to turn your head homewards to the sheepfold when the evening falls ? Yet today you are the last of all. Are you grieved for your master's eye, blinded by a wicked man and his accursed friends, when he had robbed me of my wits with wine ? Nobody was his name ; and I swear that he has not yet saved his skin ! Ah, if only you could feel as I do and find a voice to tell me where he's hiding from my fury ! Wouldn't I hammer him and splash his brains all over the floor of the cave, till that miserable Nobody had eased my heart of the suffering I owe to him !'

"So he passed the ram out ; and when we had put a little distance between ourselves and the courtyard of the cave, I first freed myself from under my ram and next untied my men from theirs. Then, quickly, though with many a backward look, we drove our long-legged sheep right down to the ship — and a rich, fat flock they made. My dear companions were overjoyed when they caught sight of us survivors, though their relief soon changed to lamentation for their slaughtered friends. I would have none of this weeping, however, and with a nod made clear my will to each, bidding them make haste instead to tumble all the fleecy sheep on board and put to sea. So in they jumped, ran to the benches, sorted themselves out, and plied the grey water with their oars.

"But before we were out of earshot, I let Polyphemus have a piece of my mind. 'Cyclops!' I called. 'So he was not such a weakling after all, the man whose friends you meant to overpower and eat in that snug cave of yours! And your crimes came home to roost, you brute, who have not even the decency to refrain from devouring your own guests. Now Zeus and all his fellow-gods have paid you out.'

"My taunts so exasperated the angry Cyclops that he tore the top off a great pinnacle of rock and hurled it at us. The rock fell just ahead of our blue-painted bows. As it plunged in, the water rose and the backwash, like a swell from the open sea, swept us landward and nearly drove us on the beach. Seizing a long pole, I succeeded in punting her off, at the same time rousing my crew with urgent nods to dash in with their oars and save us from disaster. They buckled to and rowed with a will ; but when they had brought us across the water to twice our previous distance I was for giving the Cyclops some more of my talk, though from all parts of the ship my men's voices were raised in gentle remonstrance.

"'Aren't you rash, sir,' they said, 'to provoke this savage ? The rock he threw into the sea just now drove the ship back to the land, and we thought we were done for then and there. Had he heard a cry, or so much as a word, from a single man, he'd have smashed in our heads and the ship's timbers with another jagged boulder from his hand. You have seen how he can throw!'

"But all this went for nothing with me. My spirit was up, and in my rage I called to him once more:

"'Cyclops, if anyone ever asks you how you came by your unsightly blindness, tell him your eye was put out by Odysseus, Sacker of Cities, the son of Laertes, who lives in Ithaca.'

"The Cyclops gave a groan. 'Alas!' he cried. 'So the old prophecy has come home to me with a vengeance! We had a prophet with us once, a fine upstanding man, Telemus son of Eurymus, who was an excellent seer and grew old among us in the practice of his art. All of that has now happened he foretold, when he warned me that a man called Odysseus would rob me of my sight. But I always expected some big and handsome fellow of tremendous strength to come along. And now, a puny, good for nothing, little runt fuddles me with wine and then puts out my eye! But come here, Odysseus, so that I may make you some friendly gifts and prevail on the great Earthshaker to see you safely home. For I am his son, and he is not ashamed to call himself my father. He is the one who will heal me if he's willing — a thing no other blessed god nor any man on earth could do.'

"To which I shouted in reply: 'I only wish I could make as sure of robbing you of life and breath and sending you to Hell, as I am certain that not even the Earthshaker will ever heal your eye.'

"At this the Cyclops lifted up his hands to the heavens that hold the stars and prayed to the Lord Poseidon: 'Hear me, Poseidon, Girdler of Earth, god of the sable locks. If I am yours indeed and you accept me as your son, grant that Odysseus, who styles himself Sacker of Cities and son of Laertes, may never reach his home in Ithaca. But if he is destined to reach his native land, to come once more to his own house and see his friends again, let him come late, in evil plight, with all his comrades dead, and when he is landed, by a foreign ship, let him find trouble in his home.'

"So Polyphemus prayed; and the god of the sable locks heard his prayer. Then once again the Cyclops picked a boulder up — bigger by far, this time — and hurled it with a swing, putting such boundless force into his throw that the rock fell only just astern of our blue-painted ship, missing the end of the steering-oar by inches. The water heaved up as it ploughed into the sea; but the wave that it raised carried us on toward the farther shore. And so we reached our island, where the rest of our good ships were awaiting us in a body, while their crews sat round disconsolate and kept a constant watch for our return. Once there, we beached our ship, jumped out on the shore, and unloaded the Cyclops' sheep from the hold. We then divided our spoil so that no one, as far as I could help it, should go short of his proper share. But my comrades-in-arms did me the special honour, when the sheep were distributed, of presenting me with the big ram in addition. Him I sacrificed on the beach, burning slices from his thighs as an offering to Zeus of the Black Clouds, the Son of Cronos, who is lord of us all. But Zeus took no notice of my sacrifice; his mind must already have been full of plans for the destruction of all my gallant ships and my trusty band."

The Hindu Tradition

"Hinduism" is the term that Westerners have used to describe the religion of most people living on the subcontinent of India. Many other religions have originated and flourished in India, however, including Buddhism, Jainism, and Sikhism. The religion of Islam has also been a major part of Indian life since about A.D. 1000. However, Hinduism encompasses more than just religion; it includes an entire way of life.

As the Hindus settled down and spread throughout the Indian subcontinent, they developed a sophisticated culture between about 200 B.C. and A.D. 400. Hinduism promoted a well-rounded view of life. It focused on the idea that there were four legitimate goals for which all men and women should strive.

The first and most basic goal was pleasure (*kama*). Much pleasure was derived by wealthy people and commoners alike from very elaborate craft traditions in art, music, drama, and literature. Even the joys of food and sex were developed into highly sophisticated forms, and treatises such as the *Kama Sutra* were written to cultivate refinement in these areas.

The second goal was the acquisition and maintenance of wealth (*artha*). Much Hindu writing on this topic (the *Artha Shastra*, for example) centered on politics and kingship; wealth was secure only when a king could achieve and preserve power by maintaining order within his kingdom and against external aggressors.

The third goal was to abide by law or duty (*dharma*). Hindu law was believed to be eternal and unchanging, revealed to human seers or prophets at the beginning of time (for example, Manu was the recipient of the *Laws of Manu*). The essential structure of the law was the fourfold division of social classes — from priests and warriors at the top to the commoners and servile class (the conquered, darker-skinned people) at the bottom. This structure was the basis of the "caste system," whereby one's occupation and social status were completely determined at birth. Hindu law also postulated that after death each person would enter a new life form based on the good or evil done in the previous life. This process is called transmigration or reincarnation (*samsara*).

A final goal of the Hindus was the quest for liberation (*moksha*) from the process of transmigration. This goal involved a quest for transcending the normal human condition of trying to do good and avoid evil, only to be reborn again in another life where the struggle would continue indefinitely. Some Hindus sought, and believed they could attain, a condition of god-like perfection that would be an end to such a cycle.

The Hindu tradition described three valid paths to end transmigration. The first was the path of action (*karma*), which meant properly performing religious rituals as well as doing one's prescribed duty. Most Hindu thinkers, however, believed that following such a path could only partially lead a person to the ultimate goal. Therefore a second, and more favored, path was that of knowledge (*jñāna*), first described in the *Upanishads*, beginning around 700 B.C. This path involved calm contemplation of the universe and the self until one realized that God was present everywhere — including *within* the self. Only a small percentage of all Hindus would ever reach, or even attempt to reach, this mystical experience of oneness with God and the universe. The journey was a long and difficult one that required sacrificing all usual ways of living and thinking for long hours of private meditation.

The final path to liberation involved devotion (*bhakti*) to God. After the time of the *Rig Veda*,[1] the Hindus gradually developed the concept that only one God existed. But Hindus did not all agree on the identity of this God; some believed Vishnu was supreme (as did the writer of the *Bhagavad Gita*), while others favored Shiva. However, they did agree that a person totally devoted to God, in thinking and love, would be saved by God and granted liberation from transmigration. The worship of the supreme deity, the outpouring of love toward God, and the prayerful hope for divine compassion became the major driving forces of Hinduism. The following text selections can give only a small sample of the great variety of writing produced by Hindu India.

19

Essence of the Universe

This selection, from one of the earliest *Upanishads* (the *Chandogya Upanishad*), takes the form of a dialogue between a teacher and pupil. It presents the view that the *Brahman* — the Self of the universe, the abstract, divine power that is present everywhere — is the same as the soul or self (*atman*) dwelling within each individual.

QUESTIONS TO CONSIDER

1. How does the dialogue explain the essential reality underlying the world?
2. How essential is this dialogue in the understanding of Hinduism? Why?

"In the beginning, my dear, this world was just being (*sat*), one only, without a second. Some people, no doubt, say: 'In the beginning, verily, this world was just nonbeing (*asat*), one only, without a second; from that nonbeing, being was produced.' But how, indeed, my dear, could it be so?" said he. "How could being be

From W. de Bary et al., *Sources of Indian Tradition*, vol. 1 (New York: Columbia University Press, 1958), pp. 31–34. Reprinted by permission of Columbia University Press.

1. The *Rig Veda* is an anthology of over a thousand hymns of praise arranged in ten books. The hymns are chanted by Brahmans to the various Aryan gods of nature. The *Rig Veda* is the oldest of the four earliest Indian literary works known as *Vedas* (*Knowledge*). Vedic India covers the period from about 1500 to 1000 B.C.

produced from nonbeing? On the contrary, my dear, in the beginning this world was being alone, one only, without a second. Being thought to itself: 'May I be many; may I procreate.' It produced fire. That fire thought to itself: 'May I be many, may I procreate.' It produced water. Therefore, whenever a person grieves or perspires, then it is from fire [heat] alone that water is produced. That water thought to itself: 'May I be many; may I procreate.' It produced food. Therefore, whenever it rains, then there is abundant food; it is from water alone that food for eating is produced. . . .

"Bring hither a fig from there." "Here it is, sir." "Break it." "It is broken, sir." "What do you see there?" "These extremely fine seeds, sir." "Of these, please break one." "It is broken, sir." "What do you see there?" "Nothing at all, sir." Then he said to Shvetaketu: "Verily, my dear, that subtle essence which you do not perceive — from that very essence, indeed, my dear, does this great fig tree thus arise. Believe me, my dear, that which is the subtle essence — this whole world has that essence for its Self; that is the Real [*satya*, truth]; that is the Self; that [subtle essence] art thou, Shvetaketu." "Still further may the venerable sir instruct me." "So be it, my dear," said he.

"Having put this salt in the water, come to me in the morning." He did so. Then the father said to him: "That salt which you put in the water last evening — please bring it hither." Even having looked for it, he did not find it, for it was completely dissolved. "Please take a sip of water from this end," said the father. "How is it?" "Salt." "Take a sip from the middle," said he. "How is it?" "Salt." "Take a sip from that end," said he. "How is it?" "Salt." "Throw it away and come to me." Shvetaketu did so thinking to himself: "That salt, though unperceived, still persists in the water." Then Aruni said to him: "Verily, my dear, you do not perceive Being in this world; but it is, indeed, here only: That which is the subtle essence — this whole world has that essence for its Self. That is the Real. That is the Self. That art thou, Shvetaketu."

20

Transmigration

This selection is from the *Laws of Manu,* the most important law book of classical India, completed in its present form around the second century A.D. The excerpt displays in detail the workings of transmigration and the law of karma — good deeds will be automatically rewarded and evil ones inevitably punished in the next life.

QUESTIONS TO CONSIDER

1. How does the Hindu concept of transmigration compare with the Christian belief of retribution?
2. What constitute sinful acts in the Laws of Manu as given in the selection below? What are the karmic consequences of such acts?

3. Compare the Laws of Manu with the Ten Commandments (see Reading 11), the Book of Covenant (see Reading 12), and the Golden Rule and God's Will (see Reading 42).

1. O sinless One, the whole sacred law, (applicable) to the four castes, has been declared by thee ; communicate to us (now), according to the truth, the ultimate retribution for (their) deeds."

2. To the great sages (who addressed him thus) righteous Bhrigu [a seer], sprung from Manu, answered, "Hear the decision concerning this whole connexion with actions."

3. Action [*karma*], which springs from the mind, from speech, and from the body, produces either good or evil results ; by action are caused the (various) conditions of men, the highest, the middling, and the lowest.

4. Know that the mind is the instigator here below, even to that (action) which is connected with the body, (and) which is of three kinds, has three locations, and falls under ten heads.

5. Coveting the property of others, thinking in one's heart of what is undesirable, and adherence to false (doctrines), are the three kinds of (sinful) mental action.

6. Abusing (others, speaking) untruth, detracting from the merits of all men, and talking idly, shall be the four kinds of (evil) verbal action.

7. Taking what has not been given, injuring (creatures) without the sanction of the law, and holding criminal intercourse with another man's wife, are declared to be the three kinds of (wicked) bodily action.

8. (A man) obtains (the result of) a good or evil mental (act) in his mind, (that of) a verbal (act) in his speech, (that of) a bodily (act) in his body.

9. In consequence of (many) sinful acts committed with his body, a man becomes (in the next birth) something inanimate, in consequence (of sins) committed by speech, a bird, or a beast, and in consequence of mental (sins he is re-born in) a low caste.

10. That man is called a (true) tridandin in whose mind these three, the control over his speech . . . , the control over his thoughts . . . , and the control over his body . . . , are firmly fixed.

11. That man who keeps this threefold control (over himself) with respect to all created beings and wholly subdues desire and wrath, thereby assuredly gains complete success. . . .

52. In consequence of attachment to (the objects of) the senses, and in consequence of the non-performance of their duties, fools, the lowest of men, reach the vilest births.

53. What wombs this individual soul enters in this world and in consequence of what actions, learn the particulars of that at large and in due order.

54. Those who committed mortal sins . . . , having passed during large numbers of years through dreadful hells, obtain, after the expiration of (that term of punishment), the following births.

From G. Buhler, trans., *The Laws of Manu*, Sacred Books of the East, vol. 25 (New York : Dover Publications, 1969 ; orig. pub. 1886), pp. 483–485, 496–497.

55. The slayer of a Brâhma*n*a enters the womb of a dog, a pig, an ass, a camel, a cow, a goat, a sheep, a deer, a bird, a Candala, and a Pukkasa [two low-caste groups].
56. A Brâhma*n*a who drinks (the spirituous liquor called) Sura shall enter (the bodies) of small and large insects, of moths, of birds, feeding on ordure, and of destructive beasts.
57. A Brâhma*n*a who steals (the gold of a Brâhma*n*a shall pass) a thousand times (through the bodies) of spiders, snakes and lizards, of aquatic animals and of destructive Pishacas [ghosts].
58. The violator of a Guru's bed (enters) a hundred times (the forms) of grasses, shrubs, and creepers, likewise of carnivorous (animals) and of (beasts) with fangs and of those doing cruel deeds.
59. Men who delight in doing hurt (become) carnivorous (animals); those who eat forbidden food, worms; thieves, creatures consuming their own kind; those who have intercourse with women of the lowest castes, Pretas [another kind of ghost].

21

The Path to Liberation

This selection from the *Laws of Manu* explains that a person should seek the ultimate experience of liberation from transmigration only after fulfilling the duty of a householder (that is, raising a family and earning a living). When this responsibility is satisfied, an individual may renounce social life, retire to the forest alone, and begin the rigorous pursuit of final liberation.

QUESTIONS TO CONSIDER

1. What is final liberation in Hindu-Buddhist thought? Can one achieve the final liberation simply by ending one's life in this world? How?
2. Compare the Hindu goal of liberation from transmigration with the Judaic, Christian, and Islamic ideas of salvation?

Having thus lived a householder's life according to the prescribed rules, a twice-born householder should, making a firm resolve and keeping his sense-organs in subjection, live in a forest as recommended in the Sacred Law.

From W. de Bary et al., *Sources of Indian Tradition*, vol. 1 (New York: Columbia University Press, 1958), pp. 229–230. Reprinted by permission of Columbia University Press.

When a householder sees his skin wrinkled and his hair gray and when he sees the son of his son, then he should resort to the forest.

Having given up food produced in villages [by cultivation] and abandoning all his belongings, he should depart into the forest, either committing his wife to the care of his sons or departing together with her. . . .

He should be constantly engaged in study and should be self-controlled, friendly toward all, spiritually composed, ever a liberal giver and never a receiver, and compassionate toward all beings. . . .

Having consigned the sacred fires [used for sacrifices to the gods] into himself in accordance with the prescribed rules, he should live without a fire, without a house, a silent sage subsisting on roots and fruit. . . .

Having thus passed the third part of his life in the forest, he should renounce all attachments to worldly objects and become an ascetic during the fourth part of his life. . . .

He should always wander alone, without any companion, in order to achieve spiritual perfection — clearly seeing that such attainment is possible only in the case of the solitary man, who neither forsakes nor is forsaken. . . .

The student, the householder, the hermit, and the ascetic — these constitute the four separate stages of life, originating from and depending upon the householder's life.

All these stages of life, adopted successively and in accordance with the Shāstras [law books], lead the brāhman following the prescribed rules to the highest state.

Of all these, verily, according to the precepts of the Veda and the Smriti [tradition] the householder is said to be the most excellent, for he supports the other three.

22

Duties of the Social Classes

The following selection from the *Laws of Manu* summarizes the duties required of each social class.

QUESTIONS TO CONSIDER

1. What reasons does Hinduism give people — from the servile and common classes up to priests and kings — for abiding by the law and doing their prescribed duty?
2. What are the possible positive features of these laws? Why? What are the negative aspects?

For the sake of the preservation of this entire creation, [Purusha, the creator God], the exceedingly resplendent one, assigned separate duties to the classes which had sprung from his mouth, arms, thighs, and feet.

Teaching, studying, performing sacrificial rites, so too making others perform sacrificial rites, and giving away and receiving gifts — these he assigned to the brāhmans.

Protection of the people, giving away of wealth, performance of sacrificial rites, study, and nonattachment to sensual pleasures — these are, in short, the duties of a kshatriya [warrior].

Tending of cattle, giving away of wealth, performance of sacrificial rites, study, trade and commerce, usury, and agriculture — these are the occupations of a vaishya [commoner].

The Lord has prescribed only one occupation [karma] for a shūdra [conquered person], namely, service without malice of even these other three classes.

Man is stated to be purer above the navel than below it; hence his mouth has been declared to be the purest part by the Self-existent One [Purusha].

On account of his origin from the best limb of the Cosmic Person [Purusha], on account of his seniority, and on account of the preservation by him of the Veda [brahman] — the brāhman is in respect of dharma [law] the lord of this entire creation.

For the Self-Existent One, having performed penance, produced the brāhman first of all, from his own mouth, for the sake of the conveying of the offerings intended for the gods and those intended for the manes [deceased ancestors] and for the sake of the preservation of this entire universe.

What created being can be superior to him through whose mouth the gods always consume the oblations intended for them and the manes those intended for them?

Of created beings, those which are animate are the best; of the animate, those who subsist by means of their intellect; of the intelligent, men are the best; and of men, the brāhmans are traditionally declared to be the best;

Of the brāhmans, the learned ones are the best; of the learned, those whose intellect is fixed upon ritual activity; of those whose intellect is fixed upon ritual activity, those who carry out ritual activity; of those who carry out ritual activity, those who realize the Brahman.

The very birth of a brāhman is the eternal incarnation of dharma. For he is born for the sake of dharma and tends toward becoming one with the Brahman. . . .

For the sake of the discussion of the brāhman's duties and of those of the other classes according to their precedence, wise Manu, the son of the Self-existent One, produced this treatise. . . .

In this treatise there are expounded in entirety dharma, the merits and demerits of [human] actions, and the eternal code of conduct of the four classes.

The code of conduct — prescribed by scriptures and ordained by sacred tradition [the Sacred Law] — constitutes the highest dharma; hence a twice-born person [member of first three social classes], conscious of his own Self [seeking spiritual salvation], should be always scrupulous in respect of it.

From W. de Bary et al., *Sources of Indian Tradition,* vol. 1 (New York: Columbia University Press, 1958), pp. 220–221. Reprinted by permission of Columbia University Press.

23

Bhagavad-Gita

The *Bhagavad-Gita*, "The Song of God," is one of the most popular and revered books in Hindu religious literature. For more than two millennia, it has been the principal source of religious inspiration for many millions of South Asian people. It consists of more than 700-line verses in the form of a long philosophical dialogue primarily between Krishna, a manifestation of the Supreme Deity in human form, and Arjuna, a warrior-prince, dealing with questions regarding the relationship between man's real self or soul and the body and life and destiny as a whole. In the first of the following two excerpts from the *Bhagavad-Gita*, Krishna explains the deathless life and the indestructibility of the soul and the importance of caste duties, concepts so central to Hindu religious belief, to Arjuna, who is torn by the feelings of worldly and spiritual obligations. In the second excerpt, the importance of devotion to God in achieving salvation in Hindu religion is described.

QUESTIONS TO CONSIDER

1. Explain what Arjuna's worldly and spiritual obligations are and the reason for his dilemma.
2. What spiritual justifications does Krishna offer to Arjuna for killing the enemy in the battle field?

Deathless Life and Caste Obligation

How can I use my arrows in battle against Bhīshma, my grandsire, and Drona, my venerable teacher, who are worthy rather to be worshipped, O Destroyer of all opponents?

Surely would it be better to eat the bread of beggary in this life than to slay these great-souled masters!

If I kill them, all enjoyment of wealth, all gratified desire, is stained by their blood!

Indeed, scarcely can I tell which would be better, that they or we should conquer, for to destroy those sons of Dhritarāshtra who oppose us, would be to extinguish forever the savor of life.

Overpowered by my helplessness, and with a mind in confusion, I supplicate Thee! Make clear to me that which is my good; I am Thy disciple. Instruct me, who have sought my refuge in Thee!

There is naught to dispel this sorrow which overpowereth my senses. Were I to obtain undisputed and powerful dominion over all the earth, and mastery over the gods, what then would that avail me?

Arjuna, having thus spoken to Kṛishṇa, Lord of the Senses, made end, saying:

'I shall not fight!' and with these words fell silent.

But as he remained sorrowing thus in the midst of the two armies, Kṛishṇa, smiling a little, spoke to him as follows:

Thou hast grieved for those undeserving of grief, Arjuna! Although thou speakest wisely, those who are still wiser mourn neither for the living nor for the dead.

For never hath it been that I was not, nor thou, nor these Kings; nor shall we cease to be, ever.

The self is not interrupted while childhood, youth and old age pass through the flesh; likewise in death the self dieth not, but is released to assume another shape. By this the calm soul is not deluded.

The impressions of the senses, quickened to heat and cold, pain and pleasure, are transitory. Forever on the ebb and flow, they are by their very nature impermanent. Bear them then patiently, O Descendant of Kings!

For the wise man who is serene in pain and pleasure, whom these disturb not, he alone is able to attain Immortality, O Great amongst men!

The unreal can never be; the real can never cease to be. Those who know the truth know that this is so.

The Uunnamable Principle which pervadeth all things, none hath power to destroy: know thou certainly that It is indestructible.

By *That,* immortal, inexhaustible, illimitable, Indweller, is the mortality of this flesh possessed. Fight therefore O Descendant of brave Kings!

He who conceiveth this Indweller, this Self, as slayer, or who conceiveth It as slain, is without knowledge. The Self neither slayeth nor is It slain.

It is never born, nor doth It die, nor having once existed, doth It ever cease to be. Ancient, eternal, changeless, ever Itself, It perisheth not when the body is destroyed.

How can that man who knoweth It to be indestructible, changeless, without birth, and immutable, how can he, Arjuna, either slay or cause the slaying of another?

As a man casteth off an old garment and putteth on another which is new, so the Self casteth off its outworn embodiment and entereth into a new form.

This Self, weapons cut not; This, fire burneth not; This, water wetteth not; and This, the winds dry not up.

This Self cannot be cut, it cannot be burnt, it cannot be wetted, it cannot be dried. Changeless, all-pervading, unmoving, Eternal, it is the Unalterable Self.

This Self is invisible, inconceivable, and changeless. Knowing that It is such, cease, therefore, to grieve!

But whether thou believest this Self of eternal duration or subjected constantly to birth and death, yet Mighty-armèd One, hast thou no cause to grieve.

For, to that which is born, death is certain ; to that which dieth, birth is certain, and the unavoidable, giveth not occasion for grief.

Nothing may be perceived in its beginning ; in its middle state only is it known, and its end again is undisclosed. What herein, Arjuna, is cause for grief?

One man perceiveth the Self as a thing of wonder ; another speaketh of It as a wonder ; others hear of It as a wonder, but though seeing, speaking, hearing, none comprehendeth It at all.

This, which is the Indweller in all beings, is forever beyond harm. Then, for no creature, Arjuna, hast thou any cause to grieve.

Examine thy duty and falter not, for there is no better thing for a warrior than to wage righteous war.

Fortunate indeed are the soldiers, Arjuna, who, fighting in such a battle, reach this unsought, open gate to heaven.

But to refuse this just fight and forego thine own duty and honour, is to incur sin.

By so doing the world will also hold thee ever in despite. To the honourable, dishonour is surely worse than death.

The great charioteer warriors will believe that through fear thou hast withdrawn from the battle. Then shalt thou fall from their esteem, who hast hitherto been highly regarded.

Thine enemies moreover, cavilling at thy great prowess, will say of thee that which is not to be uttered. What fate, indeed, could be more unbearable than this?

Dying thou gainest heaven ; victorious, thou enjoyest the earth. Therefore, Arjuna, arise, resolved to do battle.

Look upon pain and pleasure, gain and loss, conquest and defeat, as the same, and prepare to fight ; thus shalt thou incur no evil.

Now hath been declared unto thee the understanding of the Self. Hearken thou moreover to the Way,[1] following which, O son of Kings, thou shalt break through the fateful bondage of thine act.[2]

On this Way nothing that is begun is lost, nor are there any obstacles, and even a very little progress thereon bringeth security against great fear.

Devotion to God

But those who adore Me, and Me alone, and all beings who are steadfast and supremely dedicated in their worship, I augment in their fullness and fill them up in their emptiness.

Even those who devotedly worship other gods because of their love, worship Me ; but the path they follow is not My path.

For I alone am the Deity of all sacrifices, and those who worship other gods than Me reach the end of merit and return to the world, where they must set forth anew upon the way.

---

1. Yoga. The exact meaning of Yoga depends on its context. It signifies any consistent way of spiritual life.
2. "The bondage of thine act," Karma. "The doctrine of true knowledge and of emancipation by means of it."

One pursueth the gods and attaineth the sphere of the gods suitable to the merit of his works ; another worshippeth the Fathers and yet another worshippeth attributes and incarnations, each attaining unto his own place ; but he who worshippeth Me cometh unto Me.

Whosoever with devotion offereth Me leaf, flower, fruit, or water, I accept it from him as the devout gift of the pure-minded.

Whatsoever thou doest, Arjuna, whatsoever thou eatest, whatsoever thou givest away, whatsoever thou offerest up as sacrifice, and whatsoever austerity thou shalt practice, do it as an offering unto Me.

Thus shalt thou be released from the fateful bonds of thine acts, and the cage of good and evil. Thine heart shall renounce itself, and being liberated, shall come unto Me.

To Me none is hateful, none dear ; but those who worship Me with devotion dwell in Me, and I also in them.

Even a very wicked man who worshippeth Me, eschewing all else in his devotion to Me, shall be regarded as worthy of merit, for great is his faith.

He shall attain righteousness in a short time, Arjuna, and compel everlasting Peace ; therefore, proclaim it aloud that no one of My devotees is destroyed.

They also who might be considered of inferior birth, women, tradesmen, as well as day-laborers, even they shall master this world and attain Me, Arjuna, if they seek Me with single mind.

What need, then, to describe priests and kings who have attained holiness ? Therefore, Arjuna, in this transient, joyless world, worship thou Me!

Make thy mind My dwelling place ; consecrate thyself to Me ; sacrifice unto Me, bow down unto Me, make thy heart steadfast in Me thy Supreme Destination, and thou too shalt assuredly come unto Me.

24

Duties of a King

This selection and the next are from the *Artha Shastra*, a manual written by Kautiliya (c. fourth century B.C.). These guidelines were intended to give practical advice to kings on how to stay in power. The tone is not always very high minded because the author knew that realistically the "law of the fishes" prevails — that is, big fish eat little ones.

QUESTIONS TO CONSIDER

1. How does this selection compare with Niccolò Machiavelli's *The Prince and the Discourses on Titus Livy* (see Reading 84)?

2. Are these guidelines and advice consistent with Hindu-Buddhist religious precepts? How? Use King Ashoka's thoughts (see Reading 31).

Only if a king is himself energetically active, do his officers follow him energetically. If he is sluggish, they too remain sluggish. And, besides, they eat up his
works. He is thereby easily overpowered by his enemies. Therefore, he should
ever dedicate himself energetically to activity.

He should divide the day as well as the night into eight parts . . . During the
first one-eighth part of the day, he should listen to reports pertaining to the organization of law and order and to income and expenditure. During the second, he
should attend to the affairs of the urban and the rural population. During the
third, he should take his bath and meal and devote himself to study. During
the fourth, he should receive gold and the departmental heads. During the fifth,
he should hold consultations with the council of ministers through correspondence and also keep himself informed of the secret reports brought by spies. During the sixth, he should devote himself freely to amusement or listen to the
counsel of the ministers. During the seventh, he should inspect the military formations of elephants, cavalry, chariots, and infantry. During the eighth, he, together
with the commander-in-chief of the army, should make plans for campaigns of
conquest. When the day has come to an end he should offer the evening prayers.

During the first one-eighth part of the night, he should meet the officers of
the secret service. During the second, he should take his bath and meals and also
devote himself to study. During the third, at the sounding of the trumpets, he
should enter the bed chamber and should sleep through the fourth and fifth.
Waking up at the sounding of the trumpets, he should, during the sixth part, ponder over the teachings of the sciences and his urgent duties for the day. During the
seventh, he should hold consultations and send out the officers of the secret service for their operations. During the eighth, accompanied by sacrificial priests,
preceptors, and the chaplain, he should receive benedictions; he should also have
interviews with the physician, the kitchen-superintendent, and the astrologer.
Thereafter, he should circumambulate by the right a cow with a calf and an ox and
then proceed to the reception hall. Or he should divide the day and the night into
parts in accordance with his own capacities and thereby attend to his duties.

When he has gone to the reception hall, he should not allow such persons, as
have come for business, to remain sticking to the doors of the hall [i.e., waiting in
vain]. For, a king, with whom it is difficult for the people to have an audience, is
made to confuse between right action and wrong action by his close entourage.
Thereby he suffers from the disaffection of his own subjects or falls prey to the enemy. Therefore he should attend to the affairs relating to gods, hermitages, heretics, learned brāhmans, cattle, and holy places as also those of minors, the aged,
the sick, those in difficulty, the helpless, and women — in the order of their enu-
meration or in accordance with the importance or the urgency of the affairs.

From W. de Bary et al., *Sources of Indian Tradition*, vol. 1 (New York: Columbia University Press,
1958), pp. 241–243. Reprinted by permission of Columbia University Press.

A king should attend to all urgent business, he should not put it off. For what has been thus put off becomes either difficult or altogether impossible to accomplish. . . .

In the happiness of the subjects lies the happiness of the king ; in their welfare, his own welfare. The welfare of the king does not lie in the fulfillment of what is dear to him ; whatever is dear to the subjects constitutes his welfare.

Widow Burning: Two Views of Sati

In many ancient cultures, men were interred upon their death with their widows, horses, and other cherished possessions in the belief that the deceased men might have them in the next world. One of the widely practiced Hindu funeral rites in traditional India for over two millennia was sati (or as it is sometimes spelled, suttee), the self-immolation of widows on the deceased husband's funeral pyre. A Hindu legend has it that Sati, wife of the Hindu deity Siva, committed suicide in protest against her father Daksha's insult to her husband. The actual meaning of the Sanskrit word *sati* is "virtuous wife," one who remains unmarried in expression of her faithfulness to her husband even after his death. Subsequently, it came to mean suicide of widows by the flame of the pyre on which their husbands' bodies were cremated. By the early centuries of the common era, many Hindu lawgivers sanctioned such a practice as commendable for widows since their widowhood was looked upon as sinful. Sati was regarded as a way for a widow to achieve salvation not only for herself but also for her husband. In the early period, this custom was practiced primarily by the widows of members of the upper castes such as princes and warriors, but with the passage of time, this custom spread to the wives of the lower castes as well. By the sixth and seventh centuries, this custom was widely practiced voluntarily and, perhaps, more often involuntarily, as a duty for widowed women in India.

One of the earliest references to the practice of sati is found in the great Hindu epic poems *Mahabharata* (c. 300 B.C.–A.D. 300). The account in the epic describes the self-immolation of Madri, the second wife of King Pandu, who died while he was making love to her.[1]

1. J. A. B. van Buitenen, trans. and ed., *The Mahabharata, 1 The Book of the Beginning* (Chicago : University of Chicago Press, 1973), pp. 259–262.

25

A Greek General's View

This account is one of the earliest recorded accounts in the Greek chronicles. It is an eyewitness account of the sati of one of the wives of an Indian general who was killed in battle in modern day Iran while fighting the Greek General Antigonus in 316 B.C. The Greek generals allowed only the younger wife to immolate herself on the pyre since the elder wife was with child.

QUESTIONS TO CONSIDER

1. Why was widowhood looked upon as sinful? Why would such a custom survive in India until the twentieth century?
2. Did the Greek generals make the correct decision in permitting one of the Indian widows to immolate herself on her husband's funeral pyre?

[At this, the elder woman] went away lamenting, with the band about her head rent, and tearing her hair, as if tidings of some great disaster have been brought her; and the other departed, exultant at her victory, to the pyre, crowned with fillets by the women who belonged to her, and decked out splendidly as for a wedding. She was escorted by her kinsfolk who chanted a song in praise of her virtue. When she came near to the pyre, she took off her adornments and distributed them to her familiars and friends, leaving a memorial of herself, as it were, to those who had loved her. Her adornments consisted of a multitude of rings on her hands set with precious gems of diverse colours, about her head golden stars not a few, variegated with different sorts of stones, and about her neck a multitude of necklaces, each a little larger than the one above it. In conclusion, she said farewell to her familiars and was helped by her brother onto the pyre, and there to the admiration of the crowd which had gathered together for the spectacle she ended her life in heroic fashion. Before the pyre was kindled, the whole army in battle array marched round it thrice. She meanwhile lay down beside her husband, and as the fire seized her no sound of weakness escaped her lips. The spectators were moved, some to pity and some to exuberant praise. But some of the Greeks present found fault with such customs as savage and inhumane.

E. J. Rapson, ed., *The Cambridge History of India,* vol. I, *Ancient India* (Cambridge, England: Cambridge University Press, 1935), p. 415. Reprinted with permission.

26

Jean Baptice Tavernier, *Travels in India*

This account, published in 1676, was written by Jean Baptice Tavernier, an inveterate French traveler who visited India five times between 1638 and 1668.

QUESTIONS TO CONSIDER

1. Despite the differences in time, are there any similarities between the Greek and French views of sati?
2. How would you compare these two views of sati with the Viking practice of burning women (see Reading 58)? Do you know of other cultures that burned women in funeral ceremonies?

It is also an ancient custom among the idolaters of India that on a man dying his widow can never remarry; as soon, therefore, as he is dead she retires to weep for her husband, and some days afterwards her hair is shaved off, and she despoils herself of all the ornaments with which her person was adorned; she removes from her arms and legs the bracelets which her husband had given her, when espousing her, as a sign that she was to be submissive and bound to him, and she remains for the rest of her life without any consideration, and worse than a slave, in the place where previously she was mistress. This miserable condition causes her to detest life, and prefer to ascend a funeral pile to be consumed alive with the body of her deceased husband, rather than be regarded by all the world for the remainder of her days with opprobrium and infamy. Besides this the Brāhmans induce women to hope that by dying in this way, with their husbands, they will live again with them in some other world with more glory and more comfort than they have previously enjoyed. These are the two reasons which make these unhappy women resolve to burn themselves with the bodies of their husbands; to which it should be added that the priests encourage them with the hope that at the moment they are in the fire, before they yield up their souls, Rām will reveal wonderful things to them, and that after the soul has passed through several bodies it will attain to an exalted degree of glory for all eternity.

I have seen women burned in three different ways, according to the customs of different countries. In the Kingdom of Gujarāt, and as far as Agra and Delhi, this is how it takes place: On the margin of a river or tank, a kind of small hut, about twelve feet square, is built of reeds and all kinds of faggots, with which some pots of oil and other drugs are placed in order to make it burn quickly. The

Jean Baptice Tavernier, *Travels in India*, trans. V. Ball (London : Macmillan and Co., 1889), II :208–216 passim.

woman is seated in a half-reclining position in the middle of the hut, her head reposes on a kind of pillow of wood, and she rests her back against a post, to which
she is tied by her waist by one of the Brāhmans, for fear lest she should escape on
feeling the flame. In this position she holds the dead body of her husband on her
knees, chewing betel all the time ; and after having been about half an hour in this
condition, the Brāhman who has been by her side in the hut goes outside, and she
calls out to the priests to apply the fire ; this the Brāhmans, and the relatives and
friends of the woman who are present immediately do, throwing into the fire
some pots of oil, so that the woman may suffer less by being quickly consumed.
After the bodies have been reduced to ashes, the Brāhmans take whatever is found
in the way of melted gold, silver, tin, or copper, derived from the bracelets, earrings, and rings which the woman had on ; this belongs to them by right, as I have
said.

In the Kingdom of Bengal women are burned in another manner. A woman
in that country must be very poor if she does not come with the body of her husband to the bank of the Ganges to wash it after he is dead, and to bathe herself before being burned. I have seen them come to the Ganges more than twenty days'
journey, the bodies being by that time altogether putrid, and emitting an unbearable odour. There was one of them who came from the north, near the frontiers of
the Kingdom of Bhutān, with the body of her husband which she had conveyed in
a carriage, and travelled all the way on foot herself, without eating for fifteen or
sixteen days, till she arrived at the Ganges, where after washing the body of her
husband, which stank horribly, and bathing herself also, she had herself burned
with him with a determination which surprised those who saw it. I was there at the
time. As throughout the course of the Ganges, and also in all Bengal, there is but
little fuel, these poor women send to beg for wood out of charity to burn themselves with the dead bodies of their husbands. A funeral pile is prepared for them,
which is like a bed, with its pillow of small wood and reeds, in which pots of oil and
other drugs are placed in order to consume the body quickly. The woman who intends to burn herself, preceded by drums, flutes, and hautboys, and adorned with
her most beautiful jewels, comes dancing to the funeral pile, and ascending it she
places herself, half-lying, half-seated. Then the body of her husband is laid across
her, and all the relatives and friends bring her, one a letter, another a piece of
cloth, this one flowers, that one pieces of silver or copper, asking her to give this
from me to my mother, or to my brother, or to some relative or friend, whoever
the dead person may be whom they have most loved while alive. When the woman
sees that they bring her nothing more, she asks those present three times whether
they have any more commissions for her, and if they do not reply she wraps all
they have brought in a taffeta, which she places between her lap and the back of
the body of her dead husband, calling upon the priests to apply fire to the funeral
pile. This the Brāhmans and the relatives do simultaneously. There is, as I have remarked, but little wood in the Kingdom of Bengal ; so as soon as these miserable
women are dead and half burned, their bodies are thrown into the Ganges with
those of their husbands, where they are eaten by the crocodiles.

Let us see now what is the practice along the coast of Coromandel when
women are going to be burned with the bodies of their deceased husbands. A
large hole of nine or ten feet deep, and twenty-five or thirty feet square, is dug,

into which plenty of wood is thrown, with many drugs to make it burn quickly. When the hole is well heated, the body of the husband is placed on the edge, and then his wife comes dancing, and chewing betel, accompanied by all her relatives and friends, and with the sound of drums and cymbals. The woman then makes three turns round the hole, and at each time she embraces all her relatives and friends. When she completes the third turn the Brāhmans throw the body of the deceased into the fire, and the woman, with her back turned towards the hole, is pushed by the Brāhmans, and falls in backwards. Then all the relatives throw pots of oil and other drugs of that kind, as I have said is elsewhere done, so that the bodies may be the sooner consumed. In the greater part of the same Coromandel coast the woman does not burn herself with the body of her deceased husband, but allows herself to be interred, while alive, with him in a hole which the Brāh-mans dig in the ground, about one foot deeper than the height of the man or woman. They generally select a sandy spot, and when they have placed the man and woman in the hole, each of their friends fills a basket of sand, and throws it on the bodies until the hole is full and heaped over, half a foot higher than the ground, after which they jump and dance upon it till they are certain that the woman is smothered.

The Buddhist Tradition

Buddhism represents one of the few truly unifying threads in the diverse cultures of Asia. From its origins in Northeast India around 500 B.C., this religion spread throughout the subcontinent and beyond, into Sri Lanka and Southeast Asia. The patronage of missionary activity by the Indian king of the Mauryan dynasty, Ashoka (269–232 B.C.), particularly promoted the dissemination of Buddhism. Around the beginning of the Christian Era, this religion was introduced into China, and from there it passed via Korea into Japan by the sixth century A.D. By the seventh century, Buddhism had become the dominant religion of Tibet.

Throughout this long, complex history, Buddhists have focused on the essential elements of their faith by devising a few key formulas. First, all Buddhists believe in the "Three Jewels" (or "Three Refuges"): the Buddha, his Teaching (*Dharma*), and the Community of Monks (*Sangha*). Moreover, the major events in the life of the Buddha (563–483 B.C.) were frequent themes in Buddhist art and literature. For example, many biographical accounts were written (such as the *Buddhacarita*), enabling followers to envision the details of the Buddha's life from his birth, through his early life as the pampered prince Gautama of the Shakya clan, to his renunciation of social life and quest for enlightenment. The Buddha's insight into human suffering and the path to overcome it earned him his title, which means the Enlightened One.

The many sermons with which the Buddha taught his followers during his long ministry in the Ganges Valley were memorized by some of the monks. These sermons were later collected to form one part of the Buddhist sacred scriptures, the *Tripitika*, committed to writing by the first century B.C. in India and Sri Lanka. Two other parts deal with rules for the monks and advanced analyses of the Buddha's teaching.

The Buddha's teaching emphasized that life in the endless cycle of transmigration (*samsara*) is inherently fraught with suffering and frustration. The cause of this suffering is our desire for material things and our ignorance of the fact that there is no "self." Our false notions prompt us to action in search of satisfaction for our "selves"; and all of these actions (which the Buddhists and Hindus call *karma*) produce good or bad consequences, depending on whether they involve good or evil deeds. The results push us into another life in the cycle of transmigration, where we will receive our due rewards. However, the Buddha believed that we are only heaps of *skandhas*, material components, which obey natural laws of causation and which eventually disintegrate like all matter. So, the Buddha reasoned, if people could only abandon the false notion of self and give up all desire, they would be liberated from the effects of actions and, therefore, from the cycle of transmigration. Once liberated, people would achieve a condition of absolute peace and tranquility, which the Buddhists call *nirvana.* To achieve this state, the Buddha provided an Eightfold Path for living a disciplined life of calm detachment.

Only monks and nuns, who constitute the Sangha, completely follow this path to reach nirvana. These rare men — and a few women — totally give up their worldly possessions and ways. Historically, most monks lived in monasteries where they spent their time learning and discussing the Buddha's teaching and meditating in order to achieve a deep, inner calm. The Buddhist laypersons (that is, those who lived normal lives outside the monastery) greatly respected the monks and gained merit by providing them food for their one meal a day. This religious practice still prevails in Sri Lanka and Southeast Asia.

Buddhism began mainly as a path for the extraordinary few who sought liberation from the normal human condition; however, in time it developed into a humane way of life for the entire society. The first and best example involved the famous Indian king, Ashoka, who (as shown in Reading 31) was inspired by Buddhism to renounce violence as a political tool. In place of violence, Ashoka promoted compassion and righteousness throughout his vast empire. After his death, Ashoka was remembered as the ideal of the Buddhist monarch, and he was emulated by the kings of Sri Lanka and Southeast Asia.

Reading 29 shows a new ideal that came to prominence about 500 years after the Buddha, called the Bodhisattva (or Buddha-to-be). Rather than emphasizing the calm reflection on reality that allowed the Buddha, and the community of monks following him, to achieve the total dispassion of nirvana, the Bodhisattva strove for perfection in compassion. The Bodhisattva was dedicated to selflessly helping as many other creatures as possible and delayed achieving nirvana and becoming a Buddha. Guanyin is one of the most popular Bodhisattvas. This form of Buddhism, in which the Bodhisattva predominates, is called the *Mahayana* or Greater Vehicle, since it provides more people with easier access to liberation than the older form of Buddhism (called the *Hinayana*, Lesser Vehicle, or *Theravada*, Doctrine of the Elders), in which the monks were the central element.

27

Enlightenment of the Buddha

This selection is from the best-known biography of the Buddha, called the *Buddhacarita* and written by the Indian poet Ashvaghosha before A.D. 200. The reading begins with Prince Gautama already having abandoned family and home, intent on conquering the cause of human suffering. This Buddha-to-be decides to sit alone under a tree until an answer to his problem is clear. The episode ends with his achieving enlightenment — insight into the cause of suffering and the way to overcome it. This experience turns him into a Buddha, an Enlightened One.

QUESTIONS TO CONSIDER

1. Compare the achievements of the Buddha with those of Jesus, Muhammad, and Confucius.
2. How important is meditation in achieving enlightenment in Buddhism? Why?

The Bodhisattva [Buddha-to-be], possessed of great skill in Transic meditation, put himself into trance, intent on discerning both the ultimate reality of things and the final goal of existence. After he had gained complete mastery over all the degrees and kinds of trance:

1. In the *first watch* of the night he recollected the successive series of his former births. 'There was I so and so; that was my name; deceased from there I came here' — in this way he remembered thousands of births, as though living them over again. When he had recalled his own births and deaths in all these various lives of his, the Sage, full of pity, turned his compassionate mind towards other living beings, and he thought to himself: 'Again and again they must leave the people they regard as their own, and must go on elsewhere, and that without ever stopping. Surely this world is unprotected and helpless, and like a wheel it turns round and round.' As he continued steadily to recollect the past thus, he came to the definite conviction that this world of Samsara is as unsubstantial as the pith of a plantain tree.

2. Second to none in valour, he then, in the *second watch* of the night, acquired the supreme heavenly eye, for he himself was the best of all those who have sight. Thereupon with the perfectly pure heavenly eye he looked upon the entire

world, which appeared to him as though reflected in a spotless mirror. He saw that the decease and rebirth of beings depend on whether they have done superior or inferior deeds. And his compassionateness grew still further. It became clear to him that no security can be found in this flood of Samsaric existence, and that the threat of death is ever-present. Beset on all sides, creatures can find no resting place. In this way he surveyed the five places of rebirth with his heavenly eye. And he found nothing substantial in the world of becoming, just as no core of heart-wood is found in a plantain tree when its layers are peeled off one by one.

3. Then, as the *third watch* of that night drew on, the supreme master of trance turned his meditation to the real and essential nature of this world : 'Alas, living beings wear themselves out in vain! Over and over again they are born, they age, die, pass on to a new life, and are reborn! What is more, greed and dark delusion obscure their sight, and they are blind from birth. Greatly apprehensive, they yet do not know how to get out of this great mass of ill.' He then surveyed the twelve links of conditioned co-production, and saw that, beginning with ignorance, they lead to old age and death, and, beginning with the cessation of ignorance, they lead to the cessation of birth, old age, death, and all kinds of ill.

When the great seer had comprehended that where there is no ignorance whatever, there also the karma-formations are stopped — then he had achieved a correct knowledge of all there is to be known, and he stood out in the world as a Buddha. He passed through the eight stages of Transic insight, and quickly reached their highest point. From the summit of the world downwards he could detect no self anywhere. Like the fire, when its fuel is burnt up, he became tranquil. He had reached perfection, and he thought to himself : 'This is the authentic Way on which in the past so many great seers, who also knew all higher and all lower things, have travelled on to ultimate and real truth. And now I have obtained it!'

4. At that moment, in the *fourth watch* of the night, when dawn broke and all the ghosts that move and those that move not went to rest, the great seer took up the position which knows no more alteration, and the leader of all reached the state of all-knowledge. When, through his Buddhahood, he had cognized this fact, the earth swayed like a woman drunken with wine, the sky shone bright with the Siddhas who appeared in crowds in all the directions, and the mighty drums of thunder resounded through the air. Pleasant breezes blew softly, rain fell from a cloudless sky, flowers and fruits dropped from the trees out of season — in an effort, as it were, to show reverence for him. Mandarava flowers and lotus blossoms, and also water lilies made of gold and beryl, fell from the sky on to the ground near the Shakya sage, so that it looked like a place in the world of the gods. At that moment no one anywhere was angry, ill, or sad ; no one did evil, none was proud ; the world became quite quiet, as though it had reached full perfection. Joy spread through the ranks of those gods who longed for salvation ; joy also spread among those who lived in the regions below. Everywhere the virtuous were strengthened, the influence of Dharma increased, and the world rose from the dirt of the passions and the darkness of ignorance. Filled with joy and wonder at the Sage's work, the seers of the solar race who had been protectors of men, who had been royal seers, who had been great seers, stood in their mansions in the heavens and showed him their reverence. The great seers among the hosts of invisible beings could be heard widely proclaiming his fame. All living things rejoiced and sensed that things went well.

28

The Four Holy Truths

This selection presents the most succinct formulation of the Buddha's teaching. The reading comes from the collection of the Buddha's sermons in the *Sutra* section of the *Tripitika*, which is the earliest canon of Buddhist sacred scriptures. The excerpt is, in fact, believed to be the message he preached in his very first sermon.

QUESTIONS TO CONSIDER

1. Is Buddhism pessimistic about life? Or does this religion seem to offer hope? In what way?
2. How do the Four Holy Truths compare with the Ten Commandments in Reading 11?

What then is the Holy Truth of Ill? Birth is ill, decay is ill, sickness is ill, death is ill. To be conjoined with what one dislikes means suffering. To be disjoined from what one likes means suffering. Not to get what one wants, also that means suffering. In short, all grasping at any of the five Skandhas involves suffering.

What then is the Holy Truth of the Origination of Ill? It is that craving which leads to rebirth, accompanied by delight and greed, seeking its delight now here, now there, i.e., craving for sensuous experience, craving to perpetuate oneself, craving for extinction.

What then is the Holy Truth of the Stopping of Ill? It is the complete stopping of that craving, the withdrawal from it, the renouncing of it, throwing it back, liberation from it, non-attachment to it.

What then is the Holy Truth of the steps which lead to the stopping of Ill? It is this holy eightfold Path, which consists of right views, right intentions, right speech, right conduct, right livelihood, right effort, right mindfulness, right concentration.

29

Guanyin: Compassion of the Bodhisattva[1]

Guanyin is one of the most popular Bodhisattvas in the Far East. Guanyin means "the one who hears the cry" or "The Regarder of the Cries of the World." Guanyin is believed to be infinitely compassionate and able to deliver all beings from any sort of danger or misfortune. Guanyin appears in many different forms. In early iconography, he appears in male form, but the female form is more popular. As the Goddess of Mercy, she is believed to protect women and children. For example, it is widely believed that women who desire to become mothers and invoke her name will have their prayers answered. Legends and stories about miracles as a result of the intervention by this protectress abound in East Asia; temples and statues in honor of Guanyin are found throughout this part of the world. The following selection from *The Lotus Sutra* tells how compassionate and merciful this Bodhisattva is.

QUESTIONS TO CONSIDER

1. How do you compare the concept of compassion expressed in this selection with the Christian teachings given in the selections from the Beatitudes and St. Francis (see Readings 40 and 63)?
2. Why do you think Guanyin's role is so relevant to Mahayanistic Buddhism?

Thereafter the Bodhisattva Mahasattva Akshayamati rose from his seat, put his upper robe upon one shoulder, stretched his joined hands towards the Lord, and said: For what reason, O Lord, is the Bodhisattva Mahasattva Avalokitesvara called Avalokitesvara [Guanyin]? So he asked, and the Lord answered to the Bodhisattva Mahasattva Akshayamati: All the hundred thousands of myriads of kotis[1] of creatures, young man of good family, who in this world are suffering troubles will, if they hear the name of the Bodhisattva Mahasattva Avalokitesvara, be released from that mass of troubles. Those who shall keep the name of this Bodhisattva Mahasattva Avalokitesvara, young man of good family, will, if they fall into a great mass of fire, be delivered therefrom by virtue of the lustre of the Bodhisattva Mahasattva. In case, young man of good family, creatures, carried off by the current of river, should implore the Bodhisattva Mahasattva Avalokitesvara all rivers will afford them a ford. In case, young man of good family, many hundred thousand myriads of kotis of creatures, sailing in a ship on the

H. Kern, trans., *Saddharma-Pundarika or The Lotus of the True Law* (Oxford: Clarendon Press, 1984), pp. 406–409.

1. Also spelled as Kuan Yin or Kwan-shi-yin in Chinese, Kannon in Japanese, and Avalokitesvara in Sanskrit.
   1. A figure varying from 100,000 to 10,000,000,000.

ocean, should see their bullion, gold, gems, pearls, lapis lazuli, conch shells, stones, corals, emeralds, Musaragalvas,[2] and other goods lost, and the ship by a vehement, untimely gale cast on the island of Giantesses,[3] and if in that ship a single being implores Avalokitesvara, all will be saved from that island of Giantesses. For that reason, young man of good family, the Bodhisattva Mahasattva Avalokitesvara is named Avalokitesvara.

If a man given up to capital punishment implore Avalokitesvara, young man of good family, the swords of the executioners shall snap asunder. Further, young man of good family, if the whole triple chiliocosm[4] were teeming with goblins and giants, they would by virtue of the name of the Bodhisattva Mahasattva Avalokitesvara being pronounced lose the faculty of sight in their wicked designs. If some creature, young man of good family, shall be bound in wooden or iron manacles, chains, or fetters, be he guilty or innocent, then those manacles, chains, or fetters shall give way as soon as the name of the Bodhisattva Mahasattva Avalokitesvara is pronounced. Such, young man of good family, is the power of the Bodhisattva Mahasattva Avalokitesvara. If this whole triple chiliocosm, young man of good family, were teeming with knaves, enemies, and robbers armed with swords, and if a merchant leader of a caravan marched with a caravan rich in jewels; if then they perceived those robbers, knaves, and enemies armed with swords, and in their anxiety and fright thought themselves helpless; if, further, that leading merchant spoke to the caravan in this strain : Be not afraid, young gentlemen, be not frightened; invoke, all of you, with one voice the Bodhisattva Mahasattva Avalokitesvara, the giver of safety; then you shall be delivered from this danger by which you are threatened at the hands of robbers and enemies; if then, the whole caravan with one voice invoked Avalokitesvara with the words : Adoration, adoration be to the giver of safety, to Avalokitesvara Bodhisattva Mahasattva! then by the mere act of pronouncing the name, the caravan would be released from all danger. Such, young man of good family, is the power of the Bodhisattva Mahasattva Avalokitesvara. In case creatures act under the impulse of impure passion, young man of good family, they will, after adoring the Bodhisattva Mahasattva Avalokitesvara, be freed from passion. Those who act under the impulse of hatred will, after adoring the Bodhisattva Mahasattva Avalokitesvara, be freed from hatred. Those who act under the impulse of infatuation will, after adoring the Bodhisattva Mahasattva Avalokitesvara, be freed from infatuation. So mighty, young man of good family, is the Bodhisattva Mahasattva Avalokitesvara. If a woman, desirous of male offspring, young man of good family, adores Bodhisattva Mahasattva Avalokitesvara, she shall get a son, nice, handsome, and beautiful; one possessed of the characteristics of a male child, generally beloved and winning, who has planted good roots. If a woman is desirous of getting a daughter, a nice, handsome, beautiful girl shall be born to her; one possessed of the (good) characteristics of a girl, generally beloved and winning, who has planted good roots. Such, young man of good family, is the power of the Bodhisattva Mahasattva Avalokitesvara.

2. It is believed to be a kind of precious stone.
3. Modern day Ceylon or Sri Lanka.
4. The triple world is supposed to consist of the Realm of Desire, the Realm of Form, and the Formless Realm.

30

The Free Will: "The Burning House"

The importance of the free will of those who wish to attain salvation is stressed in Mahayana Buddhism.[1] In the following selection from *The Lotus of the Wonderful Law* or simply *The Lotus Sutra*, a Mahayanist scripture which is one of the most popular and influential religious books in Asia, Buddha reveals his wisdom in the form of a parable to his closest disciple, Sariputra. He tells him that although as the Buddha he is compassionate, he limits his omnipotence in helping people achieve their salvation.

QUESTIONS TO CONSIDER

1. Compare this parable with "The City of God" by St. Augustine of Hippo (Reading 47).
2. What part of this story is central to the idea of the free will?

"Sariputra! Suppose, in a (certain) kingdom, city, or town, there is a great elder, old and worn, of boundless wealth, and possessing many fields, houses, slaves, and servants. His house is spacious and large, but it has only one door, and many people dwell in it, one hundred, two hundred, or even five hundred in number. Its halls and chambers are decayed and old, its walls crumbling down, the bases of its pillars rotten, the beams and roof-trees toppling and dangerous. On every side, at the same moment, fire suddenly starts and the house is in conflagration. The boys of the elder, say ten, twenty, or even thirty, are in the dwelling. The elder, on seeing this conflagration spring up on every side, is greatly startled and reflects thus: 'Though I am able to get safely out of the gate of this burning house, yet my boys in the burning house are pleasurably absorbed in amusements without apprehension, knowledge, surprise, or fear. Though the fire is pressing upon them and pain and suffering are instant, they do not mind or fear and have no impulse to escape.'

"Sariputra! This elder ponders thus: 'I am strong in my body and arms. Shall I get them out of the house by means of a flower-vessel, or a bench, or a table?' Again he ponders: 'This house has only one gate, which moreover is narrow and small. My children are young, knowing nothing as yet and attached to their place of play; perchance they will fall into the fire and be burnt. I must speak to them on this dreadful matter (warning them) that the house is burning, and

W. E. Soothil, trans., *The Lotus of the Wonderful Law* or *The Lotus Sutra Gospel* (Oxford: The Clarendon Press, 1930), pp. 86–91. Reprinted by Permission.

1. One of the two major branches of Buddhism. It means the "Greater Vehicle," and it is "greater" in the sense of its all-inclusiveness. All are to be saved through faith. The other branch is called Hinayana or the "Lesser Vehicle," or Theravada, the "Doctrine of the Elders," whereby the few are to be saved by works.

that they must come out instantly lest they are burnt and injured by the fire.' Having reflected thus, according to his thoughts, he calls to his children : 'Come out quickly, all of you !'

"Though their father, in his pity, lures and admonishes with kind words, yet the children, joyfully absorbed in their play, are unwilling to believe him and have neither surprise nor fear, nor any mind to escape ; moreover, they do not know what is the fire (he means), or what the house, and what he means by being lost, only run hither and thither in play, no more than glancing at their father. Then the elder reflects thus : 'This house is burning in a great conflagration. If I and my children do not get out at once, we shall certainly be burnt up by it. Let me now, by some expedient, cause my children to escape this disaster.' Knowing that to which each of his children is predisposed, and all the various attractive playthings and curiosities to which their natures will joyfully respond, the father tells them saying : '(Here are) rare and precious things for your amusement — if you do not (come) and get them, you will be sorry for it afterwards. So many goat-carts, deer-carts, and bullock-carts are now outside the gate to play with. All of you come quickly out of this burning house, and I will give you whatever you want.' Thereupon, the children, hearing of the attractive playthings mentioned by their father, and because they suit their wishes, everyone eagerly, each pushing the other, and racing one against another, comes rushing out of the burning house.

"Then the elder seeing his children have safely escaped and are all in the square, sits down in the open, no longer embarrassed, but with a mind at ease and ecstatic with joy. Then each of the children says to their father : 'Father ! Please now give us those playthings you promised us, goat-carts, deer-carts, and bullock-carts.' Sariputra ! Then the elder gives to his children equally each a great cart, lofty and spacious, adorned with all the precious things, surrounded with railed seats, hung with bells on its four sides, and covered with curtains, splendidly decorated also with various rare and precious things, draped with strings of precious stones, hung with garlands of flowers, thickly spread with beautiful mats, and supplied with rosy pillows. It is yoked with whiter bullocks of pure (white) skin, of handsome appearance, and of great muscular power, which walk with even steps, and with the speed of the wind, and also has many servants and followers to guard them. Wherefore ? Because this great elder is of boundless wealth and all his various store-houses are full to overflowing. So he reflects this : 'My possessions being boundless, I must not give my children inferior small carts. All these children are my sons, whom I love without partiality. Having such great carts made of the seven precious things,[1] infinite in number, I should with equal mind bestow then on each one without discrimination. Wherefore ? Because, were I to give them to the whole nation, these things of mine would not run short — how much less so to my children !' Meanwhile each of the children rides on his great cart, having received that which he had never before had and never expected to have.

"Sariputra ! What is your opinion ? Has that elder, in (only) giving great carts of the precious substances to his children equally, been in any way guilty of falsehood ?"

---

1. Gold, silver, crystal, shell, agate, ruby, lapis lazuli.

"No, World-honored One!" says Sariputra. "That elder only caused his children to escape the disaster of fire and preserved their bodies alive — he committed no falsity. Why? He thus preserved their bodies alive, and in addition gave them the playthings they obtained; moreover, it was by his expedient that he saved them from that burning house! World-honored One! Even if that elder did not give them one of the smallest carts, still he is not false. Wherefore? Because that elder from the first formed this intention, 'I will, by an expedient, cause my children to escape.' For this reason he is not false. How much less so seeing that, knowing his own boundless wealth and desiring to benefit his children, he gives them great carts equally!"

"Good! Good!" replies the Buddha to Sariputra. "It is even as you say. Sariputra! The Tathagatha[2] is also like this, for he is the Father of all worlds, who has for ever entirely ended all fear, despondency, distress, ignorance, and enveloping darkness, and has perfected boundless knowledge, strength, and fearlessness. He is possessed of great supernatural power and wisdom-power, has completely attained the Paramitas[3] of adaptability and wisdom, and is the greatly merciful and greatly compassionate, ever tireless, ever seeking the good, and benefiting all being. He is born in this triple world,[4] the old decayed burning house, to save all living creatures from the fires of birth, age, disease, death, grief, suffering, foolishness, darkness, and the Three Poisons,[5] and teach them to obtain Perfect Enlightenment. He sees how all living creatures are scorched by the fires of birth, age, disease, death, grief, and sorrow, and suffer all kinds of distress by reason of the five desires[6] and the greed of gain; and how, by reason of the attachments of desire and its pursuits, they now endure much suffering and hereafter will suffer in hell, or as animals or hungry spirits. Even if they are born in a heaven, or amongst men, there are all kinds of sufferings, such as the bitter straits of poverty, the bitterness of parting from loved ones, the bitterness of association with the detestable. Absorbed in these things, all living creatures rejoice and take their pleasure, while they neither apprehend, nor perceive, are neither alarmed, nor fear, and are without satiety, never seeking to escape, but, in the burning house of this triple world, running to and fro, and although they will meet with great suffering, count it not as cause for anxiety.

"Sariputra! The Buddha, having seen this, reflects thus: 'I am the Father of all creatures and must snatch them from suffering and give them the bliss of the infinite, boundless Buddha-wisdom for them to play with.' . . .

"Sariputra! Even as that elder, though with strength in body and arms, yet does not use it, but only by diligent tact, resolutely saves his children from the calamity of the burning house, and then gives each of them great carts adorned with precious things, so is it with the Tathagata. Though he has power and fearlessness, he does not use them, but only by his wise tact does he remove and save all living creatures from the burning house of the triple world. . . ."

2. One who comes, or goes, as he should, a term for a Buddha.
3. The six virtues leading to nirvana: renunciation, purity, endurance, advance, concentrated meditation, and wisdom.
4. The Realm of Desire, the Realm of Form (gods living there have forms and no desire), and the Formless Realm (in which only mind exists, no form).
5. Greed, anger, and stupidity.
6. The desires to have the pleasures of the five senses.

31

The Ideal of Buddhist Kingship

This statement was one of several rock inscriptions Ashoka had erected in public so that everyone could be instructed. While the content is not particularly Buddhist, the material was inspired by the Buddhist ideal of compassion. The ideal of rule by *dharma*, a just and humane order, is emphasized.

QUESTIONS TO CONSIDER

1. In what other cases have political leaders been inspired by a religion to promote a humane and just society, as was King Ashoka?
2. Why is the statement of Ashoka in this selection not considered particularly Buddhist? What specific aspects are not Buddhist?

The Kaliṅga country was conquered by King Priyadarśī [Ashoka], Beloved of the Gods, in the eighth year of his reign. One hundred and fifty thousand persons were carried away captive, one hundred thousand were slain, and many times that number died.

Immediately after the Kaliṅgas had been conquered, King Priyadarśī became intensely devoted to the study of Dharma, to the love of Dharma, and to the inculcation of Dharma.

The Beloved of the Gods, conqueror of the Kaliṅgas, is moved to remorse now. For he has felt profound sorrow and regret because the conquest of a people previously unconquered involves slaughter, death, and deportation.

But there is a more important reason for the King's remorse. The Brāhmaṇas and Śramaṇas [the priestly and ascetic orders] as well as the followers of other religions and the householders — who all practiced obedience to superiors, parents, and teachers, and proper courtesy and firm devotion to friends, acquaintances, companions, relatives, slaves, and servants — all suffer from the injury, slaughter, and deportation inflicted on their loved ones. Even those who escaped calamity themselves are deeply afflicted by the misfortunes suffered by those friends, acquaintances, companions, and relatives for whom they feel an undiminished affection. Thus all men share in the misfortune, and this weighs on King Priyadarśī's mind. . . .

Therefore, even if the number of people who were killed or who died or who were carried away in the Kaliṅga war had been only one one-hundredth or one one-thousandth of what it actually was, this would still have weighed on the King's mind.

King Priyadarśī now thinks that even a person who wrongs him must be forgiven for wrongs that can be forgiven.

From N. Nikam and R. McKeon, eds. and trans., *The Edicts of Asoka* (Chicago : University of Chicago Press, 1959), pp. 27–30. © 1959 by The University of Chicago Press. Reprinted by permission.

King Priyadarśi seeks to induce even the forest peoples who have come under his dominion [that is, primitive peoples in the remote sections of the conquered territory] to adopt this way of life and this ideal. He reminds them, however, that he exercises the power to punish, despite his repentance, in order to induce them to desist from their crimes and escape execution.

For King Priyadarśi desires security, self-control, impartiality, and cheerfulness for all living creatures.

King Priyadarśi considers moral conquest [that is, conquest by Dharma, *Dharma-vijaya*] the most important conquest. He has achieved this moral conquest repeatedly both here and among the peoples living beyond the borders of his kingdom, even as far away as six hundred *yojanas* [about three thousand miles], where the Yōna [Greek] king Antiyoka rules, and even beyond Antiyoka in the realms of the four kings named Turamaya, Antikini, Maka, and Alikasudara, and to the south among the Cholas and Pāṇḍyas [in the southern tip of the Indian peninsula] as far as Ceylon. . . .

Even in countries which King Priyadarśi's envoys have not reached, people have heard about Dharma and about his Majesty's ordinances and instructions in Dharma, and they themselves conform to Dharma and will continue to do so.

Wherever conquest is achieved by Dharma, it produces satisfaction. Satisfaction is firmly established by conquest by Dharma [since it generates no opposition of conquered and conqueror]. Even satisfaction, however, is of little importance. King Priyadarśi attaches value ultimately only to consequences of action in the other world.

This edict on Dharma has been inscribed so that my sons and great-grandsons who may come after me should not think new conquests worth achieving. If they do conquer, let them take pleasure in moderation and mild punishments. Let them consider moral conquest the only true conquest.

This is good, here and hereafter. Let their pleasure be pleasure in morality [*Dharma-rati*]. For this alone is good, here and hereafter.

The Golden Age of Chinese Thought

The Eastern Chou[1] [Eastern Zhou] dynasty ruled China from 770 to 221 B.C. During the dynasty's last centuries, however, the land was beset by political and social disintegration and bitter civil war. Ironically, despite the chaotic conditions, this time was the most remarkable golden age of Chinese thought. Many of the philosophies developed during this period had a last-

---

1. There are at least two ways to transcribe Chinese in the English-speaking world : the Wade-Giles system and the Pinyin system. The Wade-Giles system was first developed by an English Sinologist, Thomas F. Wade, in 1867 and was later modified by Herbert Giles in 1912. It became the standard way of transcribing Chinese. But this system has now either been replaced or is in the process of being replaced by Pinyin, the official transcription system of the People's Republic of China. Hereafter, the Pinyin transcriptions will be provided in brackets on the first occurrence of Chinese terms in each reading where they occur. If no transcription appears, the term is the same in both systems.

ing influence on the cultures of East Asia, similar to the influence Classical Greece had on European civilization. This great age of intellectual ferment is also known as the age of "The Hundred Schools."

During this period, many philosophical schools such as the Naturalists, Logicians, Mohists, Taoists, [Daoist], Confucianists, and Legalists evolved in China. They questioned old values and institutions and sought new meaning and purpose in life and society. The following selections represent the three most important schools of philosophy that emerged during this period.

32

Confucius, *Analects*

Perhaps the one individual who was most responsible for molding Chinese mind and institutions was Confucius (551–479 B.C.). The name "Confucius" is the Latinized version of K'ung Fu-tzu [Kong Fuzi] (or Master Kung). His family name was K'ung [Kong] and his given name was Chiu [Jiu]. As a transmitter of the wisdom of the past and a creator of new ideas, his primary concern was the fundamental issue of creating utopia. He believed in the perfectibility of all people and used the word "chün-tzu," [junzi] literally meaning "ruler's son," to describe a perfect or morally superior person. This individual possessed among other qualities the five inner virtues of (1) integrity (*chih*) [zhi]; (2) righteousness (*i*) [yi]; (3) loyalty and conscientiousness toward others (*chung*) [zhong]; (4) altruism and reciprocity (*shu*); and (5) virtue, love, and human heartedness (*jen*) [ren]. The chün-tzu also possessed culture or polish (*wen*), and ritual or proper etiquette (*li*). Confucius' ideal of a well-ordered society was one based on mutual moral obligations in the five basic human relationships. These bonds were between ruler and subject, husband and wife, father and son, elder and younger brother, and friend and friend. All had assigned roles to play in a hierarchical society.

The teachings of Confucius were not accepted widely during his lifetime; for the ensuing few centuries, the Confucian school remained only one among many Chinese schools of philosophy. But for over 2000 years, from around the second century B.C. to the twentieth century, Confucianism was the official creed of the Chinese Empire. The great influence of this philosophy on the civilizations of the East Asian peoples was unmatched by any other body of thinking.

Among the Confucian classics, the most important work is the *Analects (Lun Yü)* [Lunyu], a collection of sayings by Confucius and his disciples. These sayings were selected and compiled, perhaps in the fourth century B.C., long after Confucius' death, by his disciples' followers. The *Analects* consist of 20 chapters (or "books") with 497 proverbial-style verses.

QUESTIONS TO CONSIDER

1. Compare and contrast the tenets of Confucianism with those of Taoism (Reading 33), and Legalism (Reading 34).
2. How do you compare the ideas of Confucius with those developed during the golden age of Greek thought (see Reading 38)?
3. What kind of person is "superior" in the Confucian sense?

The Superior Man

1. Tsze-kung [Zigong] asked what constituted the superior man. The Master said, "He acts before he speaks, and afterwards speaks according to his actions."

2. The Master said, "The superior man is catholic and no partizan. The mean man is a partizan and not catholic."

3. (a) The Master said, "Riches and honours are what men desire. If it cannot be obtained in the proper way, they should not be held. Poverty and meanness are what men dislike. If it cannot be obtained in the proper way, they should not be avoided."

(b) "If a superior man abandons virtue, how can he fulfil the requirements of that name?"

(c) "The superior man does not, even for the space of a single meal, act contrary to virtue. In moments of haste, he cleaves to it. In seasons of danger, he cleaves to it."

4. The Master said, "The superior man, in the world, does not set his mind either for anything, or against anything; what is right he will follow."

5. The Master said, "The superior man thinks of virtue; the small man thinks of comfort. The superior man thinks of the sanctions of law; the small man thinks of favours which he may receive."

6. The Master said, "The mind of the superior man is conversant with righteousness; the mind of the mean man is conversant with gain."

7. The Master said, "The superior man wishes to be slow in his speech and earnest in his conduct."

8. The Master said of Tsze-ch'an [Zichan] that he had four of the characteristics of a superior man: — in his conduct of himself, he was humble; in serving his superiors, he was respectful; in nourishing the people, he was kind; in ordering the people, he was just."

9. The Master said, "The superior man, extensively studying all learning, and keeping himself under the restraint of the rules of propriety, may thus likewise not overstep what is right."

10. The Master said, "The superior man is satisfied and composed; the mean man is always full of distress."

11. (a) Sze-ma Niu [Sima Niu] asked about the superior man. The Master said, "The superior man has neither anxiety nor fear."

From James Legge, trans., *The Chinese Classics*, vol. 1 (Taipei: Wen-she-che, 1971), pp. 139, 146, 150, 152, 165, 166, 168, 169, 172, 173, 190, 193, 207, 250, 251, 252, 254, 262, 266, 273, 274, 292, 299, 314, 320, 352–354.

(b) "Being without anxiety or fear!" said Niu ; — "does this constitute what we call the superior man ?"

(c) The Master said, "When internal examination discovers nothing wrong, what is there to be anxious about, what is there to fear ?"

12. The Master said, "The superior man is affable, but not adulatory ; the mean man is adulatory, but not affable."

13. The Master said, "The superior man has a dignified ease without pride. The mean man has pride without a dignified ease."

14. Tsze-lu [Zilu] asked what constituted the superior man. The Master said, "The cultivation of himself in reverential carefulness." "And is this all ?" said Tsze-lu. "He cultivates himself so as to give rest to others," was the reply. "And is this all ?" again asked Tsze-lu. The Master said, "He cultivates himself so as to give rest to all the people. He cultivates himself so as to give rest to all the people : — even Yao and Shun were still solicitous about this."

15. Confucius said, "The superior man has nine things which are subjects with him of thoughtful consideration. In regard to the use of his eyes, he is anxious to see clearly. In regard to the use of his ears, he is anxious to hear distinctly. In regard to his countenance, he is anxious that it should be benign. In regard to his demeanour, he is anxious that it should be respectful. In regard to his speech, he is anxious that it should be sincere. In regard to his doing business, he is anxious that it should be reverently careful. In regard to what he doubts about, he is anxious to question others. When he is angry, he thinks of the difficulties (his anger may involve him in). When he sees gain to be got, he thinks of righteousness."

Virtue

16. The Master said, "Fine words and an insinuating appearance are seldom associated with true virtue."

17. The Master said, "Those who are without virtue cannot abide long either in a condition of poverty and hardship, or in a condition of enjoyment. The virtuous rest in virtue ; the wise desire virtue."

18. The Master said, "It is only the (truly) virtuous man, who can love, or who can hate, others."

19. The Master said, "Virtue is not left to stand alone. He who practises it will have neighbours."

20. (a) Yen Yuan asked about perfect virtue. The Master said, "To subdue one's self and return to propriety, is perfect virtue. If a man can for one day subdue himself and return to propriety, all under heaven will ascribe perfect virtue to him. Is the practice of perfect virtue from a man himself, or is it from others ?"

(b) Yen Yuan said, "I beg to ask the steps of that process." The Master replied, "Look not at what is contrary to propriety ; listen not to what is contrary to propriety ; speak not what is contrary to propriety ; make no movement which is contrary to propriety." Yen Yuan then said, "Though I am deficient in intelligence and vigour, I will make it my business to practise this lesson."

21. Chung-kung [Zonggong] asked about perfect virtue. The Master said, "It is, when you go abroad, to behave to every one as if you were receiving a great

guest ; to employ the people as if you were assisting at a great sacrifice ; not to do to others as you would not wish done to yourself ; to have no murmuring against you in the country, and none in the family." Chung-kung said, "Though I am deficient in intelligence and vigour, I will make it my business to practise this lesson."

22. Tsze-chang [Zizhang] asked Confucius about perfect virtue. Confucius said, "To be able to practise five things everywhere under heaven constitutes perfect virtue." He begged to ask what they were, and was told, "Gravity, generosity of soul, sincerity, earnestness, and kindness. If you are grave, you will not be treated with disrespect. If you are generous, you will win all. If you are sincere, people will repose trust in you. If you are earnest, you will accomplish much. If you are kind, this will enable you to employ the services of others."

Virtuous Government

23. The Master said, "He who exercises government by means of his virtue may be compared to the north polar star, which keeps its place and all the stars turn towards it."

24. (a) The Master said, "If the people be led by laws, and uniformity sought to be given them by punishments, they will try to avoid the punishment, but have no sense of shame."

(b) "If they be led by virtue, and uniformity sought to be given them by the rules of propriety, they will have the sense of shame, and moreover will become good."

25. The duke Ai asked, saying, "What should be done in order to secure the submission of the people ?" Confucius replied, "Advance the upright and set aside the crooked, then the people will submit. Advance the crooked and set aside the upright, then the people will not submit."

26. Chi K'ang [Ji Kang] asked how to cause the people to reverence their ruler, to be faithful to him and to go on to nerve themselves to virtue. The Master said, "Let him preside over them with gravity ; — then they will reverence him. Let him be filial and kind to all ; — then they will be faithful to him. Let him advance the good and teach the incompetent ; — then they will eagerly seek to be virtuous."

27. The Master said, "Is a prince able to govern his kingdom with the complaisance proper to the rules of propriety, what difficulty will he have ? If he cannot govern it with that complaisance, what has he to do with the rules of propriety ?"

28. (a) Tsze-kung [Zigong] asked about government. The Master said, "The requisites of government are that there be sufficiency of food, sufficiency of military equipment, and the confidence of the people in their ruler."

(b) Tsze-kung said, "If it cannot be helped, and one of these must be dispensed with, which of the three should be foregone first ?" "The military equipment," said the Master.

(c) Tsze-kung again asked, "If it cannot be helped, and one of the remaining two must be dispensed with, which of them should be foregone ?" The Master answered, "Part with the food. From of old, death has been the lot of all men ; but if the people have no faith in their rulers, there is no standing for the State."

29. The Master said, "When a prince's personal conduct is correct, his government is effective without the issuing of orders. If his personal conduct is not correct, he may issue orders, but they will not be followed."

30. (a) Tsze-chang [Zizhang] asked Confucius, saying, "In what way should a person in authority act in order that he may conduct government properly?" The Master replied, "Let him honour the five excellent, and banish away the four bad, things; — then may he conduct government properly." Tsze-chang said, "What are meant by the five excellent things?" The Master said, "When the person in authority is beneficent without great expenditure; when he lays tasks on the people without their repining; when he pursues what he desires without being covetous; when he maintains a dignified ease without being proud; when he is majestic without being fierce."

(b) Tsze-chang said, "What is meant by being beneficent without great expenditure?" The Master replied, "When the person in authority makes more beneficial to the people the things from which they naturally derive benefit; — is not this being beneficent without great expenditure? When he chooses the labours which are proper, makes them labour on them, who will repine? When his desires are set on benevolent government, and he secures it, who will accuse him of covetousness? Whether he has to do with many people or few, or with things great or small, he does not dare to indicate any disrespect; — is not this to maintain a dignified ease without any pride? He adjusts his clothes and cap, and throws a dignity into his looks, so that, thus dignified, he is looked at with awe; — is not this to be majestic without being fierce?"

(c) Tsze-chang then asked, "What are meant by the four bad things?" The Master said, "To put the people to death without having instructed them; — this is called cruelty. To require from them, suddenly, the full tale of work, without having given them warning; — this is called oppression. To issue orders as if without urgency, at first, and, when the time comes, to insist on them with severity; — this is called injury. And, generally, in the giving pay or rewards to men, to do it in a stingy way; — this is called acting the part of a mere official."

33

Taoism [Daoism]: *Lao Tzu* [Lao Zi]

Taoism was probably the second most important and influential philosophy after Confucianism in traditional China. It was antithetical to Confucianism. Taoism emphasized individual life, tranquillity, nonconformity, and transcendental spirit, while Confucianism taught the importance of regulated social order, an active life, conformity, and worldliness. Taoism had two famous founders: Lao Tzu (meaning "Venerable Master"), a sixth-century B.C. mythical sage whose historicity is questioned, and Chuang-tzu [Zhuang Zi] (369–286 B.C.). The two most important Taoist texts are *Lao Tzu* or *Tao-te-*

ching [Dao de Jing] (Classics of the Way and Its Virtue) and *Chuang Tzu*, probably written in the third century B.C.

Taoism attacked moral idealism and political realism, encouraging people to merge with Tao [Dao], meaning "the Way." Tao was conceived as a natural process, the universal force in the natural world. Tao, which could only be intuitively sensed, was the source of everything — all life, both human and natural.

The way to merge with Tao was through nonaction (*wu-wei*). This concept did not mean complete inaction but rather taking no action contrary to nature. It meant: "Do nothing and nothing will be not done."

According to this theory, human effort to reform morals or to improve nature was a waste of time and destroyed the harmonies of the universe. Taoism taught that the universe was amoral and operated on its own harmonious principles, which ignored human desires or standards of conduct. This philosophy also stressed passivity, simplicity, and a laissez-faire attitude for the individual. Taoism advised the ruler that "The least government is the best government."

The following selections are from *Lao Tzu* or *Tao-te-ching*, a small classic of about 5250 words. No other Chinese book of this size has had so much influence on the Chinese mind, and no other Chinese book has been translated into English more often than this one. This Chinese classic is a combination of poetry, philosophical speculation, and mystical reflection written in vague, subtle, and cryptic language.

QUESTIONS TO CONSIDER

1. What is the Taoist view of the universe? How do Taoists define human happiness?
2. Why is Taoism considered to be antithetical to Confucian philosophy?
3. Does the Taoist way of life have modern day relevance? How?

Tao, The Way

The Way is a void.
Used but never filled:
An abyss it is,
Like an ancestor
From which all things come.

It blunts sharpness,
Resolves tangles;
It tempers light,
Subdues turmoil.

From *The Way of Life* by Lao Tzu, translated by R. B. Blakney (New York: New American Library, 1955), pp. 55, 56, 90, 95, 96, 133. Copyright © 1955, 1983 by Raymond B. Blakney. Reprinted by permission of the publisher, New American Library, a division of Penguin Books USA Inc.

A deep pool it is,
Never to run dry!
Whose offspring it may be
I do not know:
It is like a preface to God.

The Way begot one,
And the one, two;
Then the two begot three
And three, all else.

All things bear the shade on their backs
And the sun in their arms;
By the blending of breath
From the sun and the shade,
Equilibrium comes to the world.

Orphaned, or needy, or desolate, these
Are conditions much feared and disliked;
Yet in public address, the king
And the nobles account themselves thus.
So a loss sometimes benefits one
Or a benefit proves to be loss.

What others have taught
I also shall teach:
If a violent man does not come
To a violent death,
I shall choose him to teach me.

Wu Wei (Non-Action)

The Way is always still, at rest,
And yet does everything that's done.
If then the king and nobles could
Retain its potency for good,
The creatures all would be transformed.

But if, the change once made in them,
They still inclined to do their work,
I should restrain them then
By means of that unique
Original simplicity
Found in the Virgin Block,
Which brings disinterest,
With stillness in its train,
And so, an ordered world.

The softest of stuff in the world
Penetrates quickly the hardest;
Insubstantial, it enters
Where no room is.

By this I know the benefit
Of something done by quiet being;
In all the world but few can know
Accomplishment apart from work,
Instruction when no words are used.

Government

If those who are excellent find no preferment,
The people will cease to contend for promotion.
If goods that are hard to obtain are not favored,
The people will cease to turn robbers or bandits.
If things much desired are kept under cover,
Disturbance will cease in the minds of the people.

The Wise Man's policy, accordingly,
Will be to empty people's hearts and minds,
To fill their bellies, weaken their ambition,
Give them sturdy frames and always so,
To keep them uninformed, without desire,
And knowing ones not venturing to act.

Be still while you work
And keep full control
Over all.

The ideal land is small
Its people very few,
Where tools abound
Ten times or yet
A hundred-fold
Beyond their use;
Where people die
And die again
But never emigrate;
Have boats and carts
Which no one rides.
Weapons have they
And armor too,
But none displayed.
The folk returns
To use again

The knotted cords.
Their meat is sweet;
Their clothes adorned,
Their homes at peace,
Their customs charm.

And neighbor lands
Are juxtaposed
So each may hear
The barking dogs,
The crowing cocks
Across the way;
Where folks grow old
And folks will die
And never once
Exchange a call.

34

Legalism: The Writings of Han Fei Tzu [Han Feizi]

During the warring state period (403–221 B.C.) in ancient China, the most radical school of philosophy — and the one with the most influence on political life — was Legalism (*Fa-chia*) [Fajia]. Legalism became the state ideology of the feudal state of Ch'in [Qin] (221–206 B.C.), which overthrew the Chou [Zhou] dynasty and created the first unified Chinese empire (221 B.C.).

Two leading Legalists were Kung-sun Yang [Gongsun Yang] (d. 300 B.C.), also called Wei Yang or Shang Yang (Lord Shang), and Han Fei Tzu (d. 223 B.C.). Both served in the government of Ch'in and were political strategists rather than philosophers. These Legalists, rejecting the moral and ethical basis of human conduct and society, accepted Hsün-tzu's [Xun Zi] (300–237 B.C.) view that human nature was basically evil but potentially improvable. They advocated rule by force rather than persuasion and favored a strong centralized government under an absolute ruler.

The main concern of this philosophy was how to make the state a powerful instrument in achieving whatever the ruler desired. The Legalists encouraged war, aggression, and regimentation to strengthen the power of the ruler. To make people obedient and loyal, the Legalists advised the ruler to manipulate two presumably basic human drives: greed and fear. Han Fei Tzu proposed the principle of the "Two Handles" by which the ruler could control others: proportional rewards and harsh punishments. According to this theory, proportional rewards would encourage what was beneficial to the state, and harsh punishments would restrain evil. Because Legalists viewed human nature as basically evil and selfish, and officials as self-seeking and untrustworthy, they advised the ruler to draw up an exhaustive set of laws and regulations to define everyone's duties and responsibilities clearly. Any slight infraction was to be dealt with severely. Thus, they strictly regulated the life and thought of the Chinese people. In the following excerpts, Han Fei Tzu provides a summary of Legalist doctrines.

QUESTIONS TO CONSIDER

1. Why did Legalism gain influence among the rulers of China during the last phase of the Chou period, a politically chaotic time?
2. How does the Legalistic philosophy compare with modern day totalitarian ideologies?

The Way of the Ruler

The Way is the beginning of all beings and the measure of right and wrong. Therefore the enlightened ruler holds fast to the beginning in order to understand the wellspring of all beings, and minds the measure in order to know the source of good and bad. He waits, empty and still, letting names define themselves and affairs reach their own settlement. Being empty, he can comprehend the true aspect of fullness; being still, he can correct the mover. Those whose duty it is to speak will come forward to name themselves; those whose duty it is to act will produce results. When names and results match, the ruler need do nothing more and the true aspect of all things will be revealed.

Hence it is said: The ruler must not reveal his desires; for if he reveals his desires his ministers will put on the mask that pleases him. He must not reveal his will; for if he does so his ministers will show a different face. So it is said: Discard likes and dislikes and the ministers will show their true form; discard wisdom and while and the ministers will watch their step. Hence, though the ruler is wise, he hatches no schemes from his wisdom, but causes all men to know their place. Though he has worth, he does not display it in his deeds, but observes the motives of his ministers. Though he is brave, he does not flaunt his bravery in shows of indignation, but allows his subordinates to display their valor to the full. Thus, though he discards wisdom, his rule is enlightened; though he discards worth, he achieves merit; and though he discards bravery, his state grows powerful. When the ministers stick to their posts, the hundred officials have their regular duties, and the ruler employs each according to his particular ability, this is known as the state of manifold constancy.

Hence it is said: "So still he seems to dwell nowhere at all; so empty no one can seek him out." The enlightened ruler reposes in nonaction above, and below his ministers tremble with fear.

From Burton Watson, trans., *Basic Writings of Mo Tzu, Hsün Tzu, and Han Fei Tzu* (New York: Columbia University Press, 1967), pp. 16–20, 30–34. Copyright © 1964, Columbia University Press. Reprinted by permission.

This is the way of the enlightened ruler : he causes the wise to bring forth all their schemes, and he decides his affairs accordingly ; hence his own wisdom is never exhausted. He causes the worthy to display their talents, and he employs them accordingly ; hence his own worth never comes to an end. Where there are accomplishments, the ruler takes credit for their worth ; where there are errors, the ministers are held responsible for the blame ; hence the ruler's name never suffers. Thus, though the ruler is not worthy himself, he is the leader of the worthy ; though he is not wise himself, he is the corrector of the wise. The ministers have the labor ; the ruler enjoys the success. This is called the maxim of the worthy ruler.

The Way lies in what cannot be seen, its function in what cannot be known. Be empty, still, and idle, and from your place of darkness observe the defects of others. See but do not appear to see ; listen but do not seem to listen ; know but do not let it be known that you know. When you perceive the trend of a man's words, do not change them, do not correct them, but examine them and compare them with the results. Assign one man to each office and do not let men talk to each other, and then all will do their utmost. Hide your tracks, conceal your sources, so that your subordinates cannot trace the springs of your action. Discard wisdom, forswear ability, so that your subordinates cannot guess what you are about. Stick to your objectives and examine the results to see how they match ; take hold of the handles of government carefully and grip them tightly. Destroy all hope, smash all intention of wresting them from you ; allow no man to covet them.

If you do not guard the door, if you do not make fast the gate, then tigers will lurk there. If you are not cautious in your undertakings, if you do not hide their true aspect, then traitors will arise. They murder their sovereign and usurp his place, and all men in fear make common cause with them : hence they are called tigers. They sit by the ruler's side and, in the service of evil ministers, spy into his secrets : hence they are called traitors. Smash their cliques, arrest their backers, shut the gate, deprive them of all hope of support, and the nation will be free of tigers. Be immeasurably great, be unfathomably deep ; make certain that names and results tally, examine laws and customs, punish those who act willfully, and the state will be without traitors.

The ruler of men stands in danger of being blocked in five ways. When the ministers shut out their ruler, this is one kind of block. When they get control of the wealth and resources of the state, this is a second kind of block. When they are free to issue orders as they please, this is a third kind. When they are able to do righteous deeds in their own name, this is a fourth kind. When they are able to build up their own cliques, this is a fifth kind. If the ministers shut out the ruler, then he loses the effectiveness of his position. If they control wealth and resources, he loses the means of dispensing bounty to others. If they issue orders as they please, he loses the means of command. If they are able to carry out righteous deeds in their own name, he loses his claim to enlightenment. And if they can build up cliques of their own, he loses his supporters. All these are rights that should be exercised by the ruler alone ; they should never pass into the hands of his ministers.

The way of the ruler of men is to treasure stillness and reserve. Without handling affairs himself, he can recognize clumsiness or skill in others ; without laying plans of his own, he knows what will bring fortune or misfortune. Hence he need speak no word, but good answers will be given him ; he need exact no promises, but good works will increase. When proposals have been brought before him, he takes careful note of their content; when undertakings are well on their way, he takes careful note of the result; and from the degree to which proposals and results tally, rewards and punishments are born. Thus the ruler assigns undertakings to his various ministers on the basis of the words they speak, and assesses their accomplishments according to the way they have carried out the undertaking. When accomplishments match the undertaking, and the undertaking matches what was said about it, then he rewards the man; when these things do not match, he punishes the man. It is the way of the enlightened ruler never to allow his ministers to speak words that cannot be matched by results.

The enlightened ruler in bestowing rewards is as benign as the seasonable rain; the dew of his bounty profits all men. But in doling out punishment he is as terrible as the thunder; even the holy sages cannot assuage him. The enlightened ruler is never overliberal in his rewards, never overlenient in his punishments. If his rewards are too liberal, then ministers who have won merit in the past will grow lax in their duties; and if his punishments are too lenient, then evil ministers will find it easy to do wrong. Thus if a man has truly won merit, no matter how humble and far removed he may be, he must be rewarded; and if he has truly committed error, no matter how close and dear to the ruler he may be, he must be punished. If those who are humble and far removed can be sure of reward, and those close and dear to the ruler can be sure of punishment, then the former will not stint in their efforts and the latter will not grow proud.

The Two Handles

The enlightened ruler controls his ministers by means of two handles alone. The two handles are punishment and favor. What do I mean by punishment and favor? To inflict mutilation and death on men is called punishment; to bestow honor and reward is called favor. Those who act as ministers fear the penalties and hope to profit by the rewards. Hence, if the ruler wields his punishments and favors, the ministers will fear his sternness and flock to receive his benefits. But the evil ministers of the age are different. They cajole the ruler into letting them inflict punishment themselves on men they hate and bestow rewards on men they like. Now if the ruler of men does not insist upon reserving to himself the right to dispense profit in the form of rewards and show his sternness in punishments, but instead hands them out on the advice of his ministers, then the people of the state will all fear the ministers and hold the ruler in contempt, will flock to the ministers and desert the ruler. This is the danger that arises when the ruler loses control of punishments and favors.

The tiger is able to overpower the dog because of his claws and teeth, but if he discards his claws and teeth and lets the dog use them, then on the contrary he will be overpowered by the dog. In the same way the ruler of men uses punishments and favors to control his ministers, but if he discards his punishments and favors and lets his ministers employ them, then on the contrary he will find himself in the control of his ministers.

T'ien Ch'ang [Tian Chang] petitioned the ruler for various titles and stipends, which he then dispensed to the other ministers, and used an extra large measure in doling out grain to the common people. In this way the ruler, Duke

Chien [Jian], lost the exclusive right to dispense favors, and it passed into T'ien Ch'ang's hands instead. That was how Duke Chien came to be assassinated.

Tzu-han [Zihan] said to the ruler of Sung [Song], "Since the people all delight in rewards and gifts, you should bestow them yourself; but since they hate punishments and death sentences, I beg to be allowed to dispense these for you." Thereupon the ruler of Sung gave up the exclusive right to hand out penalties and it passed into the hands of Tzu-han. That was how the ruler of Sung came to be intimidated.

T'ien Ch'ang got to bestow favors as he pleased, and Duke Chien was assassinated; Tzu-han got to hand out punishments as he pleased, and the ruler of Sung was intimidated. Hence, if the ministers of the present age are permitted to share in the right to hand out punishments and favors, the rulers of the time will put themselves in greater peril than Duke Chien and the lord of Sung. Invariably when rulers are intimidated, assassinated, obstructed, or forced into the shade, it has always come about because they relinquished the rights to administer punishment and favor to their ministers, and thus brought about their own peril and downfall.

If the ruler of men wishes to put an end to evil-doing, then he must be careful to match up names and results, that is to say, words and deeds. The ministers come forward to present their proposals; the ruler assigns them tasks on the basis of their words, and then concentrates on demanding the accomplishment of the task. If the accomplishment fits the task, and the task fits the words, then he bestows reward; but if they do not match, he doles out punishment. Hence, if one of the ministers comes forward with big words but produces only small accomplishments, the ruler punishes him, not because the accomplishments are small, but because they do not match the name that was given to the undertaking. Likewise, if one of the ministers comes forward with small words but produces great accomplishments, he too is punished, not because the ruler is displeased at great accomplishments, but because he considers the discrepancy in the name given to the undertaking to be a fault too serious to be outweighed by great accomplishments.

Once in the past Marquis Chao [Zhao] of Han got drunk and fell asleep. The keeper of the royal hat, seeing that the marquis was cold, laid a robe over him. When the marquis awoke, he was pleased and asked his attendants, "Who covered me with a robe?" "The keeper of the hat," they replied. The marquis thereupon punished both the keeper of the royal hat and the keeper of the royal robe. He punished the keeper of the robe for failing to do his duty, and the keeper of the hat for overstepping his office. It was not that he did not dislike the cold, but he considered the trespass of one official upon the duties of another to be a greater danger than cold.

Hence an enlightened ruler, in handling his ministers, does not permit them to gain merit by overstepping their offices, or to speak words that do not tally with their actions. Those who overstep their offices are condemned to die; those whose words and actions do not tally are punished. If the ministers are made to stick to their proper duties and speak only what is just, then they will be unable to band together in cliques to work for each other's benefit.

The ruler of men has two worries: if he employs only worthy men, then his ministers will use the appeal to worthiness as a means to intimidate him; on the other hand, if he promotes men in an arbitrary manner, then state affairs will be bungled and will never reach a successful conclusion. Hence, if the ruler shows a fondness for worth, his ministers will all strive to put a pleasing façade on their actions in order to satisfy his desires. In such a case, they will never show their true colors, and if they never show their true colors, then the ruler will have no way to distinguish the able from the worthless. Because the king of Yüeh [Yue] admired valor, many of his subjects defied death; because King Ling of Ch'u [Chu] liked slim waists, his state was full of half-starved people on diets. Because Duke Huan of Ch'i [Chi] was jealous and loved his ladies in waiting, Shu-tiao [Shudiao] castrated himself in order to be put in charge of the harem; because the duke was fond of unusual food, Yi-ya [Yiya] steamed his son's head and offered it to the duke. Because Tzu-k'uai [Zikuai] of Yen admired worthy men, Tzu-chih [Zizhi] insisted that he would not accept the throne even if it were offered to him.

Thus, if the ruler reveals what he dislikes, his ministers will be careful to disguise their motives; if he shows what he likes, his ministers will feign abilities they do not have. In short, if he lets his desires be known, he gives his ministers a clue as to what attitude they had best assume.

Hence Tzu-chih, by playing the part of a worthy, was able to snatch power from his sovereign; Shu-tiao [Shudiao] and Yi-ya, by catering to the ruler's desires, were able to invade his authority. As a result, Tzu-k'uai died in the chaos that ensued, and Duke Huan was left unburied for so long that maggots came crawling out the door of his death chamber.

What caused this? It is an example of the calamity that comes when the ruler reveals his feelings to his ministers. As far as the feelings of the ministers go, they do not necessarily love their ruler; they serve him only in the hope of substantial gain. Now if the ruler of men does not hide his feelings and conceal his motives, but instead gives his ministers a foothold by which they may invade his rights, then they will have no difficulty in doing what Tzu-chih and T'ien Ch'ang did. Hence it is said: Do away with likes, do away with hates, and the ministers will show their true colors. And when the ministers have shown their true colors, the ruler of men will never be deceived.

Greek and Roman Classics

Athenian democracy reached its fullest development in the half century following the Persian Wars. The success of Pericles (c. 495–429 B.C.) in centering the Delian League's treasury and judicial system in Athens brought added income and power. The Athenians used their new wealth well: The classic works of architecture, sculpture, and drama set standards for ages to come.

Three great playwrights — Aeschylus (525–456 B.C.), Sophocles (496–406 B.C.), and Euripides (485–406 B.C.) — developed the art of composing tragedies to be performed at Athenian religious festivals. Periclean Athens also produced the first writing of history as we use the term: In his *Histories*, Herodotus (c. 485–430 B.C.) gave an account of major events in the history of the world accessible to him, events culminating in the great conflict to defend Greek freedom against the Persian threat. The Age of Pericles ended in the great Peloponnesian War, fought between groups of city-states headed by Athens and Sparta from 431 to 404 B.C., although it was interrupted by truces. All modern accounts of that war still rely heavily on the classic work of Thucydides (c. 455–400 B.C.) as their principal source. His *Peloponnesian War* is far more critical and fact-oriented than Herodotus's work, and his style conveys the impression of total objectivity in his descriptions. At the same time, his frequent use of speeches and dialogue makes his narrative colorful and readable.

The highpoint of Greek philosophy came after art, architecture, and drama had reached their peak in the Age of Pericles. Socrates (c. 469–399 B.C.), his student Plato (427–347 B.C.), and Plato's student Aristotle (384–322 B.C.) are the three greatest philosophers of classical Greece. Philosophy to the Greeks simply meant "love of wisdom," and a philosopher was someone who seriously pursued knowledge relating to human concerns or cosmic matters.

The literature of the Romans did not raise the same order of original questions about the nature of man that had characterized Greek literature and philosophy. Most Roman classics followed Greek models, although in legal philosophy and commentary the Romans showed more originality. The best Roman historiography resembles that of Thucydides in recounting events with interpretive insights and plenty of lively speeches attributed verbatim to participants.

Although the modern world tends to rate the Greek classics higher than those of Rome, the impact of the surviving Roman classics was probably greater on succeeding ages until the end of the eighteenth century. The Roman Republic and early Roman Empire they described and reflected were of special interest to people in the medieval and early modern world. Then, too, the Latin language of the Romans was a much earlier and more substantial part of Western education than was Greek — an important factor before the day of readily available translations.

35

Herodotus, *Persian Dialogue*

Herodotus the fifth-century B.C. Greek writer has at least three major claims to fame. Often called "The Father of History," he is also the first writer of prose and the first Western political scientist whose work survives. Greeks before him all wrote in verse, since lines in poetic meter are easier to memorize than ordinary sentences. Although Herodotus is known to have read his *Histories* aloud to audiences, the scope of his work and his striving for factual accuracy led him to abandon the poetic form for prose. A great cultural geographer along with everything else, he stated his intention of writing about the varied cultural achievements and the great men among the Greeks as well as the "barbarians" (Asians and Africans).

In his *Histories*, Herodotus presents all earlier world history as funneling into the great conflict between Europe and Asia in the form of the Persian attempts to conquer Greece ; so, we usually entitle his sweeping *Histories*, "The Persian Wars." This source focuses on stories of how the freedom-loving Greeks feared the despotic system of the Persians enough to undergo great sacrifices and to defeat many times their own number of invading forces. Writing in the afterglow of the historic Persian Wars, Herodotus felt very positive about democracy, which he tended to equate with Greek freedom. While he shared the prejudice of his ethnocentric countrymen that Greeks had higher ideals than the less-than-free Asians (represented by the Persians), he still had abiding respect for foreign things such as the antiquity of Egyptian civilization and the strength with order preserved by Persian society. His basically democratic political philosophy includes the notion that what works best for one people does not necessarily work best for all peoples.

In the following selection, Herodotus records an episode from Persian history, in which, after a break in monarchical rule, three leading Persians — Otanes, Megabyzos, and Darius — who overthrew Magi usurpers debate rather much like stereotypical Greeks before deciding on the best form of government for Persia. The three forms of government described here, monarchy, aristocracy (oligarchy), and democracy remained as the basic options in speculative political thought through the eighteenth century.

QUESTIONS TO CONSIDER

1. Which of the three advocates, Otanes, Megabyzos, or Darius, defends "his" system with the strongest arguments in your view ? Which with the weakest ? Why ?
2. Do the twentieth-century terms *dictatorship, elite rule,* and *democracy* mean about the same thing to us that *monarchy, aristocracy,* and *democracy* meant to the ancient Greeks ? Why or why not ?

Otanes advised putting governmental power in the hands of the Persian people, saying : "I cannot think about one of us becoming a sole monarch with any pleasure or optimism. You can all see how far Cambyses' arrogance of power drove him. You also had to suffer the same thing under the Magi. How can absolute monarchy be compatible with ethical behavior when it allows the king to do whatever he wants with no accountability ? Even the very best man picked for this position would abandon the character traits which made us choose him. Envy is something everyone is born with. Limit-breaking pride will overwhelm him from the very fullness of his power and wealth. Envy heightened by pride will implant all other vices in him. Overwhelming pride and envy will lead him into commit-

Herodotus, *Histories*, Book III, ed. H. Stein (Berlin : Weidmann, 1856), pp. 76–82. Translated by Henry A. Myers.

ting foolish crimes. Logically, of course, an absolute monarch should be free of all malice; after all, he owns all the goods in his realm. The truth of the matter, however, is that he will behave in the very opposite way towards citizens. He will envy the very best people for the very fact that they are better than he. He will be attracted to the worst people and eager to listen to slander. The most contradictory thing about him is that he will be annoyed when people admire him in moderation, since they are not showing him enough humility in doing so. But if you express really strong admiration for him, then he will be put off by your flattery. Now I have been saving the worst for last: He will trample traditional laws into the ground. He will have our women seized for his own pleasure and men killed without trials.

"When the people rule, on the other hand, first of all their regime is called 'equality before the law,' and there can be no more pleasant sounding name than that. Secondly, democracy is free of all the vices of absolute monarchy. It assigns offices by lot and keeps office-holders responsible. All decisions are put before the whole people. And so I am of the opinion that we should abolish monarchy and give the people power, for the people and the state really should be thought of as the same thing."

That was the case made by Otanes. Megabyzos, however, advocated oligarchy, saying: "I support Otanes in opposing one-man rule; however, he is wrong in advising us to make the multitude into a ruler. There is really nothing less reasonable or more arrogant than the blind masses: It would be unbearable to flee the deadly whims of a sole ruler only to end up with the conceit of a mob, who recognizes no limits. A king at least knows what he is doing, but a mob does not. Where are common people supposed to get reasoning power from? They are not born with it, nor have they met up with it in their experiences. Instead the multitude hurls itself like a mountain stream into politics and washes everything away before it. We should form a government by giving the very best men power: We will be among them ourselves. The best men will make the best decisions as a matter of course." That opinion was presented by Megabyzos.

Darius was the third to speak, saying: "I concur with what Megabyzos just said about the masses, but not what he says about oligarchy. There are three possible constitutional forms. If we examine them in their purest forms, that is, the purest democracy, the purest oligarchy and the purest monarchy, the last one towers over the other two in my opinion. There is obviously nothing better than sole government by the best man: Nothing will keep him from looking after his people. Decisions against enemies of the people are best kept secret by a single ruler. In an oligarchy on the other hand, violent personal feuds arise when a good number of men compete for distinction. Everybody tries to force himself ahead. That way, real enemies are made. Out of this, factional conflicts arise, leading to assassinations. It will all end up with a return to monarchy again, and so you can see how much better monarchy is than any other form of government. When the people rule, it is impossible to prevent corruption. When conspiracies occur in a democracy, it is not a matter of hostility among the worst elements but the wrong kind of friendships: Those who work against the common good will do so in cooperation with each other, putting their heads together. That will go on until a leader of the people puts an end to their abuses. The people will admire him for that, and the admired man will lead you back again to one-man rule. Again we see monarchy emerge as the best constitution. To sum it all up briefly : How did the Persian Empire become free ? Who gave Persia her freedom : the people, an oligarchy, or the monarchy ? The answer certainly convinces me, and we must stick with that system. Anyway, we would be very foolish to discard our ancient and traditional laws, when they have served us so well, since any change is bound to be for the worse."

36

Sophocles, *Antigone*

In modern times, Athenian tragedies have enjoyed substantial revivals — remarkable given the fact that they were intended to be performed only once. What keeps them in modern repertoires is their concern with conflicts having universal interest. Some themes appear much more frequently than others, to be sure. For example, the Greek tragic hero is typically hounded by a fate inherited from the misdeeds of his forebears. Very often, too, he brings doom upon himself with *hubris*, a mortal's false pride leading to acts that no mortal can get away with.

In Greek drama, the Chorus often recites or chants odes. These relate events on stage to the will of the gods, punishments for those guilty of hubris, the implacability of fate, or similar cosmic concerns. The Chorus leader (or *Choragos*) enters the dialogue with questions and observations.

Sophocles' *Antigone*, from which the following selection is taken, remains a twentieth-century favorite. Along with the themes of implacable fate and punishment for hubris, this excerpt stresses the recurring conflict — truly global in the history of civilization — between the official, promulgated laws of a governing body and the laws believed by an individual to outweigh the claims of the governing body. Athenians saw this problem as a conflict between nature and convention. Later ages would label the conflict as natural law versus positive law (that is, law set down by people) or, returning close to Sophocles' own phrasing, God-made law versus man-made law.

In the play, Creon, King of Thebes, has declared that Polyneices, a member of the royal family, should not be buried. Polyneices — with considerable justification — had led an attack to take Thebes and was killed in single combat by his own brother, Eteocles. In popular Greek belief, the unburied dead found no rest ; therefore, Antigone, sister of Polyneices and Eteocles, violates Creon's decree by giving Polyneices burial rites. Ismene, her sister, had shown sympathy for Antigone but lacked the courage to join her in the deed. The guard who appears in this selection is one of a group sent earlier to guard the unburied body ; they had failed the first time to stop Antigone as she slipped by them unnoticed.

QUESTIONS TO CONSIDER

1. What is Antigone's attitude toward her "crime" and the death penalty she is facing?
2. How does Creon bring male/female relations into the heated discussion with Antigone?
3. Is Creon guilty of hubris (the crime of overweening pride)? Could Antigone be accused of hubris as well?
4. Was Odysseus guilty of hubris in shouting taunts at Polyphemus as he sailed away from the land of the Cyclopes (see Reading 18)?
5. When have you heard similar arguments in our own time concerning the existence of laws higher than those humans make?

Chorus: But I know her . . . ! Antigone, the ill-fated daughter of the ill-fated Oedipus: why is she under arrest?

Guard: We have the culprit here! We seized her right when she was burying him. Now where is the king?

Chorus: Coming from the palace right now. (*Creon enters.*)

Creon: What is all this . . . ?

Guard: Sire, no man should ever swear he'll never do a thing. After all your threats, I swore you'd never see me return. But being so surprised and so very glad when we captured the one who did it just made a liar out of me . . . I am bringing you the woman we caught in the very act of burying him. Take her and judge her guilt any way you like. I've done my part and ought to be relieved of any further responsibility.

Creon: Just what was she doing when you arrested her? Tell me.

Guard: Burying him. It's that simple. . . .

Creon: You there, standing with your head bowed, do you admit the truth of what he charges you with or not?

Antigone: I did it. I don't deny it.

Creon (to Guard):   Feel free to go. . . . (*Guard exits.*)

   (*to Antigone*):   Did you know that I gave the order that he should not be buried? Just tell me yes or no.

Antigone: I knew your order just as everyone else knew it.

Creon: Then you knowingly broke the law?

Antigone: I knew what I was doing. Zeus would not have approved such an order. Diké [goddess of justice], whose justice rules the world, has other decrees than such laws of men. I did not feel that your royal strength was enough to nullify the unwritten but eternal laws of the gods, laws which were not declared today or yesterday but have kept their living force from origins no mortal can trace or question. . . .

From Sophokles, *Antigone* (Gothae: F. A. Perthes, 1883), lines 382–768, passim. Translated by Martha B. Caldwell and Henry A. Myers.

Creon: This girl has outdone herself in insolence: she broke the law, and now she's boasting about breaking it. If she can get away with that, she is the man, not I.

Antigone: Do you want something else besides my execution?

Creon: No, that will be enough for me.

Antigone: Then why wait? Have me killed. Your words are having no effect on me, and you must be getting tired of mine, although you shouldn't be. I deserve all honor for burying my brother. These men right here would all congratulate me for my courage if their fear of you did not keep them quiet. Kings are really fortunate in being able to adjust laws so that whatever they want to do or say is covered by them.

Creon: Not one single Theban thinks that way but you.

Antigone: They think as I do, but you intimidate them.

Creon: Aren't you ashamed to be the only one talking like that?

Antigone: To show respect for a dead kinsman is nothing to be ashamed of. . . . Be what may, Hades requires the rite of burial.

Creon: Not so that good and bad men will be treated equally.

Antigone: Why do you think you know how the gods below will judge this?

Creon: An enemy does not become a friend by dying.

Antigone: Nature inclines me to love, not to hate.

Creon: Go ahead and die then! Love the dead in the world below if you must!

Chorus: Will you really steal your own son's bride from him?

Creon: Hades will take her, not I.

Chorus: Then she really is to die. . . . Now here comes Haemon, your last surviving son. Isn't it grief bringing him here? He's sad and bitter over Antigone's doom. (*Haemon enters.*)

Creon: We'll find out soon enough. . . . Son, have you heard about your bride's death sentence? Have you come here raving mad, or will you accept my decision as an act of love?

Haemon: Father, I belong to you. Your good judgment will steer me, and I will obey. No marriage will mean more to me than your loving guidance.

Creon: That's the right way to act, recognizing your father's authority like a proper son. Men pray for dutiful sons, each one harming his father's enemies and doing good to his father's friends. . . . So you have made the right choice, not to let this woman cloud your mind. You would find her embraces turning cold, Haemon, and then you'd be left with a hateful armful. What is worse than a false love? Let Hades find her a husband! I will not go back on my word to the state, since she alone among my people disobeyed my law. . . . She must surely die. Let her sing her appeal to Zeus who helps guard family ties. If I let my own family rebel, I would be encouraging lawlessness on a grand scale. The man who heads an orderly household is the right one to help with administering the city-state. I will not put up with anyone who wants to bend the law and dictate to his rulers. The ruler entrusted with the power of the state must be obeyed, whether he happens to be right or wrong. . . . There is no greater evil than disrespect for authority, which destroys homes and city-states alike, demoralizing and defeating armies. Discipline makes life orderly and good. With it we will preserve authority and not be led astray by a woman. If I am overthrown, I want it said at least that I was beaten by a man rather than outmaneuvered by a woman.

Chorus: Unless old age is taking its toll, my mind tells me you are speaking sensibly and justly.

Haemon: Father, reason is the greatest gift of the gods to mankind. It's not my place to say you are not using your share of it; however, there are other men around who reason well, and as your son I feel responsible for telling you their thoughts when they pertain to you. The people are afraid of making you angry and will not let you know what they really think, but I have overheard them whispering their complaints and their grief over this girl's fate. You should know how the people are mourning, saying she is doomed to die a shameful death for a glorious deed. They say she refused to leave her brother's body unburied for the vultures and dogs, and they ask: "Doesn't she deserve a prize of gold?" That's what the people are really saying. . . .

Withdraw your anger, and reverse your decree! Young as I am, I do know this: The ideal would be to have absolute wisdom at all times, but since nature doesn't work like that the next best thing is to pay attention to wisdom and reason in good advice.

Chorus: Sire, if what he says makes sense, you would do well to listen. Haemon, you in turn should consider your father's words. Both of you have spoken well.

Creon: You think it's right for a man to take instruction from a boy?

Haemon: Not if I did not have right on my side, but if I do you shouldn't hold my age against me.

Creon: Are you asking me to condone lawlessness?

Haemon: I'm not asking you to protect lawbreakers.

Creon: Isn't that just what this girl is?

Haemon: The people of Thebes don't think so.

Creon: And so the citizens are going to dictate my decrees?

Haemon: It is you now who are talking like a youngster.

Creon: Am I to rule or let others do it?

Haemon: No true city-state obeys one man alone.

Creon: A city-state belongs to its ruler.

Haemon: You might rule well alone in a desert.

Creon: I can tell this boy is under the woman's influence.

Haemon: That's true if you're a woman. I am thinking of your own interests.

Creon: Good for nothing! Getting into a fight of words with your father . . . ! All your arguing is for her sake!

Haemon: For yours and mine, too, and for the sake of the gods below.

Creon: You will never marry her while she's alive.

Haemon: She must die then, but another death will follow hers.

Creon: Another? Are you going so far as to make threats?

Haemon: I'm only trying to keep you from carrying out your vain plan.

Creon: You vain fool: you'll regret condescending talk like that.

Haemon: If you weren't my father, I'd say you were crazy. . . .

Creon: That's enough! I swear by Olympus you will not get away with your raving insults! Bring out the hateful creature: She will die this moment before her bridegroom's very eyes, right close to him.

Haemon: Don't deceive yourself. She will not die with me looking on, and you will never see my face again. Keep on raving as long as you think you have a friend to listen. (*Haemon exits.*)

Chorus: He's gone, Sire. A young man made furious can do great harm.

37

Thucydides, *Peloponnesian War*

As Athenian commerce began to dominate the Aegean Sea trade, Athenian naval power kept member states from leaving the Delian League. Trouble came with increasing discontent over this Athenian domination. There was also a perceived (perhaps real, perhaps imagined) Athenian threat to the freedom of the remaining independent Greek city-states. Many of those city-states allied with Sparta in the Peloponnesian League.

Thucydides, whose *Peloponnesian War* is the classic account of the ensuing conflict, was an Athenian general who failed to carry out his mission of relieving the city of Amphipolis from a Peloponnesian siege; in harmony with Athenian democratic principles and practice, he was relieved of his duties by authority of the people. In his history, Thucydides gives detailed information on troop numbers, types of equipment used, and other data in year-by-year accounts of battles until 411 B.C., when his book breaks off unfinished. He makes his work more vivid with speeches by leading figures on both sides. Although Thucydides was not present to hear many of the speeches, which are presented as extended verbatim quotations, he claims to give their approximate content accurately.

In the first excerpt below, we find Pericles highlighting the greatness of Athenian democracy in a funeral oration after the first battle casualties. But, two years later, Pericles died in a plague, and Athenian democracy became more extreme. As Thucydides saw it, the Athenian people began to suppose that whatever they said was law. In the second excerpt below, Thucydides writes about a confrontation with the Melians in the sixteenth year of the war. In this account, the Athenians seem to believe that might makes right, and that the Athenian Empire is mighty enough to enforce its policies — even genocidal ones — on all would-be enemies.

QUESTIONS TO CONSIDER

1. What does "democracy" appear to mean to Pericles apart from broad partici-
   pation in government?
2. Does Pericles state or imply that the rights of nonconformists or dissenters in
   Athens are protected under Athenian democracy?
3. What does Pericles appear to have in mind when he speaks of Athens as a
   model for all of Greece?
4. These selections contrast Athens as an educational model for Greece (in the
   first excerpt) and as a state demanding compliance through deadly force (in the
   second excerpt). Do you think the contrast is too neat to be true?
5. Does Thucydides — the fired Athenian general — give the impression of writing more as dramatist than historian when stressing evils in the system that rejected him? Or does he convey the image of a realistic historian regretfully
   documenting the twisting of democratic ideals?

Pericles' Funeral Oration

Pericles . . . was chosen to give the funeral oration for the first who had fallen.
When the proper time arrived, he advanced from the tomb . . . and spoke as
follows:

"I shall begin with our ancestors. . . . They dwelt in this country without in-
terruption from generation to generation, and handed it down to the present time
by their bravery. . . .

"Our constitution does not copy the laws of neighboring states; we are
rather a model for others than imitators ourselves. Its administration favors the
many instead of the few; this is why it is called a democracy. If we look at the laws,
they afford equal justice to all in settling private differences. As for prestige, advancement in public life goes to men with reputations for ability: class considera-
tions are not allowed to interfere with merit, nor again does poverty bar the way. If
a man is able to serve the state, he is not hindered by obscure origins or poverty.
The freedom we enjoy in our government extends also to our private life. There
. . . we do not feel called upon to be angry with our neighbor for doing what he
likes, or even to indulge in those injurious looks which cannot fail to be offensive,
although they inflict no actual harm. But all this ease in our private relations does
not make us lawless as citizens. . . . We obey the magistrates and the laws, particularly those for the protection of the injured, whether they are actually on the stat-
ute book, or belong to that code which, although unwritten, yet cannot be broken
without acknowledged disgrace.

"Further, we provide plenty of means for the mind to refresh itself from
business. We celebrate games and sacrifices all the year round, and the elegance of
our private establishments forms a daily source of pleasure and helps to banish our
cares. Then, too, the magnitude of our city draws the produce of the world into

From Thucydides, *Peloponnesian War*, trans. Richard Crawley (London: J. M. Dent & Co., 1903), Vol.
I, pp. 120–128, Vol. II, pp. 59–67; language modernized.

our harbor, so that to the Athenian the products of other countries are as familiar a luxury as those of his own.

"If we turn to our military policy, there also we differ from our antagonists. We throw open our city to the world, and never pass laws to exclude foreigners from any opportunity of learning or observing, although the eyes of the enemy may occasionally profit from our liberality. We rely less on secrecy than on the native spirit of our citizens. In education, where our rivals from their very cradles seek after manliness through a very painful discipline, at Athens we live as we please, and yet are just as ready to encounter every legitimate danger. . . . And yet if with habits not of labor but of ease, and with courage which is not artificial but real, we are still willing to encounter danger, we have the double advantage of escaping the experience of hardships in anticipation and of facing them in the hour of need as fearlessly as those who are never free from them.

"We cultivate refinement without extravagance and knowledge without effeminacy; wealth we employ more for use than for show, and place the real disgrace of poverty not in admitting the fact of it but in declining the struggle against it. Our public men have, besides politics, their private affairs to tend to, and our ordinary citizens, though occupied with the pursuits of industry, are still fair judges of public matters. Unlike any other nation, we regard a man who takes no part in these duties not as unambitious but as useless. . . . Instead of looking on discussion as a stumbling block in the way of action, we Athenians consider it an indispensable preliminary to any wise action at all.

"In generosity we are equally singular, acquiring our friends by conferring, not receiving, favors. Yet, of course, the doer of the favor is the firmer friend of the two, in order by continued kindness to keep the recipient in his debt; while the debtor feels less keenly from the very consciousness that the return he makes will be a repayment, not a free gift, and it is only the Athenians who, fearless of consequences, confer their benefits not from calculations of expediency, but in the confidence of liberality.

"In short, I say that as a city we are the school of Hellas; while I doubt if the world can produce a man who is equal to so many emergencies where he has only himself to depend upon, and who is graced by so happy a versatility as the Athenian. . . . For Athens alone of her contemporaries is found when tested to be greater than her reputation, and alone gives no occasion to her assailants to blush at the antagonist by whom they have been worsted, or to her subjects to question her title by merit to rule. Rather, the admiration of the present and succeeding ages will be ours, since we have not left our power without witness, but have shown it by mighty proofs; and far from needing a Homer for our panegyrist, or another poet whose verses might charm for the moment only for the impression which they gave, to melt at the touch of fact, we have forced every sea and land to be the highway of our daring, and everywhere, whether for evil or for good, have left imperishable monuments behind us. Such is the Athens for which these men, in the assertion of their resolve not to lose her, nobly fought and died; and well may every one of their survivors be ready to suffer in her cause.

"If I have dwelt at some length upon the character of our country, it has been to show that our stake in the struggle is not the same as theirs who have no such blessings to lose, and also that the praise of the men over whom I am now speaking might be confirmed by definite proofs. My speech is now largely complete ; for the Athens that I have celebrated is only what the heroism of these and others like them have made her, men whose fame, unlike that of most Hellenes, will be found to be only proportionate to what they deserve. And if a test of worth be wanted, it is to be found in their last scene, and this not only in the cases in which it set the final seal upon their merit, but also in those in which it gave the first intimation of their having any. For there is justice in the claim that steadfastness in his country's battles should be as a cloak to cover a man's other imperfections, since the good more than outweighed his demerits as an individual. . . . And while committing to hope the uncertainty of final success, in the business before them they thought fit to act boldly and trust in themselves. Thus choosing to die resisting, rather than to live submitting.

"So died these men as became Athenians. You, their survivors, must be determined to have as unfaltering a resolution in the field, though you may pray that it may have a happier outcome. . . . You must yourselves realise the power of Athens, and feed your eyes upon her from day to day, till the love of her fills your hearts ; and then when all her greatness shall break upon you, you must reflect that it was by courage, sense of duty, and a keen feeling of honor in action that men were enabled to win all this, and that no personal failure in an enterprise could make them consent to deprive their country of their bravery except as a sacrifice of the most serious contribution they could offer. For this offering of their lives made in common by them all, each of them individually receives that renown which never grows old, and for a tomb, not so much that in which their bones have been deposited, but that noblest of shrines wherein their glory is laid up to be eternally remembered upon every occasion on which deed or story shall call for its commemoration. . . . Take these as your model, and recognize that happiness comes from freedom and freedom comes from courage ; never decline the dangers of war. For it is not the miserable who have the most reason to risk their lives ; they have nothing to hope for : instead, it is they to whom continued life may bring reverses as yet unknown, and to whom a fall, if it came, would be most tremendous in its consequences. Surely, to a man of spirit, the degradation of cowardice must be immeasurably more grievous than the unfelt death which strikes him in the midst of his strength and patriotism.

"Comfort, therefore, not condolence, is what I have to offer to the parents of the dead who may be here. Numberless are the chances to which, as they know, the life of man is subject ; but fortunate indeed are they who draw their lot a death so glorious as that which has caused your mourning, and to whom life has been so exactly measured as to terminate in the happiness in which it has been passed. . . . My task is now finished. I have performed it to the best of my ability, and in words at least the requirements of the law are now satisfied. If deeds be in question, those who are here interred have received part of their honors already, and for the rest, their children will be brought up till manhood at the public expense : thus the state offers a valuable prize as the garland of victory in this race of valor, for the reward both of those who have fallen and their survivors. And where the rewards for merit are greatest, there the best citizens are found.

"And now that you have brought to a close your lamentations for your relatives, you may depart."

The Melian Conference

The Melians are a colony of Lacedæmon that would not submit to the Athenians like the other islanders, and at first remained neutral and took no part in the struggle, but afterwards upon the Athenians using violence and plundering their territory, assumed an attitude of open hostility. . . . The generals, encamping in their territory . . . before doing any harm to their land, sent envoys to negotiate. These the Melians did not bring before the people, but bade them state the object of their mission to the magistrates and the few ; upon which the Athenian envoys spoke as follows : . . .

Athenians : "For ourselves, we shall not trouble you with specious pretences — either of how we have a right to our empire because we overthrew the Mede, or are now attacking you because of wrong that you have done us — and make a long speech which would not be believed ; and in return we hope that you, instead of thinking to influence us by saying that you did not join the Lacedæmonians, although their colonists, or that you have done us no wrong, will aim at what is feasible, holding in view the real sentiments of us both ; since you know as well as we do that right, as the world goes, is only in question between equals in power, while the strong do what they can and the weak suffer what they must."

Melians : "As we think, at any rate, it is expedient — we speak as we are obliged, since you enjoin us to let right alone and talk only of interest — that you should not destroy what is our common protection, the privilege of being allowed in danger to invoke what is fair and right, and even to profit by arguments not strictly valid if they can be got to pass current. And you are as much interested in this as any, as your fall would be a signal for the heaviest vengeance and an example for the world to meditate upon."

Athenians : "The end of our empire, if end it should, does not frighten us : a rival empire like Lacedæmon, even if Lacedæmon was our real antagonist, is not so terrible to the vanquished as subjects who by themselves attack and overpower their rulers. . . . We will now proceed to show you that we are come here in the interest of our empire, and that we shall say what we are now going to say for the preservation of your country ; as we would fain exercise that empire over you without trouble, and see you preserved for the good of us both."

Melians : "And how, pray, could it turn out as good for us to serve as for you to rule ?"

Athenians : "Because you would have the advantage of submitting before suffering the worst, and we should gain by not destroying you."

Melians : "So that you would not consent to our being neutral, friends instead of enemies, but allies of neither side."

Athenians : "No ; for your hostility cannot so much hurt us as your friendship will be an argument to our subjects of our weakness, and your enmity of our power."

Melians : "Is that your subjects' idea of equity, to put those who have nothing to do with you in the same category with peoples that are most of them your own colonists, and some conquered rebels ?"

Athenians: "As far as right goes they think one has as much of it as the other, and that if any maintain their independence it is because they are strong, and that if we do not molest them it is because we are afraid; so that besides extending our empire we should gain in security by your subjection; the fact that you are islanders and weaker than others rendering it all the more important that you should not succeed in baffling the masters of the sea." . . .

Melians: "Well then, if you risk so much to retain your empire, and your subjects to get rid of it, it were surely great baseness and cowardice in us who are still free not to try everything that can be tried, before submitting to your yoke."

Athenians: "Not if you are well advised, the contest not being an equal one, with honour as the prize and shame as the penalty, but a question of self-preservation and of not resisting those who are far stronger than you are."

Melians: "But we know that the fortune of war is sometimes more impartial than the disproportion of numbers might lead one to suppose; to submit is to give ourselves over to despair, while action still preserves for us a hope that we may stand erect."

Athenians: "Hope, danger's comforter, may be indulged in by those who have abundant resources, if not without loss at all events without ruin; but its nature is to be extravagant, and those who go so far as to put their all upon the venture see it in its true colours only when they are ruined. . . ."

Melians: "You may be sure that we are as well aware as you of the difficulty of contending against your power and fortune, unless the terms be equal. But we trust that the gods may grant us fortune as good as yours, since we are just men fighting against unjust, and that what we want in power will be made up by the alliance of the Lacedæmonians. . . ."

Athenians: "When you speak of the favour of the gods, we may as fairly hope for that as yourselves; neither our pretensions nor our conduct being in any way contrary to what men believe of the gods, or practise among themselves. Of the gods we believe, and of men we know, that by a necessary law of their nature they rule wherever they can. . . . But when we come to your notion about the Lacedæmonians, which leads you to believe that shame will make them help you, here we bless your simplicity but do not envy your folly. The Lacedæmonians, when their own interests or their country's laws are in question, are the worthiest men alive; of their conduct towards others much might be said, but no clearer idea of it could be given than by shortly saying that of all the men we know they are most conspicuous in considering what is agreeable honourable, and what is expedient just. Such a way of thinking does not promise much for the safety which you now unreasonably count upon."

Melians: "But it is for this very reason that we now trust to their respect for expediency to prevent them from betraying the Melians, their colonists, and thereby losing the confidence of their friends in Hellas and helping their enemies." . . .

Athenians: "Yes, but what an intending ally trusts to, is not the goodwill of those who ask his aid, but a decided superiority of power for action; and the Lacedæmonians look to this even more than others. At least, such is their distrust of their home resources that it is only with numerous allies that they attack a neighbour ; now is it likely that while we are masters of the sea they will cross over to an island ? . . . Your strongest arguments depend upon hope and the future, and your actual resources are too scanty, as compared with those arrayed against you, for you to come out victorious. You will therefore show great blindness of judgment, unless, after allowing us to retire, you can find some counsel more prudent than this. You will surely not be caught by that idea of disgrace, which in dangers that are disgraceful, and at the same time too plain to be mistaken, proves so fatal to mankind. . . . You will not think it dishonourable to submit to the greatest city in Hellas, when it makes you the moderate offer of becoming its tributary ally, without ceasing to enjoy the country that belongs to you ; nor when you have the choice given you between war and security, will you be so blinded as to choose the worse. And it is certain that those who do not yield to their equals, who keep terms with their superiors, and are moderate towards their inferiors, on the whole succeed best. Think over the matter, therefore, after our withdrawal, and reflect once and again that it is for your country that you are consulting, that you have not more than one, and that upon this one deliberation depends its prosperity or ruin."

The Athenians now withdrew from the conference ; and the Melians, left to themselves, came to a decision corresponding with what they had maintained in the discussion, and answered, "Our resolution, Athenians, is the same as it was at first. We will not in a moment deprive of freedom a city that has been inhabited these seven hundred years ; but we put our trust in the fortune by which the gods have preserved it until now, and in the help of men, that is, of the Lacedæmonians ; and so we will try and save ourselves. Meanwhile we invite you to allow us to be friends to you and foes to neither party, and to retire from our country after making such a treaty as shall seem fit to us both."

Such was the answer of the Melians. The Athenians now departing from the conference said, "Well, you alone, as it seems to us, judging from these resolutions, regard what is future as more certain than what is before your eyes, and what is out of sight, in your eagerness, as already coming to pass ; and as you have staked most on, and trusted most in, the Lacedæmonians, your fortune, and your hopes, so will you be most completely deceived."

The Athenian envoys now returned to the army ; and the Melians showing no signs of yielding, the generals at once betook themselves to hostilities. . . . Subsequently the Athenians returned with most of their army, leaving behind them a certain number of their own citizens and of the allies to keep guard by land and sea. The force thus left stayed on and besieged the place. . . .

Summer was now over. The next winter the Lacedæmonians intended to invade the Argive territory, but arriving at the frontier found the sacrifices for crossing unfavourable, and went back again. . . . About the same time the Melians again took another part of the Athenian lines which were but feebly garrisoned. Reinforcements afterwards arriving from Athens, . . . the siege was now pressed vigorously ; and some treachery taking place inside, the Melians surrendered at discretion to the Athenians, who put to death all the grown men whom they took, and sold the women and children for slaves, and subsequently sent out five hundred colonists and inhabited the place themselves.

38

Plato, *The Republic*

Socrates wrote nothing himself but devoted much of his later life to disputations in which he sought to define and illustrate matters of essential human interest, such as beauty, love, and immortality. Socrates was a master of the "dialectic," defined then as the art of posing and answering questions to separate error and half-truths from reality. Plato wrote many dialogues in which Socrates is the main speaker and practitioner of the dialectic; however, it is impossible to know whether the statements attributed to Socrates were actually his own or Plato's. But because Plato was such a devoted admirer of Socrates, it seems likely that most of his summaries of Socrates' ideas were accurate. Aristotle, by way of contrast, occasionally rejected some of the learning he had acquired from Plato during some 20 years of study.

Five years after the end of the Peloponnesian War (431–404 B.C.), Socrates was convicted by an Athenian court of denying the existence of Greek gods and of corrupting the youth of Athens. The trial and ensuing death sentence were probably the results of Socrates' having antagonized too many prominent Athenians for too long. However, the charge that he rejected the Greek gods was not altogether false: While Socrates deeply believed in divine beings, these seldom resembled traditional Greek gods.

In the following selections from Plato's *The Republic*, Socrates (the main speaker) attempts to lead his respondents to the discovery of true justice. These excerpts demonstrate the range of subject matter and style that Plato, inspired by Socrates, was able to use in his dialogues. The first selection exemplifies the dialectical pursuit of human excellence (or "virtue" in this and most other translations). The second selection uses forceful arguments for the political equality of women, an idea completely rejected by Aristotle, whose unabashed male chauvinism was much more in keeping with the times. The third selection presents an allegory or parable, which attempts to show the real meaning of Socrates' death by contrasting the actual position of philosophers in society with the position they deserve to have in an ideal world.

QUESTIONS TO CONSIDER

1. What are the four main aspects of human excellence (or cardinal virtues) for Socrates/Plato?
2. What is the example about bleaching cloth and dyeing it purple intended to illustrate?
3. Does Socrates/Plato define justice as you would? Why or why not?
4. How does Socrates/Plato attempt to prove the basic equality of women and men?

5. How does "The Allegory of the Cave" illustrate the story of Socrates? How does this allegory show the role of public opinion in a democracy?
6. How would you compare the concept of *virtue* in the *Analects* of Confucius (see Reading 32) with that in Plato's work?

The Search for the Four Cardinal Virtues

[T]he city we have founded — if we have built rightly — will be good in the fullest sense of the word.

That is certain.

It means that the city is wise, courageous, temperate, and just.

Necessarily. . . .

[W]e inquire into the four virtues in our city. Of these virtues, wisdom is evidently the first. But I must add that there appears to be some peculiarity connected with it.

What?

Well, let us see. The city is certainly wise, for it abounds in good counsel. Good counsel, in turn, is a sort of skill or proficiency, something generated from knowledge and not from ignorance.

Of course.

But there are many diverse skills in the city and many proficiencies. Consider those practiced by carpenters, smiths, and farmers. Are these the skills that produce wisdom and prudence in governing?

No. They could only serve to produce and teach excellence in cabinetry, ironworking, and agriculture.

All right, then. Is there any form of skill or knowledge possessed by some of the citizens of the city we recently founded that attends not to particular interests but to the general interest, to the city as a whole in both its domestic and foreign policies?

Yes.

What is it, and where is it to be found?

It is the art of guardianship practiced by the city's rulers whom we recently described as guardians in the fullest sense.

What description will fit the city possessing this kind of knowledge?

A city that is prudent and truly wise. . . .

If we follow the same approach, I think we can discover the nature of courage, where it is situated, and how it imparts its spirit to the entire city. Now whoever calls a city brave or cowardly will think first about its armed forces. This is so because the character of the city is not determined by the bravery or cowardice of the citizenry as a whole. The city is brave because there is a part of it that is steadfast in its convictions about what is to be feared and what is not to be feared. These convictions constitute an integral part of the education prescribed by the city's founder. They also define the meaning of courage.

Would you please say that again? I don't think I understand.

Reprinted from Plato, *The Republic*, A New Translation by Richard W. Sterling and William C. Scott (New York: W. W. Norton, 1985), pp. 123–129, 142–146, 210–211. Reprinted by permission of W. W. Norton & Company, Inc. Copyright © 1985 by Richard W. Sterling and William C. Scott.

Courage is a preservative. Strengthened by education, it preserves convictions about the things that are legitimately to be feared and those that are not. Courage makes a man hold fast to these convictions no matter whether he is threatened by danger or lured by desire. Neither pain nor pleasure will move him. If you like, I shall try to illustrate what I mean with a comparison.

I would like that.

Well, then, consider dyers. When they wish to dye wool so that it will hold fast the true sea-purple color, they begin by choosing a white wool. Then they prepare and dress the wool with great care so that the white may perfectly absorb the purple. Only then does the dyeing begin. What is dyed in this way is color-fast, and neither soap nor lye can dull the color's brilliance. But if these procedures are neglected, you know what purple or any other color will look like.

Yes, it will be faded and ugly.

So we make this comparison with the dyers to illustrate the results we were trying to achieve in selecting our soldiers and educating them in music and gymnastic. We were contriving influences that would lead them to take on the colors of our institutions like a dye. With the right temperament and the right education their convictions about danger would be indelibly fixed. They would resist all solvents : pleasure, for instance, which can corrode the will more effectively than any caustic agent. They would likewise refuse to yield their convictions because of sorrow, fear, or desire, the strongest of the other solvents. The quality I call courage, then, is the strength to hold fast to the proper convictions about what is worth fearing and what is not. . . .

[A]fter wisdom and courage we wanted to search out two further virtues in the city. One is temperance — or moderation. . . .

To begin with, temperance seems more clearly related to peace and harmony than wisdom and courage.

How so ?

It appears to me that temperance is the ordering or controlling of certain pleasures and desires. This is what is implied when one says that a man is master of himself. It is a curious expression because it suggests that a man is both his own master and his own servant. But I believe the proper meaning of the phrase is that there is both good and bad in the soul of man. When the good part governs the bad, a man is praised for being master of himself. But if bad education or bad company subjects the good (and smaller part) of the soul to the bad (and larger) part, a man will be blamed for being unprincipled and a slave of self.

Now look at our newly founded city. If temperance and self-mastery are in charge, if the better part rules the worse, we may well say that the city is master of itself.

I agree.

We may say that the mass of diverse appetites, pleasures, and pains is to be found chiefly among children, women, slaves, and the many so-called freemen from the lower classes. But the simple and temperate desires governed by reason, good sense, and true opinion are to be found only in the few, those who are the best born and the best educated.

Yes.

Both the few and the many have their place in the city. But the meaner desires of the many will be held in check by the virtue and wisdom of the ruling few.

It follows that if any city may claim to be master of its pleasures and desires — to be master of itself — it will be ours. For all these reasons, we may properly call our city temperate.

Now we have inquired into three of the four chief qualities of our city. The fourth and final quality is justice. But here we must take care that it does not elude us. We must be like hunters who surround a thicket to make sure that the quarry doesn't escape. Justice is clearly somewhere hereabouts. Look sharp, and call me if you see it first.

I wish I could. But I am only your follower, with sight just keen enough to see what you show me. . . .

The wood is dark and almost impenetrable. We will have a hard time flushing out the quarry. Still, we must push on. . . . There, I see something. Glaucon! I think we're on the track. Now it won't escape us.

Good news.

But we have really been stupid.

How so?

Because a long time ago, at the beginning of our inquiry, justice was right in front of us, and we never saw it. We were like people who look in the distance for what they already have in their grasp. We looked away from what we were seeking and trained our eyes instead on distant objects. And that is why we did not find it.

What do you mean?

I mean that all this time we have been talking about justice without realizing that our discussion has already begun to disclose its substance.

I am getting weary of your lengthy preambles.

All right. Tell me now whether I am right or wrong. You remember the original principle we laid down at the founding of the city: each citizen should perform that work or function for which his nature best suits him. This is the principle, or some variation of it, that we may properly call justice.

We often said that.

We also said that justice was tending to one's own business and not meddling in others'.

Yes.

So minding one's own business really appears, in one sense, at least, to be justice. Do you know how I reached this conclusion?

No.

You remember we were inquiring into the four cardinal virtues of a city. We examined temperance, courage, and wisdom; now justice remains the one still to be considered. What we will find is that justice sustains and perfects the other three; justice is the ultimate cause and condition of their existence.

Now that we have wisdom, courage, temperance, and justice fairly before us, it would be hard to decide which of the four virtues effectually contributes most to the excellence of the city. Is it the harmony existing between rulers and subjects? Is it the soldier's fidelity to what he has learned about real and fictitious dangers? Or wisdom and watchfulness in the rulers? Or, finally, is it the virtue that is found in everyone — children, women, slaves and freemen, craftsmen, rulers, and subjects — which leads them each to do his own work and not to interfere with others? These are questions not easily answered.

Yes. They are very perplexing.

But we can at least accept the conclusion that the fourth virtue of minding one's own business rivals the other three virtues in contributing to the city's excellence. That is to say that justice is at least the equal of wisdom, courage, and temperance.

Position of Women in the Ideal State

[I]t is time to speak of women. . . . Let us assume that the birth and education of women will be governed by the same guidelines we prescribed for the man. We can decide later whether or not this procedure seems appropriate.

What do you mean?

This. Do we separate off male and female dogs from one another, or do we expect both to share equally in standing guard and in going out to hunt? Should all activities be shared, or do we expect the females to remain indoors on the grounds that bearing and nursing the pups incapacitate them for anything else, leaving to the males the exclusive care and guarding of the flocks?

There should be no such differentiation. The only distinction between them is that we consider males to be stronger and females weaker.

Now then, can one get any animal to perform the same functions as another without giving both the same guidance and training?

No.

Then if women are to do the same things as men, we must also teach them the same things.

Yes.

The men were taught music and gymnastics, were they not?

Yes.

It follows that we must teach the women the same two arts, as well as learning and practice in the art of war.

From what you have said I suppose it does follow.

Perhaps conventional wisdom would ridicule some of these proposals if we tried to put them into practice.

It surely would.

Well, what do you think would be the most obvious target for ridicule? Perhaps the idea of women attending the wrestling schools and exercising naked with the men, especially when they are no longer young? The whole scene would resemble the behavior of those zealous old men who still persist in going off to exercise in the gymnasium despite all their wrinkles and ugliness.

Our present notions would call the whole thing absurd.

Yet we have vowed to speak our minds. Therefore we must not be daunted by all the wisecracks that will greet such innovations. Nor must we mind what the resident wits say about women studying music and gymnastics, about women bearing arms, nor, above all, what they say about women riding astride horses.

You are right. . . .

The basic question concerns the nature of women : can a woman perform all or none of the tasks a man performs? Can she manage some but not others? Is she really capable of waging war? . . .

We can clarify our meaning by observing, for example, that a man and a woman who both have the qualifications to be a physician have the same nature. Do you agree?

Yes.

But two men, one a physician and one a carpenter, have different natures?

Oh, entirely different.

So, then, those men and women who display distinct aptitudes for any given kind of work will be assigned to do that work. If a critic can do no more than bring up the one distinction between man and woman — that the one begets and the other bears children — we shall say that for our purposes he has offered no proof of difference at all. . . .

And we shall be right in doing so. . . .

Then we must conclude that sex cannot be the criterion in appointments to government positions. No office should be reserved for a man just because he is a man or for a woman just because she is a woman. All the capabilities with which nature endows us are distributed among men and women alike. Hence women will have the rightful opportunity to share in every task, and so will men, even though women are the weaker of the two sexes.

Agreed. . . .

The Allegory of the Cave

Here allegory may show us best how education — or the lack of it — affects our nature. Imagine men living in a cave with a long passageway stretching between them and the cave's mouth, where it opens wide to the light. Imagine further that since childhood the cave dwellers have had their legs and necks shackled so as to be confined to the same spot. They are further constrained by blinders that prevent them from turning their heads; they can see only directly in front of them. Next, imagine a light from a fire some distance behind them and burning at a higher elevation. Between the prisoners and the fire is a raised path along whose edge there is a low wall like the partition at the front of a puppet stage. The wall conceals the puppeteers while they manipulate their puppets above it.

So far I can visualize it.

Imagine, further, men behind the wall carrying all sorts of objects along its length and holding them above it. The objects include human and animal images made of stone and wood and all other material. Presumably, those who carry them sometimes speak and are sometimes silent.

You describe a strange prison and strange prisoners.

Like ourselves. Tell me, do you not think those men would see only the shadows cast by the fire on the wall of the cave? Would they have seen anything of themselves or of one another?

How could they if they couldn't move their heads their whole life long?

Could they see the objects held above the wall behind them or only the shadows cast in front?

Only the shadows.

If, then, they could talk with one another, don't you think they would impute reality to the passing shadows?

Necessarily.

Imagine an echo in their prison, bouncing off the wall toward which the prisoners were turned. Should one of those behind the wall speak, would the prisoners not think that the sound came from the shadows in front of them?

No doubt of it.

By every measure, then, reality for the prisoners would be nothing but shadows cast by artifacts.

It could be nothing else.

Imagine now how their liberation from bondage and error would come about if something like the following happened. One prisoner is freed from his shackles. He is suddenly compelled to stand up, turn around, walk, and look toward the light. He suffers pain and distress from the glare of the light. So dazzled is he that he cannot even discern the very objects whose shadows he used to be able to see. Now what do you suppose he would answer if he were told that all he had seen before was illusion but that now he was nearer reality, observing real things and therefore seeing more truly? What if someone pointed to the objects being carried above the wall, questioning him as to what each one is? Would he not be at a loss? Would he not regard those things he saw formerly as more real than the things now being shown him?

He would.

Again, let him be compelled to look directly at the light. Would his eyes not feel pain? Would he not flee, turning back to those things he was able to discern before, convinced that they are in every truth clearer and more exact than anything he has seen since?

He would.

Then let him be dragged away by force up the rough and steep incline of the cave's passageway, held fast until he is hauled out into the light of the sun. Would not such a rough passage be painful? Would he not resent the experience? And when he came out into the sunlight, would he not be dazzled once again and unable to see what he calls realities?

He could not see even one of them, at least not immediately.

Habituation, then, is evidently required in order to see things higher up. In the beginning he would most easily see shadows; next, reflections in the water of men and other objects. Then he would see the objects themselves. From there he would go on to behold the heavens and the heavenly phenomena — more easily the moon and stars by night than the sun by day.

Yes.

Finally, I suppose, he would be able to look on the sun itself, not in reflections in the water or in fleeting images in some alien setting. He would look at the sun as it is, in its own domain, and so be able to see what it is really like.

Yes.

It is at this stage that he would be able to conclude that the sun is the cause of the seasons and of the year's turning, that it governs all the visible world and is in some sense also the cause of all visible things.

This is surely the next step he would take.

Now, supposing he recalled where he came from. Supposing he thought of his fellow prisoners and of what passed for wisdom in the place they were inhabiting. Don't you think he would feel pity for all that and rejoice in his own change of circumstance?

He surely would.

Suppose there had been honors and citations those below bestowed upon one another. Suppose prizes were offered for the one quickest to identify the shadows as they go by and best able to remember the sequence and configurations in which they appear. All these skills, in turn, would enhance the ability to guess what would come next. Do you think he would covet such rewards? More, would he envy and want to emulate those who hold power over the prisoners and are in turn reverenced by them? Or would he not rather hold fast to Homer's words that it is "better to be the poor servant of a poor master," better to endure anything, than to believe those things and live that way?

I think he would prefer anything to such a life.

Consider, further, if he should go back down again into the cave and return to the place he was before, would not his eyes now go dark after so abruptly leaving the sunlight behind?

They would.

Suppose he should then have to compete once more in shadow watching with those who never left the cave. And this before his eyes had become accustomed to the dark and his dimmed vision still required a long period of habituation. Would he not be laughed at? Would it not be said that he had made the journey above only to come back with his eyes ruined and that it is futile even to attempt the ascent? Further, if anyone tried to release the prisoners and lead them up and they could get their hands on him and kill him, would they not kill him?

Of course.

Now, we must apply the allegory as a whole to all that has been said so far. The prisoners' cave is the counterpart of our own visible order, and the light of the fire betokens the power of the sun. If you liken the ascent and exploration of things above to the soul's journey through the intelligible order, you will have understood my thinking, since that is what you wanted to hear. God only knows whether it is true. But, in any case, this is the way things appear to me: in the intelligible world the last thing to be seen — and then only dimly — is the idea of the good. Once seen, however, the conclusion becomes irresistible that it is the cause of all things right and good, that in the visible world it gives birth to light and its sovereign source, that in the intelligible world it is itself sovereign and the author of truth and reason, and that the man who will act wisely in private and public life must have seen it. . . .

39

Titus Livy, *Early History of Rome*

Titus Livy (59 B.C.–A.D. 17), a slightly younger contemporary of Emperor Augustus Caesar, wrote a monumental history of Rome, from its legendary founding by Romulus and Remus to his own days. Of his history's 142 books, the first 10 and 25 others have survived. Livy's last books were too controversial to be released during the first Emperor's own lifetime, but even his very early ones nostalgically contrast the heroism and public spirit of the Republic with the selfishness and greed of the new Empire. His history is, of course, full of myth as he deals with the earliest centuries of Rome. Livy — living in a sophisticated and rather sceptical age — treats stories involving the intervention of the gods with conscious disbelief; however, he portrays the patriotic devotion of heroes to the Republic without similar expressions of doubt. While there is also plenty of evil and treachery recorded in Livy's early history of Rome, the determination of his heroes usually sees them through.

Livy's fame as a historian was immediate and lasting. His work superseded all earlier Roman histories; therefore, the Middle Ages and early modern times basically received their pre-Christian Roman history from him. Some 1500 years after Livy wrote, Machiavelli composed his own lengthy work, *Discourses on the First Ten Books of Titus Livy*, which described how republics prosper despite threats of destruction. Nearly 300 years after Machiavelli's work, Thomas Jefferson's correspondence indicated that he regarded Livy's work as substantially more valuable than Plato's.

In the following excerpts, Rome's early citizens are intent on defending their Republic after the excesses of the Tarquin family had led to the fall of the Tarquin dynasty and the abolition of the old Roman monarchy. The heroic exploits of Horatius Cocles at the bridge and Gaius Mucius Scaevola before Lars Porsena illustrate a simple but favorite point among the Romans: Their Republic was destined to survive as long as its citizens were willing to risk their lives for it.

QUESTIONS TO CONSIDER

1. How did the Romans prepare for the invasion led by Lars Porsena?
2. How did Horatius Cocles contribute to the defense of Rome?
3. How did Lars Porsena proceed when his attempt to take Rome by assault had failed?
4. How did Gaius Mucius Scaevola contribute to the defense of Rome?
5. What made Porsena abandon his attempt to re-establish the Tarquins as kings of Rome?

The Tarquins, meanwhile, had taken refuge at the court of Lars Porsena, the king of Clusium. By every means in their power they tried to win his support, now begging him not to allow fellow Etruscans, men of the same blood as himself, to continue living in penniless exile, now warning him of the dangerous consequences of letting republicanism go unavenged. The expulsion of kings, they urged, once it had begun, might well become common practice; liberty was an attractive idea,

From Titus Livy, *The Early History of Rome*, trans. Aubrey de Selincourt (New York: Penguin, 1960, 1975), pp. 114–122, passim. Copyright © The Estate of Aubrey de Selincourt, 1960. Reproduced by permission of Penguin Books Ltd.

and unless reigning monarchs defended their thrones as vigorously as states now seemed to be trying to destroy them, all order and subordination would collapse ; nothing would be left in any country but flat equality ; greatness and eminence would be gone for ever. Monarchy, the noblest thing in heaven or on earth, was nearing its end. Porsena, who felt that his own security would be increased by restoring the monarchy in Rome, and also that Etruscan prestige would be enhanced if the king were of Etruscan blood, was convinced by these arguments and lost no time in invading Roman territory.

Never before had there been such consternation in the Senate, so powerful was Clusium at that time and so great the fame of Porsena. Nor was the menace of Porsena the only cause for alarm : the Roman populace itself was hardly less to be feared, for they might well be scared into admitting the Tarquins into the city and buying peace even at the price of servitude. To secure their support, therefore, the Senate granted them a number of favours, especially in the matter of food supplies. Missions were sent to Cumae and the Volscians to purchase grain ; the monopoly in salt, the price of which was high, was taken from private individuals and transferred wholly to state control ; the commons were exempted from tolls and taxes, the loss of revenue being made up by the rich, who could afford it ; the poor, it was said, made contribution enough if they reared children. These concessions proved wonderfully effective, for during the misery and privation of the subsequent blockade the city remained united — so closely, indeed, that the poorest in Rome hated the very name of 'king' as bitterly as did the great. Wise government in this crisis gave the Senate greater popularity, in the true sense of the word, than was ever won by a demagogue in after years.

On the approach of the Etruscan army, the Romans abandoned their farmsteads and moved into the city. Garrisons were posted. In some sections the city walls seemed sufficient protection, in others the barrier of the Tiber. The most vulnerable point was the wooden bridge, and the Etruscans would have crossed it and forced an entrance into the city, had it not been for the courage of one man, Horatius Cocles — that great soldier whom the fortune of Rome gave to be her shield on that day of peril. Horatius was on guard at the bridge when the Janiculum was captured by a sudden attack. The enemy forces came pouring down the hill, while the Roman troops, throwing away their weapons, were behaving more like an undisciplined rabble than a fighting force. Horatius acted promptly : as his routed comrades approached the bridge, he stopped as many as he could catch and compelled them to listen to him. 'By God,' he cried, 'can't you see that if you desert your post escape is hopeless ? If you leave the bridge open in your rear, there will soon be more of them in the Palatine and the Capitol than on the Janiculum.' Urging them with all the power at his command to destroy the bridge by fire or steel or any means they could muster, he offered to hold up the Etruscan advance, so far as was possible, alone. Proudly he took his stand at the outer end of the bridge ; conspicuous amongst the rout of fugitives, sword and shield ready for action, he prepared himself for close combat, one man against an army. The advancing enemy paused in sheer astonishment at such reckless courage. Two other men, Spurius Lartius and Titus Herminius, both aristocrats with a fine military record, were ashamed to leave Horatius alone, and with their support he won through the first few minutes of desperate danger. Soon, however, he forced them to save themselves and leave him ; for little was now left of the bridge, and the demolition squads were calling them back before it was too late. Once more Horatius stood alone ; with defiance in his eyes he confronted the Etruscan chivalry, challenging one after another to single combat, and mocking them all as tyrants' slaves who, careless of their own liberty, were coming to destroy the liberty of others. For a while they hung back, each waiting for his neighbour to make the first move, until shame at the unequal battle drove them to action, and with a fierce cry they hurled their spears at the solitary figure which barred their way. Horatius caught the missiles on his shield and, resolute as ever, straddled the bridge and held his ground. The Etruscans moved forward, and would have thrust him aside by the sheer weight of numbers, but their advance was suddenly checked by the crash of the falling bridge and the simultaneous shout of triumph from the Roman soldiers who had done their work in time. The Etruscans could only stare in bewilderment as Horatius, with a prayer to Father Tiber to bless him and his sword, plunged fully armed into the water and swam, through the missiles which fell thick about him, safely to the other side where his friends were waiting to receive him. It was a noble piece of work — legendary, maybe, but destined to be celebrated in story through the years to come.

For such courage the country showed its gratitude. A statue of Horatius was placed in the Comitium, and he was granted as much land as he could drive a plough round in a day. In addition to public honours many individuals marked their admiration of his exploit in the very hard times which were to follow, by going short themselves in order to contribute something, whatever they could afford, to his support.

Thwarted in his attempt to take the city by assault, Porsena now turned to siege operations. He garrisoned the Janiculum, took up a position on the flat ground near the river, and collected a number of vessels to prevent supplies from being brought into Rome and also to ferry troops across whenever, or wherever, an opportunity for a raid should present itself. His control over the whole outlying territory was soon so complete that, in addition to other sorts of property, all cattle had to be brought within the defences of the city, and nobody dared to drive them out to pasture. . . .

. . . [F]ood in the city was scarce and dear, and Porsena's hopes rose of being able to starve it into submission without risking an assault. It was in these circumstances that the young aristocrat Gaius Mucius performed his famous act of heroism. In the days of her servitude under the monarchy Rome had never, in any war, suffered the humiliation of a siege, and Mucius was so deeply conscious of the shame of the present situation, when, after winning their liberty, the Romans were blockaded by — of all people — the Etruscans, whom they had so often defeated in the field, that he determined to vindicate the national pride by a bold stroke. His first thought was to make his way, on his own initiative, into the enemy lines ; but there was a risk, if he attempted this without anybody's knowledge and without the authorization of the consuls, of being arrested by the guards as a deserter — a charge only too plausible, conditions in Rome being what they were. Accordingly he changed his mind, and presented himself in the Senate. 'I wish,' he said, 'to cross the river and to enter, if I can, the enemy's lines. My object is neither plunder nor reprisals, but, with the help of God, something more important than either.'

The Senate granted him permission to proceed and he started on his way, a dagger concealed in his clothing. Arrived at the Etruscan camp, he took his stand, in the crowd, close to the raised platform where the king was sitting. A great many people were present, as it was pay-day for the army. By the side of the king sat his secretary, very busy ; he was dressed much like his master, and, as most of the men addressed themselves to him, Mucius could not be sure which was the secretary and which the king. Fearing to inquire, lest his ignorance should betray him, he took a chance — and stabbed the secretary. There was a cry of alarm ; he was seized by the guards as he tried to force his way through the crowd with his blood-stained dagger, and dragged back to where Porsena was sitting. Help there was none, and his situation was desperate indeed : but he never flinched and, when he spoke, his proud words were those of a man who inspires fear, but feels none. 'I am a Roman,' he said to the king ; 'my name is Gaius Mucius. I came here to kill you — my enemy. I have as much courage to die as to kill. It is our Roman way to do and to suffer bravely. Nor am I alone in my resolve against your life ; behind me is a long line of men eager for the same honour. Gird yourself, if you will, for the struggle — a struggle for your life from hour to hour, with an armed enemy always at your door. That is the war we declare against you ; you need fear no action in the field, army against army ; it will be fought against you alone, by one of us at a time.'

Porsena in rage and alarm ordered the prisoner to be burnt alive unless he at once divulged the plot thus obscurely hinted at, whereupon Mucius, crying : 'See how cheap men hold their bodies when they care only for honour !' thrust his right hand into the fire which had been kindled for a sacrifice, and let it burn there as if he were unconscious of the pain. Porsena was so astonished by the young man's almost superhuman endurance that he leapt to his feet and ordered his guards to drag him from the altar. 'Go free,' he said ; 'you have dared to be a worse enemy to yourself than to me. I should bless your courage, if it lay with my country to dispose of it. But, as that cannot be, I, as an honourable enemy, grant you pardon, life, and liberty.'

'Since you respect courage,' Mucius replied, as if he were thanking him for his generosity, 'I will tell you in gratitude what you could not force from me by threats. There are three hundred of us in Rome, all young like myself, and all of noble blood, who have sworn an attempt upon your life in this fashion. It was I who drew the first lot ; the rest will follow, each in his turn and time, until fortune favour us and we have got you.'

The release of Mucius (who was afterwards known as Scaevola, or the Left-Handed Man, from the loss of his right hand) was quickly followed by the arrival in Rome of envoys from Porsena. The first attempt upon his life, foiled only by a lucky mistake, and the prospect of having to face the same thing again from every one of the remaining conspirators, had so shaken the king that he was coming forward with proposals for peace. . . .

The next consuls were Spurius Lartius and Titus Herminius, followed by Publius Lucretius and Publius Valerius Publicola. In the latter year Porsena made his final effort to procure Tarquin's restoration to power. His envoys on their arrival in Rome were told that the Senate would dispatch a mission to the king, and this was immediately done. The members of the mission were all senators of the highest distinction. It would have been easy enough, they declared, to give a curt refusal, on the spot, to Porsena's overtures. That was not the reason why Rome had sent representatives of such distinction rather than answer the Etruscan envoys directly; the reason was that the Romans wished the whole question of the restoration to be closed once and for all. Relations between Rome and Clusium were now excellent; it would be a pity, therefore, to risk the mutual irritation of a repeated request, on the one side, met, on the other, by a repeated refusal; and this would be bound to occur if Porsena continued to ask for what was incompatible with Roman liberty, and the Romans — short of allowing their good nature to prove their ruin — continued to refuse it to a man to whom they would not willingly refuse anything. Rome was no longer a monarchy; she enjoyed free institutions. The people of Rome would sooner open their gates to an enemy than to a king. There was not a man in the city who did not pray that the end of liberty, should it come, might also be the end of Rome. They urged Porsena, therefore, if he had the good of Rome at heart, to accept the fact that she would never surrender her liberties.

Porsena was deeply impressed. 'Since,' he said, 'it is clear that nothing can shake your determination, I will no longer weary you with requests which I now know to be useless; nor shall I deceive the Tarquins with the hope of aid which I have no power to give. They must find — by force of arms or otherwise, as they please — some other place to spend their exile in; for nothing must disturb the friendly relations between myself and Rome.'

CHRISTIANITY TO ISLAM

The Rise of Christianity

In the last century of the Roman Republic, religious and civil conflicts made Palestine vulnerable to Roman intervention in Jewish affairs. Pompey the Great stormed Jerusalem in 63 B.C. and aided an Idumean named Antipater in being named foreign minister to the temple state. Thereafter, Antipater's son, Herod, became friends with Julius Caesar, Mark Antony, and Augustus Caesar. In return for his loyalty and obedience, the Romans permitted Herod to resurrect the monarchy (37–4 B.C.).

Herod's reign was a prosperous one : He was able to rebuild Jerusalem with a great palace, the Second Temple, and to add many forts throughout the kingdom. Nonetheless, many Jews hated Herod because they saw him as pro-Roman, a murderer of his family, and — above all — not wholly Jewish.

Factions also dominated Judea, where Jesus was born. There were the Sadducees, supported by the upper classes, who controlled the Temple priesthood and were strict supporters of the Torah. Their opponents were the Pharisees, who were seen as more liberal. They supported public education, believed in personal immortality, and sponsored scribal commentaries on the Laws. Other groups, such as the Essenes, had withdrawn from secular life completely and became ascetics in desert communities. One of these latter, the New Covenanters, expected an end to the wicked age and the establishment of a new kingdom of righteousness.

Jesus was born some time near the end of Herod's rule — not, as the later Christians believed, in the year A.D. 1. Although we cannot establish a true date, his parents, Joseph and Mary, had to leave their village of Nazareth and proceed to Bethlehem. They were displaced because Caesar Augustus had ordered a census of the empire, requiring that everyone register in the city of his or her family. In the Gospels, Jesus' lineage is traced back to Bethlehem, the home of David, from whose line the Hebrew prophets had predicted a Messiah would come.

Little information is recorded in the Gospels about the middle years of Jesus' life. Not until he was baptized by his cousin, John the Baptist, would Jesus begin his public ministry. From that time until his crucifixion three years later, Jesus gathered his apostles, preached a new religious message, and worked his miracles.

As Jesus' fame increased in Galilee and Judea, the religious authorities feared disturbances. The Sadducees accused him of religious blasphemy, arrested him, and handed him over to the Roman governor of Judea, Pontius Pilate. Jesus was tried and executed for sedition against Rome.

Within a short period, the apostles announced that Jesus had risen from the grave and would shortly return in the Second Coming, which would inaugurate the Messianic Kingdom. In order to amplify this theology, the Apostle Paul identified Jesus as the son of God, or God-made flesh, whose sacrifice on the Cross made salvation from sin possible for all humanity. The apostles traveled from city to city with these messages, appealing first to the Jews and then to the Gentiles. This was the true foundation of the Christian religion.

Readings 40–42 are from one of the most famous sermons delivered by Jesus, called "The Sermon on the Mount." Here he describes the humble, the poor, and the peacemakers — not the great and privileged — as worthy of heavenly rewards. He explains that he has come to amplify, not destroy, the Laws of Moses. He then teaches his disciples how to recite the Lord's Prayer. And, finally, Jesus gives the Golden Rule to humankind as a guide ; he says that those who hear and live these words will be following God's Will.

40

Beatitudes and the Law

In this selection, Jesus describes the attributes of those whom he believes worthy of the Kingdom of God. His believers must not only follow the Old Law but also undergo an inward change of heart.

QUESTIONS TO CONSIDER

1. For whom was Jesus' message intended and why?
2. What is righteousness and what are its rewards?
3. What new interpretation of Law did Jesus give his listeners?
4. Compare the Christian teachings with the Hindu (see Readings 19–22), Buddhist (see Readings 27–29), and Hebrew (see Readings 11–15) teachings.

And seeing the multitudes, he went up into a mountain : and when he was set, his disciples came unto him :
 And he opened his mouth, and taught them, saying,
 Blessed are the poor in spirit : for their's is the kingdom of heaven.
 Blessed are they that mourn : for they shall be comforted.

From Matthew, 5:1–48 (King James Version) ; slightly modernized.

Blessed are the meek : for they shall inherit the earth.

Blessed are they which do hunger and thirst after righteousness : for they shall be filled.

Blessed are the merciful : for they shall obtain mercy.

Blessed are the pure in heart : for they shall see God.

Blessed are the peacemakers : for they shall be called the children of God.

Blessed are they which are persecuted for righteousness' sake : for their's is the kingdom of heaven.

Blessed are ye, when men shall revile you, and persecute you, and shall say all manner of evil against you falsely, for my sake.

Rejoice, and be exceeding glad : for great is your reward in heaven : for so persecuted they the prophets which were before you.

Ye are the salt of the earth : but if the salt have lost his savour, wherewith shall it be salted ? it is thenceforth good for nothing, but to be cast out, and to be trodden under foot of men.

Ye are the light of the world. A city that is set on an hill cannot be hid.

Neither do men light a candle, and put it under a bushel, but on a candlestick ; and it giveth light unto all that are in the house.

Let your light so shine before men, that they may see your good works, and glorify your Father, which is in heaven.

Think not that I am come to destroy the law, or the prophets : I am not come to destroy, but to fulfil.

For verily I say unto you, Till heaven and earth pass, one jot or one tittle shall in no wise pass from the law, till all be fulfilled.

Whosoever therefore shall break one of these least commandments, and shall teach men so, he shall be called the least in the kingdom of heaven : but whosoever shall do and teach them, the same shall be called great in the kingdom of heaven.

For I say unto you, That except your righteousness shall exceed the righteousness of the scribes and Pharisees, ye shall in no case enter into the kingdom of heaven.

Ye have heard that it was said by them of old time, Thou shalt not kill : and whosoever shall kill shall be in danger of the judgment :

But I say unto you, That whosoever is angry with his brother without a cause shall be in danger of the judgment : and whosoever shall say to his brother, Raca, shall be in danger of the council : but whosoever shall say, Thou fool, shall be in danger of hell fire.

Therefore if thou bring thy gift to the altar, and there rememberest that thy brother hath ought against thee :

Leave there thy gift before the altar, and go thy way : first be reconciled to thy brother, and then come and offer thy gift.

Agree with thine adversary quickly, whiles thou art in the way with him ; lest at any time the adversary deliver thee to the judge, and the judge deliver thee to the officer, and thou be cast into prison.

Verily I say unto thee, Thou shalt by no means come out thence, till thou hast paid the uttermost farthing.

Ye have heard that it was said by them of old time, Thou shalt not commit adultery :

But I say unto you, That whosoever looketh on a woman to lust after her hath committed adultery with her already in his heart.

And if thy right eye offend thee, pluck it out, and cast it from thee : for it is profitable for thee that one of thy members should perish, and not that thy whole body should be cast into hell.

And if thy right hand offend thee, cut it off, and cast it from thee : for it is profitable for thee that one of thy members should perish, and not that thy whole body should be cast into hell.

It hath been said, Whosoever shall put away his wife, let him give her a writing of divorcement :

But I say unto you, That whosoever shall put away his wife, saving for the cause of fornication, causeth her to commit adultery : and whosoever shall marry her that is divorced committeth adultery.

Again, ye have heard that it hath been said by them of old time, Thou shalt not forswear thyself, but shalt perform unto the Lord thine oaths :

But I say unto you, Swear not at all ; neither by heaven ; for it is God's throne :

Nor by the earth ; for it is his footstool : neither by Jerusalem ; for it is the city of the great King.

Neither shalt thou swear by thy head, because thou canst not make one hair white or black.

But let your communication be, Yea, yea ; Nay, nay : for whatsoever is more than these cometh of evil.

Ye have heard that it hath been said, An eye for an eye, and a tooth for a tooth :

But I say unto you, That ye resist not evil : but whosoever shall smite thee on thy right cheek, turn to him the other also.

And if any man will sue thee at the law, and take away thy coat, let him have thy cloak also.

And whosoever shall compel thee to go a mile, go with him twain.

Give to him that asketh thee, and from him that would borrow of thee turn not thou away.

Ye have heard that it hath been said, Thou shalt love thy neighbour, and hate thine enemy.

But I say unto you, Love your enemies, bless them that curse you, do good to them that hate you, and pray for them which despitefully use you, and persecute you ;

That ye may be the children of your Father which is in heaven : for he maketh his sun to rise on the evil and on the good, and sendeth rain on the just and on the unjust.

For if ye love them which love you, what reward have ye ? do not even the publicans the same ?

And if ye salute your brethren only, what do ye more than others ? do not even the publicans so ?

Be ye therefore perfect, even as your Father which is in heaven is perfect.

41

The Lord's Prayer and Righteousness

In these passages, Jesus teaches humanity the right way to pray.

QUESTIONS TO CONSIDER

1. Why is a Christian urged to pray in secret?
2. Why is materialism a hinderance to salvation?
3. Compare Jesus' teaching on righteousness with the Hindu teaching (see Readings 22–25).

Take heed that ye do not your alms before men, to be seen of them : otherwise ye have no reward of your Father which is in heaven.

Therefore when thou doest thine alms, do not sound a trumpet before thee, as the hypocrites do in the synagogues and in the streets, that they may have glory of men. Verily I say unto you, They have their reward.

But when thou doest alms, let not thy left hand know what thy right hand doeth :

That thine alms may be in secret : and thy Father which seeth in secret himself shall reward thee openly.

And when thou prayest, thou shalt not be as the hypocrites are : for they love to pray standing in the synagogues and in the corners of the streets, that they may be seen of men. Verily I say unto you, They have their reward.

But thou, when thou prayest, enter into thy closet, and when thou hast shut thy door, pray to thy Father which is in secret ; and thy Father which seeth in secret shall reward thee openly.

But when ye pray, use not vain repetitions, as the heathen do : for they think that they shall be heard for their much speaking.

Be not ye therefore like unto them : for your Father knoweth what things ye have need of, before ye ask him.

After this manner therefore pray ye : Our Father which art in heaven, Hallowed be thy name.

Thy kingdom come. Thy will be done in earth, as it is in heaven.

Give us this day our daily bread.

And forgive us our debts, as we forgive our debtors.

And lead us not into temptation, but deliver us from evil : For thine is the kingdom, and the power, and the glory, forever. Amen.

For if ye forgive men their trespasses, your heavenly Father will also forgive you :

From Matthew, 6:1–34 (King James Version) ; slightly modernized.

But if ye forgive not men their trespasses, neither will your Father forgive your trespasses.

Moreover when ye fast, be not, as the hypocrites, of a sad countenance : for they disfigure their faces, that they may appear unto men to fast. Verily I say unto you, They have their reward.

But thou, when thou fastest, anoint thine head, and wash thy face ;

That thou appear not unto men to fast, but unto thy Father which is in secret : and thy Father, which seeth in secret, shall reward thee openly.

Lay not up for yourselves treasures upon earth, where moth and rust doth corrupt, and where thieves break through and steal :

But lay up for yourselves treasures in heaven, where neither moth nor rust doth corrupt, and where thieves do not break through nor steal :

For where your treasure is, there will your heart be also.

The light of the body is the eye : if therefore thine eye be single, thy whole body shall be full of light.

But if thine eye be evil, thy whole body shall be full of darkness. If therefore the light that is in thee be darkness, how great is that darkness!

No man can serve two masters : for either he will hate the one, and love the other ; or else he will hold to the one, and despise the other. Ye cannot serve God and mammon.

Therefore I say unto you, Take no thought for your life, what ye shall eat, or what ye shall drink ; nor yet for your body, what ye shall put on. Is not the life more than meat, and the body than raiment ?

Behold the fowls of the air : for they sow not, neither do they reap, nor gather into barns ; yet your heavenly Father feedeth them. Are ye not much better than they ?

Which of you by taking thought can add one cubit unto his stature ?

And why take ye thought for raiment ? Consider the lilies of the field, how they grow ; they toil not, neither do they spin :

And yet I say unto you, That even Solomon in all his glory was not arrayed like one of these.

Wherefore, if God so clothe the grass of the field, which to day is, and tomorrow is cast into the oven, shall he not much more clothe you, O ye of little faith ?

Therefore take no thought, saying, What shall we eat ? or, What shall we drink ? or, Wherewithal shall we be clothed ?

(For after all these things do the Gentiles seek :) for your heavenly Father knoweth that ye have need of all these things.

But seek ye first the kingdom of God, and his righteousness ; and all these things shall be added unto you.

Take therefore no thought for the morrow : for the morrow shall take thought for the things of itself. Sufficient unto the day is the evil thereof.

42

The Golden Rule and God's Will

In this passage, Jesus explains that the person who hears and does God's Will is fulfilling the Law.

QUESTIONS TO CONSIDER

1. What are the Lord's requirements of a true believer?
2. Why are not all prophets acceptable?
3. Compare Jesus' Sermon on the Mount with the teachings of Buddha (see Readings 27–28) and the Hindu beliefs (see Readings 21–22).

Judge not, that ye be not judged.

For with what judgment ye judge, ye shall be judged : and with what measure ye mete, it shall be measured to you again.

And why beholdest thou the mote that is in thy brother's eye, but considerest not the beam that is in thine own eye?

Or how wilt thou say to thy brother, Let me pull out the mote out of thine eye : and, behold, a beam is in thine own eye?

Thou hypocrite, first cast out the beam out of thine own eye ; and then shalt thou see clearly to cast out the mote out of thy brother's eye.

Give not that which is holy unto the dogs, neither cast ye your pearls before swine, lest they trample them under their feet, and turn again and rend you.

Ask, and it shall be given you : seek, and ye shall find : knock, and it shall be opened unto you :

For every one that asketh receiveth : and he that seeketh findeth : and to him that knocketh it shall be opened.

Or what man is there of you, whom if his son ask bread, will he give him a stone?

Or if he ask a fish, will he give him a serpent?

If ye then, being evil, know how to give good gifts unto your children, how much more shall your Father which is in heaven give good things to them that ask him?

Therefore all things whatsoever ye would that men should do to you, do ye even so to them : for this is the law and the prophets.

Enter ye in at the strait gate : for wide is the gate, and broad is the way, that leadeth to destruction, and many there be which go in there :

Because strait is the gate, and narrow is the way, which leadeth unto life, and few there be that find it.

From Matthew, 7:1–29 (King James Version) ; slightly modernized.

Beware of false prophets, which come to you in sheep's clothing, but inwardly they are ravening wolves.

Ye shall know them by their fruits. Do men gather grapes of thorns, or figs of thistles?

Even so every good tree bringeth forth good fruit; but a corrupt tree bringeth forth evil fruit.

A good tree cannot bring forth evil fruit, neither can a corrupt tree bring forth good fruit.

Every tree that bringeth not forth good fruit is hewn down, and cast into the fire.

Wherefore by their fruits ye shall know them.

Not every one that saith unto me, Lord, Lord, shall enter into the kingdom of heaven; but he that doeth the will of my Father which is in heaven.

Many will say to me in that day, Lord, Lord, have we not prophesied in thy name? and in thy name have cast out devils? and in thy name done many wonderful works?

And then will I profess unto them, I never knew you: depart from me, ye that work iniquity.

Therefore whosoever heareth these sayings of mine, and doeth them, I will liken him unto a wise man, which built his house upon a rock:

And the rain descended, and the floods came, and the winds blew, and beat upon that house; and it fell not: for it was founded upon a rock.

And every one that heareth these sayings of mine, and doeth them not, shall be likened unto a foolish man, which built his house upon the sand:

And the rain descended, and the floods came, and the winds blew, and beat upon that house; and it fell: and great was the fall of it.

And it came to pass, when Jesus had ended these sayings, the people were astonished at his doctrine:

For he taught them as one having authority, and not as the scribes.

43

The Writings of St. Paul on Women

Women in many ancient societies were subordinate to men in legal, political, and religious rights. And at first glance, this might appear to be the case in the Old and New Testaments where woman (Eve) is depicted as the source of "Original Sin" or compared to Israel, God's unfaithful wife; however, woman is also viewed in the Old Testament as the faithful companion of God and in the Gospels as the way to salvation through the New Eve, Mary.

When all the Gospel accounts are taken as a whole, they seem to reflect a significant change in human relations and an increased importance for women. Jesus' teachings emphasize the idea that men and women have equal duties in marriage ; just as divorce is forbidden for both, so adultery is not limited to women. Women such as Mary Magdalene were attracted to Jesus' ministry, and it was to women that Jesus appeared at his tomb. They were also important as helpers (deaconesses) or patrons in the newly established Christian communities.

The ideas of St. Paul reflect both the Old Testament and the Gospel views of women. Born into a Jewish family, which had acquired Roman citizenship, Saul of Tarsus (Paul) at first rejected Christianity and joined in the persecution of early Christians. Later, according to his own account, a blinding light appeared to him on the road to Damascus, where God commanded him to stop harming Christians and to begin preaching the Gospel. Under his Roman name of Paul, he became such an effective Christian preacher and teacher that he was listed among the Apostles. His letters became an important part of Christian theology.

St. Paul changed the course of Christianity as he preached to the gentile communities of the Roman world instead of concentrating exclusively on Jews. When doctrinal disputes arose within Christian groups, Paul attempted to settle these problems in his letters through interpretation and application of Jesus' teachings.

St. Paul was frequently in trouble with Jewish leaders, who saw him as a traitor. Roman authorities at first had nothing against Christians but later took a dim view of religious figures, such as Paul, whose speeches provoked an uproar. When some confusion resulted in Paul's being arrested in Palestine, he used his Roman citizenship to appeal his case to the emperor. According to Church tradition, he was sent to the capital and released after several years of captivity. However, some seven or eight years later, he was one of the Christians executed during Nero's persecution.

The following excerpts from Paul's letters to the Galatians and Corinthians illustrate some of his teachings. These include the equality of men and women in Christ through baptism but their inequality in marriage and sexuality.

QUESTIONS TO CONSIDER

1. What was life like for women in the ancient world ? Are there any exceptions ?
2. How did the Hebrew religion influence the Christian view of women (see Reading 3 from Genesis) ?
3. How does St. Paul argue for equality for all persons ?
4. Does St. Paul address himself only to men in the area of freedom and responsibilities in marriage ?
5. Many authors say that St. Paul subordinates women to men in 1 Corinthians 11 :2–16. Could his statements express his view of a "natural law" governing men and women ?

Baptism and Faith

Wherefore the law was our schoolmaster to bring us unto Christ, that we might be justified by faith.

But after that faith is come, we are no longer under a schoolmaster.

For you are all the children of God by faith in Christ Jesus.

For as many of you as have been baptized into Christ have put on Christ.

There is neither Jew nor Greek, there is neither bond [slave] nor free, there is neither male nor female : for you are all one in Christ Jesus.

Marriage

Now concerning the things whereof you wrote unto me : It is good for a man not to touch a woman.

Nevertheless, to avoid fornication, let every man have his own wife, and let every woman have her own husband.

Let the husband render unto the wife due benevolence : and likewise also the wife unto the husband.

The wife has no power of her own body, but the husband : and likewise also the husband has not power of his own body, but the wife.

Do not refuse one another except by agreement for a time, that you may give yourselves to fasting and prayer ; and come together again, lest that Satan tempt you through lack of self-control.

But I speak this by permission, and not of commandment.

For I wish that all men were even as I myself. But every man has his proper gift of God, one after this manner, another after that.

I say therefore to the unmarried and widows, it is good for them if they remain even as I.

But if they cannot contain, let them marry : for it is better to marry than to burn.

And to the married I command, yet not I, but the Lord, Let not the wife depart from her husband :

But and if she depart, let her remain unmarried, or be reconciled to her husband : and let not the husband put away his wife.

But to the rest I speak, not the Lord : If any brother has an unbelieving wife, and she is pleased to live with him, let him not put her away.

And the woman who has an unbelieving husband, and if he is pleased to live with her, let her not leave him.

For the unbelieving husband is sanctified by the wife, and the unbelieving wife is sanctified by the husband : otherwise your children were unclean ; but now they are holy.

But if the unbelieving departs, let him depart. A brother or sister is not under bondage in such cases : but God has called us to peace.

For what do you know, Oh wife, whether you shall save your husband ? or how do you know, Oh man, whether you shall save your wife ?

First section from Galatians, 3:24–28. The second is from 1 Corinthians 7:1–17, 25–28, 32–40. The third section is from 1 Corinthians 11:2–16. (King James Version ; slightly modernized).

But as God has distributed to every man, as the Lord has called every one, so let him walk. And so I ordain in all churches. . . .

Now concerning virgins I have no commandment of the Lord: yet I give my judgment, as one that has obtained mercy of the Lord to be faithful.

I suppose therefore that this is good for the present distress, I say, that it is good for a man so to be.

Art you bound to a wife? seek not to be freed. Art you freed from a wife? seek not a wife.

But if you marry, you have not sinned; and if a virgin marry, she has not sinned. Nevertheless such shall have trouble in the flesh: but I spare you.

But this I say, brothers, the time is short: it remains that both they who have wives be as though they had none; . . .

But I would have you without carefulness. He that is unmarried cares for the things that belong to the Lord, how he may please the Lord:

But he that is married cares for the things that are of the world, how he may please his wife.

There is difference also between a wife and a virgin. The unmarried woman cares for the things of the Lord, that she may be holy both in body and in spirit: but she who is married cares for the things of the world, how she may please her husband.

And this I speak for your own profit; not that I may cast a snare on you, but for that which is proper, and that you may attend upon the Lord without distraction.

But if any man thinks that he behaves improperly toward his virgin, if she is passed the flower of her age, and need requires it, let him do what he will, he does not sin; let them marry.

Nevertheless he that stands steadfast in his heart, having no necessity, but has power over his own will, and has so decreed in his heart that he will keep his virgin, does well.

So then he that gives her in marriage does well; but he that does not give her in marriage does better.

The wife is bound by the law as long as her husband lives; but if her husband is dead, she is at liberty to be married to whomever she will; only in the Lord.

But she is happier if she so abide, after my judgment: and I think also that I have the Spirit of God.

Physical Differences of Sexes

Now I praise you, brothers, that you remember me in all things, and keep the ordinances, as I delivered them to you.

But I would have you know, that the head of every man is Christ; and the head of the woman is the man; and the head of Christ is God.

Every man praying or prophesying, having his head covered, dishonors his head.

But every woman who prays or prophesies with her head uncovered dishonors her head: for that is even all one as if she were shaven.

For if the woman is not covered, let her be shorn: but if it is a shame for a woman to be shorn or shaven, let her be covered.

For a man indeed ought not to cover his head, as he is the image and glory of God: but the woman is the glory of man.

For the man is not of the woman; but the woman of the man.

Neither was the man created for the woman; but the woman for the man.

For this cause ought the woman to have power on her head because of the angels.

Nevertheless neither is the man without the woman, neither the woman without the man, in the Lord.

For as the woman is of the man, even so is the man also by the woman; but all things of God.

Judge in yourselves: is it seemly that a woman pray unto God uncovered?

Does not even nature itself teach you, that, if a man has long hair, it is his shame?

But if a woman has long hair, it is a glory to her: for her hair is given her for a covering.

But if any man seems to be quarrelsome, we have no such custom, neither the churches of God.

Rome and the Christians

For three hundred years, the Roman government showed an unusual tolerance in the area of personal religion. In rare instances, such as during the Great Fire of A.D. 64, the Christians were persecuted; however, the persecution occurred not only for their religious practices. The Emperor Nero needed scapegoats to stop the rumors that he had started the fire. Most persecutions took place in the provinces and were very sporadic. They were undertaken by local governors who saw the Christians as unlicensed groups, practicing barbaric rites, such as cannibalism and child sacrifice, and refusing to make public sacrifices to the emperors. In the second century, the official government position was established by Emperor Trajan who decreed that only convicted traitors were to be punished; the Christians as a group were to be tolerated. As the empire crumbled in the last half of the third century, Emperor Diocletian viewed the Christians as a danger to the unity of the empire and began the Great Persecution (A.D. 303–311). However, after Constantine (306–337) conquered the western half of the Roman empire, he issued a declaration of religious toleration in 313 that became the governmental policy until 392 when Emperor Theodosius I made Christianity the sole religion.

The following three selections concerning the Roman treatment of Christians come from Tacitus's *Annals,* Pliny the Younger's *Letters,* and M. Minucius Felix's *Octavius.* Tacitus (A.D. 55–117?), who wrote such works as *Agricola, Germania* and the *Histories,* is considered the greatest historian of the empire. In the *Annals,* his purpose was to depict the imperial court from Tiberius through Nero in a series of vivid, unforgettable character sketches. As a moralist, he depicted those vices that led to Rome's decline. This is evident when he described the Great Fire in A.D. 64 which Nero was rumored to have started because he wished to renovate the city of Rome. Nero's subsequent treatment of Christians earned Tacitus's disapproval.

The second selection is from Pliny the Younger (A.D. 62–113), whose ten books of *Letters* illustrate travel, court and daily life, and politics at the turn of the first century. About A.D. 110, Emperor Trajan appointed Pliny proconsul or special imperial representative in the province of Bithynia, which lay along the south coast of the Black Sea. Pliny's task was to deal with irregularities in politics and public finances and to maintain public order. When he began to have a problem with Christians in his province, Pliny immediately wrote to Emperor Trajan, asking if he had acted in accord with the emperor's wishes. The emperor's response demonstrated a great deal of humanity.

The third selection, *Octavius,* is attributed to M. Minucius Felix, a Christian lawyer of the late second or early third century. It is in the form of a debate between a pagan, Q. Caecilius Natalis, and a Christian, Octavius Januarius, on their beliefs. Its merit lies in the depiction of Roman social and religious conditions and the spread of Christianity among the upper classes.

The next two sections, St. Augustine's *City of God* and The Rule of St. Benedict, date from the Late Western Roman Empire when the Christian Church emerged as the only stable institution amidst the defunct governmental, social, and religious traditions of the past. St. Augustine of Hippo (354–430) was educated by his parents in Africa and Milan to be a teacher of rhetoric. He was not a Christian until after 384 when he listened to the sermons of St. Ambrose, Bishop of Milan. Augustine became a priest and returned to Africa where he was made the Bishop of Hippo in 390.

Augustine began to write against various Christian heresies and developed explanations on predestination, grace, and free will that became the primary Christian doctrines. His most famous work, *City of God,* was an attempt to create a philosophy of history with the belief that citizens should place their trust in God, or the Heavenly City, not the City of Man.

The last selection concerns monasticism as formulated by St. Benedict (480–545). In contrast to the East where monks often led solitary lives filled with extreme fasts or self-inflicted torments, Benedict's rule prescribed moderation. Each monk took the vows of poverty, chastity, and obedience, but the rule also provided for simple meals, clothing, recreation, and adequate sleep. The most important of monk's duties was prayer, but manual labor was instituted as all monasteries were to be self-sufficient.

44

Tacitus, *The Annals*

In the late summer of A.D. 64, a fire began and burned for six days, devastating the heart of Rome. Tacitus describes Emperor Nero's persecution of Christians as an attempt to dispel the rumor that he had set the fire himself.

QUESTIONS TO CONSIDER

1. From a historical viewpoint, why is Tacitus's report important to Christianity?
2. Why did Tacitus disapprove of Nero's actions?
3. What does Tacitus think is the real reason that Nero persecuted the Christians?
4. What is the contrast between the actions of Nero and Emperor Trajan (see Reading 45) on the treatment of Christians?

The Great Fire

38 There followed a catastrophe, whether through accident or the design of the emperor is not sure, as there are authorities for both views, but it was the most disastrous and appalling of all the calamities brought on this city through the violence of fire. It had its beginning in the part of the Circus[1] next to the Palatine and Caelian hills among the shops where inflammable merchandise is sold. Here the fire broke out and, immediately gaining strength, was fanned by the wind and swept through the length of the Circus. No houses surrounded by enclosures or temples girded by walls or any other obstruction served as a check. First the blaze, as it rushed ahead, overran the level stretches, then rose to higher ground and again descended to devastate the low-lying areas, moving so swiftly in its destructive path as to outstrip all efforts to fight it, and aided by the fact that the city was vulnerable to fire because of the narrow streets winding in every direction and the irregular blocks of houses, such as old Rome had. . . .

39 During this time Nero was at Antium and did not come back to Rome until the fire approached his palace, with which he had joined the Palatine. . . . Even so the fire could not be stopped until the Palatine and the palace and everything in the area were devastated. To relieve the homeless refugees he opened up the Campus Martius and the public buildings of Agrippa and even his own gardens, and he built temporary structures to shelter the helpless multitude. Supplies were brought up from Ostia and the neighboring towns and the price of wheat was reduced. . . . These measures, though in the public interest, were wasted, because a rumor had spread abroad that at the very time when the city was burning, Nero had mounted on his private stage and sung of the destruction of Troy, comparing the present disaster with that ancient catastrophe. . . .

. . . But no amount of human effort, no acts of generosity on the part of the emperor or appeasement of the gods could save Nero's reputation from the general belief that the fire had been set at his command.

In order to put an end to these rumors Nero provided scapegoats and visited most fearful punishments on those popularly called Christians, a group hated because of their outrageous practices. The founder of this sect, Christus, was executed in the reign of Tiberius by the procurator Pontius Pilatus. Thus the pernicious superstition was suppressed for the while, but it broke out again not only in Judaea, where this evil had its origin, but even in Rome, to which all ob-

"Selections from Tacitus," trans. Harry J. Leon, in *The Annals*, Book XLV, pp. 38, 44, in *Classics in Translation*, Vol. II : *Latin Literature*, ed. Paul MacKendrick and Herbert M. Howe (Madison : The University of Wisconsin Press, 1952), pp. 390, 392. Reprinted by permission.

1. Circus Maximus.

noxious and disgraceful elements flow from everywhere in the world and receive a large following. The first ones to be seized were those who confessed ; then on their information a vast multitude was convicted, not so much on the charge of incendiarism as because of their hatred of humanity. Their executions were made into a sport in that they were covered with skins of wild beasts and torn to pieces by dogs, or they were fastened to crosses or wrapped with inflammable materials, so that when the daylight waned, they could be burned to serve as torches in the night. Nero, who had offered his own gardens for this spectacle, gave a chariot-racing exhibition in which he mingled with the crowd dressed as a charioteer or drove a chariot. The result was that despite the fact that these people were criminals worthy of the worst kind of punishment, a feeling of sympathy arose for them, since they were being destroyed not for the public good but to satisfy the cruelty of one man.

45

Pliny the Younger, *Letters to Emperor Trajan*

After a senatorial career and consulship, Pliny the Younger was sent by Emperor Trajan as a special representative to the Roman province of Bithynia in Asia Minor. His task was to keep the peace. When he had trouble dealing with the Christians, Pliny wrote to the emperor asking how he should proceed against them. The emperor replied with a surprisingly humanitarian approach.

QUESTIONS TO CONSIDER

1. What caused Pliny to write to Emperor Trajan for advice?
2. How was Emperor Trajan's approach in dealing with Christians different from that of Nero (see Reading 44)?
3. Why did a misunderstanding of Christian rites lead Roman authorities to accuse the Christians of outlandish practices (see Readings 44 and 46)?
4. Why did the Christian religion appeal to all classes and sexes?

The Official Treatment of the Christians

It is my custom, Sire, to refer to you all matters in which I am in doubt. For who can better guide my hesitancy or instruct my ignorance ? I have never been present at trials of Christians ; therefore I do not know what is sought and punished,

"Selected Letters of the Younger Pliny," trans. John Paul Heironimus, in *Letters*, Book X, pp. 96–7, in *Classics in Translation*, Volume II : *Latin Literature*, ed. Paul MacKendrick and Herbert M. Howe (Madison : The University of Wisconsin Press, 1952), pp. 366–367. Reprinted by permission.

nor to what extent. I have been puzzled in no small degree as to whether there is any difference in the treatment of ages or if the young, no matter how young, are treated just like more mature defendants; whether pardon is given to those who repent or it avails not at all to have given up the aberration if one has once been a Christian; whether the name itself, if free from criminal practices, is punished or only the abominations that are associated with the name.

For the present I have followed this procedure in the case of those who were denounced to me as Christians: I asked the defendants in person whether they were Christians. If they admitted it I asked them for a second and third time, threatening punishment: if they persisted, I ordered them to be executed. For I had no doubt that whatever it was they were confessing, their persistence and unbending stubbornness deserved to be punished. There were others of similar folly whom I sent to Rome, since they were Roman citizens. Soon the accusation became common, as usual, from the very fact that cases were being tried, and several variations appeared. An anonymous information was lodged listing a number of names. If defendants who denied that they were now Christians or had been in the past would, following my example, pray to the gods and offer incense and wine to your statue, which I had had placed beside those of the gods for this purpose, and if they would curse Christ, they should, I thought, be dismissed; for it is declared that real Christians cannot be compelled to do any of these acts. Others, named by an informer, said that they were Christians but later denied it; they had indeed been, but had given up the practice, some of them several years ago, one even twenty years ago. All of these also worshipped your image and the statues of the gods, and cursed Christ. However, they asserted that their guilt or mistake had amounted to no more than this, that they had been accustomed on a set day to gather before dawn and to chant in antiphonal form a hymn to Christ as if to a god, and to bind themselves by a pledge, not for the commission of any crime, but rather that they would not commit theft nor robbery nor adultery nor break their promises, nor refuse to return on demand any treasure that had been entrusted to their care; when this ceremony had been completed, they would go away, to reassemble later for a feast, but an ordinary and innocent one. They had abandoned even this custom after my edict in which, following your instruction, I had forbidden the existence of fellowships. So I thought it the more necessary to extract the truth even by torture from two maidservants who were called deaconesses. I found nothing save a vile superstition carried to an immoderate length.

So, postponing further trials, I have resorted to consulting you. For it seemed to me a subject worthy of consultation, especially because of the number of people charged. For many of every age and rank, and of both sexes, are being brought to trial, and will be. The contagion of the superstition has pervaded not only the cities but the villages and country districts as well. Yet it seems that it can be halted and cured. It is well agreed that temples almost desolate have begun to be thronged again, and stated rites that had long been abandoned are revived; and a sale is found for the fodder of sacrificial victims, though hitherto buyers were rare. So it is easy to conjecture what a great number of offenders may be reformed, if a chance to repent is given.

The Emperor's Answer About the Christians

You have followed the proper course, my friend, in examining the cases of those who have been denounced to you as Christians. It is impossible to establish a hard and fast procedure for general use. They are not to be sought out; if they are accused, and the case is proved, they are to be punished, with the restriction, however, that if one denies that he is a Christian and makes it manifest in very deed, that is, by offering sacrifice to our gods, he shall be pardoned because of his repentance, however suspicious his past conduct was. Information lodged anonymously ought not to be regarded in dealing with any charge; it is of an abominable tendency, and not consonant with our enlightened age.

46

M. Minucius Felix, *Octavius*

Ancient Romans, like ancient Greeks, were broadly tolerant of diverse religious views. They did draw the line, however, at any physical display of disrespect for their divinities or their temples, calling such an act "sacrilege," and there were limits to how much of a blanket denial of all divinities they would put up with. At first, Christians suffered the same dislike within the Roman Empire as had the Jews for what the Romans took to be the unspeakable arrogance of considering their God to be the one and only deity. Mild forms of emperor-worship, such as throwing a bit of incense on a flame in front of an imperial statue, had become patriotic gestures, rather much like pledges of allegiance. When Christians rejected these as idolatry, Roman resentment turned into persecution. Until the end of the third century, however, Roman persecution of Christians was an on-again, off-again phenomenon, which put the sincerity of Christians to a severe test when it was going on but which was never sweeping enough to suppress Christianity or even keep it from growing.

Still, the anti-Christian decrees with at least occasional enforcement behind them made Christians wary of too much public exposure. Pagan Roman authorities had Christians coming and going. Since Christians were outlaws, they had no choice but to hold their meetings in secret. Yet Roman authorities were apt to take the very secrecy which the bans necessitated as proof that the Christians were at least hostile to Roman public culture, as the Jews were known to be, or up to no good and practicing perverse or criminal rites.

In the following selection from his dialogue, "Octavius," Marcus Minucius Felix lets the Roman pagan, Caecilius, set forth the reasons for denouncing Christians which were making the rounds, before he is overcome in the argument by Octavius, a Christian. Minucius Felix wrote in the late second or early third century; he is one of the earliest defenders of Christianity to write a Latin literary work that survives. While his Caecilius has the function within the dialogue of making outrageous charges for his Christian adversary to refute, the passages in which he does so vividly portray the sort of thing pagan Romans were willing to attribute to Christians before the fourth century.

QUESTIONS TO CONSIDER

1. Although Christians never had anything like the "initiation feasts" which Caecilius describes, what do you suppose did give rise to the rumor that they ate the flesh and drank the blood of innocent human victims?
2. In what aspects was (or is) the Christian view of immortality different from the Roman one? How far off base is Caecilius in describing the Christian view of the afterlife?
3. How do you suppose a pagan with the mind set of Caecilius would have responded to the Christians' assertion that they were not secretive with their worship services because they wanted to be?

[Caecilius is speaking:] "Considering how the Athenians banished Protagoras . . . and destroyed his writings, when he brought divinities into question only in philosophical arguments — not out-and-out profaning them — won't you agree that it is really a disgrace that among us a miserable gang of desperate outlaws (please excuse my language, but I am speaking with conviction) can organize open attacks on the gods? They enlist men from the very sewers and recruit gullible women, easy to fool as females normally are, and establish a group of secretive, unholy low-lifes united in their nocturnal gatherings, ritual fasts and the feasts unworthy of human beings which follow them, all for the sake of criminal rites, not for any recognizably sacred ones.

["These Christians] are a secretive group who flee the light, silent in public but with plenty to say in their cubby-holes. They despise the temples as if they were mere tombs, they spit upon the gods themselves, and they make fun of all that is sacred. Wretches to feel sorry for, they say — get this now — *they* feel sorry for our priests. They hold office-holders and official robes in contempt, going around half naked themselves. What amazing foolishness! What incredible arrogance! They are not worried about receiving the tortures they deserve here and now, but they fear unknown torments in the future. They fear a death after death; in the meantime, they are not afraid to die. Their false hope of being reborn happy flatters them into ignoring real terrors.

"Today . . . with immorality reaching epidemic proportions, their unholy league is spreading itself throughout the wide world. It must be exposed and eliminated. They recognize each other by occult signs and symbols, and they *love* each

From *Octavius*, ed. by J. P. Waltzing (Louvain: C. Peeters, 1905), pp. 211–231, *passim*. Translated by Henry A. Myers.

other even before they get acquainted. As they go their ways, they introduce a religion of physical desire, calling themselves 'brothers and sisters,' but their real ties to each other are those of lust, which use holy words to convert ordinary sex into incest, and so their vain and mindless superstition leads them to glory in their crime. If there were not some truth in what is told of them, the more intelligent public would not be spreading tales of their unspeakably gross practices. I hear that in a totally irresponsible mental state they worship the 'consecrated' head of an ass, for what reason I don't know — although actually a fitting religious practice for them, when you consider the immoral impulses which gave birth to their cult. Others say that they venerate the genitals of their priests and worship them, as if they had fathered their own selves. I don't know : that could be an exaggeration, but we are justified in being suspicious of occult and nocturnal rites. If we say that a dead felon and wood from the cross on which he was executed are prime objects of their veneration, we demonstrate the kind of worship characteristic of them, and so they deserve their bad reputation.

"Their initiation rite is as detestable as it is well known. They cake raw dough around an infant and set it in front of their recruit. He or she is directed to stab what looks deceptively like a dough image to an unwary person, and so, without knowing it, the recruit performs the initiation rite by inflicting wounds on the child until it is dead. Then they eagerly drink — how disgusting — its blood ; they hand around pieces of the body to eat, and the act of consuming the victim binds them together. Then, knowing full well the likely consequences of that crime, they pledge themselves to mutual silence. These 'sacred rites' are more criminally perverse than mere acts of sacrilege.

"Their regular feasts are adding to their bad reputation also. They get together at a set time [after dark] with all their children, sisters and mothers. Then, after much eating and drinking, to heat up their incestuous desires, they throw a scrap of meat in sight and smell of a dog, but the dog is tied to a candelabra, giving the only light, by a cord too short to reach the meat scrap, and so the dog jumps and pulls the candelabra over, putting out the light which would reveal their doings. Then in the shameless darkness, love-making takes place on a random basis, and while they may not all get to *do* it, they all become accomplices to incest by implicitly consenting to it.

" . . . The secrecy of this depraved religion confirms that all or most of these things are true. Why go to all the trouble of hiding whatever they are worshipping, when honest worship is always a matter for *public* rejoicing : evil things are the objects of secrets. Why do they have no altars, no temples, no images that you can recognize ? Why do they never speak in public or congregate in the open air unless whatever they are worshipping is either criminal or shameful?

"Where do they get this 'One God' of theirs, solitary, and pitiful, whom no free people, no kingdom, not even any superstition we Romans know of has accepted ? The wretched Jewish nation did worship that single god, but at least publicly, with temples, altars, and sacrificial victims, although he turned out to be a deity so weak, that he and his own chosen people are now in bondage to Rome. The Christian god, who can neither be seen nor shown, is one who eagerly seeks to know about the morals and deeds of men, even their words and secret thoughts. He sails everywhere and *is* everywhere. They see him as a troublesome, restless, and shamelessly prying being who interferes in everything.

"Then they consign the universe — the whole world and its stars — to total, fiery destruction, as if . . . the eternal order of nature established by divine laws could be disturbed. . . . Not content with this insane stance, they embellish it with fairy tales. They claim they are born again after death from their ashen remains, and with supreme confidence — which I don't know where they get — they reinforce each other's lies. You would think that they were already brought to life a second time. . . . They are deluded enough to consider themselves the good people who will be granted an eternity of bliss, with all others condemned to eternal punishment as evil."

47

Saint Augustine of Hippo, *The City of God*

In A.D. 410, the Visigothic armies of Alaric sacked Rome. Not only was this a major military defeat for the Empire in the West, but the victory of Arian Goths also undermined a basic doctrine widely held in Church circles since the time of Constantine : that people of the wrong religion could not prevail against orthodox Christian rulers.

Saint Augustine (A.D. 354–430) of Hippo in North Africa began the task of explaining the Roman debacle in the first of what were to become twenty-two books of *The City of God*. At the outset, he attempted to refute pagan claims that Rome had done better under its old gods than under the Christian God by recalling positive experiences for the Empire under its Christian rulers and arguing that Christian morality led these emperors, with God's aid and direction, to provide a happier life for Romans than their pagan predecessors had achieved. At the same time, he stressed that true Christians lose nothing of value in worldly calamities, which, of course, rendered the havoc of barbarian invasions relatively unimportant.

For Saint Augustine, the City of God, or the Heavenly City, includes God, the angels, and mortals predestined for salvation among its citizens. Those citizens of the Heavenly City who are making their way through earthly life pay no attention to material interests. Consequently, if churchgoers show too much concern about loss of property and physical suffering, they are probably citizens of the Earthly City in this life and doomed to hell in the hereafter. Citizens of the Earthly City are identified through their interests, which are limited to those earthly concerns that are insignificant to saved Christians.

Saint Augustine worked on *The City of God* for thirteen years. Early in the project, he seems to have realized that comprehensive proof of the relative happiness of Christian times should be presented more systematically than he was doing, and so he entrusted that part of his work to Paulus Orosius, a young priest from Spain, who had come to serve him and study with him. Orosius fulfilled his research and writing assignment with *Seven Books of History Against the Pagans,* in which he selected, reordered, and interpreted historical facts in such a way as to make Christian times appear happier, more peaceful, and more blessed by Roman military victories than pagan times. For over a thousand years, this work enjoyed great success in the West as the most readable and comprehensive Christian world history.

Orosius did not succeed in pleasing Saint Augustine with his finished product, however. By the time Orosius was through, Saint Augustine was writing the later books of *The City of God* and had lost interest in associating victory, or anything of the sort, with Christian times and rulers. Instead he focused on the concept of peace within the Heavenly City and the nature of coexistence between the Heavenly City and the Earthly City.

The first selections that follow are from the early books of *The City of God*; the last two from the much later Book XIX. Two different and very influential Christian theories of history emerge in the work of Saint Augustine and Orosius. In the early books of *The City of God* and consistently in *Seven Books of History Against the Pagans,* God rewards Christian emperors and peoples for faith and good works, rather much as Jahweh rewarded the Children of Israel for the same thing. Then, in *The City of God* as a whole, particularly the later books, a theory unfolds more consistent with New Testament values: The Christian kingdom is not of this world, and true Christians should not worry much about even such momentous, earthly happenings as lost wars and falling empires.

QUESTIONS TO CONSIDER

1. Why does Saint Augustine view the sack of Rome as a cause for heightened, rather than diminished, respect for Christianity?
2. Compare Kautilya's statement from the *Duties of a King* (Reading 24): "In the happiness of the subjects lies the happiness of the king ... " with Saint Augustine's statement on the happiness of Christian emperors.
3. Why is a temporary peace observable between the City of God and the Earthly City?
4. Why does Saint Augustine say that the City of God or the Heavenly City is in a state of pilgrimage on earth?
5. What was going on in the years A.D. 410–423, in which Saint Augustine was writing *The City of God,* that might well have led him to modify his original stance that people enjoyed a better quality of peace under Christian emperors than under their predecessors?

Elements of Christian Emperors' Real Happiness

We call the Christian emperors happy if they rule justly; if they are not carried away by conceit in the midst of voices praising them extravagantly and by men hailing them with a debasing show of excess humility, but remember that they are men; if they turn their power to the service of the Divine Majesty, by using it to spread the worship of God as far as they can; and if they fear love, and worship

De civitate Dei libri xxii, ed. Emanuel Hoffman (Vienna: F. Tempsky, 1899–1900), extracts from Books I–V and Book XIX, passim. Translated by Henry A. Myers.

God. We call them happy if they are relatively slow with punishments, inflicting them only when pressed by the requirements of governing and defending the state, but are all the more quick with pardons, not to let crimes go unpunished but in the hope of rehabilitating the offenders; and if they make up for often necessarily harsh decrees with kindness and mercy and with sweeping generosity. We call them happy if they restrict their luxury all the more as their wealth lets them afford it; if they prefer ruling over low desires within themselves to ruling over any nation at all; and if they do all this not out of a passion for vain glory but out of a love for eternal happiness, without failing to offer the sacrifice of humility, mercy and prayer for their sins to their own true God.

The Prosperity God Granted Emperor Constantine

On Emperor Constantine . . . God bestowed such an abundance of earthly favors as no man would dare wish for. He permitted him to found a city to share in the imperial rule of Rome, a daughter, so to speak, of Rome herself but without any temples or images of the demons.[1] He reigned for a long time, maintaining the whole Roman world as sole emperor. He was most victorious in directing and waging wars, and he was always successful in putting down usurpers. He was very old when he died of sickness and age, and he left sons to rule after him.

The Faith and Piety of Emperor Theodosius [I]

Theodosius . . . put down the usurper Eugenius, who had illegally installed himself in that emperor's place, prevailing against his very powerful army more by prayer than by the sword. Some soldiers who were there have told me that all the spears they were throwing were snatched from their hands by a very strong wind, which blew away from Theodosius' side in the enemy's direction, and that it not only gave greater force to whatever they threw against them but even turned back the spears which the enemy soldiers were throwing into their own bodies. . . .

About the War in Which King Radagais of the Goths, a Worshipper of Demons, Was Defeated with His Huge Army in a Single Day

When Radagais, King of the Goths, was already threatening the Romans' very necks with his huge and savage army encamped near the city, he was beaten in one day with such speed and in such a way that not one single Roman was wounded, let alone killed, while well over a hundred thousand of his soldiers were struck down, and he was captured and soon put to a deserved death. For if such a godless man with such equally godless troops had entered Rome, who would have been spared by him? What shrines of the martyrs would he have respected? In dealing with what person would the fear of God have restrained him? Whose blood would he have wanted to leave unshed and whose chastity unravaged?

1. Reference is to Constantinople, founded by Constantine upon the site of Byzantium, which, of course, had previously contained pagan temples, although Constantine tried to make the new capital a purely Christian city.

**Whether the Sweep of Imperial Command ... Is among Things of Value
for Wise and Happy Men**

It makes sense that if the true God is worshipped and served with true rites and
good morals, it is a benefit for good men to have long reigns over great territories.
This is actually not of so much use to themselves as it is to their subjects, because as
far as they themselves are concerned their own true faith and righteousness,
which are great gifts from God, are enough to give them the true happiness that
lets them live this life well and attain eternal life afterwards. Thus the reign of
good men here on earth does not serve their own good so much as it does human
concerns.

**The Harsh Brutality in the Sack of Rome Corresponded with Established Customs
of War, While the Mercy Shown Revealed the Power of Christ's Name**

All the destruction, killing, looting, burning, and suffering which took place in
the recent sack of Rome happened in accordance with the customs of waging war.
What was altogether new and previously unheard of, however, was that the barbarian brutality [of the Goths] was so tamed that they picked the largest of the ba-
silicas and allowed them to remain sanctuaries, where no one could be struck
down and from which no one could be dragged away. Many people were led there
to freedom and safety by soldiers showing sympathy for them. ... Anyone who
does not see fit to credit this to the name of Christ — yes, to Christian times — is
blind. Anyone who sees this new turn of events but fails to praise it is most
ungrateful.

The Saints Lose Nothing of Value in Losing Material Goods

In the sack of Rome faithful and godly men ... "lost everything they had." How
about their faith? How about their godliness? How about the goods of the inner
being which make a person rich before God? Listen to what the Apostle Paul says
about the riches of Christianity: "... Godliness with contentment is great gain,
for we brought nothing into this world and certainly we can carry nothing out. If
we have food and clothing, let us be content with them. People who want to be rich
fall into temptations and traps. They fall into foolish and harmful desires which
drown men in destruction and perdition."[2]

**The Universal Peace, Which the Law of Nature Preserves through All
Disturbances, and the Condition Which Each Person Deserves to Find
Himself in, according to the Way He Has Used His Will and according
to the Decision of the Just Judge**

... Domestic peace is a harmonious arrangement in matters of command and obedience among those of the same household, and the peace of a [normal] city is a

2. I *Timothy,* 6:6–10.

similar one among its citizens. The peace of the Heavenly City is the most perfectly and harmoniously designed communal relationship in the enjoyment of God and in the fellowship resulting from union with God. Peace for all beings is tranquillity within order. Order is the arrangement of equal and unequal things, with each assigned its proper place.

And so we see that miserable people [lacking faith and godliness] . . . in the very fact that they justly deserve their misery are confined to a condition of misery by the principle of order. This keeps them from being united with saved people. When they live without obvious disturbances they adapt to their bondage, and so there is a bit of tranquil order among them, and so they enjoy a peace of sorts. They still remain miserable, however, since, in spite of not suffering constantly from a total lack of security, they are not within that realm where there is no cause to worry about either suffering or security. . . .

Where Peace and Discord between the Heavenly and Earthly Cities Come From

The Earthly City, which does not live by faith, desires an earthly peace, seeking to bring it about through harmony of command and obedience among citizens, even though its scope is limited to uniting people's wills on matters pertaining to this mortal life.

The Heavenly City, however, or, to be more precise, those of its members who are living by faith during their mortal pilgrimages, must make use of this peace, although only until they are through with their transient status on earth, which requires it. For this reason, the Heavenly City sojourning either as a captive or a wandering stranger in the Earthly City does not hesitate to obey earthly authority in matters required by the communal life of mortals. With mortal life common to the people of both Cities, a certain harmony between them may be maintained in relation to its requirements.

While the Heavenly City sojourns on earth, it recruits members from all peoples and forms a pilgrim society of men and women speaking all different languages, which pays no attention to the diversity of customs, laws, and institutions among them, by which earthly peace is established and maintained.

48

Monastic Life: The Rule of Saint Benedict

In the midst of a disorderly world, medieval monasteries established communities devoted to achieving salvation. Saint Benedict of Nursia (A.D. 480–543), the most influential figure in Western European monastic history, came from a wealthy Italian family; but at age 20, he renounced all worldly temptations and withdrew to the mountains to live as a hermit. His reputation for holiness led others to seek him out, and in time they became his devoted disciples.

Saint Benedict eventually decided that a communal setting was a better environment for most men trying to lead a life pleasing to God. He founded 12 monasteries in Italy before he and his followers built a large one at Monte Cassino around 529, where he applied his "Rule" and lived the rest of his life. Requiring vows of chastity, poverty, and obedience, Saint Benedict's Rule became the basis for monastic life in the West.

Unlike the stricter Celtic monasticism of Saint Columban, the strength of Saint Benedict's Rule lies in its combination of religious commitment, encouragement of good works along with faith, and common-sense moderation in discipline. In contrast, the more extreme Celtic rules required severe punishment for even unintentional lapses. The Benedictine model is the family, with the abbot in the role of a strict, but patient and loving, father. Other members of the community overcome un-Christian willfulness through continual acts of humility; they complete their tasks in a mutually supportive fashion as brothers. In the year before Saint Benedict died, his sister, Scholastica, founded a convent near Monte Cassino. With appropriate modifications, the Benedictine Rule guided nuns as well as monks in the medieval West.

QUESTIONS TO CONSIDER

1. What should the monk do in order to achieve progressively greater degrees of humility?
2. What are Saint Benedict's guidelines for correcting the faults of those who commit offenses?
3. What is Saint Benedict's basic attitude toward providing food, drink, and other necessities of life for the monks?

What Kind of Man the Abbot Ought to Be

An abbot who is worthy to rule over the monastery ought always to remember what he is called, and correspond to his name of superior by his deeds. For he is believed to hold the place of Christ in the monastery, since he is called by his name, as the apostle says: 'You have received the spirit of the adoption of children, in which we cry Abba, Father.' And, therefore, the abbot ought not (God forbid) to teach, or ordain, or command anything contrary to the law of the Lord; but let his bidding and his doctrine be infused into the minds of his disciples like the leaven of divine justice.

Let the abbot be ever mindful that at the dreadful judgment of God an account will have to be given both of his own teaching and of the obedience of his disciples. And let him know that to the fault of the shepherd shall be imputed any

From "The Rule of Saint Benedict," trans. Dom Oswald Hunter Blair, in Emmanuel Heufelder, *The Way to God According to the Rule of St. Benedict* (Kalamazoo, MI: Cistercian Publications, 1983), pp. 224–266, passim. Reprinted by permission of Fort Augustus Abbey.

lack of profit which the father of the household may find in his sheep. Only then shall he be acquitted, if he shall have bestowed all pastoral diligence on his unquiet and disobedient flock, and employed all his care to amend their corrupt manner of life: then shall he be absolved in the judgment of the Lord.

For the abbot in his doctrine ought always to observe the bidding of the apostle, wherein he says: 'Reprove, entreat, rebuke'; mingling, as occasions may require, gentleness with severity; showing now the rigor of a master, now the loving affection of a father, so as sternly to rebuke the undisciplined and restless, and to exhort the obedient, mild, and patient to advance in virtue. And such as are negligent and haughty we charge him to reprove and correct. Let him not shut his eyes to the faults of offenders; but as soon as they appear, let him strive with all his might to root them out, remembering the fate of Eli, the priest of Shiloh. Those of good disposition and understanding let him, for the first or second time, correct only with words; but such as are forward and hard of heart, and proud, or disobedient, let him chastise with bodily stripes at the very first offence, knowing that it is written: 'The fool is not corrected with words.' . . .

Of Obedience

The first degree of humility is obedience without delay. This becomes those who hold nothing dearer to them than Christ, and who on account of the holy servitude which they have taken upon them, either for fear of hell or for the glory of life everlasting, as soon as anything is ordered by the superior, suffer no more delay in doing it than if it had been commanded by God himself. It is of these that the Lord says: 'At the hearing of the ear he has obeyed me.' And again, to teachers he says: 'He that hears you hears me.'

Such as these, therefore, leaving immediately their own occupations and forsaking their own will, with their hands disengaged, and leaving unfinished what they were about, with the speedy step of obedience follow by their deeds the voice of him who commands; and so as it were at the same instant the bidding of the master and the perfect fulfilment of the disciple are joined together in the swiftness of the fear of God by those who are moved with the desire of attaining eternal life.

Of the Practice of Silence

Let us do as says the prophet: 'I said, I will take heed to my ways, that I sin not with my tongue, I have placed a watch over my mouth; I became dumb and was silent, and held my peace even from good things.' Here the prophet shows that if we ought at times to refrain even from good words for the sake of silence, how much more ought we to abstain from evil words, on account of the punishment due to sin. Therefore, on account of the importance of silence, let leave to speak be seldom granted even to perfect disciples, although their conversation be good and holy and tending to edification; because it is written: 'In much speaking you shall not avoid sin.' . . . But as for buffoonery or idle words, such as move to laughter, we utterly condemn them in every place, nor do we allow the disciple to open his mouth in such discourse. . . .

Of Humility

The Holy Scripture cries out to us, brothers, saying : 'Every one that exalts himself shall be humbled, and he who humbles himself shall be exalted.' . . .

The first degree of humility, then, is that a man, always keeping the fear of God before his eyes, avoid all forgetfulness ; and that he be ever mindful of all that God has commanded, bethinking himself that those who despise God will be consumed in hell for their sins, and that life everlasting is prepared for them that fear him. . . .

The second degree of humility is, that a man love not his own will, nor delight in fulfilling his own desires ; but carry out in his deeds that saying of the Lord : 'I came not to do mine own will, but the will of him who sent me.' And again Scripture says : 'Self-will has punishment, but necessity wins the crown.'

The third degree of humility is, that a man for the love of God submit himself to his superior in all obedience ; imitating the Lord, of whom the apostle says : 'He was made obedient even unto death.'

The fourth degree of humility is, that if in this very obedience hard and contrary things, nay even injuries, are done to him, he should embrace them patiently with a quiet conscience, and not grow weary or give in, as the Scripture says : 'He that shall persevere to the end shall be saved.' And again : 'Let your heart be comforted, and wait for the Lord.'

The fifth degree of humility is, not to hide from one's abbot any of the evil thoughts that beset one's heart, or the sins committed in secret, but humbly to confess them. Concerning which the Scripture exhorts us, saying : 'Make known your way unto the Lord, and hope in him.' . . .

The sixth degree of humility is for a monk to be contented with the meanest and worst of everything, and in all that is enjoined him to esteem himself a bad and worthless laborer, saying with the prophet : 'I have been brought to nothing, and I knew it not : I am become as a beast before you, yet I am always with you.'

The seventh degree of humility is that he should not only call himself with his tongue lower and viler than all, but also believe himself in his inmost heart to be so, humbling himself, and saying with the prophet : 'I am a worm and no man, the shame of men and the outcast of the people : I have been exalted, and cast down, and confounded.' . . .

The eighth degree of humility is for a monk to do nothing except what is authorized by the common rule of the monastery, or the example of the seniors.

The ninth degree of humility is, that a monk refrain his tongue from speaking, keeping silence until a question be asked him, as the Scripture shows : 'In much talking you shall not avoid sin,' and, 'The talkative man shall not be directed upon the earth.'

The tenth degree of humility is, that he be not easily moved and prompt to laughter ; because it is written : 'The fool lifts up his voice in laughter.' . . .

Having, therefore, ascended all these degrees of humility, the monk will presently arrive at that love of God which, being perfect, casts out fear. . . .

Of Those Who, Being Often Corrected, Do Not Amend

If any brother who has been frequently corrected for some fault, or even ex-communicated, does not amend, let a more severe chastisement be applied: that is, let the punishment of stripes be administered to him. But if even then he does not correct himself, or perchance (which God forbid), puffed up with pride, even wishes to defend his deeds, then let the abbot act like a wise physician. If he has applied fomentations and the unction of his admonitions, the medicine of the Holy Scriptures, and the last remedy of excommunication or corporal chastisement, and if he see that his labors are of no avail, let him add what is still more powerful, his own prayers and those of all the brothers for him, that God, who is all-powerful, may work the cure of the sick brother. But if he be not healed even by this means, then at length let the abbot use the sword of separation, as the apostle says: 'Put away the evil one from you.' And again: 'If the faithless one depart, let him depart,' lest one diseased sheep should taint the whole flock. . . .

What Kind of Man the Cellarer of the Monastery Is to Be

Let there be chosen out of the community, as cellarer of the monastery, a man wise and of mature character, temperate, not a great eater, not haughty, nor head-strong, nor arrogant, not slothful, nor wasteful, but a Godfearing man, who may be like a father to the whole community. Let him have the care of everything, but do nothing without leave of the abbot. Let him take heed to what is commanded him, and not sadden his brothers. If a brother ask him for anything unreasonably, let him not treat him with contempt and so grieve him, but reasonably and with all humility refuse what he asks for amiss. Let him be watchful over his own soul, re-membering always that saying of the apostle, that 'he that has ministered well, pur-chases to himself a good degree.' Let him have special care of the sick, of the children, of guests and of the poor, knowing without doubt that he will have to render an account of them all on the day of judgment. . . .

Whether Monks Ought to Have Anything of Their Own

The vice of private ownership is above all to be cut off from the monastery by the roots. Let none presume to give or receive anything without leave of the abbot, nor to keep anything as their own, either book or writing-tablet or pen, or anything whatsoever; since they are permitted to have neither body nor will in their own power. But all that is necessary they may hope to receive from the father of the monastery; nor are they allowed to keep anything which the abbot has not given, or at least permitted them to have. Let all things be com-mon to all, as it is written: 'Neither did anyone say that anything which he pos-sessed was his own.' But if anyone should be found to indulge in this most baneful vice, and after one or two admonitions does not amend, let him be sub-jected to correction. . . .

Whether All Ought Alike to Receive What Is Needful

As it is written : 'Distribution was made to every man, according as he had need.'
Herein we do not say that there should be respecting of persons — God forbid —
but consideration for infirmities. Let him, therefore, that has need of less give
thanks to God and not be grieved ; and let him who requires more be humbled for
his infirmity and not made proud by the kindness shown to him ; and so all members of the family shall be at peace. Above all, let not the evil of murmuring show
itself by the slightest word or sign on any account whatever. If anyone be found
guilty herein, let him be subjected to severe punishment. . . .

Of the Weekly Servers in the Kitchen

Let the brothers wait on one another in turn, so that none be excused from the
work of the kitchen, except he be prevented by sickness or by some more necessary employment ; for thus is gained a greater reward and an increase of charity.
But let assistance be given to the weak, that they may not do their work with sadness ; and let all have help according to the number of the community and the situation of the place. If the community be large, let the cellarer be excused from
work in the kitchen, and also those, as already mentioned, who are occupied in
more urgent business. Let the rest serve each other in turn with all charity. Let
him who ends his week in the kitchen make all things clean on Saturday and wash
the towels with which the brothers dry their hands and feet. Let both him who
goes out and him who is coming in wash the feet of all. Let him hand over to the
cellarer the vessels of his office, clean and whole ; and let the cellarer deliver the
same to him who enters, that he may know what he gives and what he receives.
     Let the weekly servers each take a cup of drink and a piece of bread over and
above the appointed portion, one hour before the time for refection, that so they
may serve their brothers when the hour comes without murmuring or great
labor. . . .

Of Old Men and Children

Although human nature is of itself drawn to feel pity for these two times of life,
namely, old age and infancy, yet the authority of the Rule should also provide for
them. Let their weakness be always taken into account, and the strictness of the
Rule respecting food be by no means kept in their regard ; but let a kind consideration be shown for them, and let them eat before the regular hours. . . .

Of the Measure of Food

We think it sufficient for the daily meal, whether at the sixth or the ninth hour,
that there be at all seasons of the year two dishes of cooked food, because of the
weakness of different people ; so that he who perchance cannot eat the one, may
make his meal of the other. Let two dishes, then, suffice for all the brothers ; and if

there be any fruit or young vegetables, let a third be added. Let one pound weight of bread suffice for the day, whether there be but one meal or both dinner and supper. . . .

Of the Measure of Drink

Everyone has his proper gift from God, one after this manner, another after that. And, therefore, it is with some misgiving that we appoint the measure of other men's living. Yet, considering the infirmity of the weak, we think that one pint of wine a day is sufficient for each ; but let those to whom God gives the endurance of abstinence know that they shall have their proper reward. If, however, the situation of the place, the work, or the heat of summer require more, let it be in the power of the superior to grant it, taking care in every thing that surfeit or drunkenness creep not in. And although we read that wine ought by no means to be the drink of monks, yet since in our times monks cannot be persuaded of this, let us at least agree to drink not to satiety, but sparingly ; because 'wine makes even the wise to fall away.' But where the necessity of the place allows not even the aforesaid measure, but much less, or none at all, let those who dwell there bless God and not murmur. This above all we admonish, that there be no murmuring among them.

The Reign of Emperor Justinian

Upon the death of his uncle Justin I, Justinian (A.D. 527–565) became Roman Emperor and immediately had his wife, Theodora (a former prostitute), crowned Empress. Together they worked hard to meet the challenges of imperial rule. In A.D. 532, Theodora's timely advice helped Justinian successfully suppress the Nika tax riots in Constantinople.

Justinian's central policy was to reunite the Western Roman Empire, which had fallen to various barbarian Germanic peoples, with the East. This goal was accomplished with the aid of many great generals ; for example, Belisarius conquered Vandal-held Africa and led the first invasions of Ostrogothic Italy. In addition to the Western reunification, there were a series of confrontations with the Sassanid Persian Empire in Syria-Palestine and Armenia. In these latter engagements, Justinian sent his armies but preferred to reach a series of very expensive truces with Persia rather than any definitive conclusion.

Another imperial objective was peace within the Christian Church, which was disturbed by heretics called Monophysites. These Christians rejected the orthodox view that Christ had two natures, human and divine ; they rejected Christ's humanity and stressed only his divine nature. After attempting a series of compromises, Justinian finally resorted to religious persecution that only increased the dissatisfaction of orthodox and heretics alike.

Our major source for Justinian's reign is Procopius of Caesarea. Born about A.D. 500, he went to Constantinople, where he became the private secretary (c. 527) to General Belisarius. From his pen came three known works: *History of the Wars, On the Buildings,* and the *Secret History.* The first book details the events concerning Justinian's wars in Africa, Italy, and Persia. The second work praises the emperor for his architectural contributions such as the rebuilding of Santa Sophia, which had been destroyed in the Nika riots. Yet it is Procopius' third and smallest book — the *Secret History* or *Anecdota* — that has given him the most fame. It records in vitriolic splendor the "crimes," vices, and scandals of Justinian, Theodora, General Belisarius, and his wife Antonina.

49

Procopius, *History of the Wars*

In A.D. 532, citizens of Constantinople revolted against the tax policies of Emperor Justinian. The following selection reveals Empress Theodora's part in controlling this uprising.

QUESTIONS TO CONSIDER

1. Why was Empress Theodora one of the most influential women in Byzantine history?
2. Compare Procopius' description of Theodora's early life with the present selection (see Reading 50). What are the most significant differences in his views?
3. What other women in history had so much influence?

At this same time an insurrection broke out unexpectedly in Byzantium among the populace, and, contrary to expectation, it proved to be a very serious affair, and ended in great harm to the people and to the senate, as the following account will show. In every city the population has been divided for a long time past into the Blue and the Green factions; but within comparatively recent times it has come about that, for the sake of these names and the seats which the rival factions occupy in watching the games, they spend their money and abandon their bodies to the most cruel tortures, and even do not think it unworthy to die a most shameful death. And they fight against their opponents knowing not for what end they imperil themselves, but knowing well that, even if they overcome their enemy in the fight, the conclusion of the matter for them will be to be carried off straightway to the prison, and finally, after suffering extreme torture, to be destroyed. So there grows up in them against their fellow men a hostility which has no cause, and

Reprinted by permission of the publishers and the Loeb Classical Library from Procopius, *History of the Wars*, Book I, trans. H. B. Dewing (Cambridge, MA: Harvard University Press, 1914/1961), pp. 219, 223, 231, 233.

at no time does it cease or disappear, for it gives place neither to the ties of marriage nor of relationship nor of friendship, and the case is the same even though those who differ with respect to these colours be brothers or any other kin. They care neither for things divine nor human in comparison with conquering in these struggles; and it matters not whether a sacrilege is committed by anyone at all against God, or whether the laws and the constitution are violated by friend or by foe; nay even when they are perhaps ill supplied with the necessities of life, and when their fatherland is in the most pressing need and suffering unjustly, they pay no heed if only it is likely to go well with their "faction"; for so they name the bands of partisans. And even women join with them in this unholy strife, and they not only follow the men, but even resist them if opportunity offers, although they neither go to the public exhibitions at all, nor are they impelled by any other cause; so that I, for my part, am unable to call this anything except a disease of the soul. This, then, is pretty well how matters stand among the people of each and every city.

But at this time the officers of the city administration in Byzantium were leading away to death some of the rioters. But the members of the two factions, conspiring together and declaring a truce with each other, seized the prisoners and then straightway entered the prison and released all those who were in confinement there, whether they had been condemned on a charge of stirring up sedition, or for any other unlawful act. And all the attendants in the service of the city government were killed indiscriminately; meanwhile, all of the citizens who were sane-minded were fleeing to the opposite mainland, and fire was applied to the city as if it had fallen under the hand of an enemy. The sanctuary of Sophia and the baths of Zeuxippus, and the portion of the imperial residence from the propylaea as far as the so-called House of Ares were destroyed by fire, and besides these both the great colonnades which extended as far as the market place which bears the name of Constantine, in addition to many houses of wealthy men and a vast amount of treasure. During this time the emperor and his consort with a few members of the senate shut themselves up in the palace and remained quietly there. Now the watchword which the populace passed around to one another was Nika,[1] and the insurrection has been called by this name up to the present time. . . .

Now the emperor and his court were deliberating as to whether it would be better for them if they remained or if they took to flight in the ships. And many opinions were expressed favouring either course. And the Empress Theodora also spoke to the following effect: "As to the belief that a woman ought not to be daring among men or to assert herself boldly among those who are holding back from fear, I consider that the present crisis most certainly does not permit us to discuss whether the matter should be regarded in this or in some other way. For in the case of those whose interests have come into the greatest danger nothing else seems best except to settle the issue immediately before them in the best possible way. My opinion then is that the present time, above all others, is inopportune for flight, even though it bring safety. For while it is impossible for a man who has seen the light not also to die, for one who has been an emperor it is unendurable to be a fugitive. May I never be separated from this purple, and may I not live that

1. Conquest or victory.

day on which those who meet me shall not address me as mistress. If, now, it is your wish to save yourself, O Emperor, there is no difficulty. For we have much money, and there is the sea, here the boats. However consider whether it will not come about after you have been saved that you would gladly exchange that safety for death. For as for myself, I approve a certain ancient saying that royalty is a good burial-shroud." When the queen had spoken thus, all were filled with boldness, and, turning their thoughts towards resistance, they began to consider how they might be able to defend themselves if any hostile force should come against them.

50

Procopius, *The Secret History*

Belisarius was Justinian's most important general. However, Procopius relates how easily Belisarius was deceived by his unscrupulous wife Antonina.

QUESTIONS TO CONSIDER

1. Why would Procopius not want his *Secret History* published in his lifetime?
2. How were the depictions of Belisarius and Justinian less than flattering?
3. Compare Procopius' views of women in *The Secret History* with those in *History of the Wars.*

Belisarius had a wife, whom I have had occasion to mention in the previous books; her father and grandfather were charioteers who had given exhibitions of their skill in both Byzantium and Thessalonica, and her mother was one of the prostitutes attached to the theatre. This woman, having in her early years lived a lewd sort of a life and having become dissolute in character, not only having consorted much with the cheap sorcerers who surrounded her parents, but also having thus acquired the knowledge of what she needed to know, later became the wedded wife of Belisarius, after having already been the mother of many children. Straightway, therefore, she decided upon being an adulteress from the very start, but she was very careful to conceal this business, not because she was ashamed of her own practices, nor because she entertained any fear so far as her husband was concerned (for she never experienced the slightest feeling of shame for any action whatsoever and she had gained complete control of her husband by means of many tricks of magic), but because she dreaded the punishment the Empress might inflict. . . .

Reprinted by permission of the publishers and the Loeb Classical Library from Procopius, *The Secret History or Anecdota*, Vol. 6, trans. H. B. Dewing (Cambridge, MA : Harvard University Press, 1935/1960), pp. 7, 13, 95, 107, 111.

There was a certain youth from Thrace in the household of Belisarius, Theodosius by name. . . . Now when Belisarius was about to embark on the voyage to Libya, he bathed this youth in the sacred bath, from which he lifted him with his own hands, thus making him the adopted child of himself and his wife, as is customary for Christians to make adoptions, and consequently Antonina loved Theodosius, as she naturally would, as being her son through the sacred word, and with very particular solicitude she kept him near herself. And straightway she fell extraordinarily in love with him in the course of this voyage, and having become insatiate in her passion, she shook off both fear and respect for everything both divine and human and had intercourse with him, at first in secret, but finally even in the presence of servants of both sexes. For being by now possessed by this passion and manifestly smitten with love, she could see no longer any obstacle to the deed. And on one occasion Belisarius caught them in the very act in Carthage, yet he willingly allowed himself to be deceived by his wife. For though he found them both in an underground chamber and was transported with rage, she, without either playing the coward or attempting to conceal the deed, remarked "I came down here in order to hide with the aid of the boy the most valuable of our booty, so that it may not get to the knowledge of the Emperor." Now she said this as a mere pretext, but he, appearing to be satisfied, dropped the matter, though he could see that the belt which supported the drawers of Theodosius, covering his private parts, had been loosened. For under compulsion of love for the woman, he would have it that the testimony of his own eyes was absolutely untrustworthy.

> In another section of *The Secret History,* Procopius describes the nature and moral character of the emperor.

And I think it not inappropriate to describe the appearance of this man. He was neither tall in stature nor particularly short, but of a medium height, yet not thin but slightly fleshy, and his face was round and not uncomely ; for his complexion remained ruddy even after two days of fasting. But that I may describe his appearance as a whole in few words, I would say that he resembled Domitian, son of Vespasian, very closely, an Emperor who so impressed the Romans who suffered under him that even after they had chopped his whole body into pieces they felt that they had not satisfied their rage against him. . . .

Such was Justinian in appearance ; but his character I could not accurately describe. For this man was both an evil-doer and easily led into evil, the sort of a person whom they call a moral pervert, never of his own accord speaking the truth to those with whom he conversed, but having a deceitful and crafty intent behind every word and action, and at the same time exposing himself, an easy prey, to those who wished to deceive him. And a certain unusual mixture had developed in him, compounded of both folly and wickedness. And possibly this illustrated a saying uttered by one of the Peripatetic philosophers in earlier times, to the effect that the most opposite elements are found in man's nature, just as in mixed colours. (I am now writing, however, of matters in which I have not been able to attain competency.) But to resume, this Emperor was insincere, crafty, hypocritical, dissembling his anger, double-dealing, clever, a perfect artist in acting out an opinion which he pretended to hold, and even able to produce tears, not from joy or sorrow, but contriving them for the occasion according to the need of the moment, always playing false, yet not carelessly but adding both his signature and the most terrible oaths to bind his agreements, and that too in dealing with his own subjects. But he departed straightway from his agreements and his oaths, just like the vilest slaves, who, through fear of the tortures hanging over them, are induced to make confession of acts which they had denied on oath. He was a fickle friend, a truceless enemy, an ardent devotee of assassination and of robbery, quarrelsome and an inveterate innovator, easily led astray into wrong, but influenced by no counsel to adopt the right, keen to conceive and to execute base designs, but looking upon even the hearing about good things as distasteful. How could any man be competent to describe adequately the character of Justinian? These faults and many others still greater he manifestly possessed to a degree not in accord with human nature. On the contrary, Nature seemed to have removed all baseness from the rest of mankind and to have concentrated it in the soul of this man. And in addition to his other shortcomings, while he was very easy-going as to lending an ear to slanders, yet he was severe as to inflicting punishment. For he never paused for a thorough investigation before reaching a decision, but straightway upon hearing what the slanderer said, he would make his decision and order it published. And he did not hesitate to write orders that called for the capture of towns and the burning of cities and the enslavement of whole peoples, for no reason whatever. Consequently, if one should care to estimate all the misfortunes which have befallen the Romans from the earliest times and then to balance against them those of the present day, it seems to me that he would find a greater slaughter of human beings to have been perpetrated by this man than has come to pass in all the preceding time. And while he had no scruples whatever against the quiet acquisition of other men's money — for he never even made any excuse, putting forward justice as a screen in trespassing upon things which did not belong to him — yet when once these had become his own, he was perfectly ready to shew his contempt for the money, with a prodigality in which there was no trace of calculation, and for no reason at all to fling it away to the barbarians. And, to sum up the whole matter, he neither had any money himself, nor would he allow anyone else in the world to have it, as though he were not a victim of avarice, but simply consumed by envy of those who possessed money. Consequently he lightly banished wealth from the Roman world and became the creator of poverty for all.

In the following section of *The Secret History,* Procopius describes Theodora's unsavory life before she met and married Justinian.

The traits, then, of Justinian's character, as far as we are able to state them, were roughly these. And he married a wife concerning whom I shall now relate how she was born and reared and how, after being joined to this man in marriage, she overturned the Roman State to its very foundations. There was in Byzantium a certain Acacius, keeper of the animals used in the circus, an adherent of the Green Faction, a man whom they called Master of the Bears. This man had died a natural death during the reign of Anastasius, leaving three girls, Comito, Theodora and Anastasia, the eldest of whom was not yet seven years of age. And the woman, now reduced to utter distress, entered into marriage with another husband, who, she thought, would later on assist her in both the care of the household and in her first husband's occupation. But the Dancing Master of the Greens, a man named Asterius, was bribed by another man to remove these persons from that office and to make no difficulty about putting in the position the man who had given him the money. For the Dancing Masters had authority to administer such matters as they wished. But when the woman saw the whole populace gathered in the Circus, she put garlands on the heads and in both hands of the three girls and caused them to sit as suppliants. And though the Greens were by no means favourable to receiving the supplication, the Blues conferred this position of honour upon them, since their Master of the Bears also had recently died. And when these children came of age, the mother immediately put them on the stage there — since they were fair to look upon — not all three at the same time, but as each one seemed to her to be ripe for this calling. Now Comito, the first one, had already scored a brilliant success among the harlots of her age ; and Theodora, the next in order, clothed in a little sleeved frock suitable to a slave girl, would follow her about, performing various services and in particular always carrying on her shoulders the stool on which her sister was accustomed to sit in the assemblies. Now for a time Theodora, being immature, was quite unable to sleep with a man or to have a woman's kind of intercourse with one, yet she did engage in intercourse of a masculine type of lewdness with the wretches, slaves though they were, who, following their masters to the theatre, incidentally took advantage of the opportunity afforded them to carry on this monstrous business, and she spent much time in the brothel in this unnatural traffic of the body. But as soon as she came of age and was at last mature, she joined the women of the stage and straightway became a courtesan, of the sort whom men of ancient times used to call "infantry." For she was neither a flute-player nor a harpist, nay, she had not even acquired skill in the dance, but she sold her youthful beauty to those who chanced to come along, plying her trade with practically her whole body. Later on she was associated with the actors in all the work of the theatre, and she shared their performances with them, playing up to their buffoonish acts intended to raise a laugh. For she was unusually clever and full of gibes, and she immediately became admired for this sort of thing. For the girl had not a particle of modesty, nor did any man ever see her embarrassed, but she undertook shameless services without the least hesitation, and she was the sort of a person who, for instance, when being flogged or beaten over the head, would crack a joke over it and burst into a loud laugh ; and she would undress and exhibit to any who chanced along both her front and her rear naked, parts which rightly should be unseen by men and hidden from them.

And as she wantoned with her lovers, she always kept bantering them, and by toying with new devices in intercourse, she always succeeded in winning the hearts of the licentious to her ; for she did not even expect that the approach should be made by the man she was with, but on the contrary she herself, with wanton jests and with clownish posturing with her hips, would tempt all who came along, especially if they were beardless youths. Indeed there was never anyone such a slave to pleasure in all forms ; for many a time she would go to a community dinner with ten youths or even more, all of exceptional bodily vigour who had made a business of fornication, and she would lie with all her banquet companions the whole night long, and when they all were too exhausted to go on, she would go to their attendants, thirty perhaps in number, and pair off with each one of them ; yet even so she could not get enough of this wantonness.

On one occasion she entered the house of one of the notables during the drinking, and they say that in the sight of all the banqueters she mounted to the projecting part of the banqueting couch where their feet lay, and there drew up her clothing in a shameless way, not hesitating to display her licentiousness. And though she made use of three openings, she used to take Nature to task, complaining that it had not pierced her breasts with larger holes so that it might be possible for her to contrive another method of copulation there. And though she was pregnant many times, yet practically always she was able to contrive to bring about an abortion immediately.

And often even in the theatre, before the eyes of the whole people, she stripped off her clothing and moved about naked through their midst, having only a girdle about her private parts and her groins, not, however, that she was ashamed to display these too to the populace, but because no person is permitted to enter there entirely naked, but must have at least a girdle about the groins. Clothed in this manner, she sprawled out and lay on her back on the ground. And some slaves, whose duty this was, sprinkled grains of barley over her private parts, and geese, which happened to have been provided for this very purpose, picked them off with their beaks, one by one, and ate them. And when she got up, she not only did not blush, but even acted as if she took pride in this strange performance. For she was not merely shameless herself, but also a contriver of shameless deeds above all others. . . .

The Rise of Islam

Arabia in the sixth century A.D. was inhabited primarily in the southern area of Yemen, along the western slopes of the Hejaz Mountains, and along scattered desert oases. Large-scale international trade in dates and imported spices from Africa and India was made possible through the use of camel caravans. Religion was well developed; the people worshipped the Moon, planets, spirits, stone idols, and rocks.

The major center of religious worship and pilgrimage, however, was the city of Mecca. Within the city there was a sacred precinct containing a well, called the Zamzam, and the holy shrine, referred to as the Kaaba. A great variety of religions were connected with the Kaaba, which housed approximately 300 idols, including statues of Jesus.

Politically, the Byzantines and Persians, each of whom had launched several invasions to gain control of Arabia, were fierce competitors. Yet, despite these struggles, no major power had secured total domination of the independent peoples.

Muhammad (A.D. 570?–632) was born into the Kuraysh clan, which was one of the leading camel-caravan trading groups in Mecca. Unfortunately, before Muhammad's birth his father died. The child was left in the care of his mother until she too died when he was six. At this time, he was placed under the protection of his paternal uncle.

There is little information about Muhammad's life until 595, when he became an overseer for a wealthy, older caravan owner, a woman named Khadija. Muhammad did so well at his job that soon Khadija asked him to marry her ; this marriage of convenience turned to true affection and lasted until Khadija's death in 619. After her death, Muhammad married many times, in each case to bind new converts to his religion. Despite his numerous marriages, Muhammad never had a son who lived beyond infancy ; however, he later adopted a cousin as a foster son.

During the month of Ramadan (Fasting) in the year 610, Muhammad said he was called by God (Allah) to become his prophet. Through the messages of the Archangel Gabriel, which Muhammad received for the rest of his life, he formed the religion called Islam (meaning submission to the Will of God). Muhammad was instructed to preach the message of Allah to the Meccans. At first he was able to convert only members of his family and some young men in the city, while most Meccans resisted his teachings.

Persecution of Muhammad and his small group of followers intensified. When he finally decided to leave Mecca, his Hegira (migration) took him to a small date-palm oasis called Yathrib (Medina), some 250 miles north. Once in Yathrib, Muhammad became a political as well as a religious leader for his Muslims ; as such, he resorted to the time-honored tradition of raiding caravans that passed near Yathrib. These actions brought swift retaliation from Mecca, but the Meccans were never able to defeat Muhammad, whose prestige continually increased. Finally, the Meccans ended their opposition to Muhammad and allowed him into the city to perform the act of "pilgrimage" (or Hajj). Once inside Mecca, he cleansed the Kaaba of idolatry and rededicated it to the sole worship of Allah.

51

The Life of Muhammad

The writer of this selection, Muhammad ibn Ishaq ibn Yasar (c. A.D. 768), was born in Medina and died at a very old age in Baghdad. His *Life of Muhammad* was the first serious compilation of traditional oral accounts (*hadiths*) of the Prophet's life and preaching. The following excerpts deal with several miracles surrounding the Prophet, his relations with Jews and Christians in Medina, and the purification of the Kaaba.

QUESTIONS TO CONSIDER

1. Why were miracles important in the life of Muhammad ? Why are miracles important in other religions ?
2. Why is Jerusalem important to Islam, Judaism, and Christianity ?
3. Why is Abraham revered by Muslims and Hebrews alike ?

What Was Said to Āmina When She Had Conceived the Apostle

It is alleged in popular stories . . . that Amina d. Wahb, the mother of God's apostle, used to say when she was pregnant with God's apostle that a voice said to her, 'You are pregnant with the lord of this people and when he is born say, "I put him in the care of the One from the evil of every envier ; then call him Muhammad."' As she was pregnant with him she saw a light come forth from her by which she could see the castles of Buṣrā in Syria. Shortly afterwards 'Abdullah the apostle's father died while his mother was still pregnant.

The Birth of the Apostle and His Suckling

The apostle was born on Monday, 12th Rabī'u'l-awwal, in the year of the elephant. . . .

After his birth his mother sent to tell his grandfather 'Abdu'l-Muṭṭalib that she had given birth to a boy and asked him to come and look at him. When he came she told him what she had seen when she conceived him and what was said to her and what she was ordered to call him. . . .

Thaur b. Yazīd . . . told me that some of the apostle's companions asked him to tell them about himself. He said : 'I am what Abraham my father prayed for and the good news of (. . . my brother) Jesus. When my mother was carrying me she saw a light proceeding from her which showed her the castles of Syria. I was suckled among the B. Sa'd b. Bakr, and while I was with a brother of mine behind our tents shepherding the lambs, two men in white raiment came to me with a gold basin full of snow. Then they seized me and opened up my belly, extracted my heart and split it ; then they extracted a black drop from it and threw it away ; then they washed my heart and my belly with that snow until they had thoroughly cleaned them. Then one said to the other, weigh him against ten of his people ; they did so and I outweighed them. Then they weighed me against a hundred and then a thousand, and I outweighed them. He said, "Leave him alone, for by God, if you weighed him against all his people he would outweigh them."'. . .

The Prophet's Mission

Wahb b. Kaisān told me . . . : Every year during that month the apostle would pray in seclusion and give food to the poor that came to him. And when he completed the month and returned from his seclusion, first of all before entering his house he would go to the Ka'ba and walk round it seven times or as often as it pleased God ; then he would go back to his house until in the year when God sent him, in the month of Ramaḍān in which God willed concerning him what He willed of His grace, the apostle set forth to Ḥirā' as was his wont, and his family with him. When it was the night on which God honoured him with his mission and showed mercy on His servants thereby, Gabriel brought him the command of God. 'He came to me,' said the apostle of God, 'while I was asleep, with a coverlet

From Muhammad ibn Ishaq, *The Life of Muhammad*, trans. A. Guillaume (Karachi : Oxford University Press, 1978), pp. 69, 72, 105–106, 181, 186–187, 260, 268, 552–553. Reprinted by permission.

of brocade whereon was some writing, and said, "Read!" I said, "What shall I read?" He pressed me with it so tightly that I thought it was death; then he let me go and said, "Read!" I said, "What shall I read?" He pressed me with it again so that I thought it was death; then he let me go and said "Read!" I said, "What shall I read?" He pressed me with it the third time so that I thought it was death and said "Read!" I said, "What then shall I read?" — and this I said only to deliver myself from him, lest he should do the same to me again. . . . So I read it, and he departed from me. And I awoke from my sleep, and it was as though these words were written on my heart. (. . . I thought, Woe is me poet or possessed — Never shall Quraysh say this of me! I will go to the top of the mountain and throw myself down that I may kill myself and gain rest. So I went forth to do so and then) when I was midway on the mountain, I heard a voice from heaven saying, "O Muhammad! thou art the apostle of God and I am Gabriel." I raised my head towards heaven to see (who was speaking), and lo, Gabriel in the form of a man with feet astride the horizon, saying, "O Muhammad! thou art the apostle of God and I am Gabriel." I stood gazing at him, . . . moving neither forward nor backward; then I began to turn my face away from him, but towards whatever region of the sky I looked, I saw him as before. And I continued standing there, neither advancing nor turning back, until Khadīja sent her messengers in search of me and they gained the high ground above Mecca and returned to her while I was standing in the same place.'. . .

The Night Journey and the Ascent to Heaven

According to what I have heard . . . Burāq, the animal whose every stride carried it as far as its eye could reach on which the prophets before him used to ride was brought to the apostle and he was mounted on it. His companion (Gabriel) went with him to see the wonders between heaven and earth, until he came to Jerusalem's temple. There he found Abraham the friend of God, Moses, and Jesus assembled with a company of the prophets, and he prayed with them. . . .

I was told . . . that the apostle said: 'While I was sleeping in the Ḥijr Gabriel came and stirred me with his foot. I sat up but saw nothing and lay down again. He came a second time and stirred me with his foot. I sat up but saw nothing and lay down again. He came to me the third time and stirred me with his foot. I sat up and he took hold of my arm and I stood beside him and he brought me out to the door of the mosque and there was a white animal, half mule, half donkey, with wings on its sides with which it propelled its feet, putting down each forefoot at the limit of its sight and he mounted me on it. Then he went out with me keeping close to me.

. . . 'When I came up to mount him he shied. Gabriel placed his hand on its mane and said, Are you not ashamed, O Burāq, to behave in this way? By God, none more honourable before God than Muhammad has ever ridden you before. The animal was so ashamed that he broke out into a sweat and stood still so that I could mount him.'

. . . 'Then I was taken up to the second heaven and there were the two maternal cousins Jesus, Son of Mary, and John, son of Zakariah. Then to the third heaven and there was a man whose face was as the moon at the full. This was my brother Joseph, son of Jacob. Then to the fourth heaven and there was a man called Idrīs. "And we have exalted him to a lofty place." Then to the fifth heaven and there was a man with white hair and a long beard, never have I seen a more handsome man than he. This was the beloved among his people Aaron son of 'Imrān. Then to the sixth heaven, and there was a dark man. . . . This was my brother Moses, son of 'Imrān. Then to the seventh heaven and there was a man sitting on a throne at the gate of the immortal mansion. Every day seventy thousand angels went in not to come back until the resurrection day. Never have I seen a man more like myself. This was my father Abraham. Then he took me into Paradise.' . . .

The apostle said : 'On my return I passed by Moses and what a fine friend of yours he was! He asked me how many prayers had been laid upon me and when I told him fifty he said, "Prayer is a weighty matter and your people are weak, so go back to your Lord and ask him to reduce the number for you and your community." I did so and He took off ten. Again I passed by Moses and he said the same again ; and so it went on until only five prayers for the whole day and night were left. Moses again gave me the same advice. I replied that I had been back to my Lord and asked him to reduce the number until I was ashamed, and I would not do it again. He of you who performs them in faith and trust will have the reward of fifty prayers.' . . .

Jewish and Christian Disputes

When the Christians of Najrān came to the apostle the Jewish rabbis came also and they disputed one with the other before the apostle. Rāfi' said, 'You have no standing,' and he denied Jesus and the Gospel ; and a Christian said to the Jews, 'You have no standing' and he denied that Moses was a prophet and denied the Torah. So God sent down concerning them : 'The Jews say the Christians have no standing ; and the Christians say that Jews have no standing, yet they read the scriptures. They do not know what they are talking about. God will judge between them on the day of resurrection concerning their controversy,' i.e. each one reads in his book the confirmation of what he denies, so that the Jews deny Jesus though they have the Torah in which God required them by the word of Moses to hold Jesus true ; while in the Gospel is what Jesus brought in confirmation of Moses and the Torah he brought from God : so each one denies what is in the hand of the other. . . .

The apostle entered a Jewish school where there was a number of Jews and called them to God. Al-Nu'mān b. 'Amr and al-Hārith b. Zayd said to him :

'What is your religion, Muhammad ?'

'The religion of Abraham.'

'But Abraham was a Jew.'

'Then let the Torah judge between us.'

They refused, and so God sent down concerning them : 'Hast thou not seen how those who have received a portion of scripture when invited to God's book that it may judge between them, a party of them turn their backs in opposition. That is because they say, The fire will not touch us except for a limited time. What they were inventing has deceived them in their religion.'

The Jewish rabbis and the Christians of Najrān, when they were together before the apostle, broke into disputing. The rabbis said that Abraham was nothing but a Jew. The Christians said he was nothing but a Christian; so God revealed concerning them: 'O Scripture folk, Why do you argue about Abraham when the Torah and the Gospel were not sent down until after his time? Can it be that you do not understand? Behold, you are they who argue of what you know something, but why do you argue about what you know nothing? God knows but you do not know. Abraham was neither a Jew nor a Christian but he was a Muslim *hanīf* and he was not a polytheist.[1] Those who are the nearest to Abraham are those who follow him and this prophet and those who believe, God being the friend of believers.' . . .

Abū Yāsir and Nāfi' b. Abū Nāfi' and 'Azir and Khālid and Zayd and Izār and Ashya' came to the apostle and asked him about the apostles he believed in. So the apostle said: 'We believe in God and what he has sent down to us and what was sent down to Abraham and Ishmael and Isaac and Jacob and the tribes and what was given to Moses and Jesus and what was given to the prophets from their Lord; we make no difference between any one of them. And we are submissive unto Him.' When he mentioned Jesus, Son of Mary, they denied that he was a prophet, saying, 'We do not believe in Jesus, Son of Mary, or in anyone who believes in him.' So God sent down concerning them: 'O Scripture folk, do you blame us for anything but our belief in God and what He has sent down to us and what was sent down aforetime and because most of you are evil-doers?'

Rāfi' b. Ḥāritha and Sallām b. Mishkam and Mālik b. al-Sayf and Rāfi' b. Ḥuraymila came to him and said: 'Do you not allege that you follow the religion of Abraham and believe in the Torah which we have and testify that it is the truth from God?' He replied, 'Certainly, but you have sinned and broken the covenant contained therein and concealed what you were ordered to make plain to men, and I dissociate myself from your sin.' They said, 'We hold by what we have. We live according to the guidance and the truth and we do not believe in you and we will not follow you.' So God sent down concerning them: 'Say, O Scripture folk, you have no standing until you observe the Torah and the Gospel and what has been sent down to you from your Lord. What has been sent down to thee from thy Lord will assuredly increase many of them in error and unbelief. But be not sad because of the unbelieving people.'

Muhammad and the Kaaba

Muhammad b. Ja'far b. al-Zubayr . . . told me that the apostle after arriving in Mecca when the populace had settled down went to the temple and encompassed it seven times on his camel touching the black stone with a stick which he had in his hand. This done he summoned 'Uthmān b. Talḥa and took the key of the Ka'ba from him, and when the door was opened for him he went in. There he found a dove made of wood. He broke it in his hands and threw it away. Then he stood by the door of the Ka'ba while the men in the mosque gathered to him.

The apostle entered Mecca on the day of the conquest and it contained 360 idols which Iblīs[2] had strengthened with lead. The apostle was standing by them

1. Hanifs were pre-Islamic monotheists.
2. The Devil.

with a stick in his hand, saying, 'The truth has come and falsehood has passed away ; verily falsehood is sure to pass away.' . . . Then he pointed at them with his stick and they collapsed on their backs one after the other.

When the apostle prayed the noon prayer on the day of the conquest he ordered that all the idols which were round the Ka'ba should be collected and burned with fire and broken up. . . .

From Ḥakīm b. 'Abbād b. Ḥanīf and other traditionists : Quraysh had put pictures in the Ka'ba including two of Jesus son of Mary and Mary (on both of whom be peace !). I. Shihāb said . . . that a woman of Ghassān joined in the pilgrimage of the Arabs and when she saw the picture of Mary in the Ka'ba she said, 'My father and my mother be your ransom ! You are surely an Arab woman !' The apostle ordered that the pictures should be erased except those of Jesus and Mary.

A traditionist told me that the apostle stood at the door of the Ka'ba and said : 'There is no God but Allah alone ; He has no associate. He has made good His promise and helped His servant. He has put to flight the confederates alone. Every claim of privilege or blood or property are abolished by me except the custody of the temple and the watering of the pilgrims. The unintentionally slain in a quasi-intentional way by club or whip, for him the bloodwit is most severe : a hundred camels, forty of them to be pregnant. O Quraysh, God has taken from you the haughtiness of paganism and its veneration of ancestors. Man springs from Adam and Adam sprang from dust.' Then he read to them this verse : 'O men, We created you from male and female and made you into peoples and tribes that you may know one another : of a truth the most noble of you in God's sight is the most pious' to the end of the passage. Then he added, 'O Quraysh, what do you think that I am about to do with you ?' They replied, 'Good. You are a noble brother, son of a noble brother.' He said, 'Go your way for you are the freed ones.'

52

The Koran

The Koran is the Holy Scripture and basis of the Islamic religion. The work comprises 114 chapters (or suras) arranged according to their length, running from the longest to the shortest. The Koran is believed to be the word of God, transmitted by the Archangel Gabriel to the prophet Muhammad. The prophet, in turn, preached these messages, first in Mecca, then in Medina, to his small group of converts (Muslims). Only after Muhammad's death were the messages gathered together and given their final arrangement by the third caliph,[1] Othman.

The basic beliefs of Islam are drawn from contacts with both Jews and Christians, and then adapted for the Arab peoples. Essential to the religion is the need for each person to submit to the one and only god, Allah. Accord-

---

1. *Caliph* means "Successor of the Apostle of God (Muhammad)." A caliph was the head of state, a judge, leader in worship, and commander of the army.

ing to this religion, Allah knows and sees everything. He has determined each person's fate; however, lest one fall into fatalism, each person must account for his or her actions on the Day of Last Judgment.

Drawing upon the scriptures of the "Peoples of the Book" (Jews and Christians), Muhammad preached that Allah had described to his 28 prophets — including Adam, Noah, Moses, John the Baptist, and Jesus — the method in which He was to be worshipped. However, Muhammad thought that the Jews and Christians had deliberately distorted the original messages. Muhammad claimed that the Koran was the most perfect guide for worshipping Allah, and that he was the final prophet or "Seal."

In the following Koranic selections, note the descriptions of Muhammad's call to God's Word, the Last Judgment, the Islamic view of the "Peoples of the Book," and the duties that each Muslim must follow. Today the Koran governs approximately 800 million lives.

QUESTIONS TO CONSIDER

1. What are some of the basic beliefs and duties in Islam?
2. What are significant similarities and differences between Islam, Judaism, and Christianity?
3. Why was the description of Paradise so appealing in Arabia?
4. How were women to be treated according to the Koran?

The Clot

In the Name of Allah, the Beneficent, the Merciful

1. Read in the name of your Lord Who created.
2. He created man from a clot.
3. Read and your Lord is Most Honorable,
4. Who taught (to write) with the pen,
5. Taught man what he knew not.
6. Nay! man is most surely inordinate,
7. Because he sees himself free from want.

The Food

In the Name of Allah, the Beneficent, the Merciful

97. Allah has made the Kaaba, the sacred house, a maintenance for the people, and the sacred month and the offerings and the sacrificial animals with gar-

From *Holy Qur'an*, trans. M. H. Shakir (Elmhurst, NY: Tahrike Tarsile Qur'an, 1985), Surahs 96:1–7, 5:97, 56:1–44, 61:6, 62:1–9, 3:45–71, 4:34, 24:31–32, 2:174–185, 187, 196–197, 219–220. Reprinted by permission of Tahrike Tarsile Qur'an, Inc.

lands; this is that you may know that Allah knows whatever is in the heavens and whatever is in the earth, and that Allah is the Knower of all things.

The Great Event

In the Name of Allah, the Beneficent, the Merciful

1. When the great event comes to pass,
2. There is no belying its coming to pass —
3. Abasing (one party), exalting (the other),
4. When the earth shall be shaken with a (severe) shaking,
5. And the mountains shall be made to crumble with (an awful) crumbling,
6. So that they shall be as scattered dust.
7. And you shall be three sorts.
8. Then (as to) the companions of the right hand; how happy are the companions of the right hand!
9. And (as to) the companions of the left hand; how wretched are the companions of the left hand!
10. And the foremost are the foremost,
11. These are they who are drawn nigh (to Allah),
12. In the gardens of bliss.
13. A numerous company from among the first,
14. And a few from among the latter.
15. On thrones decorated,
16. Reclining on them, facing one another.
17. Round about them shall go youths never altering in age,
18. With goblets and ewers and a cup of pure drink;
19. They shall not be affected with headache thereby, nor shall they get exhausted;
20. And fruits such as they choose,
21. And the flesh of fowl such as they desire.
22. And pure, beautiful ones,
23. The like of the hidden pearls:
24. A reward for what they used to do.
25. They shall not hear therein vain or sinful discourse,
26. Except the word peace, peace.
27. And the companions of the right hand; how happy are the companions of the right hand!
28. Amid thornless lote-trees,
29. And banana-trees (with fruits), one above another.
30. And extended shade,
31. And water flowing constantly,
32. And abundant fruit,
33. Neither intercepted nor forbidden,
34. And exalted thrones.
35. Surely We have made them to grow into a (new) growth,
36. Then We have made them virgins,

37. Loving, equals in age,
38. For the sake of the companions of the right hand.
39. A numerous company from among the first,
40. And a numerous company from among the last.
41. And those of the left hand, how wretched are those of the left hand!
42. In hot wind and boiling water,
43. And the shade of black smoke,
44. Neither cool nor honorable. . . .

The Ranks

In the Name of Allah, the Beneficent, the Merciful

6. And when Jesus son of Mary said: O children of Israel! surely I am the apostle of Allah to you, verifying that which is before me of the Torah and giving the good news of an Apostle who will come after me, his name being Ahmad,[1] but when he came to them with clear arguments they said: This is clear magic.

Friday

In the Name of Allah, the Beneficent, the Merciful

1. Whatever is in the heavens and whatever is in the earth declares the glory of Allah, the King, the Holy, the Mighty, the Wise.
2. He it is Who raised among the inhabitants of Mecca an Apostle from among themselves, who recites to them His communications and purifies them, and teaches them the Book and the Wisdom, although they were before certainly in clear error,
3. And others from among them who have not yet joined them; and He is the Mighty, the Wise.
4. That is Allah's grace; He grants it to whom He pleases, and Allah is the Lord of mighty grace.
5. The likeness of those who were charged with the Torah, then they did not observe it, is as the likeness of the ass bearing books, evil is the likeness of the people who reject the communications of Allah; and Allah does not guide the unjust people.
6. Say: O you who are Jews, if you think that you are the favorites of Allah to the exclusion of other people, then invoke death if you are truthful.
7. And they will never invoke it because of what their hands have sent before; and Allah is Cognizant of the unjust.
8. Say: (As for) the death from which you flee, that will surely overtake you, then you shall be sent back to the Knower of the unseen and the seen, and He will inform you of that which you did.
9. O you who believe! when the call is made for prayer on Friday, then hasten to the remembrance of Allah and leave off trading; that is better for you, if you know. . . .

1. Muhammad.

The Family of Imram

In the Name of Allah, the Beneficent, the Merciful

45. When the angels said: O Mary, surely Allah gives you good news with a Word from Him (of one) whose name is the Messiah, Jesus son of Mary, worthy of regard in this world and the hereafter and of those who are made near (to Allah).

46. And he shall speak to the people when in the cradle and when of old age, and (he shall be) one of the good ones.

47. She said: My Lord! when shall there be a son (born) to me, and man has not touched me? He said: Even so, Allah creates what He pleases; when He has decreed a matter, He only says to it, Be, and it is.

48. And He will teach him the Book and the wisdom and the Torah and the Gospel.

49. And (make him) an apostle to the children of Israel: That I have come to you with a sign from your Lord, that I determine for you out of dust like the form of a bird, then I breathe into it and it becomes a bird with Allah's permission and I heal the blind and the leprous, and bring the dead to life with Allah's permission and I inform you of what you should eat and what you should store in your houses; most surely there is a sign in this for you, if you are believers.

50. And a verifier of that which is before me of the Torah, and that I may allow you part of that which has been forbidden you, and I have come to you with a sign from your Lord, therefore be careful of (your duty to) Allah and obey me.

51. Surely Allah is my Lord and your Lord, therefore serve Him; this is the right path.

52. But when Jesus perceived unbelief on their part, he said: Who will be my helpers in Allah's way? The disciples said: We are helpers (in the way) of Allah: We believe in Allah and bear witness that we are submitting ones.

53. Our Lord! we believe in what Thou hast revealed and we follow the apostle, so write us down with those who bear witness.

54. And they planned and Allah (also) planned, and Allah is the best of planners.

55. And when Allah said: O Jesus I am going to terminate the period of your stay (on earth) and cause you to ascend unto Me and purify you of those who disbelieve and make those who follow you above those who disbelieve to the day of resurrection; then to Me shall be your return, so I will decide between you concerning that in which you differed.

56. Then as to those who disbelieve, I will chastise them with severe chastisement in this world and the hereafter, and they shall have no helpers.

57. And as to those who believe and do good deeds, He will pay them fully their rewards; and Allah does not love the unjust.

58. This We recite to you of the communications and the wise reminder.

59. Surely the likeness of Jesus is with Allah as the likeness of Adam; He created him from dust, then said to him, Be, and he was.

60. (This is) the truth from your Lord, so be not of the disputers.

61. But whoever disputes with you in this matter after what has come to you of knowledge, then say: Come let us call our sons and your sons and our women and your women and our near people and your near people, then let us be earnest in prayer, and pray for the curse of Allah on the liars.

62. Most surely this is the true explanation, and there is no god but Allah ; and most surely Allah — He is the Mighty, the Wise.

63. But if they turn back, then surely Allah knows the mischief-makers.

64. Say : O followers of the Book ! come to an equitable proposition between us and you that we shall not serve any but Allah and (that) we shall not associate aught with Him, and (that) some of us shall not take others for lords besides Allah ; but if they turn back, then say : Bear witness that we are Muslims.

65. O followers of the Book ! why do you dispute about Abraham, when the Torah and the Gospel were not revealed till after him ; do you not then understand ?

66. Behold ! you are they who disputed about that of which you had knowledge ; why then do you dispute about that of which you have no knowledge ? And Allah knows while you do not know.

67. Abraham was not a Jew nor a Christian but he was (an) upright (man), a Muslim, and he was not one of the polytheists.

68. Most surely the nearest of people to Abraham are those who followed him and this Prophet and those who believe and Allah is the guardian of the believers.

69. A party of the followers of the Book desire that they should lead you astray, and they lead not astray but themselves, and they do not perceive.

70. O followers of the Book ! Why do you disbelieve in the communications of Allah while you witness (them) ?

71. O followers of the Book ! Why do you confound the truth with the falsehood and hide the truth while you know ?

Women

In the Name of Allah, the Beneficent, the Merciful

34. Men are the maintainers of women because Allah has made some of them to excel others and because they spend out of their property ; the good women are therefore obedient, guarding the unseen as Allah has guarded ; and (as to) those on whose part you fear desertion, admonish them, and leave them alone in the sleeping-places and beat them ; then if they obey you, do not seek a way against them ; surely Allah is High, Great.

The Light

In the Name of Allah, the Beneficent, the Merciful

31. And say to the believing women that they cast down their looks and guard their private parts and do not display their ornaments except what appears thereof, and let them wear their head-coverings over their bosoms, and not display their ornaments except to their husbands or their fathers, or the fathers of their husbands, or their sons, or the sons of their husbands, or their brothers, or their brothers' sons, or their sisters' sons, or their women, or those whom their

right hands possess, or the male servants not having need (of women), or the children who have not attained knowledge of what is hidden of women ; and let them not strike their feet so that what they hide of their ornaments may be known ; and turn to Allah all of you, O believers ! so that you may be successful.

32. And marry those among you who are single and those who are fit among your male slaves and your female slaves ; if they are needy, Allah will make them free from want out of His grace ; and Allah is Ample-giving, Knowing.

The Cow

In the Name of Allah, the Beneficent, the Merciful

174. Surely those who conceal any part of the Book that Allah has revealed and take for it a small price, they eat nothing but fire into their bellies, and Allah will not speak to them on the day of resurrection, nor will He purify them, and they shall have a painful chastisement.

175. These are they who buy error for the right direction and chastisement for forgiveness ; how bold they are to encounter fire.

176. This is because Allah has revealed the Book with the truth ; and surely those who go against the Book are in a great opposition.

177. It is not righteousness that you turn your faces towards the East and the West, but righteousness is this that one should believe in Allah and the last day and the angels and the Book and the prophets, and give away wealth out of love for Him to the near of kin and the orphans and the needy and the wayfarer and the beggars and for (the emancipation of) the captives, and keep up prayer and pay the poor-rate ; and the performers of their promise when they make a promise, and the patient in distress and affliction and in time of conflicts — these are they who are true (to themselves) and these are they who guard (against evil).

178. O you who believe ! retaliation is prescribed for you in the matter of the slain ; the free for the free, and the slave for the slave, and the female for the female, but if any remission is made to any one by his (aggrieved) brother, then prosecution (for the bloodwit) should be made according to usage, and payment should be made to him in a good manner ; this is an alleviation from your Lord and a mercy ; so whoever exceeds the limit after this, he shall have a painful chastisement.

179. And there is life for you in (the law of) retaliation, O men of understanding, that you may guard yourselves.

180. Bequest is prescribed for you when death approaches one of you, if he leaves behind wealth for parents and near relatives, according to usage, a duty (incumbent) upon those who guard (against evil).

181. Whoever then alters it after he has heard it, the sin of it then is only upon those who alter it ; surely Allah is Hearing, Knowing.

182. But he who fears an inclination to a wrong course or an act of disobedience on the part of the testator, and effects an agreement between the parties, there is no blame on him. Surely Allah is Forgiving, Merciful.

183. O you who believe ! fasting is prescribed for you, as it was prescribed for those before you, so that you may guard (against evil).

184. For a certain number of days; but whoever among you is sick or on a journey, then (he shall fast) a (like) number of other days; and those who are not able to do it may effect a redemption by feeding a poor man; so whoever does good spontaneously it is better for him; and that you fast is better for you if you know.

185. The month of Ramadan is that in which the Quran was revealed, a guidance to men and clear proofs of the guidance and the distinction; therefore whoever of you is present in the month, he shall fast therein, and whoever is sick or upon a journey, then (he shall fast) a (like) number of other days; Allah desires ease for you, and He does not desire for you difficulty, and (He desires) that you should complete the number and that you should exalt the greatness of Allah for His having guided you and that you may give thanks. . . .

187. It is made lawful to you to go into your wives on the night of the fast; they are an apparel for you and you are an apparel for them; Allah knew that you acted unfaithfully to yourselves, so He has turned to you (mercifully) and removed from you (this burden); so now be in contact with them and seek what Allah has ordained for you, and eat and drink until the whiteness of the day becomes distinct from the blackness of the night at dawn, then complete the fast till night, and have not contact with them while you keep to the mosques; these are the limits of Allah, so do not go near them. Thus does Allah make clear His communications for men that they may guard (against evil). . . .

196. And accomplish the pilgrimage and the visit for Allah, but if you are prevented, (send) whatever offering is easy to obtain, and do not shave your heads until the offering reaches its destination; but whoever among you is sick or has an ailment of the head, he (should effect) a compensation by fasting or alms or sacrificing; then when you are secure, whoever profits by combining the visit with the pilgrimage (should take) what offering is easy to obtain; but he who cannot find (any offering) should fast for three days during the pilgrimage and for seven days when you return; these (make) ten (days) complete; this is for him whose family is not present in the Sacred Mosque, and be careful (of your duty) to Allah, and know that Allah is severe in requiting (evil).

197. The pilgrimage is (performed in) the well-known months; so whoever determines the performance of the pilgrimage therein, there shall be no intercourse nor fornication nor quarrelling amongst one another; and whatever good you do, Allah knows it; and make provision, for surely the provision is the guarding of oneself, and be careful (of your duty) to Me, O men of understanding. . . .

219. They ask you about intoxicants and games of chance. Say: In both of them there is a great sin and means of profit for men, and their sin is greater than their profit. And they ask you as to what they should spend. Say: What you can spare. Thus does Allah make clear to you the communications, that you may ponder.

220. On this world and the hereafter. And they ask you concerning the orphans. Say: To set right for them (their affairs) is good, and if you become co-partners with them, they are your brethren; and Allah knows the mischief-maker and the peacemaker; and if Allah had pleased, He would certainly have caused you to fall into a difficulty; surely Allah is Mighty, Wise.

Commentaries on Islamic Law and Culture

53

Wills, Slave Emancipation, and Clientship

Islam developed during the lifetime of the Prophet Muhammad not only as a religion in the sense of a way of worship and a systematic elaboration of the relationship between man and his creator; through the circumstances of its incubation, it also evolved as a social and political institution which claimed divine authority for the regulation of relations between man and man, believer and nonbeliever. The Koran, the revealed word of God, was the prime and unchanging authority. The early generations of Muslims could also recall decisions made by the Prophet, whose teachings were considered a supplement to and commentary on the divine text. Soon, however, as the community of Islam expanded and embraced former subjects of Byzantium, Sassanid Iran, and others as far west as Spain and as far east as India who belonged to many different nations and cultures, the need arose to formalize the social teachings of Islam and to unify its rituals.

The evolution of Islamic law took place largely in the second and third centuries of Islam (c. A.D. 750–950), and a number of distinct systems emerged based on the teachings of various scholars. By a self-selecting process, these were eventually reduced (among Sunni Muslims) to four law-schools, each of which was considered to be equally authoritative. To the Koran and the sayings of the Prophet — the Ḥadīth (diligently amassed in written collections) — were added a number of other subsidiary principles — notably analogical reasoning — and by the fourth century of Islam (A.D. 10th century), we see the appearance of manuals enunciating agreed positions on all the main issues in ritual, personal status (marriage, divorce, inheritance etc.), commercial transactions, and criminal and moral law (e.g., theft, adultery, drinking intoxicating liquors). The *Risāla* of Ibn Abī Zayd, a jurisprudent of Qayrawan (modern Tunisia) who died in A.D. 996 is one such manual. It reflects the views of the law school of Malik ibn Anas (d. 797) which is dominant in North and West Africa and the upper Nile valley. As with the Jewish Talmud, the Islamic law manuals have been commented upon by later generations of scholars, and the commentaries themselves have been further elucidated by other scholars. This is reflected in the first selection by the use of square brackets [ ]. In the second selection, the brackets reflect explanatory words of the translator, who thus, in effect, becomes yet another commentator.

Slavery was an ancient institution in the Middle East and Islam acknowledged its validity while mitigating its effects. Neither the Koran nor the law speaks about enslavement as such, although it came to be agreed that prisoners taken in a war waged on behalf of the faith — a *jihād* — could be made slaves. The Koran stresses kind treatment to slaves and enumerates ways for their emancipation, and this is echoed in the Prophetic *Hadīth*. The law-books devote a section to emancipation and to clientship — the lingering bonds of attachment of a slave to his master's family after emancipation — but otherwise deal with slaves' rights and disabilities only incidentally under appropriate sections, such as marriage, pilgrimage, punishments, and so on — the slave generally having only half the rights of a free man and, often, suffering only half the penalties.

QUESTIONS TO CONSIDER

1. In what ways might a slave have gained his or her freedom?
2. Did slaves have any legal rights under Islamic law?
3. Was it possible for slaves to acquire property?
4. Are there any similarities between Islamic law and the laws of Hammurabi (see Reading 7)?

It is fitting that he who has something to bequeath should draw up a will. There can be no bequest in favor of an heir. Bequests come out of the disposable one-third of the estate. Any bequests exceeding the one-third should be given back [to the designated heirs], unless they authorize otherwise. The specified emancipation of a slave is to be dealt with before proceeding to bequests. [A declaration that] a slave is to be emancipated on the owner's death made when the owner was in good health takes precedence over a declaration made when he was [gravely] ill referring to emancipation or other [dispositions regarding the slave such as being given as a gift or a charitable donation]. It also takes precedence over the payment of outstanding alms-tax (*zakāt*) which a man decides to pay off from his estate. Such latter payments come out of the disposable third and take precedence over other bequests. A declaration of emancipation on the owner's death made when the owner was in good health, however, takes precedence.

If the disposable one-third is insufficient [to cover all the bequests made], the legatees whose bequests have no precedence the one over the other, take proportionate shares. A man may annul a legacy, whether it involves emancipation or any other matter.

The formula for declaring a slave free upon the master's death is: 'You are *mudabbar*.' or 'You are free after my demise.' After this the master cannot sell him or give him away. The master may make use of the slave's services until he dies, at which point the slave is free. The master may confiscate his slave's possessions, so long as the slave is not [gravely] ill. The master may have sexual relations with his female slave, but he may not do so with one to whom emancipation has been

From the *Risāla* of Ibn Abī Zayd al-Qayrawānī with the commentary of Abū 'l-Ḥasan al-Mālikī and the supercommentary of ʿAlī al-Saʿīdī al-ʿAdawī, Cairo : Muṣṭafā al-Bābī al-Ḥalabī, 1937, ii, 177–99. Edited and translated by John O. Hunwick, Professor of History, Northwestern University.

promised after a stated lapse of time, nor can he sell her. However, he may enjoy her labor and he has the right to confiscate her possessions, provided the time of her emancipation is not close.

When a master dies the value of his *mudabbar* slave is considered part of the disposable one-third, whereas the value of a slave to be emancipated after a fixed lapse of time is reckoned as a part of the total estate. The slave with whom a contract of emancipation has been agreed remains a slave while he owes any portion [of the agreed price of his freedom]. A contract may be drawn up stipulating any sum of money agreed upon by the master and the slave, to be paid in installments, either few or many. If the slave becomes unable to pay, he becomes a simple slave again. What the master has taken from him [by way of installments] may lawfully be retained [by the master]. If a slave refuses [to acknowledge his insolvency] only the civil authority has the power to declare him insolvent [unilaterally] after first granting him a respite [during which he might become solvent].

The offspring of a woman [other than by her master] assume her status, whether she is a slave with whom a contract of manumission has been drawn up, a *mudabbar* slave, or one to be emancipated after a fixed lapse of time, or one who has been given as a pledge. The child born to an *umm walad* (i.e., a slave woman who has already borne her master's child) fathered by some one other than her master shares his mother's rights and disabilities [if born after she became *umm walad*].

A slave's possessions belong to him, unless the master confiscates them from him. If the master frees him unconditionally or contractually and does not exclude the slave's possessions [from such emancipation], then the master cannot confiscate them.

A master may have sexual relations with a female slave under contract of manumission. Any offspring fathered by a male or born to a female slave under contract of manumission partakes in the contract with them and becomes free at the time of their emancipation.

It is permissible to draw up a contract of emancipation with a group [of slaves], but none of them becomes free until all have paid [the price of] their freedom. A slave under contract of emancipation cannot free his own slave or dissipate his wealth until he attains freedom; neither may he marry or travel to a distant destination without his master's permission. Should he die [before paying for his freedom in full], having a child, the child takes his place and pays from the [dead slave's] wealth whatever sum remains outstanding [in the emancipation contract], this now being considered a debt whose repayment has fallen due. [If anything remains], those of his sons conjoined with him [in contractual freedom] inherit the surplus. If the wealth the slave leaves is insufficient to pay off the contractual debt of emancipation, the slave's offspring, if they are adult, should work to pay off the debt by installments. If they are minors and the legacy of their deceased slave father is insufficient to pay the installments up to the time when they will be old enough to work, they are immediately returned to unconditional slavery. If [the slave under contract of emancipation dies] having no offspring conjoined with him in the contract, his master inherits him [even if his estate is greater than his debt].

Whoever fathers a child from his female slave has the right to continue having sexual relations with her for the rest of his life and she is freed out of his total estate after his death. She cannot be sold, nor can her master demand service from her, nor can he hire out her services to others, though he may demand service and hire out the services of a child of hers from another man [born after she became *umm walad*]. Such a child shares its mother's status and becomes free when she does. Whatever she aborts which is recognized to be a child [by the testimony of midwives] causes her thereby to become *umm walad*. The master's protestations of *coitus interruptus* shall be of no avail if he denies paternity but admits having had sexual relations with her. If he claims that he had her declared free of pregnancy [before purchasing her] and did not thereafter have sexual relations with her, then the offspring to which she gives birth will not be considered his.

A man so deeply in debt [that he has no inheritance to leave] may not free a slave. If a man partially frees his slave [either a fraction of him or a particular limb, for example], the slave's freedom is to be made complete [by judicial decree]. If another person has a share in the slave, the one who freed a portion of his half shall pay the price of his partner's share according to the value of the slave on the day he took the action and [both halves of the slave having been emancipated] the slave shall be free. If a man who freed a part of his half of the slave does not have the means to pay his partner's share, the partner's half of the slave remains enslaved.

Whoever punishes his slave by disfiguring him in an obvious fashion, e.g., by amputating a limb, is compelled to free the slave.

If any of the following relatives of a man come into his possession as a slave, they are to be freed without compensation : one or both parents, a son or daughter, the child of a son or daughter, a grandfather or a grandmother, a full brother or a half-brother. If a pregnant woman is emancipated her foetus is emancipated along with her.

The following categories of slave are not to be freed when emancipation is a religious obligation [in expiation of unintentional homicide] : one who is already a *mudabbar* ; one who is already in a contract of emancipation ; anyone who belongs to a similar category, such as an *umm walad* or a slave to be freed at the expiry of a fixed term ; a blind slave, a slave with an amputated hand [or leg, or finger or toe] ; any slave in a similar condition [e.g., paralysed or disfigured] ; a non-Muslim slave. It is not permissible for a minor to emancipate a slave, nor for anyone who is a ward [by reason of mental illness] to do so.

Patronage belongs to the one who emancipates and it cannot be sold or given away. If a man frees the slave of another, patronage devolves upon the owner of the slave [not the one who emancipated him]. Patronage does not go to the man at whose hands a slave converts to Islam ; it goes to the [community of] Muslims. If a woman emancipates a slave she becomes that slave's patron. She is also the patron of those attracted to this status, such as the child [of the freed slave] or [the slave's] slave. A woman does not inherit from a slave whom her father, her son or her husband, etc. freed. The inheritance of a slave [who is emancipated with the formula ; 'You are like a camel] set free to roam' belongs to the community of Muslims. Patronage goes to the closest of the agnates of the dead man. If he leaves two sons they jointly inherit patronage of a client of their father. If one of these sons dies leaving two sons, the patronage goes back to the other brother rather than to the sons. If one of the two sons dies and leaves a male child, then the other dies leaving two children, the patronage is shared by these three equally.

54

Circumcision of Men and Women

This reading — on circumcision — reflects Muslims' concern with ritual purity and conformity to Prophetic practice. The attitude displayed toward excision for women, however, seems more centered in male chauvinism than in a concern for ritual purity. Though it is less obligatory than male circumcision, it continues to be widely practiced in the Muslim world and — at least in Africa — in many non-Muslim cultures.

QUESTIONS TO CONSIDER

1. Why is circumcision practiced in Islam?
2. Why do other civilizations practice circumcision?

Text: Circumcision is a *sunna* — Prophetic practice — obligatory for men, while excision for women is an ennoblement.

Commentary: *'Obligatory'* — that is 'confirmed' because of the saying of the Prophet in the two Authentic Collections [of al-Bukhārī and Muslim]: The natural state [of a man comprises] five things: circumcision, shaving of the pubic hair, clipping the mustache and plucking the hair of the armpits'. Circumcising on the day of birth or on the seventh day is disapproved unless there is fear for the child's health, since that is the custom of the Jews. It may be done [prematurely] if the child is sick and it is feared he may die. There are conflicting views over whether a boy who is born without a foreskin should be operated upon.

Supercommentary: *'The natural state . . . five things'.* i.e., the qualities whereby a man is perfected so that he displays the finest characteristics. His statement: *'should be operated upon'*: one view is that whatever there is to be cut should be cut. Others said not.

Commentary: There are conflicting views over whether an adult who becomes a Muslim should be circumcised, if he fears this might be injurious to his health. Whoever fails to be circumcised without any excuse or reason is not permitted to be an imam — leader of communal prayer — or to give formal testimony.

Supercommentary: One of the commentators said: 'It is forbidden to look at the genitals of an adult, or an adolescent or a boy who has attained puberty and no forbidden act should be committed in order to carry out a sunna. It would appear, therefore, that [the adult convert to Islam] should circumcise himself, since the

From the *Risāla* of Ibn Abī Zayd al-Qayrawānī with the commentary of Abū 'l-Hasan al-Mālikī and the supercommentary of ʿAlī al-Saʿidī al-ʿAdawī, Cairo: Mustafā al-Bābī al-Halabī, 1937, ii, 177–99. Edited and translated by John O. Hunwick, Professor of History, Northwestern University.

man who has attained the age of legal responsibility is bound to do what will make his Islam complete. You are aware that circumcision makes a man's Islam complete. The same applies to a slave who is purchased after he attains puberty or who is adolescent. His statement *'is not permitted to be an imam'* lacks authority since [the accepted view of] the law school is that for an uncircumcised man to be imam is [merely] disapproved of [not forbidden].

Commentary: Excision is removal of excess [flesh] from the woman's vulva.

Supercommentary: Ibn ᶜUmar said: 'Excision is taking away some part of the protuberance [which lies] between the two labia'.

Commentary: *'An ennoblement'* — that is to say, a Sunna like the circumcision of men. It brings back fluid to a woman's face and makes intercourse more pleasant for the husband.

Supercommentary: His statement; *'That is to say, a Sunna'* lacks authority. The reliable view is that it is [merely] 'preferred'. His statement: *'It brings back fluid to a woman's face'* appears to mean that fluid was in the face and then disappeared and was brought back by excision. However, this is not so. The meaning of its bringing back fluid to the face is that [excision] gives rise to a glamorous appearance in the face, to its glowing and shining.

Final Remark: Should an hermaphrodite be circumcised or not? Ibn Nājī said not, since on principle it is better to forbid something than to allow it, i.e., the hermaphrodite should not have either or both of its genitals operated upon.

55

Muslim Culture in Baghdad

In A.D. 750, the first Islamic dynasty, the Umayyad caliphs, were overthrown by the Abbasids, who belonged to a branch of the Prophet Muhammad's family. The Abbasids were supported by the thousands of Shiites[1] and non-Arab Muslims who had objected to their inferior status under Umayyad rule.

Once in power, the second Abbasid caliph, al-Mansur (754–775), moved the center of government from Damascus, Syria, to Iraq, and in four years time, he built a brand new city officially called Medinat al-Salam (City of Peace), better known as Baghdad. The city was built as a circular fortress surrounded by double brick walls. The center of government was a great green-domed palace protected by a ninety-foot wall and deep moat.

The height of the Abbasid empire came in the reign of Haroun al-Rashid (786–809), his family, and the first Grand Vizirs, the Barmakids. Using

---

1. The Shiites belong to the Shia Ali, or party of Ali. Ali was Muhammad's cousin. He married the Prophet's daughter Fatima and was the fourth caliph (A.D. 656–661). The Shiites never recognized any group or family other than Ali's as caliphs. The Shiites believed that Ali's descendants had been given divine power from Allah to lead Islam and were always ready to fight for their beliefs.

an economic base of agriculture and international trade, these caliphs and their courtiers built fabled palaces where they dined off solid gold dishes and covered the walls with tapestries interwoven with gems. At one marriage ceremony, the bride and groom sat on a jewel-encrusted mat of gold, while they were showered with thousands of pearls and their guests each received a ball of musk[2] containing a note for land or horses. It is no wonder that this court has caught popular imagination through the ages.

The following selection comes from a letter written by an anonymous Persian noble to his father in the late eighth century. It is an excellent eyewitness account of the affluence at court and among the upper classes.

QUESTIONS TO CONSIDER

1. Why do you think that Caliph Haroun al-Rashid might be jealous of the Barmakid family?
2. Is the author completely uncritical of Abbasid society?
3. Islamic society has been criticized as repressing women. Based on this selection, is this true?

When I wandered about in the city after a long absence, I found it in an expansion of prosperity that I had not observed before this time. The resplendent buildings that rose in the city of al-Mansûr were not sufficient for its wealthy people until they extended to the houses of the eastern quarter known as Rusâfa.[1] They built high castles and ornamented homes in this quarter, and set up markets, mosques and public baths. The attention of al-Rashid and the Barmakids was directed toward adorning it with public buildings, until the old Baghdâd became like an ancient town whose beauties were assembled in a section of the city which was created near by it.

I admired the arrival of buildings in Baghdâd because of the overcrowdedness of the people I had seen in its sections. Their billowing is like the sea in its expanses; their number is said to exceed 1,500,000, and no other city in the world has such a sum or even half its amount. Moreover, the social life of the people points to this great sum, although there are no cities to the right or the left of the place in which the people band together like sand. Then I marvelled at the arrival of comfort among the people, for I saw many of them aiming toward arts whose need is not confined to the necessities of civilization. Moreover, the usefulness of their crafts and what they produce expands to the demands of affluence

"Muslim Culture in Baghdad," trans. by John Damis, in Ilse Lichtenstadter, ed., *Introduction to Classical Arabic Literature* (New York : Twayne Publishers, Inc., 1974), pp. 357–362. Reprinted by permission of the editor.

2. Musk is a substance with a penetrating odor that comes from a male musk deer, a muskrat, or musk ox.

1. Rusafa was a section of Baghdad built on the east bank of the Tigris River in 768. It was intended to be an outer defense of the capital with a wall and a moat. With the building of a palace, mosques, and a large market area, the suburb of Rusafa became part of Baghdad proper.

which occurs among nations at the end of their rule and at the time when commanding becomes difficult.

It is difficult for me, with this pen which is of limited substance, to describe the glorious qualities of the city which are but a small part of the honor it achieves, such that it prides itself in the splendor of power. The city brings together a great many notable persons, even to the extent that if the traveler meets a group of them on the road, he does not understand where the multitude is from, although even the least of them has wealth and rank. It is difficult for the largest of cities to support its inhabitants and to extend its soldiery and its retinue and those expectant to it from every direction. The people of wealth walk with slave boys and retinue whose number the listener will fancy to be far from the truth. I witnessed at Attâbiyya station a prince who was riding with a hundred horsemen and was surrounded by slave boys, even filling the road and blocking the path of the people until they passed. I witnessed at the water hole of a sugar cane field along the Tigris a youth from the people of wealth who was going in a grand procession of horses and men, and it was as if I was with a Byzantine emperor upon his mount or a Persian king in the splendor of his procession. The number of those counted in the 'Abbâsid house is probably more than the thousand men riding in such a group as this, and all of them are of great wealth and affluence of civilization. Moreover, prosperity prevailed among the Baghdâdîs, even resembling the affluence of al-Rashid which they saw in his concern in the world for seeking comfort, even verifying the saying which says, "The people are in debt of the king." For it was he who clothed the world, throughout its expanses, with this beauty. Nor was any Caliph ever known to be more generous than he in the handing out of wealth. It is said that he spent ten thousand dirhams [a silver coin] every day for his food, and perhaps the cooks would prepare for him thirty kinds of food. Abû Yûsuf informed me that when the Caliph consummated his marriage to Zubaida, the daughter of Ja'far the Barmakid, he gave a banquet unprecedented in Islam. He gave away unlimited presents at this banquet, even giving containers of gold filled with silver, containers of silver filled with gold, bags of musk and pieces of ambergris. The total expenditure on this banquet reached 55,000,000 dirhams. The Caliph commanded that Zubaida be presented in a gown of pearls whose price no one was able to appraise. He adorned her with pieces of jewelry, so much so that she was not able to walk because of the great number of jewels which were upon her. This example of extravagance had no precedent among the kings of Persia, the emperors of Byzantium or the princes of the Umayyads, despite the great amounts of money which they had at their disposal.

Part of the beauty of the world in these days is that al-Rashid is not unique in the greatness of his spending and squandering. His wife, Zubaida, designs works which surpass the spending of the kings, as in an example of her making, a carpet of silk brocade. This carpet contained the picture of all animals of all the species, and of every bird in gold and their eyes in sapphires and jewels. It is said that she spent about 1,000,000 dînârs [a gold coin] on it. Or for example, her making vessels of gold inlaid with jewels, and dresses of exquisite embroidery whose price exceeds 50,000 dînârs and domes of silver, ebony, and sandalwood, upon which are daggers of gold adorned with embroidery, silk brocade, sable and types of silk. Or for example, her making candles of ambergris, and slippers adorned with jewels, and her taking from among the servants hirelings who followed on donkeys and tended after her needs and ran her errands. And other examples of the affairs which are recorded in the annals of the kings to enhance their position of power and the tales of the amenities which they had at their disposal.

I did not see the likes of this affluence in other houses of the Caliphate except among the glorious Barmakids, where the beauty of the kings and their radiance reached their limit. When they decided to ride out, more people gathered to see them than gathered to see the Caliph. I saw one of their young men at the Muhawwal Gate in the western quarter in a grand procession. His clothes were embroidered and he was thronged by soldiers and slave boys, offspring and notables. He placed his glance upon the mane of his horse, and the people were looking at him, but he did not turn toward them because of his eminence and loftiness. When al-Rashîd himself was in the presence of the Barmakids, he found himself amidst inlaid containers, marbled vaults, and seats of embroidery and silk brocade. Slave girls trailed garments of silk and jewels, and received him with perfumes whose scent was unknown, and it seemed to him that he was in Paradise, surrounded by beauty, jewels and perfume.

The affluence of the Barmakids reached, in the end, the highest level of enjoyment with an ampleness of comfort. Their sessions of entertainment in their houses were more splendid than those in the houses of al-Rashîd and more complete with devices of entertainment. This was because they possessed female singers who were unrivaled in the country, especially the famous Fauz, Farîda and Manna, who were the finest female singers and the best at plucking the lute.

The singing for the Barmakids was not known in the houses of princes, except for the yellow-skinned and the black-skinned. When the Barmakid children grew up, they wanted the beautiful slave girls to know how to sing in order that their beauty would increase from the influence which singing would have on souls. Nâfidh, from the account of one of their doormen, told me that when al-Rashîd visited them on one of the days of his vacation, they had the slave girls brought out to the garden. There they fell into double-column formation like soldiers, and sang and played lutes and struck tambourines until they reached the steps of the castle.

We do not know any preceding king who possessed the good things which are abundant among our kings in this age. It is as if Baghdâd had dropped its quarters onto the bed of life's richness, and, from the abundance of wealth, the causes of ease and eminence had been found for the people.

The Affluence of the Baghdâdîs and Their Immersion in the Good Things of Life

Affluence is abundant among the upper rank of those who are masters of the state. It then diminishes little by little among those of lesser rank, until only a small amount remains for the general public. As for those who do not enjoy the exalted power and breadth of bounty of the kings, they begin to equip themselves with all the good things after they have gone on journeys which gain them experience, show them wonderous things, and give them profits. The people in the provinces come to them with the grandest of all the types of their wares, until markets have become plentiful in Baghdâd. They have advanced from requesting necessities to the acquisition of things for beautification and decoration. This may be seen in the case of their purchase of arms inlaid with gold, their competing in costly jewels, ornamented vessels, and splendid furniture, and their acquisition of a large number of slave boys, female singers, and those things which they send out their retainers to seek in the provinces. When every expensive and rare thing in the country was brought to them, I realized that the beauties of the world had been assembled in Baghdâd.

I witnessed the market of the female slaves after my return from Khorâsân, when I was living in the place known as the market of the slave traders. They are the men who have the girls brought to Baghdâd from the ends of the earth. I saw among these girls Ethiopians, Greeks, Georgians, Circassians, and Arabs born in Medina, Tâ'if, Yamâma and Egypt, possessing sweet tongues and ready answers. The singers among them were known by their very fine dresses, and their headbands which they arranged with pearls and jewels and wrote upon with gold leaf.

The observer imagines on his first trip to this market that, while he is circulating among the girls, they are being sold in injustice and slavery. But he does not retain this sudden fancy after he sees how they embrace the people of ease. I had heard that some of the beautiful girls luxuriously adorned were rescued secretly from places they disliked. Then they would come to the market disguised from the eyes of the guards until a prospective buyer stopped before one of the people. Their masters are unaware of them, and the slave traders oversee their sale like merchants overseeing their goods. When their buyer stops before a man, he grabs with his hand at the hand of the slave trader, just as the custom is known in buying and selling. I had stopped that day, with the guide calling to those about him who were interested, describing for them one slave girl after another, using the best descriptions of beauty. The noise was resounding and the market was brisk.

I return now to what I had started to speak of concerning the excessive affluence of the Baghdâdîs. I saw them beautifying their chambers with magnificent furnishings and costly furniture. They cover their walls with embroidery and silk brocade, and take an interest in planting flowers in their gardens, even to the extent that they have rare flowers brought to them from India. It reaches the point that the price of one of these gardens is valued at 10,000 dînârs. They select their slave boys from the most graceful of people and the most lively in energy : they desire entertainment and amusement from their concern, which I had mentioned, for their acquisition of female singers. They indulge in luscious food to the point of buying game and fruit out of season, paying for them their weight in silver. They enjoy the taste in some of their foods from perfume which they chew, and Indian betel leaves which they mix with wet lime to improve the taste and the food, and produce delight and cheerfulness in the soul. When it is hot they place their chairs among water gushing from statues of lions and among forms of birds and apples and other forms which they chisel in marble. When their bodies have obtained sufficient water to refresh the soul, they place fans on the ceiling. They work the fans by ropes which pull them, and pulling them, they draw the cool breeze over themselves. They indulge in clothes and ornamentation and in riding horses with silk brocade and heavy finery of silvery, to a degree which no affluent nations before them have reached.

THE MEDIEVAL WEST AND THE EAST

Epics of Chivalry

The term *chivalry* originally meant *cavalry,* but under feudalism the warrior nobility fighting on horseback developed a value system all its own. Chivalry, as an ideology, stressed courageous loyalty for good reasons ; in the centuries when feudalism prevailed, the "state" (in the sense of an independent entity with a legal monopoly on the use of force) simply did not exist. Dukes, counts, and others in the feudal hierarchy were supposed to keep a semblance of law and order in their territories and assist their liege lords in doing the same, but the responsibilities were a matter of individual contract. For example, a lord promised to uphold his vassal's rights in his fief, and the vassal promised to give "aids" and counsel to his lord. For the system to work properly, it was necessary — in the absence of readily available enforcing power — for both sides to feel a strong sense of honor in carrying out their commitments. Consequently, the utmost value was attached to having sufficient loyalty and courage to stand by the feudal contract despite overwhelming threats.

The ideals of chivalry were conveyed in epics known by their French generic name, *chansons de geste* (songs of deeds), of which the *Song of Roland* is easily the most famous, but chivalric epics were written in many parts of Europe. The work that follows, as well as *The Book of Emperors and Kings* in the next section, illustrate variations on chivalric themes.

The *Nibelungenlied,* written anonymously in Germany around 1200, mixes elements of the older epic emphasis on detailed and bloody battles with elements of the new "courtly" style, in which refinement, good manners, and fine clothing come into their own. In this new courtly style, women play very active roles. Siegfried, the most heroic male figure, is a master of both helmet-splitting combat and the courtly arts. He knows just what to do, just what to say, and just what to wear to cut a fine chivalric figure. The following excerpts from the *Nibelungenlied* sample both the violence-loving older emphasis and the (by 1200 contemporary but still fairly new) emphasis on what is polite and fashionable.

To understand the second and third excerpts, it is necessary to know that Brunhilde, Queen of Iceland, was a beautiful but Amazonian figure who offered her hand in marriage to any aspiring knight who would attempt to defeat her in sports but who would be killed if he lost to her. Gunther, King of Burgundy, was no match for Brunhilde and knew it, but he enlisted the aid of Siegfried by giving him a magic helmet that gave supernatural strength and invisibility to the wearer. In return for his help, Siegfried would have the beautiful Princess Kriemhilde, Gunther's sister, as his wife. Gunther went through the motions of throwing the required spear and a huge stone, but it was the invisible Siegfried who really won the games for him. Later, on their wedding night, Brunhilde refused to yield to Gunther's embraces but rather tied him up and hung him on the wall until dawn. Gunther then enlisted Siegfried's aid again: The next night, the invisible Siegfried physically overcame Brunhilde but then turned her over to Gunther for the consummation of their marriage, after which her Amazonian features left her and she became simply the "home queen" of Burgundy. Siegfried's fatal mistake was in taking a ring and valuable belt from Brunhilde as souvenirs of his adventure and then — an even worse judgment call — giving them to his own bride, Kriemhilde.

Eventually, rivalry between the two women led Kriemhilde to tell Brunhilde that Siegfried was the first man to possess her, and Brunhilde's longing for vengeance led to her persuading Hagen, one of Gunther's vassals who was trusted by Siegfried, to murder Siegfried. Much, much later, Kriemhilde got her own revenge by bringing about the bloody deaths of Hagen and other traitors, even though she had to marry Attila the Hun to do so and lost her own life in the process of carrying out the demands of justice as she saw them.

56

The *Nibelungenlied*

QUESTIONS TO CONSIDER

1. How does the author go about making Siegfried an appealing figure for his audience?
2. How does the character of King Gunther emerge as a point of contrast with Siegfried's heroic nature?
3. Why do you suppose the author starts the conflict with the Danes and Saxons with a description of single combat and ends it with one combining single combat and mass fray?
4. Where do you suppose the author got the idea of a man risking his life on a wager on his athletic performance for the hand of a desirable woman? Have you met up with a roughly similar story in one or more earlier cultures?
5. What does the feudal structure have to do with the rivalry between Brunhilde and Kriemhilde?

I

In the Netherlands, a son of the mighty King Siegmund and Queen Sieglinde grew up. There, downstream on the Rhine, the royal castle with the city called Xanten was known far and wide for its splendor. The bold young prince was named Siegfried. His manly courage was to lead him on tests of his warrior's skill into many kingdoms; his bold strength kept him riding through the lands. . . . He was of an age now to take his own place at the royal court. The people loved to watch him ride by. Many ladies and many girls hoped that his desires might pull him in their direction. Many loved him. . . . Siegmund and Sieglinde kept him very well dressed, and wise men who knew what honor was all about instructed him in winning lands and people to rule. . . .

[Hearing tales of the great beauty and charm of the Burgundian princess, Kriemhilde, Siegfried makes a knightly journey to Worms, the Burgundian capital. While he is there, messengers of the hostile kings of Saxony and Denmark approach her brother, King Gunther :] "If you will permit us, Sire, there is no reason for us to delay in giving you our message : It is that Ludgast and Ludger, the rulers who sent us, declare the feud you have caused by kindling great hatred in them, as we have been told, as reason for marauding your land. They plan an expedition to Worms on the Rhine, and there should be no doubt that many bold knights will follow them here. . . . They will start out in twelve weeks; that is, unless you want to negotiate with them : Then offer what you can. If you choose that course, the vast armies of your mighty enemies will not ride so close to Worms, bringing conflict that will cause you sorrow because so many of your good knights will be killed."

"Give me a little time," the good king said, "until I can think all this over. I will let you know what I decide later. If I indeed have loyal vassals, I will not want to keep this from them. Such a harsh message calls for the advice of my friends."

The best of his men who could be located came to him, and he said : "Ludgast and Ludger intend to invade our lands with strong forces : Just think about the grief that this will bring us."

"Let's defend with swords," said Gernot. "He will die whose lot it is to fall. I will not forget my honor in the fight : Let us welcome our enemies to do battle here."

Then Hagen of Tronya spoke up : "That does not seem like a good idea. Ludgast and Ludger are too full of themselves. We can't get a decent army together in such a short time. Why don't you tell Siegfried about this?"

Gunther directed men to see that the messengers were given lodgings in his city. Even though they were enemies, he had them very well taken care of. His act was generous, and he was doing the right thing until he could find friends who would support him.

But then the boldest of knights [Siegfried] saw how something terrible was depressing the king. He had no way of knowing what had gone on, and so he asked King Gunther to let him know what had happened. . . .

From *Das Nibelungenlied*, ed. Friedrich Zarncke (Halle : M. Niemeyer, 1905), verses 20–843. Translated by Henry A. Myers.

"I don't want to tell everybody about the troubles I have to bear secretly, but there is nothing wrong with opening your heart to your real friends."

At this, Siegfried turned both pale and red and said to the king: "I have never turned you down in anything yet, and I will help you deal with everything that is worrying you. If you need the help of friends, count on me. Trust me to support you through it all with honor until my own end comes."

"May God reward you, Lord Siegfried! I like the way you talk. Even if you don't actually fight in my cause, I'm glad to hear that you are so supportive. If I live through all this, I will see that you are well rewarded. And so, I will let you in on what troubles me so much right now. I just learned from my enemies' messengers that they are going to invade my lands, which no knights have ever done before."

"Don't pay too much attention to that threat," said Siegfried, "and don't let it worry you. Just do what I ask you to. Send for your vassals to come to your aid, but let me win honor and victories for you. If your mighty enemies can enlist thirty thousand knights, I would still beat them even if I had only a thousand. You can count on that."

"If you do, I will see that you receive lasting rewards," said King Gunther. . . .

When the news reached Denmark [that Gunther was going to fight and that the renowned Siegfried was supporting him], the king's men hurried to assemble more and more forces until Ludgast had twenty thousand knights ready to ride under his banner. King Ludger kept recruiting in Saxony until forty thousand and more had pledged to ride against the Burgundians.

[A little later at Gunther's court] "Let your Royal Highness stay at home," said Siegfried, "since your knights are willing to follow me. Look after the ladies and be of good cheer because I will prevent those invaders from attacking you at Worms on the Rhine. They will wish they had stayed at home because we will ride so far back into their own lands that their arrogance will be turned to grief." . . .

From the Rhine, the Burgundian forces rode through Hesse toward Saxony, where the battle was soon to be fought. . . . Never had the Saxons experienced such a devastating attack as this was to be. . . . "I will ride out myself," said Siegfried the hero, "and do some reconnaissance in our enemies' direction until I can establish where their knights are." He rode directly into Saxony . . . , and there he caught sight of a great army encamped in the field. From the forward sentries' position, one noble warrior soon rode out ready for combat. That bold man had seen Siegfried, and Siegfried saw him now.

I'll tell you who that was, riding now from the vanguard and holding a light shield of gold: It was King Ludgast himself, who had come to lead his army in person! Siegfried galloped toward him in all his glory, and Ludgast sought his noble "guest" for single combat as well. . . . Spurred on, their horses bore the two royal warriors, who had lowered their lances to rest on their shields for the charge, toward each other with such lightness that the wind itself appeared to be carrying them.

[The impact did not dislodge either of them, however, and] each grim and determined foe turned his steed around and sought the other with his sword. The field echoed the sounds of clanging metal, as Siegfried struck heavy blows. Under his hero's hand, great red sparks of fire sprayed from Ludgast's helmet. For a while, each of them found the other his equal, for Ludgast struck Siegfried many severe blows, too : Gashes made by the other's sword soon marked both their shields. Thirty of Ludgast's men saw what was going on, but before they reached him, Siegfried won the combat with three deep wounds he dealt the king through his light armor : They were decisive. The cutting edge of his sword drew blood from Ludgast's wounds and destroyed his will to continue. He asked for his life and, letting Siegfried know that he was Ludgast, offered him his lands.

But then his knights, who had seen from the outpost what was happening rode up and attacked Siegfried, all thirty of them, while he was leading Ludgast away. But Siegfried's strong arm let him keep his valuable hostage for himself : That wonderful knight inflicted still more destruction on his foes. Of the thirty, he killed all but one, leaving him to ride back to tell the news of what had happened with the red on his helmet bearing testimony. Denmark's warriors were sad and grim to learn that their ruler had been captured. When his brother, Ludger, heard the news, he went into convulsions of rage and grief.

[After turning Ludgast over to Hagen at the Burgundian camp,] Siegfried told the knights there to tie their flags on their lances : "There is much more to be done on the field of battle," he said. "If I stay alive, the wife of many a fine knight will be grieving in Saxony before sundown. .·. . I can lead you to Ludger's forces. There your strong arms will split many helmets before we return." . . .

They led no more than one thousand knights and the twelve brought by Siegfried. Clouds of dust began to rise on the road as they rode over the land, but many an ornamented shield rim still gleamed from their midst.

By then the full army of the Saxons was on the march. With their well-sharpened swords . . . , the Saxons hoped to defend their towns and lands from the stranger. . . . The Danes, too, gave their hands a good try. [When the battle began,] you could hear the clang of blows on many shield rims, while the sharp swords struck many wounds. Eager for combat, the Saxons did plenty of damage, but the Burgundians pressed into the fray, slashing wide wounds everywhere. You could watch the blood flowing over the saddles as those bold and good warriors competed for honor. Yes, you could hear their sharp weapons ring loud and far as they wielded them. Those who had followed Siegfried from the Netherlands pushed forward behind their lord into the thickest combat. You could see a bloody brook flowing through the gleaming helmets split by Siegfried's strong hand until he confronted King Ludger before his comrades at arms. . . .

When brave Ludger caught sight of Siegfried swinging his wonderful sword . . . high and low and slaughtering so many of his men, rage welled up in him. Both kings' followers rushed at each other with loud sword blows, as their leaders tested each other. Hate was seething all around, but then the Saxons began to back off a little. The Saxon king was told that his brother had been captured, and this gave him sad cause to grieve. . . . Siegfried soon took such blows from Ludger's sword that he felt his horse falter under his saddle. . . . In the press of battle, many knights dismounted, as did Siegfried and Ludger, who charged each other on foot. Siegfried's blows sent the rim clasps holding Ludger's shield together flying off, and the hero from the Netherlands felt sure of winning victory. . . . King Ludger recognized the crown painted on Siegfried's shield, and, realizing that the peerless hero must be its owner, began shouting loudly to his followers : "Give up fighting, all you on my side ; I now see Siegmund's son before me. Yes, I recognize that strongest of men : The devil himself sent him against us Saxons!"

And so the Saxons lowered their battle flags. Ludger sought peace, and this was granted him with the stipulation that he must go to King Gunther's country as a hostage. Brave Siegfried's strong hand had made him a prisoner.

II

"I want to sail over the North Sea to Brunhilde," said Gunther, the king from the Rhineland. "I don't care what happens to me : I am going to put my life on the line to win her love and die if I fail to win her as my wife."

"I would advise against that," said Siegfried. "That queen has introduced a savage custom at her court : The man who seeks her love will pay dearly for it. You really should find out more what *that* trip involves."

"If you insist on going," said Hagen, "I would advise you to take Siegfried along to help you with the grave dangers there, since he seems to know so much about the ways of Brunhilde's court."

"Noble Siegfried, will you help me to win my beloved? If you do what I ask and help me win that most desirable of women for my wife, I will risk my own honor and life to repay you."

"If you give me your sister to be my queen, I will do it," answered Siegfried. "I would not want any other reward for my trouble than that exalted princess, the beautiful Kriemhilde."

"I promise!" said Gunther. "Siegfried, let me shake your hand and swear that if the beautiful Brunhilde comes here to my kingdom I will give you my sister as your wife and you shall live happily ever after with your own beautiful bride." And so those bold knights confirmed their promises with oaths.

[A little later, Gunther spoke to Kriemhilde :] "My dearest sister, we cannot make good on what we plan without your help. We are going to undertake real challenges in Brunhilde's country, and for that we will need truly magnificent clothing to wear when we appear before the women there."

The maiden answered him : "My dearest brother, rest assured that I will surely do everything in my power to help you. Kriemhilde would be very sorry indeed if someone else were to let you down. In fact, noble knight that you are, I would rather that you didn't make requests of me as if it worried you to do so. Act confident in letting me know what you would like me to do for you. You will find me not only willing but eager to carry out your wishes. . . ."

"My dear sister, we want to go there wearing the best of clothes. Your own white hands can well see to our needs, but your serving women should help you, too, so that we look splendid for this trip. We wouldn't know where to begin otherwise."

The maiden answered : "I'm glad to let you know that I have just the silk for the task. See that we get a couple of shields full of gems. When we have sewn the gems on the silks, every combination you wear will do you honor before that prized princess. But who is going along to her court with you and will need fine clothes?"

"Four of us," he said. "Siegfried and two of my vassals, Dankwart and Hagen, are going to her court with me. Now pay close attention, sister, to what I am requesting : I would like each of us to have three changes of clothes per day for four days, outfits nice enough that when we leave Brunhilde's kingdom there will be no negative comments."

With cheerful words of parting, the royal lords left her. Princess Kriemhilde then had thirty of her ladies-in-waiting come from their chambers, those who had a keen sense of craftsmanship for the work at hand. They set gems on Arabian silks, white as snow, and the fine silks from Zazamanc, green as clover. Out of these they made fine garments with that wonderful young lady, Kriemhilde, cutting the cloth herself.

They also took some hides from exotic creatures of the deep[1] to serve as bottom layers, sewing the silk on top of them and mounting gold on top of both layers to catch the eyes of their hosts in that foreign land. You can just imagine what comments of amazement those glittering outfits later received! Kriemhilde certainly demonstrated her willing support of the project. She had an abundance of the very best silks that royalty had ever heard of from Morocco and some from Libya, too. Since this was the most exalted of all kinds of expeditions, they would have considered mere ermine furs unworthy. They did use ermine, but they mounted pieces of velvet, black as coals, on it so fine and costly that it would make bold heroes even of our own day stand out at ceremonies. The ladies took great pains with their work, and within seven weeks they had completed the wardrobe, which included garments with gems set in a background of Arabian gold. . . .

III

Kriemhilde and Brunhilde, the two exalted queens, were sitting next to each other [at a palace window, looking on] as outside many knights took part in jousting. They began to speak of two very special heroes who deserved the highest praise. "I have a husband," said the lovely Kriemhilde, "who deserves control over all these domains."

"How could that come about ?" Brunhilde responded. "If no other royal kin were still living but you and Siegfried, then the lands could owe allegiance to him, but as long as Gunther is alive they never will."

"Just look at him out there," said Kriemhilde, "riding so nobly and so handsomely in front of the other knights. He displays the moon's radiance dominantly in front of the milder glow of the stars. I have to admit that I derive pleasure from that fact."

"I don't care how well-outfitted your husband is," said Brunhilde, "or how well-mannered or how good-looking, you will still have to concede a higher place to your royal brother, the noble Gunther. You know very well that he must take his place before all other kings."

---

1. Probably sharkskin.

"My husband is so great," said Kriemhilde, "that I did not exaggerate with my praise of him. He deserves the very highest respect in a good many areas. Take it from me, Brunhilde: He is Gunther's equal and maybe more than that."

[The verbal exchanges escalated in sharpness until] "You are ranking yourself too high," said Brunhilde: "I am just waiting to see if people show you as much respect in public as they do me." Both of the ladies were really getting angry. . . .

[Later the two queens confronted each other upon approaching the door of the cathedral.] The home queen could not suppress her rage and rudely told Kriemhilde to stand where she was, saying: "No vassal's woman has a right to enter before a ruling king's wife."

That infuriated Kriemhilde: "You had better learn to hold your tongue. You brought disgrace on your own lovely body. How do you think another man's mistress can ever hope to be a real queen?"

"Who are you calling 'mistress'?" asked the king's wife.

"That is my name for you," said Kriemhilde, "because it was *my* dear husband, Siegfried, who first possessed that beautiful body of yours. It just wasn't my brother that you lost your virginity to. What are you so mad about? Or are you just pretending to be hurt? Why did you let him be your lover if he is supposed to be your vassal?"

Brunhilde began to cry. Kriemhilde waited no longer before the home king's wife but strode into the cathedral followed by her retinue.

Charlemagne and Pope Leo III

In the mid-twelfth century, one or more anonymous clerics in the German city of Regensburg made the first attempt since ancient times to present history to a broad — in fact, largely illiterate — audience in its own vernacular language. *The Book of Emperors and Kings,* now referred to with greater frequency and less accuracy as *The Imperial Chronicle,* was composed for reading or chanting aloud. Although it retains the outward form of a rhymed epic, the main author states his intention of telling the true history of the Roman Empire (meaning the Holy Roman Empire as well as the ancient one) from its beginning to the present day. He makes it plain that, unlike other "songs," his will refute lies instead of spreading them.

In the following excerpt, we see this author's idea of truth. He is more concerned throughout with true models of Christian rulership and contrasting examples of falsity than with mere "facticity." For example, he is intent on portraying Charlemagne as a monumental figure of stern faith and courage who collaborated with Pope Leo III in giving new life to the Roman Empire after the Byzantine Greeks, "the preceding house," had let the Empire's fortunes slide. To explain the motivation behind their mutual support, the author makes Pope Leo III into Charlemagne's brother.

The episode in which Charlemagne threatens Saint Peter may seem extreme by modern standards, but it reminds us that ideas of contract and loyalty thoroughly permeated the religious as well as the secular value system of the feudal world. Charlemagne has kept his part of the feudal contract; when he is convinced that Saint Peter has not kept his, he acts accordingly. Saint Peter responds like a liege lord who has been late in relieving his vassal's distress.

The selection also demonstrates the ambivalence of medieval people in northern Europe toward Rome and the Romans. All of them acknowledged the Bishop of Rome, the Pope, as head of the Church, while the descent of their Empire from Rome was stressed in the German-speaking lands. Still, those loyal to the Empire regarded the current inhabitants of Rome as a frequently treacherous group, who had to be controlled from time to time by "right-thinking" rulers with armies from the "uncorrupted" countries to the north of Italy.

By the twelfth century, the tradition that electoral princes (ranking members of the nobility and clergy) chose the German King (who officially became Roman emperor when consecrated by the Pope) had become established. In describing Charlemagne's ascension to these positions, the author of *The Book of Emperors and Kings* drifts between historical accounts from learned sources and traditional accounts from his own day.

The Saint Pancras episode reflects the legal view that people of different tribes or nations were entitled to be tried according to their own native laws. At the same time, this account heightens the author's ethnic stereotypes: The brave Germanic peoples settle their disputes through trial by combat, while the less courageous Romans settle legal disputes by raising two fingers and swearing oaths. According to legend, Pancras was a youth of fourteen who was martyred during Diocletian's (A.D. 284–305) persecution of Christians. As a reward for his courage in the face of death, God gave him the power to inflict a wasting, terminal illness on any who swore a false oath at his grave.

57

The Book of Emperors and Kings

QUESTIONS TO CONSIDER

1. How does the author establish Charlemagne as a model Christian ruler?
2. What motivates the Romans to attack the Pope? Why is Charlemagne ultimately to blame for this conflict?
3. Why is the Pope's requesting mercy for his assailants unacceptable to Charlemagne?
4. Does *The Book of Emperors and Kings* give any justification for identifying most of the inhabitants of Arles as "heathens"?
5. How does Charlemagne finally win his struggle in Spain?

The Empire remained without a head. The lords of Rome set the crown on Saint Peter's Altar. Meeting all together, they swore before the people that never again would they choose a king — nor judge, nor anyone else to rule them — from the kin of the preceding house, which had proven unable to maintain faith and honor with them. They wanted kings from other lands. . . .

According to a custom of those days, young princes from all over the Empire were raised and instructed with great care at the court in Rome. The Romans gave them the sword of knighthood when the time came . . . , sending the young heirs back to their homelands. This helped keep all the dominions mindful of serving Rome.

It came to pass that Pippin, a mighty king of Karlingen,[1] had two fine sons. One of them named Leo came to hold Saint Peter's throne after being raised in Rome, while Charles, the other, stayed home.

One night when Charles fell asleep, a voice called out to him three times: "Arise, beloved Charles, and hurry to Rome! Your brother Leo needs you!" And quickly Charles made ready, saying nothing to anyone about what he intended to do until he asked leave of the King to go. . . .

When the young Prince asked for leave, his father granted it to him gladly and bestowed gifts upon his son in a manner worthy of a mighty king. . . .

Charles really undertook his journey more for [the chance to pray at the tombs of] the divine Apostles than for his brother's sake. Early and late in the day his thoughts, which he revealed to no one, were filled with love of God. . . .

When Charles arrived in Rome, he was given a fine reception by old and young. . . . Pope Leo sang a mass then in honor of the Holy Ghost and to strengthen the Prince's spirit. Then he received God's Body. All who were there praised God, finding Charles so worthy and to their liking that the law should make him their ruler.

Charles did not listen to what was being said: He had made his journey for the sake of prayer, and he let no commotion distract him. He entered churches barefoot and, imploring God's mercy, he prayed for his soul. This steadfast devotion brought him every worldly honor, too. . . .

Thus he spent four weeks so wrapped in prayer and meditation that no one could approach him to speak, until once his brother, Pope Leo, and all the people fell at his feet. Charles pointed out to God in Heaven that if he were to prove unworthy he never should have made his journey. Then he received the royal emblems, and they set a magnificent crown on his head. All those there in Rome rejoiced that day, and all said, "Amen."

Then the King sat in judgment, and the Pope made complaint before him that church properties and the collection of tithes, entrusted to him by his predecessors for his use in the saving of souls, were being granted away from his jurisdic-

From *The Book of Emperors and Kings (Der keiser und der kunige buoch)*. Translated by Henry A. Myers from text published as *Die Kaiserchronik eines Regensburger Geistlichen*, ed. Eduard Schröder, in *Monumenta Germaniae Historica, Deutsche Chroniken* (Hannover: Hahn, 1892), vol. 1, pp. 339–353, passim.

1. "Karlingen," the name given by several medieval German writers to the domain of Charlemagne and his ancestors, is probably a derivation by analogy on the assumption that the name of the great Charles (Karl) was given to his whole family domain. Similarly, his grandson Lothar's name was applied to Lorraine (Lotharingen).

tion, and that his benefices had been taken from him. His complaint angered a number of the nobles.

Then Charles spoke these true ruler's words: "Never in this world, I feel sure, did anyone make a gift to honor God in order that another might take it. That would clearly be robbery. . . . Whoever would take anything away from gifts bestowed on God's houses, through which God's work is furthered, would be despised of God and could not remain a good Christian. . . ." Then those nobles departed, full of resentment. Charles also had no desire to remain there any longer.

Charles returned to Ripuaria.[2] The Romans realized very well that he was their rightful judge, but stupid men among them ridiculed the others for ever having proclaimed him ruler. . . . In Saint Peter's Cathedral they caught the Pope and pushed his eyes out of their sockets . . . , and sent him blind to the King in Ripuaria.

Nothing remained for the Pope to do but set out on the journey in his hapless condition. He rode on a donkey and took with him two of his chaplains, desiring no other escort. . . .

The Pope arrived in Ingelheim with his two chaplains and rode into the King's courtyard. When the King saw him coming, he said to one of his men: "Someone has attacked this pilgrim, and we shall do justice in his cause if we can. He seems badly injured. Someone must have robbed him. . . ."

The King strode quickly across the courtyard . . . and said: "Good pilgrim, if you wish to stay here with me, I will gladly take you in. Tell me if your misfortune is such that I can help you with it. Why don't you dismount?"

The noble Pope wanted to draw closer to the King. His head hung at a strange angle, and his eyes stared askew. "That God should have granted me your presence!" he began. . . . "It has not been long since I sang a mass for you at Rome, when I could still see." As he spoke these words, the noble King recognized him and was so shocked that he could neither see nor hear. . . . His body went limp and he could not speak. . . .

When the Emperor had recovered, the Pope told him sorrowfully: "I have come here that you may take pity on me. It was because of you that I lost my eyes: they blinded me to get even with you. Still, Brother, you must pull yourself together, and weep no more. . . ."

The Emperor himself lifted him down and carried him across the courtyard into his private chamber. There they sat together, and Charles told his men to go outside. "Brother," he said, "how did this happen to you? Let me hear your complaint, and then my forces of justice will right the wrong."

Pope Leo answered the King: "Brother, after you left Rome, the Romans very soon betrayed their loyalty to me in a conspiracy. They caught me in the Cathedral and committed this terrible crime upon me. Brother, we must bear this patiently: I seek vengeance only in Heaven, and you must not injure any of them for this."

"It would be doing God a dishonor to spare those murderers!" the noble King replied. "Ah! How sorely that would injure Christendom. I am called 'Judge' and 'Ruler': and this means I have the duty of judging over the peoples. . . . I must

---

2. Territorial home of one historic group of the Franks on the Rhine River; for the author, this location is sometimes synonymous with "Karlingen," sometimes one of its provinces.

defend Christendom with the sword. You will have them sorely regret their crime against you. I will avenge your eyes, or I will renounce my sword."

Then he dispatched messengers to King Pippin to tell him of his great need and let the nobles of Karlingen know that if they ever wanted to render God a loving service they should hurry to him. And there were none in Karlingen but who proclaimed all with one voice: "Woe to the fatal hour that Rome was ever founded!" . . .

The messengers galloped ceaselessly from land to land and from lord to vassal: all men were willing to come to the cause of Charles. Farmers and merchants, too — no one could hold them back. They left all their belongings and set out to join Charles. The mourning and grief over the news traveled through Christendom from people to people, and the streams of warriors converged like clouds over the Great Saint Bernard Pass. . . . The book does not give a number for the total army, but it was the greatest military expedition that ever descended on Rome.

When the army had advanced to within sight of the Aventine Hill in Rome, the worthy King asked three days and nights for himself. This annoyed his great lords, who went to him to say that it ill became his office to pause there, now that they had come so close that they could see the city which had aggrieved them.

"First we must pray to God, for we must gain His leave to carry through," answered the King. "Then we shall fight with ease. . . ."

Early one morning the voice of God spoke to him: "God in Heaven commands you, King, to remain here no longer. Ride on to Rome: God has rendered judgment, and just vengeance shall overtake them."

And so the King's banner was raised, and Charles let word pass through his whole army that when the knights were prepared for battle they should keep their eyes upon the banner and ride in close formation. Hearts swelling with high spirits, Charles's men swarmed over the hill. . . .

Owî, what an army this was that besieged Rome and the Lateran for seven days and seven nights, so menacingly that no one would fight against it! On the eighth day — this is the truth I am telling you — the Romans ordered the city gates opened and offered to let the King enter with this condition: that any man who could prove himself innocent of committing, aiding, or advising the crime would remain in the King's favor, while the King would deal with the guilty ones after deciding on a just sentence. . . .

As the Emperor sat in judgment and the document naming the guilty men was read, the accused all fervently denied their guilt when they were called forward. The King ordered them to submit to trial by combat for their unwillingness to confess. But then the Romans objected that this was not according to their law, and that no Emperor had ever forced such treatment on them before; instead, they should prove their innocence by swearing with their two fingers.

Then King Charles spoke: "I doubt that any crime so great was ever committed before. Don't be overhasty now: I imagine my brother saw at the time who did it." Still, when so very many of the accused offered their oaths in the Cathedral, the King said: I will not deprive you of recourse to your own law any longer; however, I know of a youth here named Pancras. If you are willing to swear an oath at his grave and if he tolerates it, then I will be willing to believe you."

Icy fear seized the Romans at the mention of this test. As they came to the place sacred to Saint Pancras and were supposed to hold up their fingers and to keep asserting their innocence under oath, one man was overcome, and panic gripped all the rest. They retreated in fear and fled back over the bridge although a fair number went back to Saint Peter's Cathedral.

Charles hesitated no longer but rode after them angrily. For three days, he and his men struck them down, and for three days they carried them out. Then they washed down the floor stones. . . . Charles fell on his knees before Saint Peter's tomb and made his plea to Christ: "Lord God in Heaven, how can I be any good to You as King when You let such shame befall me? Sinner that I may be, I do make every attempt to judge the people in a manner worthy of You. The Romans swore allegiance to a Pope, and You granted him a portion of Your power that he might loose the people from their sins and bind them. I [ask] . . . that you give the evil people of Rome something to recognize Your hidden power by: then they will know for certain that You are a true God. Grant me this, Holy Christ!"

A second time Charles, the noble King, fell to the ground and said: "Hail noble Saint Peter! You are really a divine stalwart of God, a watchman of Christendom. Think now, my lord, what I am going through! You are a summoner of the Kingdom of Heaven. Just look at your Pope! I left him sound of body in your care. Blinded was how I found him, and if you do not heal the blind man today I shall destroy your Cathedral and ruin the buildings and grounds donated to you, and then I shall leave him for you blind as he is, and go back again to Ripuaria."

Quickly the noble Pope Leo made himself ready and said his confession. As he spoke the last word, he saw a heavenly light with both his eyes. Great are the hidden powers of God.

The Pope turned around and spoke to the multitude: "My dearest children gathered from afar, be glad of heart, for the Kingdom of God is drawing near to you. God has heard you and because of your holy prayer has turned His face toward you. Here, at this very place, you are called to be public witnesses that a great miracle has happened. . . . I can see with both eyes better than I ever saw in this world." . . .

The Pope consecrated him as Emperor and granted absolution to all his comrades in arms. Owî, what joy there was in Rome then! The whole people rejoiced then and sang: *"Gloria in excelsis Deo."*

Then Charles laid down the Imperial Law, as an angel recited the true words of God to him. . . . And so the mighty Emperor left us many good laws, which God caused to be spoken before him. . . .

The very first laws the Emperor established dealt with what seemed to him to be the most exalted matters, those concerning bishops and priests, for the Imperial Law of Constantine had been sadly neglected. At the same time, he established laws governing tithes and gifts of property to the Church. . . .

Now I shall tell you about what the peasant is to wear according to the Imperial Law: his clothes may be black or gray, and he is allowed no other. . . . He is to have shoes of cow leather only and seven yards of towcloth for his shirt and breeches. He is to spend six days at the plow and doing plenty of other work; on Sunday he is to go to Church, carrying his animal goad openly in his hand. If a sword is found on a peasant, he is to be led bound to the churchyard fence, where he is to be tied and his skin and hair are to be flayed. If he is threatened by enemies, however, let him defend himself with a pitchfork. This law King Charles established for the peasants. . . .

. . . Emperor Charles besieged a walled city called Arles [France], which actually took him more than seven years. The inhabitants had considered him unworthy of his office. By way of an underground canal, wine was conveyed to them in plentiful supply, but finally Charles's cunning succeeded in cutting off their source. When the inhabitants could not hold out any longer, they threw open the city gates and fought fiercely, offering no terms at all. So many were slain on both sides that there is no man who can tell another how many of either the Christians or the heathens were lying there dead after the battle. No one could tell the dead apart until the Emperor solved the problem with God's help : He found the Christians lying separately in well adorned coffins. Now that is a wonder really worth telling about. . . .

The Emperor and his men turned toward Galicia [in Spain], where the king of the heathens inflicted great losses upon them. The Christian soldiers were all slain, and Charles barely escaped from the battle. Today the stone stays wet on which Charles sat afterwards, weeping passionately as he lamented his sins, saying : "Hail to You, God sublime! Grant me mercy for my poor soul. Take me out of this world, so that my people will no longer be punished because of me. I can never be consoled again."

Then an angel comforted him, saying : "Charles, beloved of God, your joy will come to you quickly. Bid your messengers make haste to summon virgin women — leave the married ones at home — for God will reveal His power through them. If you will fear and love God, the maidens will win your honor back again for you."

The messengers made haste and thoroughly searched through all the lands. They gathered together the maidens and brought them together . . . where the Emperor was waiting for them. Many a young maid came to join the host, fifty-three thousand — I am telling you this as a fact — and sixty-six more. . . .

When all the maidens arrived in a valley since named for Charles, they readied themselves for battle in formations just like men. . . .

Each heathen sentry was struck by wonder as to who this people could be, for it all seemed very strange to them. They hurried back, and one of them said to their king : "Sire, even though we slew the old ones, we must tell you for a fact that the young ones have followed them here. I have the feeling they want to slake their thirst for vengeance. They are big around the chest. Sire, if you fight with them, it will not come to any good end. Their hair is long, and their gait is very graceful : They are fine knights indeed. They are a terrifying lot. . . . No force could ever be assembled on this earth to defeat them. . . ."

At the advice of his experienced counsellors, their king turned over hostages to the Emperor. The king then had himself baptized — how well he suddenly believed in God! — and all his people with him. . . . Thus God made Charles victorious without the thrust of a spear or the blow of a sword, and the maidens well realized that God in Heaven was with them.

Charles and his heroines returned to their own homes back in the Empire. On the way, the worthy maidens came to a green meadow. Tired from the expedition, the heroines stuck their spearshafts into the ground and stretched out their arms in the form of a cross, sleeping on the ground after praising God for the goodness which He had shown them. They stayed there overnight, and a great miracle occurred. Their spearshafts had turned green and had sent forth leaves and blossoms. That is why the place is called "Woods of the Spearshafts"; it can be seen to this day.

Charles, the rich and powerful, built a mighty and beautiful church for the praise of Holy Christ, the honor of Saint Mary and all God's maidens, and the solace of Christendom. Since through chastity and spiritual purity the maids achieved their victory, the church is called *Domini Sanctitas.*[3]

East-West Ethnic Images

At the present, historians attempt to write as impartially and as factually as possible, even though each is a product of his or her own culture. However, this was not the case with the historians of the distant past.

The following three selections demonstrate that most written historical accounts were xenophobic — written from fear of things alien, or derived from a view that one's own culture was somehow morally or culturally superior to that of the strange and barbaric peoples with whom one had contact. Ibn Fadlan's account of the Vikings depicted them as a filthy race, while the Vikings countered this argument with another showing that their funeral rites were superior to those of the Arabs. Luitprand's *A Mission to Constantinople* describes nothing that is good about the Byzantines (e.g., their food, clothing, or entertainments) as compared to the German court. The Christian Crusaders were seen by most Muslim authors as ruthless, unbelieving barbarians who carved out their feudal states in the Near East at the expense of the native population.

58

Ibn Fadlan's Account of Vikings in Early Russia

In 921, Al-Muktadir, the Caliph of Baghdad, sent his ambassador, Ahmed ibn Fadlan, to the King of Bulgaria to arrange for the sending of Muslim missionaries to Bulgaria. Ahmed ibn Fadlan's roundabout journey, north from Baghdad and then west to Bulgaria, took him through southeastern Russia where, near the Volga River in 922, he encountered a Viking settlement and recorded these impressions of the "Northmen."

---

3. This church is the Emperor's Chapel, the main and oldest part of the Aachen Cathedral, also called Saint Mary's.

QUESTIONS TO CONSIDER

1. How does Ibn Fadlan's account of the funeral suggest Viking religious beliefs?
2. How would you compare this funeral practice with those described in Readings 25 and 26?

They are the filthiest race that God ever created. They do not wipe themselves after going to stool, nor wash themselves after a nocturnal pollution, any more than if they were wild asses.

They come from their own country, anchor their ships in the Volga, which is a great river, and build large wooden houses on its banks. In every such house there live ten or twenty, more or fewer. Each man has a couch, where he sits with the beautiful girls he has for sale. Here he is as likely as not to enjoy one of them while a friend looks on. At times several of them will be thus engaged at the same moment, each in full view of the others. Now and again a merchant will resort to a house to purchase a girl, and find her master thus embracing her, and not giving over until he has full had his will.

Every morning a girl comes and brings a tub of water, and places it before her master. In this he proceeds to wash his face and hands, and then his hair, combing it out over the vessel. Thereupon he blows his nose, and spits into the tub, and leaving no dirt behind, conveys it all into this water. When he has finished, the girl carries the tub to the man next to him, who does the same. Thus she continues carrying the tub from one to another till each of those who are in the house has blown his nose and spit into the tub, and washed his face and hair. . . .

I was told that the least of what they do for their chiefs when they die, is to consume them with fire. When I was finally informed of the death of one of their magnates, I sought to witness what befell. First they laid him in his grave — over which a roof was erected — for the space of ten days, until they had completed the cutting and sewing of his clothes. In the case of a poor man, however, they merely build for him a boat, in which they place him, and consume it with fire. At the death of a rich man, they bring together his goods, and divide them into three parts. The first of these is for his family; the second is expended for the garments they make; and with the third they purchase strong drink, against the day when the girl resigns herself to death, and is burned with her master. To the use of wine they abandon themselves in mad fashion, drinking it day and night; and not seldom does one die with the cup in his hand.

When one of their chiefs dies, his family asks his girls and pages, 'Which one of you will die with him?' Then one of them answers, 'I.' From the time that he utters this word, he is no longer free: should he wish to draw back, he is not permitted. For the most part, however, it is the girls that offer themselves. So, when the

From Albert Stanburrough Cook, "Ibn Fadlan's Account of Scandinavian Merchants on the Volga in 922," *Journal of English and Germanic Philology* 22(1923):54–63.

man of whom I spoke had died, they asked his girls, 'Who will die with him?' One of them answered, 'I.' She was then committed to two girls, who were to keep watch over her, accompany her wherever she went, and even, on occasion, wash her feet. The people now began to occupy themselves with the dead man — to cut out the clothes for him, and to prepare whatever else was needful. During the whole of this period, the girl gave herself over to drinking and singing, and was cheerful and gay.

When the day was now come that the dead man and the girl were to be committed to the flames, I went to the river in which his ship lay, but found that it had already been drawn ashore. Four corner-blocks of birch and other woods had been placed in position for it, while around were stationed large wooden figures in the semblance of human beings. Thereupon the ship was brought up, and placed on the timbers above-mentioned. In the meantime the people began to walk to and fro, uttering words which I did not understand. The dead man, meanwhile, lay at a distance in his grave, from which they had not yet removed him. Next they brought a couch, placed it in the ship, and covered it with Greek cloth of gold, wadded and quilted, with pillows of the same material. There came an old crone, whom they call the angel of death, and spread the articles mentioned on the couch. It was she who attended to the sewing of the garments, and to all the equipment; it was she, also, who was to slay the girl. I saw her; she was dark, thick-set, with a lowering countenance.

When they came to the grave, they removed the earth from the wooden roof, set the latter aside, and drew out the dead man in the loose wrapper in which he had died. Then I saw that he had turned quite black, by reason of the coldness of that country. Near him in the grave they had placed strong drink, fruits, and a lute; and these they now took out. Except for his colour, the dead man had not changed. They now clothed him in drawers, leggings, boots, and a *kurtak* and *chaftan* of cloth of gold, with golden buttons, placing on his head a cap made of cloth of gold, trimmed with sable. Then they carried him into a tent placed in the ship, seated him on the wadded and quilted covering, supported him with the pillows, and, bringing strong drink, fruits, and basil, placed them all beside him. Then they brought a dog, which they cut in two, and threw into the ship; laid all his weapons beside him; and led up two horses, which they chased until they were dripping with sweat, whereupon they cut them in pieces with their swords, and threw the flesh into the ship. Two oxen were then brought forward, cut in pieces, and flung into the ship. Finally they brought a cock and a hen, killed them, and threw them in also.

The girl who had devoted herself to death meanwhile walked to and fro, entering one after another of the tents which they had there. The occupant of each tent lay with her, saying, 'Tell your master, "I [the man] did this only for love of you."'

When it was now Friday afternoon, they led the girl to an object which they had constructed, and which looked like the framework of a door. She then placed her feet on the extended hands of the men, was raised up above the framework, and uttered something in her language, whereupon they let her down. Then again they raised her, and she did as at first. Once more they let her down, and then lifted her a third time, while she did as at the previous times. They then handed her a hen, whose head she cut off and threw away; but the hen itself they cast into the ship. I inquired of the interpreter what it was that she had done. He replied: 'The first time she said, "Lo, I see here my father and mother"; the second time, "Lo, now I see all my deceased relatives sitting"; the third time, "Lo, there is my master, who is sitting in Paradise. Paradise is so beautiful, so green. With him are his men and boys. He calls me, so bring me to him."' Then they led her away to the ship.

Here she took off her two bracelets, and gave them to the old woman who was called the angel of death, and who was to murder her. She also drew off her two anklets, and passed them to the two serving-maids, who were the daughters of the so-called angel of death. Then they lifted her into the ship, but did not yet admit her to the tent. Now men came up with shields and staves, and handed her a cup of strong drink. This she took, sang over it, and emptied it. 'With this,' so the interpreter told me, 'she is taking leave of those who are dear to her.' Then another cup was handed her, which she also took, and began a lengthy song. The crone admonished her to drain the cup without lingering, and to enter the tent where her master lay. By this time, as it seemed to me, the girl had become dazed; she made as though she would enter the tent, and had brought her head forward between the tent and the ship, when the hag seized her by the head, and dragged her in. At this moment the men began to beat upon their shields with the staves, in order to drown the noise of her outcries, which might have terrified the other girls, and deterred them from seeking death with their masters in the future. Then six men followed into the tent, and each and every one had carnal companionship with her. Then they laid her down by her master's side, while two of the men seized her by the feet, and two by the hands. The old woman known as the angel of death now knotted a rope around her neck, and handed the ends to two of the men to pull. Then with a broad-bladed dagger she smote her between the ribs, and drew the blade forth, while the two men strangled her with the rope till she died.

The next of kin to the dead man now drew near, and, taking a piece of wood, lighted it, and walked backwards towards the ship, holding the stick in one hand, with the other placed upon his buttocks (he being naked), until the wood which had been piled under the ship was ignited. Then the others came up with staves and firewood, each one carrying a stick already lighted at the upper end, and threw it all on the pyre. The pile was soon aflame, then the ship, finally the tent, the man, and the girl, and everything else in the ship. A terrible storm began to blow up, and this intensified the flames, and gave wings to the blaze.

At my side stood one of the Northmen, and I heard him talking with the interpreter, who stood near him. I asked the interpreter what the Northman had said, and received this answer: 'You Arabs,' he said, 'must be a stupid set! You take him who is to you the most revered and beloved of men, and cast him into the ground, to be devoured by creeping things and worms. We, on the other hand, burn him in a twinkling, so that he instantly, without a moment's delay enters into Paradise.' At this he burst out into uncontrollable laughter, and then continued: 'It is the love of the Master [God] that causes the wind to blow and snatch him away in an instant.' And, in very truth, before an hour had passed, ship, wood, and girl had, with the man, turned to ashes.

59

Liutprand, Bishop of Cremona, *A Mission to Constantinople*

In theory, all medieval Christians recognized the leadership within a single church until 1054, when the leaders of what we know as the Roman Catholic Church in the West and the Greek Orthodox Church in the East broke with each other and remain separate to this day. In reality, differences in style and theology had come to alienate the Greek-oriented Easterners from their counterparts in the West well before 1054. The self-image of the Easterners was one of pride in continuing Roman civilization with sophistication and refinement; Westerners appeared rough and savage by contrast. The self-image of Westerners was one of being honest and straightforward, as well as fearless in facing enemies; Easterners appeared devious and decadent by contrast.

In 968, the Western or Holy Roman Emperor Otto I sent Bishop Liutprand of Cremona, Italy, to the court of the Eastern Emperor Nicephorus Phocas to negotiate a marriage between his son, Otto II, whom he had made his co-ruler, and Princess Theophano, the daughter of Romanus II, Byzantine emperor between 959 and 963. His hope was that the marriage would help overcome strife between Greeks and Saxons over territories in Italy claimed by both empires. Liutprand's account of his stay in Constantinople, a much-condensed version of which follows, conveys the conflict of cultural images very vividly. In reporting to the Ottos, he is determined *not* to let Easterners get away with their boasts of living on a higher plane of civilization. (Some of his complaints were also reported by Western crusaders in the following centuries.) His complaints range from an emphatic rejection of the most common Greek wine to indignation over Greek attempts to overcharge him for everything. (Even today, Western travelers in Greece are likely to remark that retsina, the resinated wine that Greeks favor above all others, "tastes a little like turpentine" or, more kindly, "is going to take a little getting used to.") Like many Westerners then and later, Liutprand found the eunuchs at the Eastern capital to be proof of the degraded and effeminate nature of Byzantine society. Wearing apparel was another source of conflict. The fur-trimmed leather garments, in which Germanic Europeans took much pride, seem to have been harshly criticized by their southern and eastern counterparts since the days of the great migrations. In the selection that follows, Liutprand is very defensive on this score. In a section not included in the reading, he refers to the long-sleeved, silky garments of the East as of a type "that only street-walkers and sorcerers wear" in the West.

Still, both East and West were moved by the feeling that they should pull toward unity, particularly in the face of the Muslim threat. Liutprand's mission foundered at the time on the shoals of mutual dislike, but the following year Nicephorus was assassinated by his nephew, John Zimisces, who became emperor and in 972 under this new Eastern regime, Otto II did, in fact, marry the Princess Theophano, whom Liutprand had attempted to secure for him as a bride. From the perspective of centuries, however, Theophano's genteel influence scarcely put a dent in East-West ethnic prejudices. The mutual excommunications of 1054 and the sacking of Constantinople by Western crusaders a hundred and fifty years after that attest to the fragile nature of East-West medieval Christian harmony.

QUESTIONS TO CONSIDER

1. How does Liutprand mentally cope with the wealth and scope of the Byzantine Empire?
2. What main elements in the Westerners' self-image emerge in Liutprand's account?
3. Nearly a thousand years after Liutprand's mission, we find *Webster's Biographical Dictionary,* which we generally recognize as a fairly dispassionate source of information, noting that when Princess Theophano married Otto and came to the West, she "had great influence at his court, introducing much of the refinement of Constantinople."[1] Liutprand died in 972 or thereabouts, but, if he had lived another 10 or 15 years, how do you suppose he would have judged the efforts of a Byzantine-born empress to upgrade the culture of the Saxon court?

When we arrived in Constantinople on June 4, we were received very shabbily as a sign of disrespect to you, and afterwards treated the same way. They shut us up in a palace of sorts, which was big enough, all right, but had no roof to keep out heat or cold. Armed soldiers stood guard outside, to keep any of my companions from going out or anyone else from coming in. We were located so far away from the palace of Nicephorus that we were always out of breath from the long walk up to it whenever we went. We found the Greek wine, which is mixed with tar, resin, and plaster unfit to drink, but we could not even *buy* water to quench our thirst. No earthly being, but only one from hell, could be compared to the warden assigned to look after our daily needs. Like a drenching cloudburst, his inventiveness soaked us with misfortunes, extortions, torture, and grief for a hundred and twenty days.

On June 7, I was led before Nicephorus, a human freak with a very wide head and eyes as small as a mole's. He is thoroughly repulsive to look at with a thick neck less than an inch in length, long and bristly hair, Ethiopian skin color, drooping paunch and short stature. He is of a type you would hope not to meet up with after dark. And his clothes! They are very costly but ancient, faded, and bad-smelling. I always thought of my own august lords and emperors as handsome, but this horrible sight made me appreciate your handsome qualities all the more. In

---

"Legatio," in *Liudprandi episcopi Cremonensis opera omnia* (Hannover : Hahn, 1877), chs. i–xl, passim. Translated and condensed by Henry A. Myers ; calendar usage modernized.

1. *Webster's Biographical Dictionary* (Springfield, MA : G. & C. Merriam, 1960), p. 1131.

the same way, I was always aware of your great magnificence, power, kindness, and virtue : How much more did being with Nicephorus make me appreciate these even more!

... Both these rulers ... , the King of the Greeks and the King of the Franks[1] are men ... , but they are as different from each other — I would exaggerate only a little if I said : as species of animals differ from each other — as people of a sound mind differ from the insane. The King of the Greeks wears long hair and a tunic with long sleeves and a hood. He is lying, scheming, without mercy, fox-like, proud, insincerely humble, stingy, and greedy. He eats garlic, onions, and leeks, and he drinks bathwater. By way of contrast, the King of the Franks wears his hair tastefully trimmed, his clothing is altogether different from a woman's, and he wears a hat. He is truthful, straightforward, merciful when this is appropriate but severe when it is not. He is always sincerely humble and never stingy. He does not live on garlic, onions, and leeks, nor does he pile up money by saving animals to sell rather than having them to eat. . . .

[Liutprand was defending the Western imperial position on governing areas in Italy claimed by the Byzantines, when Nicephorus interrupted him:][2] "It is time for the solemn procession to the church. Let us attend to the needs of the hour, and when I have some time I will take up your requests again."

And what a procession it was indeed, with craftsmen and base-born people lining both sides of the road in masses thick as walls from the palace to Saint Sophia's. They were made even uglier than they already were by the thin little shields and flimsy spears which many of them carried. The fact that they came barefooted, which I think was to honor Nicephorus, made them more disgusting than ever to look at. The nobles who passed through that multitude of low-lifes were wearing tunics that were really old. Their grandfathers must have worn those self-same garments, which were very, very old even when their grandfathers wore them. None of them was wearing any gold, not even jewels, except Nicephorus himself; however, the symbols of imperial majesty which had been made for his imperial predecessors simply made him all the more loathsome to look at. I swear by your very salvation, which I value more than my own, that one precious garment of any of your nobles is worth more than a hundred of the things his were wearing. I had to take part in this procession and ended up on a platform next to the singers.

When Nicephorus, like a slithering reptile, reached the cathedral's interior, the singers chanted loudly : "Behold the Morning Star as he approaches. His glances do reflect the sun's own rays : Nicephorus, our ruler, who brings swift death to Muslims." They kept on like that : "A long life to our ruler, Nicephorus! Worship him, O people, adore him ; bow your heads to him alone." It would have been much more appropriate if they had sung : "Come to us, burnt-out wood-ember that you are, fool who looks like an evil spirit of the forest and walks like an old woman ; you double-jointed rebel, scaly-headed, bristly of hide, totally rural,

1. By Liutprand's time, the term "Frank" no longer applied simply to the original ethnic group of that name, but to any people associated with running the Germanic or Holy Roman Empire. By the time of the Crusades, it had become a rather generic term for Westerners as opposed to inhabitants of the East, and Asians from Arabia to China called all Western peoples, "Franks."
2. Material in brackets is the editor's condensed summary of Liutprand's writing.

barbarian, rude serf-by-nature, most at home in filthy places!" And so, blown up
by the lying chants of dunces, he entered Saint Sophia's.

That day he asked me to dinner, but, acting as if I were unworthy to be
placed above any of his nobles, he assigned me a seat fifteen places away from him
without even a tablecloth in front of me. The meal was completely disgusting;
everything smelt bad. All the food was soaked in oil, and they washed it all down
with a perfectly awful kind of spicy fish juice. During that meal he asked me many
questions about you, the lands you rule, and the forces which serve you. Then
when I had given him true and straightforward answers, he accused me of lying.

Eight days later, he invited me back again, thinking no doubt that I would appreciate the food and drink he served. Many bishops were there, including the Patriarch of Constantinople. He asked me many Bible questions, which I answered
eloquently enough, but then he tried to make fun of us by comparing the great
church councils which have been held in the East with the lack of them in the
West. [The Patriarch implied that the dearth of councils held in Western cities
showed that the Christian faith there was not mature; for Luitprand, however,
councils had the function of coping with heresies, so that a lack of them meant a
lack of heresy in the region.] I answered: "It is the member of the body which is
afflicted that must be cauterized with a hot iron. All heresies have come from your
territory. We of the Western nations have strangled them and put an end to them.
The Saxon people have produced no heresies from the time they first received
baptism and the knowledge of God. With no errors of doctrine among them, they
had no need of holding church councils. I am willing to agree with you that faith
among the Saxons is young: Faith in Christ is *always* young, not old, in people who
actually live according to it. Where people do not live according to the faith,
where people scorn it and throw it away like worn-out clothes — that is where
faith is old. But let me add that I do know for sure of one council held by Saxons:
It determined that it is better to fight with swords than with pens and to submit to
death than run from the enemy. Your own army has learned the truth confirmed
by *that* council." And to myself I said: "May the Saxons soon have a chance to show
what they can do in war!"

I just hope you believe me — and, of course, I know that you will believe
me — when I tell you that [if war reoccurs in Italy] four hundred of your fighting
men can slay the whole army dispatched by Nicephorus, unless they survive by
hiding behind ditches and walls. It seems to me that it is as if to show his scorn of
you that he has given the command of this army to a kind of man — I say "kind of"
because he has ceased to be a male and has not yet been able to become a female.

[By mid-September, the outcome of Liutprand's mission seemed very much
in doubt. When Nicephorus appeared reluctant to let him leave, Luitprand indicated to a group of Byzantine nobles that Emperor Otto might consider taking
vengeance on the Greeks for having detained his messenger so long.] "If he tries
it," they said, "neither Italy, nor the poor region of Saxony, land of his birth,
where the natives go around in wild animal skins, will be able to protect him. Our
money gives us power, and with it we will rally all manner of peoples against him.
We will break him like a clay pot, which, once shattered, cannot be put back together again." [These nobles also seized some purple garments from Liutprand
and his companions in a forced purchase, saying that they were too good for peo-

ple from the West.] How totally inappropriate it is that these soft, effeminate, lying, neutered, idle creatures with their long sleeves, hoods, and veils should go around in purple, while heroes representing you, strong warriors that they are, experienced in the military arts, possessing love and the true faith — men who hold God in real reverence and are full of virtues — may not. What is this, if not horrendous vanity!

Those who seek God upon false paths shall never find Him!

The Crusaders Seen through Muslim Eyes

By the mid-tenth century, the once mighty Abbasid caliphs [the head of state] of Baghdad were puppets of their own bodyguards. About a century later, Turkish nomads, the Seljuks, who had come from central Asia into Iran and had converted to Islam, rescued the caliphs. These Seljuk sultans slowly extended their political power from Iran-Iraq through Syria and Palestine. In 1071, the Byzantine emperor, Romanus IV Diogenes, tried to stop Seljuk raids into Anatolia (modern Turkey), but he was defeated at Manzikert. The Seljuks soon took over most of Anatolia from the Byzantine government.

Soon, however, the Seljuk sultanate broke up into quarreling petty states. This situation, plus appeals from the Byzantines and the Seljuk restrictions on the number of Christian pilgrims to the Holy Land, led Pope Urban II in 1095 to call for the First Crusade (1096–1099). The Crusaders, or Franks as Muslim authors refer to them, were able to create a series of western states along the Mediterranean coast from Anatolia to Egypt. These states did not last. The Turkish lord of Mosul, Zangi, and the Kurdish warrior Saladin became the anti-Crusading champions as they recaptured northern Syria and then Jerusalem by 1187.

One Arab-Syrian who lived through this period was Usamah Ibn Munqidh. He was born in 1095 to one of the most important families of the area who controlled the Castle of Shayzar on the Orontes river, which guarded routes into northern Syria or south into Lebanon. Usamah was given such a well-rounded education by his father that he not only gained military fame in fighting the Franks but was also considered a world traveler, poet, and scholar. His fame was so great that Saladin appointed him a lecturer on Islamic law and tutor in rhetoric in one of the academies in Damascus.

60

Memoirs of Usamah Ibn-Munqidh

The following selections from Usamah's *Memoirs* relate a very personal view of the Franks. Although the Crusaders are referred to as "devils" or "infidels" whose morals were both shocking or amusing to a conservative Muslim, Usamah developed a friendship with and respect for some of the Christians.

QUESTIONS TO CONSIDER

1. Compare the culture and society of Western Europe to that of the Near East. Why did the Franks seem barbaric to the Muslims?
2. Why would the sexual customs of the Franks shock Usamah?
3. How did Western Europe and Islamic society treat women?
4. Is there any indication that relations between the Franks and Muslims were not solely as enemies?
5. Compare the present selection with the Portuguese and Spanish relations with Africa and the New World (see Readings 88–89, 91–92). What are some similar or different attitudes?

Their curious medication. — A case illustrating their curious medicine is the following:

The lord of al-Munaytirah[1] wrote to my uncle asking him to dispatch a physician to treat certain sick persons among his people. My uncle sent him a Christian physician named Thābit. Thābit was absent but ten days when he returned. So we said to him, "How quickly hast thou healed thy patients!" He said:

They brought before me a knight in whose leg an abscess had grown; and a woman afflicted with imbecility.[2] To the knight I applied a small poultice until the abscess opened and became well; and the woman I put on diet and made her humor wet. Then a Frankish physician came to them and said, "This man knows nothing about treating them." He then said to the knight, "Which wouldst thou prefer, living with one leg or dying with two?" The latter replied, "Living with one leg." The physician said, "Bring me a strong knight and a sharp ax." A knight came with the ax. And I was standing by. Then the physician laid the leg of the patient on a block of wood and bade the knight strike his leg with the ax and chop it off at one blow. Accordingly he struck it — while I was looking on — one blow, but the leg was not severed. He dealt another blow, upon which the marrow of the leg flowed out and the pa-

Philip K. Hitti, trans., *An Arab-Syrian Gentleman and Warrior in the Period of the Crusades, Memoirs of Usamah Ibn-Munqidh* (New York: Columbia University Press, 1929), pp. 162–169.

1. In Lebanon near Afqah, the source of Nahr-Ibrāhīm, i.e., ancient Adonis.
2. Ar. *nashāf*, "dryness," is not used as a name of a disease. I take the word therefore to be Persian *nishāf* — "imbecility."

tient died on the spot. He then examined the woman and said, "This is a woman in whose head there is a devil which has possessed her. Shave off her hair." Accordingly they shaved it off and the woman began once more to eat their ordinary diet — garlic and mustard. Her imbecility took a turn for the worse. The physician then said, "The devil has penetrated through her head." He therefore took a razor, made a deep cruciform [cross-shaped] incision on it, peeled off the skin at the middle of the incision until the bone of the skull was exposed and rubbed it with salt. The woman also expired instantly. Thereupon I asked them whether my services were needed any longer, and when they replied in the negative I returned home, having learned of their medicine what I knew not before.

Newly arrived Franks are especially rough : One insists that Usāmah should pray eastward. — Everyone who is a fresh emigrant from the Frankish lands is ruder in character than those who have become acclimatized and have held long association with the Moslems. Here is an illustration of their rude character.

Whenever I visited Jerusalem I always entered the Aqṣa Mosque, beside which stood a small mosque which the Franks had converted into a church. When I used to enter the Aqṣa Mosque, which was occupied by the Templars[3], who were my friends, the Templars would evacuate the little adjoining mosque so that I might pray in it. One day[4] I entered this mosque, repeated the first formula, "Allah is great," and stood up in the act of praying, upon which one of the Franks rushed on me, got hold of me and turned my face eastward saying, "This is the way thou shouldst pray !" A group of Templars hastened to him, seized him and repelled him from me. I resumed my prayer. The same man, while the others were otherwise busy, rushed once more on me and turned my face eastward, saying, "This is the way thou shouldst pray !" The Templars again came in to him and expelled him. They apologized to me, saying, "This is a stranger who has only recently arrived from the land of the Franks and he has never before seen anyone praying except eastward." Thereupon I said to myself, "I have had enough prayer." So I went out and have ever been surprised at the conduct of this devil of a man, at the change in the color of his face, his trembling and his sentiment at the sight of one praying towards the *qiblah.*[5]

Another wants to show to a Moslem God as a child. — I saw one of the Franks come to al-Amīr [chieftain] Mu'īn-al-Dīn (may Allah's mercy rest upon his soul !) when he was in the Dome of the Rock[6] and say to him, "Dost thou want to see God as a child ?" Mu'īn-al-Dīn said, "Yes." The Frank walked ahead of us until he showed us the picture of Mary with Christ (may peace be upon him !) as an infant in her lap. He then said, "This is God as a child." But Allah is exalted far above what the infidels say about him !

Franks lack jealousy in sex affairs. — The Franks are void of all zeal and jealousy. One of them may be walking along with his wife. He meets another man who takes the wife by the hand and steps aside to converse with her while the husband is standing on one side waiting for his wife to conclude the conversation. If she lingers too long for him, he leaves her alone with the conversant and goes away. . . .

3. Knights Templars were members of a military religious order called the Knights of the Temple of Solomon, named from their house in Jerusalem.
4. About 1140.
5. The direction of the Ka'bah in the holy city, Mecca.
6. The mosque standing near al-Aqṣa in Jerusalem.

We had with us a bath-keeper named Sālim, originally an inhabitant of al-Ma'arrah,[7] who had charge of the bath of my father (may Allah's mercy rest upon his soul!). This man related the following story :

> I once opened a bath in al-Ma'arrah in order to earn my living. To this bath there came a Frankish knight. The Franks disapprove of girding a cover around one's waist while in the bath. So this Frank stretched out his arm and pulled off my cover from my waist and threw it away. He looked and saw that I had recently shaved off my pubes. So he shouted, "Sālim!" As I drew near him he stretched his hand over my pubes and said, "Sālim, good! By the truth of my religion, do the same for me." Saying this, he lay on his back and I found that in that place the hair was like his beard. So I shaved it off. Then he passed his hand over the place and, finding it smooth, he said, "Sālim, by the truth of my religion, do the same to madame" (*al-dāma* in their language means the lady), referring to his wife. He then said to a servant of his, "Tell madame to come here." Accordingly the servant went and brought her and made her enter the bath. She also lay on her back. The knight repeated, "Do what thou has done to me." So I shaved all that hair while her husband was sitting looking at me. At last he thanked me and handed me the pay for my service.

Consider now this great contradiction! They have neither jealousy nor zeal but they have great courage, although courage is nothing but the product of zeal and of ambition to be above ill repute.

Their judicial trials : A duel. — I attended one day a duel in Nāblus between two Franks. The reason for this was that certain Moslem thieves took by surprise one of the villages of Nāblus. One of the peasants of that village was charged with having acted as guide for the thieves when they fell upon the village. So he fled away. The king[8] sent and arrested his children. The peasant thereupon came back to the king and said, "Let justice be done in my case. I challenge to a duel the man who claimed that I guided the thieves to the village." The king then said to the tenant who held the village in fief, "Bring forth someone to fight the duel with him." The tenant went to his village, where a blacksmith lived, took hold of him and ordered him to fight the duel. The tenant became thus sure of the safety of his own peasants, none of whom would be killed and his estate ruined.

I saw this blacksmith. He was a physically strong young man, but his heart failed him. He would walk a few steps and then sit down and ask for a drink. The one who had made the challenge was an old man, but he was strong in spirit and he would rub the nail of his thumb against that of the forefinger in defiance, as if he was not worrying over the duel. Then came the viscount, i.e., the seignior of the town, and gave each one of the two contestants a cudgel and a shield and arranged the people in a circle around them.

The two met. The old man would press the blacksmith backward until he would get him as far as the circle, then he would come back to the middle of the arena. They went on exchanging blows until they looked like pillars smeared with blood. The contest was prolonged and the viscount began to urge them to hurry, saying, "Hurry on." The fact that the smith was given to the use of the hammer proved now of great advantage to him. The old man was worn out and the smith

7. Ma'arrah-al-Nu'mān, between Ḥamāh and Aleppo.
8. Fulk of Anjou, king of Jerusalem (1131–42).

gave him a blow which made him fall. His cudgel fell under his back. The smith knelt down over him and tried to stick his fingers into the eyes of his adversary, but could not do it because of the great quantity of blood flowing out. Then he rose up and hit his head with the cudgel until he killed him. They then fastened a rope around the neck of the dead person, dragged him away and hanged him. The lord who brought the smith now came, gave the smith his own mantle, made him mount the horse behind him and rode off with him. This case illustrates the kind of jurisprudence and legal decisions the Franks have — may Allah's curse be upon them!

Ordeal by water. — I once went in the company of al-Amīr Mu'īn-al-Dīn (may Allah's mercy rest upon his soul!) to Jerusalem. We stopped at Nāblus. There a blind man, a Moslem, who was still young and was well dressed, presented himself before al-amīr carrying fruits for him and asked permission to be admitted into his service in Damascus. The amīr consented. I inquired about this man and was informed that his mother had been married to a Frank whom she had killed. Her son used to practice ruses against the Frankish pilgrims and coöperate with his mother in assassinating them. They finally brought charges against him and tried his case according to the Frankish way of procedure.

They installed a huge cask and filled it with water. Across it they set a board of wood. They then bound the arms of the man charged with the act, tied a rope around his shoulders and dropped him into the cask, their idea being that in case he was innocent, he would sink in the water and they would then lift him up with the rope so that he might not die in the water; and in case he was guilty, he would not sink in the water. This man did his best to sink when they dropped him into the water, but he could not do it. So he had to submit to their sentence against him — may Allah's curse be upon them! They pierced his eyeballs with red-hot awls [drills].

The Fourth Crusade

The purpose of the Fourth Crusade (A.D. 1202–1204), as envisioned by Pope Innocent III, was to continue the Western attack on the Muslim-held holy places in the Near East. However, the French Norman crusaders were diverted from their original task because of the Venetian desire to control the trade routes to the Near East coupled with a plea for aid from Alexius Angelus. Angelus was the son of the imprisoned, blinded, and dethroned Byzantine emperor, Isaac.

Although the crusaders were able to restore Isaac and his son to their rightful positions, the Byzantine emperors were not able to fulfill their bargain to pay the Normans for the restoration. As a result, tensions between the natives and the crusaders eventually led to the usurpation of the Byzantine throne as well as the deaths of Isaac and his son. In 1204, the crusaders decided to attack Constantinople, which fell amid scenes of violence and rapacity on the part of the Normans. In the period from 1204 to 1261, a Latin kingdom, ruled by Franks, arose in the East. The crusade also forcibly instituted Roman Catholicism in place of the Eastern Orthodox Church. These actions left a lasting religious bitterness and an Eastern empire that never recovered from the devastation.

Robert of Clari, who was among the Fourth Crusaders, left an eyewitness account from the perspective of a simple soldier. After returning home in 1205, Robert dictated his memoirs, adding one last piece concerning the death of the second Latin emperor, Henry I, in 1216.

This chronicle is the best single Western source describing the motivations and actions of the crusaders. Robert, with great accuracy, describes the Great Palace, Santa Sophia, and the Golden Gate; he also offers diversions concerning miracle cures and sacred relics such as the True Cross, the head of John the Baptist, and perhaps the Shroud of Turin, thought by many to be the burial cloth of Jesus.

61

Robert of Clari, *The Conquest of Constantinople*

QUESTIONS TO CONSIDER

1. Why was the Fourth Crusade a perversion of the crusading spirit?
2. What was the cause of the religious problems between Rome and Constantinople?
3. What caused the crusaders to sack the city?
4. What miraculous objects or places impressed the crusaders?
5. What comparison can you make between Robert of Clari's description and the Spanish conquest of Mexico (see Reading 92)?

In the meantime, while the crusaders and the Venetians were staying there [on the Dalmatian coast] that winter, the crusaders bethought them that they had spent a great deal. And they talked with one another and said that they could not go to Babylon or to Alexandria or to Syria, because they had neither provisions nor money for going there. For they had spent nearly everything, on the long delay they had made as well as on the great price they had given for the hire of the fleet. . . .

The doge of Venice saw right well that the pilgrims were in sore straits, and he spoke to them and said: "Lords, in Greece there is a land that is very rich and plenteous in all good things. If we could have a reasonable excuse for going there

From Robert of Clari, *The Conquest of Constantinople,* trans. Edgar Holmes McNeal (New York: Columbia University Press, 1936; Octagon Books, 1966), pp. 45, 57–59, 67–68, 77, 92–95, 97, 99–103, 106–107, 112–115, 128. © 1936 Columbia University Press. Reprinted by permission of Columbia University Press.

and taking provisions and other things in the land until we were well restored, it would seem to me a good plan. Then we should be well able to go oversea." . . .

Now you have heard how Isaac arose and how he became emperor and how his son went to Germany — he for whom the crusaders and the Venetians were going to send, on the advice of the marquis of Montferrat, their leader, . . . so that they might have an excuse for going to the country of Constantinople. And now we shall tell you about this youth and the crusaders, how the crusaders sent for him and how they went to Constantinople and how they conquered it. . . .

Then all the barons of the host were summoned and the Venetians. And when they were all assembled, the doge of Venice rose and spoke to them. "Lords," said the doge, "now we have a good excuse for going to Constantinople, if you approve of it, for we have the rightful heir." Now there were some who did not at all approve of going to Constantinople. Instead they said : "Bah! what shall we be doing in Constantinople? We have our pilgrimage to make, and also our plan of going to Babylon or Alexandria. Moreover, our navy is to follow us for only a year, and half of the year is already past." And the others said in answer : "What shall we do in Babylon or Alexandria, when we have neither provisions nor money to enable us to go there? Better for us before we go there to secure provisions and money by some good excuse than to go there and die of hunger. Then we shall be able to accomplish something. Moreover, he offers to come with us and to maintain our navy and our fleet a year longer at his own cost." . . . When they of Constantinople saw this fleet which was so finely arrayed, they gazed at it in wonder, and they were mounted on the walls and on the houses to look upon this marvel. And they of the fleet also regarded the great size of the city, which was so long and so wide, and they marveled at it exceedingly.

When the emperor of Constantinople learned of it, he sent good envoys to ask them what they sought there and why they were come there, and he sent word to them that if they wanted any of his gold or his silver, he would right gladly send it to them. When the high men heard this, they answered the envoys that they did not want any of his gold or his silver, but rather they wanted the emperor to surrender the empire, for he held it neither rightfully nor loyally, and they sent word to him that they had the rightful heir with them, Alexius, the son of Isaac the emperor. Thereupon the envoys answered and said that the emperor would do nothing of the sort, and with that they went away. . . .

While the French and the Venetians were talking together, there arose a great clamor in the city, for they of the city told the emperor that he ought to deliver them from the French who were besieging them, and that if he did not fight with them they would seek out the youth whom the French had brought and make him emperor and lord over them.

When the emperor heard this, he gave them his word that he would fight them on the morrow. But when it came near midnight, the emperor fled from the city with as many people as he could take with him.

When the morning was come on the morrow and they of the city knew that the emperor was fled, what do they do but go to the gates and open them and issue forth and come to the camp of the French and ask and inquire for Alexius, the son of Isaac. And they were told that they would find him at the tent of the marquis. When they came there, they found him, and his friends did him great honor and made great rejoicing over him. And they thanked the barons right heartily and said that they who had done this thing had done right well and had done a great deed of baronage. And they said that the emperor had fled, and that they [the crusaders] should come into the city and into the palace as if it all belonged to them. Then all the high barons of the host assembled, and they took Alexius, the son of Isaac, and they led him to the palace with great joy and much rejoicing. And when they were come to the palace, they had Isaac, his father, brought out of prison, and his wife also. This was the one who had been imprisoned by his brother, the recent emperor. When Isaac was out of prison, he made great rejoicing over his son and embraced and kissed him, and he gave great thanks to the barons who were there and said that it was by the help of God first and next by theirs that he was out of prison. Then they brought two golden chairs and seated Isaac on one and Alexius his son on the other beside him, and to Isaac was given the imperial seat. . . .

Afterwards the emperor sought out the barons and said to them that he had nothing save Constantinople and that this was worth little to him by itself, for his uncle held all the cities and castles that ought to be his. So he asked the barons to help him conquer some of the land around, and he would right gladly give them still more of his wealth. Then they answered that they would be very glad to do it, and that anyone who wanted to profit by this could go. Then a good half of the host went with Alexius and the other half stayed in Constantinople to receive the payment, and Isaac stayed behind to make the payment to the barons. So Alexius went with all his host and conquered full twenty cities and full forty castles or more of the land, and Alexius, the other emperor, his uncle, fled always before him. . . .

. . . When this respite was past and the French saw that the emperor was not going to pay them anything, all the counts and the high men of the host came together, and they went to the palace of the emperor and asked again for their payment. Then the emperor answered them that he could not pay them anything, and the barons answered that if he did not pay them they would seize enough of his possessions to pay themselves. . . .

. . . While these things were going on, those of the Greeks who were traitors toward the emperor and this Murzuphlus whom the emperor had freed from prison came together and plotted a great treason. For they wanted to make someone else emperor, someone who would deliver them from the French, because Alexius did not seem good to them any longer. And finally Murzuphlus said : "If you will leave it to me," said he, "and will make me emperor, I will deliver you from the French and from this emperor, so that you will never have any more trouble from them." And they said that if he would deliver them they would make him emperor, and Murzuphlus vowed to free them within a week, and they agreed to make him emperor.

Then Murzuphlus went and lost no time. He took sergeants with him and entered by night into the chamber where his lord the emperor, who had freed him from prison, was sleeping, and he had them tie a cord around his neck and strangle him and his father Isaac also. . . . It was not long afterwards that Murzuphlus sent word to the count of Flanders, to Count Louis, to the marquis, and to all the other high barons, telling them to go away and vacate his land, and letting them know that he was emperor and that if he came on them there a week from then he would slay them all. When the barons heard the message that Murzuphlus had sent, they replied: "What?" said they, "He who has treacherously murdered his lord by night has sent this word to us?" And they sent back word to him that they defied him and let him now beware of them, for they would not abandon the siege until they had avenged him whom he had murdered and had taken Constantinople again and had secured in full the payment which Alexius had promised them. . . .

Then it came about on a Friday, about ten days before Palm Sunday, that the pilgrims and the Venetians got their ships and their engines ready and prepared for the assault. So they ranged their ships side by side, and the French had their engines loaded on barges and galleys, and they set out to go toward the city, and the navy extended fully a good league along its front. . . .

When the navy was about to make land, they took strong cables and drew their ships as close as they could to the walls, and the French had their engines set up, their "cats" and "carts" and "sows," to mine the walls. And the Venetians mounted on the bridges of their ships and hardily assailed the walls and the French likewise assailed them with their engines. When the Greeks saw the French attacking them thus, they set to hurling huge blocks of stone, more than enough, onto the engines of the French, and they began to crush and break to pieces and destroy all these engines, so that no one dared to remain inside or under them. And the Venetians on their part were not able to reach the walls or the towers, they were so high. Nor ever that day were the Venetians or the French able to accomplish anything at the walls or at the city. When they saw that they could not do anything, they were greatly disheartened and drew off. When the Greeks saw them withdrawing, they began to hoot and to call out more lustily than a great deal, and they mounted on the walls and let down their clouts and showed them their backsides. . . .

Then when the bishops had preached and had shown the pilgrims that the battle was a righteous one, they all confessed themselves right well and were given communion. When it came to Monday morning, the pilgrims all made themselves ready and armed themselves right well, and the Venetians also. Then they repaired the bridges on their ships and got ready their transports and their galleys and ranged them side by side for the assault, and the navy had fully a good league of front. When they reached the shore and had drawn up as close as they could to the walls, they cast anchor. And when they were at anchor, they began to attack vigorously and to shoot and hurl stones and throw Greek fire on the towers, but the fire could not take hold on them because of the hides with which they were covered. And those within the city defended themselves right hardily, and they had fully sixty petraries [medieval military engines for discharging stones] hurling missiles, and at each cast they hit the ships, but the ships were so well covered with planks and with grapevines that they did not do them any harm, and the stones were so large that a man could not lift one of them from the ground. . . . When my lord Pierre of Amiens saw that those who were in the towers were not advancing and saw the condition of the Greeks, what does he do but descend to the land on foot, he and his people with him, on a little piece of ground that was between the sea and the wall. When they were on land, they looked ahead and saw a false postern, the door of which had been removed and it had been walled up again. . . .

... When they were come to this postern, they began to attack it hardily with their picks, and the quarrels of the crossbows were flying so thick and they were hurling so many stones down on them from the walls, that it seemed as if they would be buried under them, so many were thrown. And those below had shields and targes with which they covered those who were picking at the postern. And the others hurled down on them pots full of boiling pitch and Greek fire and immense stones, so that it was a miracle of God they were not all crushed. And my lord Pierre of Amiens and his people endured there labors and difficulties more than a great deal. So they picked away at this postern with axes and with good swords, with pieces of wood, with bars and with picks, until they made a great hole in it. . . .

When those who were defending the towers and the walls saw that the French were entered into the city and their emperor had fled away, they did not dare remain there but fled away each one as best he could. Thus was the city taken. When the city was taken in this way and the French were inside, they stayed right where they were. Then the high barons assembled and took counsel among them as to what they should do. And finally it was cried through the host that no one should dare to go on into the city, for it was a great peril to go there, lest they should cast stones on them from the palaces, which were very large and high, or lest they should slay them in the streets, which were so narrow that they would not be able to defend themselves, or lest the city should be set on fire behind them and they be burned. Because of these dangers and perils, they did not dare seek quarters or disperse, but remained there right where they were. . . .

When morning came on the morrow, what do they do, the priests and clergy in their vestments, the English, Danes, and people of other countries, but come in procession to the camp of the French and cry them mercy and tell them all that the Greeks had done, and they said that all the Greeks had fled and no one was left in the city but the poor people. When the French heard this, they were mightily glad. Then they had it cried through the host that no one should take possession of a house until it had been decided how they should be divided. Then the high men, the rich men, came together and agreed among themselves to take the best houses of the city, without the common people or the poor knights of the host knowing anything about it. And from that time on they began to betray the common people and to keep bad faith and bad comradeship with them. . . .

So they sent to seize all the best houses and the richest of the city, and they had them all taken before the poor knights and the common people of the host were aware of it. And when the poor people were aware of it, they went each one as best he could and took what they could get. . . .

When the city was captured and the pilgrims were quartered, . . . and the palaces were taken over, then they found in the palaces riches more than a great deal. And the palace of Boukoleon was very rich and was made in such a way as I shall tell you. Within this palace, . . . there were fully five hundred halls, all connected with one another and all made with gold mosaic.[1] And in it there were fully

---

1. In these terms Robert attempts to describe the great complex of buildings lying between the Hippodrome and the sea walls, which was known as the Great Palace. . . .

thirty chapels, great and small, and there was one of them which was called the Holy Chapel. . . .[2] Within this chapel were found many rich relics. One found there two pieces of the True Cross as large as the leg of a man and as long as half a *toise,* and one found there also the iron of the lance with which Our Lord had His side pierced and two of the nails which were driven through His hands and feet, and one found there in a crystal phial quite a little of His blood, and one found there the tunic which He wore and which was taken from Him when they led Him to the Mount of Calvary, and one found there the blessed crown with which He was crowned, which was made of reeds with thorns as sharp as the points of daggers. And one found there a part of the robe of Our Lady and the head of my lord St. John the Baptist and so many other rich relics that I could not recount them to you or tell you all the truth. . . .

Now I will tell you about the church of Saint Sophia, how it was made. Saint Sophia in Greek means Sainte Trinité ["Holy Trinity"] in French [*sic.*] The church of Saint Sophia was entirely round, and within the church there were domes, round all about, which were borne by great and very rich columns, and there was no column which was not of jasper or porphyry or some other precious stone, nor was there one of these columns that did not work cures. There was one that cured sickness of the reins when it was rubbed against, and another that cured sickness of the side, and others that cured other ills. . . . On the ring of the great door of the church, which was all of silver, there hung a tube, of what material no one knew ; it was the size of a pipe such as shepherds play on. This tube had such virtue as I shall tell you. When an infirm man who had some sickness in his body like the bloat, so that he was bloated in his belly, put it in his mouth, however little he put it in, when this tube took hold it sucked out all the sickness and it made the poison run out of his mouth and it held him so fast that it made his eyes roll and turn in his head, and he could not get away until the tube had sucked all of this sickness out of him. And the sicker a man was the longer it held him, and if a man who was not sick put it in his mouth, it would not hold him at all, much or little. . . .

. . . And among the rest, there was another of the churches which they called My Lady Saint Mary of Blachernae, where was kept the *sydoine* in which Our Lord had been wrapped, which stood up straight every Friday so that the features of Our Lord could be plainly seen there.[3] And no one, either Greek or French, ever knew what became of this *sydoine* after the city was taken. . . .

Afterwards it came about that all the counts and all the high men came together one day at the palace of Boukoleon, which belonged to the marquis, and they said to one another that they ought to decide on an emperor and ought to choose their ten electors, and they told the doge of Venice to choose his ten. When the marquis heard this, he wanted to put in his own men and those who he thought would choose him as emperor, and he wanted to be emperor forthwith. . . . This discord lasted a good fortnight without their ever being able to agree.

2. This is the celebrated church of the Blessed Virgin of the Pharos (lighthouse). . . .
3. Robert seems to have confused the *sudarium* (the sweat cloth or napkin, the True Image of St. Veronica) with the *sindon* (the grave cloth in which the body of Jesus was wrapped for entombment). Both relics were in the church of the Blessed Virgin in the Great Palace, and not in the church in the palace of Blachernae, as Robert says.

And there was no day on which they did not assemble for this affair, until at length they agreed that the clergy of the host, the bishops and abbots who were there, should be the electors. . . .

When the mass was chanted, the electors assembled and took counsel together, and they talked of one and of another, until the Venetians and the bishops and abbots, all twenty electors, agreed all together that it should be the count of Flanders, nor was there one of them who was against it. . . .

King John and the Barons of England

In 1215, English barons forced King John (reigned 1199–1216) to agree to the Magna Carta ("Great Charter"). This agreement was a consequence of the King's assumption of new and arbitrary royal powers, which violated feudal relationships with his vassals.

King John had gone rather far with his abuses. He had been awarding heiresses in his custody to men who offered him the highest bids of money for approving their marriage contracts. He had been requiring exorbitant "reliefs," payments by heirs who took over their fathers' fiefs. He also had been demanding scutage or "shield money" (payments in lieu of required military service) to finance military expeditions he never conducted. A main concern of the barons was to limit the king's right to demand what we would call "taxes" from them except when traditionally specified in feudal contracts.

The Magna Carta went well beyond royal-feudal disputes in its provisions, however. The agreement was probably drawn up by Stephen Langton, Archbishop of Canterbury, who assured that the charter would guarantee the independence of the Church in England from unwarranted royal interference. At the same time, Langton had foresight enough to include specific rights not only for the clergy and nobility but for all free commoners as well. Thus, the document became a landmark in securing political liberties for all the English population who counted in the Middle Ages: nobles, churchmen, and free commoners. The Magna Carta further established the important general principle that the king was under — rather than above — the law. This agreement even outlined enforcement procedures for bringing the king back into line if he should assert arbitrary powers again.

62

The Magna Carta

QUESTIONS TO CONSIDER

1. What enumerated rights show this document to be concerned with protection of the nobility from arbitrary royal power?
2. What rights does the Magna Carta guarantee to the English Church?
3. Which articles contain provisions of greatest interest to merchants and other townspeople?
4. Do you think that article 61 guarantees the right to trial by jury? What clause makes the question a slightly open one?
5. What are the main duties of the 25-baron council?

Rights of the English Clergy, Nobles, and Freemen

John, by the grace of God, king of England, lord of Ireland, duke of Normandy and Aquitaine, count of Anjou, to the archbishops, bishops, abbots, earls, barons, justiciars, foresters, sheriffs, reeves, servants and all bailiffs and his faithful people, greeting. . . .

1. In the first place, we have granted to God, and by this our present charter confirmed, for us and for our heirs forever, that the English church shall be free, and shall hold its rights entire and its liberties uninjured; and we will that it be thus observed; which is shown by this, that the freedom of elections, which is considered to be most important and especially necessary to the English church, we, of our pure and spontaneous will, granted, and by our charter confirmed, before the contest between us and our barons had arisen; and obtained a confirmation of it by the lord pope, Innocent III; which we shall observe and which we will shall be observed in good faith by our heirs forever.

We have granted, moreover, to all free men of our kingdom, for us and our heirs forever, all the liberties written below, to be had and holden by themselves and their heirs from us and our heirs.

2. If any of our earls or barons, or others holding from us in chief by military service shall have died, and when he has died his heir shall be of full age and owe relief, he shall have his inheritance by the ancient relief; that is to say, the heir or heirs of an earl for the whole barony of an earl a hundred pounds; the heir or heirs of a baron for a whole barony a hundred pounds; the heir or heirs of a knight for a whole knight's fee a hundred shillings at most; and who owes less let him give less according to the ancient custom of fiefs.

From "Extracts from the Great Charter," in Edward P. Cheyney, ed., *Readings in English History Drawn from the Original Sources* (Boston: Ginn & Co., 1908), pp. 182–187.

3. If, moreover, the heir of any one of such shall be under age, and shall be in wardship, when he comes of age he shall have his inheritance without relief and without a fine. . . .

6. Heirs shall be married without disparagement, so never-the-less, that before the marriage is contracted it shall be announced to the relatives by blood of the heir himself.

7. A widow, after the death of her husband, shall have her marriage portion and her inheritance immediately and without obstruction, nor shall she give anything for her dowry or for her marriage portion, or for her inheritance . . . and she may remain in the house of her husband for forty days after his death within which time her dowry shall be assigned to her.

8. No widow shall be compelled to marry so long as she prefers to live without a husband, provided she give security that she will not marry without our consent, if she holds from us, or without the consent of her lord from whom she hold, if she holds from another. . . .

12. No scutage or aid shall be imposed in our kingdom except by the common council of our kingdom, except for the ransoming of our body, for the making of our oldest son a knight, and for once marrying our oldest daughter ; and for these purposes it shall be only a reasonable aid. In the same way it shall be done concerning the aids of the city of London.

13. And the city of London shall have all its ancient liberties and free customs, as well by land as by water. Moreover, we will and grant that all other cities and boroughs and villages and ports shall have all their liberties and free customs.

14. And for holding a common council of the kingdom concerning the assessment of an aid otherwise than in the three cases mentioned above, or concerning the assessment of a scutage, we shall cause to be summoned the archbishops, bishops, abbots, earls, and greater barons by our letters under seal ; and besides we shall cause to be summoned generally, by our sheriffs and bailiffs, all those who hold from us in chief, for a certain day, that is at the end of forty days at least, and will express the cause of the summons, and when the summons has thus been given the business shall proceed on the appointed day, on the advice of those who shall be present, even if not all of those who were summoned have come.

15. We will not grant to any one, moreover, that he shall take an aid from his freemen, except for ransoming his body, for making his oldest son a knight, and for once marrying his oldest daughter ; and for these purposes only a reasonable aid shall be taken.

16. No one shall be compelled to perform for a knight's fee or for any other free tenement any greater service than is owed from it.

17. The common pleas shall not follow our court, but shall be held in some certain place.

18. The recognitions of *novel disseisin, mort d'ancestor,* and *darrein presentment* [these were legal "inquests" instituted by Henry II] shall be held only in their own counties and in this manner : we, or if we are outside of the kingdom, our principal justiciar, will send two justiciars through each county four times a year, who, with four knights of each county, elected by the county, shall hold in the county and on the day and in the place of the county court the aforesaid assizes of the county. . . .

28. No constable or other bailiff of ours shall take any one's grain or other chattels without immediately paying for them in money, unless he is able to obtain a postponement at the good will of the seller.

29. No constable shall require any knight to give money in place of his ward of a castle, if he is willing to furnish that ward in his own person or through another honest man, if he himself is not able to do it for a reasonable cause ; and if we shall lead or send him into the army, he shall be free from ward in proportion to the time which he has been in the army.

30. No sheriff or bailiff of ours or any one else shall take horses or wagons of any freeman for carrying purposes except on the permission of the freeman.

31. Neither we nor our bailiffs will take the wood of another man for castles, or for anything else which we are doing, except by the permission of him to whom the wood belongs. . . .

35. There shall be one measure of wine throughout our whole kingdom, and one measure of ale, and one measure of grain, that is the London quarter, and one width of dyed cloth and of russets and of halbergets, that is two ells within the selvages ; of weights, moreover, it shall be as of measures. . . .

39. No freeman shall be taken or imprisoned or dispossessed, or outlawed or banished or in any way destroyed, nor will we go upon him, nor send upon him, except by the legal judgment of his peers or by the law of the land.

40. To no one will we sell, to no one will we deny, or delay right or justice.

41. All merchants shall be safe and secure in going out from England and coming into England, and in remaining and going through England, as well by land and by water, for buying and selling, free from all evil tolls by the ancient and rightful customs, except in time of war, and if they are of a land at war with us ; and if such are found in our land at the beginning of war, they shall be attached without injury to their bodies or goods, until it shall be known from us or from our principal justiciar in what way the merchants of our land are treated who shall be then found in the country which is at war with us ; and if ours are safe there, the others shall be safe in our land. . . .

47. All forests which have been afforested in our time shall be disafforested immediately ; and so it shall be concerning river banks which in our time have been fenced in. . . .

51. And immediately after the reestablishment of peace we will remove from the kingdom all foreign-born soldiers, crossbowmen, servants, and mercenaries who have come with horses and arms for the injury of the realm.

52. If any one shall have been dispossessed or removed by us without legal judgment of his peers, from his lands, castles, franchises, or his right, we will restore them to him immediately ; and if contention arises about this then it shall be done according to the judgment of the twenty-five barons, of whom mention is made below concerning the security of the peace. Concerning all those things, however, from which any one has been removed or of which he has been deprived without legal judgment of his peers by King Henry our father, or by King Richard our brother, which we have in our hand, or which others hold, and which it is our duty to guarantee, we shall have respite till the usual term of crusaders ; excepting those things about which the suit has been begun or the inquisition made by our writ before our assumption of the cross. When, however, we shall return from our

journey, or if by chance we desist from the journey, we will immediately show full justice in regard to them. . . .

60. Moreover, all those customs and franchises mentioned above, which we have conceded in our kingdom, and which are to be fulfilled, as far as pertains to us, in respect to our men, all men of our kingdom, as well clergy as laymen, shall observe as far as pertains to them, in respect to their men.

61. Since, moreover, for the sake of God, and for the improvement of our kingdom, and for the better quieting of the hostility sprung up lately between us and our barons, we have made all these concessions; wishing them to enjoy these in a complete and firm stability forever, we make and concede to them the security described below; that is to say, that they shall elect twenty-five barons of the kingdom, whom they will, who ought with all their power to observe, hold, and cause to be observed, the peace and liberties which we have conceded to them, and by this our present charter confirmed to them.

Thus if we or our justiciar, or our bailiffs, or any of our servants shall have done wrong in any way toward any one, or shall have transgressed any of the articles of peace or security, and the wrong shall have been shown to four barons of the aforesaid twenty-five barons, let those four barons come to us, or to our justiciar, if we are out of the kingdom, laying before us the transgression, and let them ask that we cause that transgression to be corrected without delay. And if we shall not have corrected the transgression, or, if we shall be out of the kingdom, if our justiciar shall not have corrected it, within a period of forty days, counting from the time in which it has been shown to us, or to our justiciar, if we are out of the kingdom, the aforesaid four barons shall refer the matter to the remainder of the twenty-five barons, and let these twenty-five barons with the whole community of the country distress and injure us in every way they can; that is to say, by the seizure of our castles, lands, possessions, and in such other ways as they can until it shall have been corrected according to their judgment, saving our person and that of our queen, and those of our children; and when the correction has been made, let them devote themselves to us as they did before. . . .

63. Wherefore we will and firmly command that the church of England shall be free, and that the men in our kingdom shall have and hold all the aforesaid liberties, rights, and concessions, well and peacefully, freely and quietly, fully and completely, for themselves and their heirs, from us and our heirs, in all things and places, forever, as before said. It has been sworn, moreover, as well on our part as on the part of the barons, that all these things spoken of above shall be observed in good faith and without any evil intent. Witness the above at the place which is called Runnymede, between Windsor and Staines, on the fifteenth day of June, in the seventeenth year of our reign.

Apostolic Poverty

Francis of Assisi (1182–1226), founder of the Franciscan Order, is one of the most celebrated saints of medieval Europe. As the son of a prosperous merchant, young Francis enjoyed a carefree life of pleasure and paid little attention to religion. But in 1206, he underwent a conversion experience and committed the rest of his life to minister to the poorest of the poor living in the burgeoning cities of his native Italy. In imitation of the first apostles, Francis accepted a life of absolute poverty. He gave away all of his property and made his way by begging. Francis was an open, joyful man who loved animals and loved to laugh. Despite the hardships of his ministry, he naturally drew people to him. Francis was loath to establish detailed regulations for his followers, but by 1210, so many people had joined in his work that he was compelled to organize a rule for his followers. To underscore the virtue of humility, Francis called his followers the Order of Friars Minor. Unlike monks who retreated from the world to live in monasteries, his "little brothers" or friars were to live among the people. The Franciscan Friars, and the women's order of the Poor Clare nuns that he inspired, were to own nothing. Like Francis, they were to earn their way by manual labor or by begging. The focus of their ministry was the poor of the inner cities. Soon the Franciscans had established hospitals for lepers, orphanages for abandoned children, and shelters for the homeless. By 1217, Franciscan missionaries had been sent to France, Germany, Hungary, Spain, North Africa and would soon be in China (see Reading 69). By the end of the thirteenth century, 1400 Franciscan convents and friaries had been established. Because of the tremendous growth of the Franciscan movement, Francis was forced to revise his rule of 1210, and in 1223, three years before his death, he produced a more detailed rule to guide his Franciscans.

63

The Rule of St. Francis

QUESTIONS TO CONSIDER

1. Why would the Rule of St. Francis be so attractive to thousands of men and women throughout medieval Europe?
2. Why did Francis exempt his followers from certain periods of fasting and permit them to "eat whatever food is set before them"?
3. What does the success of the Franciscan order suggest about social conditions in thirteenth-century Europe?

4. How would you compare the life of a Franciscan with that of a Benedictine (see Reading 48)?

5. Why would the Franciscans excel as foreign missionaries (see Reading 69)?

1. This is the rule and life of the Minor Brothers, namely, to observe the holy gospel of our Lord Jesus Christ by living in obedience, in poverty, and in chastity. Brother Francis promises obedience and reverence to pope Honorius and to his successors who shall be canonically elected, and to the Roman Church. The other brothers are bound to obey brother Francis, and his successors.

2. If any, wishing to adopt this life, come to our brothers [to ask admission], they shall be sent to the provincial ministers, who alone have the right to receive others into the order. The provincial ministers shall carefully examine them in the catholic faith and the sacraments of the church. And if they believe all these and faithfully confess them and promise to observe them to the end of life, and if they have no wives, or if they have wives, and the wives have either already entered a monastery, or have received permission to do so, and they have already taken the vow of chastity with the permission of the bishop of the diocese [in which they live], and their wives are of such an age that no suspicion can rise against them, let the provincial ministers repeat to them the word of the holy gospel, to go and sell all their goods and give to the poor [Matt. 19:21]. But if they are not able to do so, their good will is sufficient for them. And the brothers and provincial ministers shall not be solicitous about the temporal possessions of those who wish to enter the order; but let them do with their possessions whatever the Lord may put into their minds to do. Nevertheless, if they ask the advice of the brothers, the provincial ministers may send them to God-fearing men, at whose advice they may give their possessions to the poor. Then the ministers shall give them the dress of a novice, namely: two robes without a hood, a girdle, trousers, a hood with a cape reaching to the girdle. But the ministers may add to these if they think it necessary. After the year of probation is ended they shall be received into obedience [that is, into the order], by promising to observe this rule and life forever. And according to the command of the pope they shall never be permitted to leave the order and give up this life and form of religion. For according to the holy gospel no one who puts his hand to the plough and looks back is fit for the kingdom of God [Luke 9:62]. And after they have promised obedience, those who wish may have one robe with a hood and one without a hood. Those who must may wear shoes, and all the brothers shall wear common clothes, and they shall have God's blessing if they patch them with coarse cloth and pieces of other kinds of cloth. But I warn and exhort them not to despise nor judge other men who wear fine and gay clothing, and have delicious foods and drinks. But rather let each one judge and despise himself.

3. The clerical brothers shall perform the divine office according to the rite of the holy Roman church, except the psalter, from which they may have breviaries. The lay brothers shall say 24 Paternosters at matins, 5 at lauds, 7 each at primes, terces, sexts, and nones, 12 at vespers, 7 at completorium, and prayers for

Oliver J. Thatcher and Edgar J. McNeal, eds., *A Source Book for Medieval History: Selected Documents* (New York: Charles Scribner's Sons, 1905), pp. 499–504.

the dead. And they shall fast for All Saints' day [November 1] to Christmas. They may observe or not, as they choose, the holy Lent which begins at epiphany [January 6] and lasts for 40 days, and which our Lord consecrated by his holy fasts. Those who keep it shall be blessed of the Lord, but those who do not wish to keep it are not bound to do so. But they shall all observe the other Lent [that is, from Ash-Wednesday to Easter]. The rest of the time the brothers are bound to fast only on Fridays. But in times of manifest necessity they shall not fast. But I counsel, warn, and exhort my brothers in the Lord Jesus Christ that when they go out into the world they shall not be quarrelsome or contentious, nor judge others. But they shall be gentle, peaceable, and kind, mild and humble, and virtuous in speech, as is becoming to all. They shall not ride on horseback unless compelled by manifest necessity or infirmity to do so. When they enter a house they shall say, "Peace be to this house." According to the holy gospel, they may eat of whatever food is set before them.

4. I strictly forbid all the brothers to accept money or property either in person or through another. Nevertheless, for the needs of the sick, and for clothing the other brothers, the ministers and guardians may, as they see that necessity requires, provide through spiritual friends, according to the locality, season, and the degree of cold which may be expected in the region where they live. But, as has been said, they shall never receive money or property.

5. Those brothers to whom the Lord has given the ability to work shall work faithfully and devotedly, so that idleness, which is the enemy of the soul, may be excluded and not extinguish the spirit of prayer and devotion to which all temporal things should be subservient. As the price of their labors they may receive things that are necessary for themselves and the brothers, but not money or property. And they shall humbly receive what is given them, as is becoming to the servants of God and to those who practise the most holy poverty.

6. The brothers shall have nothing of their own, neither house, nor land, nor anything, but as pilgrims and strangers in this world, serving the Lord in poverty and humility, let them confidently go asking alms. Nor let them be ashamed of this, for the Lord made himself poor for us in this world. This is that highest pitch of poverty which has made you, my dearest brothers, heirs and kings of the kingdom of heaven, which has made you poor in goods, and exalted you in virtues. Let this be your portion, which leads into the land of the living. Cling wholly to this, my most beloved brothers, and you shall wish to have in this world nothing else than the name of the Lord Jesus Christ. And wherever they are, if they find brothers, let them show themselves to be of the same household, and each one may securely make known to the other his need. For if a mother loves and nourishes her child, how much more diligently should one nourish and love one's spiritual brother? And if any of them fall ill, the other brothers should serve them as they would wish to be served.

7. If any brother is tempted by the devil and commits a mortal sin, he should go as quickly as possible to the provincial minister, as the brothers have determined that recourse shall be had to the provincial ministers for such sins. If the provincial minister is a priest, he shall mercifully prescribe the penance for him. If he is not a priest, he shall, as may seem best to him, have some priest of the order prescribe the penance. And they shall guard against being angry or irritated about it, because anger and irritation hinder love in themselves and in others.

8. All the brothers must have one of their number as their general minister and servant of the whole brotherhood, and they must obey him. At his death the provincial ministers and guardians shall elect his successor at the chapter held at Pentecost, at which time all the provincial ministers must always come together at whatever place the general minister may order. And this chapter must be held once every three years, or more or less frequently, as the general minister may think best. And if at any time it shall be clear to the provincial ministers and guardians that the general minister is not able to perform the duties of his office and does not serve the best interests of the brothers, the aforesaid brothers, to whom the right of election is given, must, in the name of the Lord, elect another as general minister. After the chapter at Pentecost, the provincial ministers and guardians may, each in his own province, if it seems best to them, once in the same year, convoke the brothers to a provincial chapter.

9. If a bishop forbids the brothers to preach in his diocese, they shall obey him. And no brother shall preach to the people unless the general minister of the brotherhood has examined and approved him and given him the right to preach. I also warn the brothers that in their sermons their words shall be chaste and well chosen for the profit and edification of the people. They shall speak to them of vices and virtues, punishment and glory, with brevity of speech, because the Lord made the word shortened over the earth [Rom. 9:28].

10. The ministers and servants shall visit and admonish their brothers and humbly and lovingly correct them. They shall not put any command upon them that would be against their soul and this rule. And the brothers who are subject must remember that for God's sake they have given up their own wills. Wherefore I command them to obey their ministers in all the things which they have promised the Lord to observe and which shall not be contrary to their souls and this rule. And whenever brothers know and recognize that they cannot observe this rule, let them go to their ministers, and the ministers shall lovingly and kindly receive them and treat them in such a way that the brothers may speak to them freely and treat them as lords speak to, and treat, their servants. For the ministers ought to be the servants of all the brothers. I warn and exhort the brothers in the Lord Jesus Christ to guard against all arrogance, pride, envy, avarice, care, and solicitude for this world, detraction, and murmuring. And those who cannot read need not be anxious to learn. But above all things let them desire to have the spirit of the Lord and his holy works, to pray always to God with a pure heart, and to have humility, and patience in persecution and in infirmity, and to love those who persecute us and reproach us and blame us. For the Lord says, "Love your enemies, and pray for those who persecute and speak evil of you" [cf. Matt. 5:44]. "Blessed are they who suffer persecution for righteousness' sake, for theirs is the kingdom of heaven" [Matt. 5:10]. He that endureth to the end shall be saved [Matt. 10:22].

11. I strictly forbid all the brothers to have any association or conversation with women that may cause suspicion. And let them not enter nunneries, except those which the pope has given them special permission to enter. Let them not be intimate friends of men or women, lest on this account scandal arise among the brothers or about brothers.

12. If any of the brothers shall be divinely inspired to go among Saracens and other infidels they must get the permission to go from their provincial minister, who shall give his consent only to those who he sees are suitable to be sent. In addition, I command the ministers to ask the pope to assign them a cardinal of the holy Roman church, who shall be the guide, protector, and corrector of the brotherhood, in order that, being always in subjection and at the feet of the holy church, and steadfast in the catholic faith, they may observe poverty, humility, and the holy gospel of our Lord Jesus Christ, as we have firmly promised to do. Let no man dare act contrary to this confirmation. If anyone should, and so on.

Scholasticism

Although the Renaissance of the Twelfth Century furthered a great revival of interest in the ancient Greek and Roman classics, Church leaders in the West occasionally expressed reservations about this enthusiastic propagation of secular learning. They were all the more concerned because many Greek philosophical and scientific works had reached Europe by way of Arab sources from Muslim Spain ; there was considerable interest at the new universities in Arab works on alchemy, astronomy, mathematics, and medicine. The most comprehensive commentary on Aristotle before 1200 was that of the Spanish Muslim Averröes.

The reservations of Church authorities concerning pagan or Muslim learning influenced Scholasticism toward attempts to harmonize useful pagan learning with Christian teachings. During the earlier Carolingian Renaissance, teachers of the liberal arts had been called "scholastics," or "school-men" ; as a loose and general term, the earlier scholasticism had signified the teaching of theology and philosophy, particularly at points where the two overlapped. During the thirteenth century, however, Scholasticism became the systematic defense of approved dogma with a combination of secular philosophy and scriptural authority.

Saint Thomas Aquinas (c. 1225–1274), a Dominican monk, was easily the greatest of the Scholastic writers. His *Summa Theologiae* uses human reason and ancient philosophy, particularly that of Aristotle, to confirm revealed religious propositions, especially those found in the letters of Saint Paul. In Thomas's work, like that of many other Scholastics, Aristotle is simply called the "Philosopher" and Saint Paul the "Apostle."

In the following selection from the *Treatise on God,* part of the *Summa Theologiae,* Saint Thomas employs the dialectic, the ancient Greek form of argumentation so effectively used by Plato in his dialogues (see Reading 38). By the thirteenth century, the dialectic had come to mean presenting a bit of theory as a question ; examining all the arguments for it, if it was a false proposition, or against it, if it was a true one ; and, finally, answering these wrong arguments with reason and evidence.

64

Saint Thomas Aquinas, "The Existence of God"

QUESTIONS TO CONSIDER

1. Why does Saint Thomas find it useful to dispute the proposition that the existence of God is self-evident?
2. What does motion have to do with Saint Thomas's proof of the existence of God?
3. How do we know, according to Saint Thomas, that one can *demonstrate* (as opposed to *believe*) that God exists?
4. The "efficient cause" for Aristotle involved the maker of a thing, such as the sculptor of a statue, who *causes* the object to be his or her handiwork. How does Saint Thomas introduce the idea of "efficient cause" among his proofs for the existence of God?
5. What are the similarities and differences between the ways Saint Thomas and Plato (see Reading 38) use the dialectic? Which approach seems more effective?

Because the principal intention of this sacred doctrine is to teach the knowledge of God not only as He is in Himself but also as He is the beginning of things and their last end, and especially of the rational creature, as is clear from what has been already said, therefore in expounding this science, we shall treat : (1) of God ; (2) of the rational creature's movement toward God ; (3) of Christ, who as man is our way to God.

In treating of God there will be a threefold division : for we shall consider those things that pertain (1) to the divine essence ; (2) to the distinctions of Persons ; (3) to the procession of creatures from Him.

Concerning the divine essence, we must consider : first, whether God exists ; secondly, the manner of His existence, or rather, what is *not* the manner of His existence ; while in the third place we shall treat of that which pertains to His operation, viz., His knowledge, will, and power.

Regarding the first, there are three problems to be dealt with : (1) whether the proposition *God exists* is self-evident ; (2) whether it is demonstrable ; (3) whether God exists.

From Saint Thomas Aquinas, *Treatise on God,* texts selected and translated by James F. Anderson (Englewood Cliffs, NJ : Prentice-Hall, 1963), pp. 6–12. Reprinted by permission of Prentice-Hall, Inc. Footnotes omitted.

Is the Existence of God Self-Evident ?

Objection 1. It seems so ; for those things are said to be "self-evident to us" the knowledge of which exists naturally in us, as is clear in the case of first principles. But as Damascene says in the beginning of his book, "the knowledge of God's existence is naturally implanted in all." Therefore the existence of God *is* self-evident.

Objection 2. Moreover, those things are said to be "self-evident" which are known as soon as the terms are grasped ; this, the Philosopher says in Book I of the *Posterior Analytics,* is true of the first principles of demonstration. Thus, when the nature of a whole and of a part is known, it is at once recognized that every whole is greater than its part. But as soon as the meaning of the word *God* is understood, it is at once seen that God exists. For by this term is signified a reality than which nothing greater can be signified. But that which exists both actually and mentally is greater than that which exists only mentally. Hence, since as soon as the name "God" is understood He exists mentally, it also follows that He exists actually. Therefore the existence of God *is* self-evident.

Objection 3. Then, too, the existence of truth is self-evident. For he who denies the existence of truth, concedes its existence. For if truth does not exist, then the proposition "Truth does not exist" is true ; and if there is anything true, there must be truth. But God is truth itself : "I am the way, the truth, and the life" *(John 14 :6).* Therefore God's existence is self-evident.

On the contrary : No one can think the opposite of what is self-evident, as the Philosopher makes clear in Book IV of the *Metaphysics* and in Book I of the *Posterior Analytics,* in regard to the first principles of demonstration. But the opposite of the proposition "God is" can be thought : "The fool said in his heart, There is no God" *(Psalm 52 :1).* Hence God's existence is not self-evident.

I answer that : A thing can be self-evident in two ways : on the one hand, self-evident in itself, though not to us ; on the other, self-evident in itself, and to us. A proposition is *self-evident* because the predicate is included in the meaning of the subject : e.g., "Man is an animal" ; for *animal* is contained in the concept of *man.* So if the meaning of the predicate and subject be known to all, the proposition will be self-evident to all : as is clear regarding the first principles of demonstrations, whose terms are certain common notions that all are acquainted with, such as being and not-being, whole and part, and the like. But if there are some to whom the meaning of the predicate and subject is unknown, the proposition will be self-evident in itself, but not to those who do not know the meaning of its predicate and subject. And so it happens, as Boethius says in his *De Hebdomadibus,* that there are some conceptions which are common and self-evident only to the learned, as that "incorporeal substances are not in space." Therefore I say that this proposition, "God exists," of itself is self-evident, for the predicate is the same as the subject, because God *is* His own existence, as will be shown presently. But because we do not know the essence of God, the proposition is not self-evident to us, but needs to be demonstrated through things that are more known to us, though less known in their nature, viz., through effects.

Reply Objection 1. To know that God exists in a general and indeterminate way is implanted in us by nature, in that God is indeed man's beatitude. For man naturally desires happiness, and what is naturally desired by man is naturally known by him. This, however, is not to know precisely that *God* exists; just as to know that *someone* is approaching is not the same as to know that *Peter* is approaching, even though it is Peter who is approaching. For there are many who suppose that man's perfect good, which is happiness, consists in riches, and others in pleasures, and others in something else.

Reply Objection 2. It may be that one who hears this name "God" does not understand it to signify something than which nothing greater can be thought; for some have believed God to be a body. But even if it be supposed that everyone understands that by this name *God* is signified something than which nothing greater can be thought, it does not follow that he understands that what the name signifies exists actually, but only that it exists mentally. Nor can it be argued that it actually exists, unless it be admitted that there actually exists something than which nothing greater can be thought. And this is just what is not admitted by those who hold that God does not exist.

Reply Objection 3. The existence of truth-in-general is self-evident, but the existence of a Primal Truth is not self-evident to us.

Can It Be Demonstrated That God Exists?

Objection 1. It seems not; for it is an article of faith that God exists. But what is of faith cannot be demonstrated, because a demonstration produces scientific knowledge, whereas faith is of the unseen, as is clear from the Apostle (*Hebrews 11:1*). So it cannot be demonstrated that God exists.

Objection 2. Moreover, what-a-thing-is, is the middle term of demonstration. But we cannot know what God is, but only what He is not, as Damascene says. Therefore we cannot demonstrate that God exists.

Objection 3. Then too, if the existence of God were demonstrated, this could only be from His effects. But His effects are not proportioned to Him because He is infinite and His effects are finite; and between the finite and infinite there is no proportion. So, since a cause cannot be demonstrated through an effect not proportioned to it, it seems that the existence of God cannot be demonstrated.

On the contrary: The Apostle says: "The invisible things of God are clearly seen, being understood by the things that are made" (*Romans 1:20*). But this would not be unless the existence of God could be demonstrated through the things that are made. For the first thing that must be known of anything is whether it exists.

I answer that: Demonstration is twofold: One type is through the cause, and is called *"propter quid"*; and this is through what is prior simply. The other is through the effect, and is called a demonstration *"quia"*; this is through what is prior relatively to us. When an effect is more manifest to us than its cause, from the effect we proceed to the knowledge of the cause. And from every effect the existence of its proper cause can be demonstrated, so long as its effects are better known to us. For, since every effect depends upon its cause, if the effect exists, the cause must pre-exist. Hence the existence of God, being not self-evident to us, can be demonstrated through effects which are known to us.

Reply Objection 1. The existence of God and other similar truths about God, which, as is said (*Romans 1:19*), can be known by natural reason, are not articles of faith, but are preambles to the articles. For faith presupposes natural knowledge, just as grace presupposes nature, and perfection the perfectible. But there is nothing to prevent a man, who does not grasp the demonstration, from accepting as a matter of faith something which in itself is capable of being demonstrated and scientifically known.

Reply Objection 2. When the existence of a cause is demonstrated from an effect, the latter must take the place of the definition of the cause in proving the cause's existence; and this is pre-eminently the case in regard to God. For in order to prove the existence of anything, it is necessary to accept as middle term the meaning of the name, and not what the thing is, because the question of *what* it is follows on the question of *whether* it is. Now the names given to God are derived from His effects, as will be later shown. Hence, in demonstrating the existence of God from His effects, we can take for the middle term the meaning of the name *God.*

Reply Objection 3. From effects not proportioned to the cause no perfect knowledge of that cause can be obtained. Yet, as we have said, from any effect manifest to us the existence of the cause can be demonstrated. And so we can demonstrate the existence of God from His effects; though from them we cannot know Him perfectly according to His essence.

Does God Exist?

Objection 1. It seems not; because if one of two contraries be infinite, the other would be wholly eliminated. But the very word *God* implies infinite goodness. So if God existed, there would be no evil discovered. But evil is found in the world. Therefore God does not exist.

Objection 2. Moreover, that which can be brought about through fewer causes has not been produced by many. But it seems that everything we see in the world can be brought about through other causes, supposing God did not exist. For all natural things can be traced to one cause, which is nature; and all voluntary things can be traced to one cause, which is human reason, or will. So there is no need to suppose *God's* existence.

On the contrary: It is said in the person of God: "I am Who am" (*Exodus 3:14*). *I answer that:* The existence of God can be proved in five ways.

The *first* and more manifest *way* is taken from motion. It is certain, and evident to our senses, that in the world some things are in motion. Now, whatever is being moved is being moved by another, for nothing is *moved* except insofar as it is in potency to that toward which it is moved; whereas a thing *moves* insofar as it is in act. For "to move" is nothing else than to reduce something from potency to act. But nothing can be reduced from potency to act except by something existing in act. Thus, that which is actually hot — such as fire — makes wood, which is potentially hot, to be actually hot, and thereby "moves" and alters it. Now it is not possible that the same thing should be at once in act and in potency in the same respect, but only in different respects: what is actually hot cannot simultaneously be potentially hot ; rather, it is simultaneously potentially cold. So it is impossible that in the same respect and in the same way a thing should be both *moving* and *moved ;* in other words, that it should *move itself.* Therefore, whatever is *being moved* must be moved by another. If that by which it is being moved be itself moved, then this also must be moved by another, and that by another again. But this cannot go on to infinity, because then there would be no *first* mover and, consequently, no other mover. For secondary movers move only because they are themselves moved by the primary one ; even as the staff moves only because it is moved by the hand. That is why it is necessary to conclude to a First Mover — which is moved by nothing else whatever. And this all understand as being "God."

The *second way* is from the nature of the efficient cause. Among sensible things in our world we find an order of efficient causes. There is no case of a thing's being the efficient cause of itself ; nor is such a thing possible, for then it would be prior to itself ; which is impossible. Now in efficient causes it is not possible to proceed to infinity, because in all efficient causes following in order, the first is the cause of the intermediate, and the intermediate is the cause of the ultimate, whether the intermediate be several or only one. Now to remove the cause is to remove the effect. So, if there be no *first* in efficient causes, there will be no last, nor any intermediate, term. But if it is possible to proceed to infinity in efficient causes, there will be no first efficient cause ; and so there will be no terminal effect, nor any intermediate efficient causes. But this is patently false. Therefore it is necessary to admit a *first* efficient cause, which all call "God."

The *third way* is taken from the possible and the necessary ; and it is this. We find in things some which are possible of being and of not-being, since they are found to be generated, and to be corrupted and, consequently, to be possible of being and of not-being. But it is impossible for all such things always to exist, for that which can not-be at some time is not. So if everything can not-be, then at one time there was nothing. But if this were true, even now there would be nothing, because that which is not does not begin to be except by something which is. So, if at one time nothing existed, it would have been impossible for anything to have begun to exist ; and thus even now nothing would be in existence — which is patently false. Therefore, not all beings are possibles, but there must be something whose existence is necessary. But every necessary entity either has its necessity caused by another, or not. Now it is impossible to proceed to infinity in necessary things whose necessity is caused, as has been already proved in regard to efficient causes. It is therefore necessary to admit the existence of a being having its necessity through itself, and not receiving it from another, but rather causing in others their necessity. This all men call "God."

The *fourth way* is taken from the grades [of perfection] found in things. Among beings there are some more and some less good, true, and noble ; and so in the case of other perfections of this kind. But "more" and "less" are predicated of diverse things according as they approach in diverse measures something which is the maximum, as a thing is hotter the more it approaches that which is hottest. There is, then, something which is truest and best and noblest and, consequently, something which is maximally a being. For those things that are greatest in truth are greatest in being, as Aristotle says in Book II of the *Metaphysics.* Now that which is predicated maximally in a genus is the cause of all in that genus ; e.g., fire, which is maximally hot, is the cause of all hot things, as is said in the same book. Hence there is a reality which is for all things the cause of their being, goodness, and every other perfection ; and this we call "God."

The *fifth way* is taken from the governance of things. For we see that certain beings devoid of knowledge, namely, natural bodies, act for an end ; and this is evident from their acting always, or almost always, in the same way, in order to obtain the best result. Hence it is clear that they achieve their end, not fortuitously, but purposefully. Now whatever lacks knowledge does not tend toward an end unless it be directed by some being endowed with knowledge and intelligence, even as the arrow is directed by the archer. It follows that some intelligent being exists by whom all natural things are directed to their end. This being we call "God."

Reply Objection 1. As Augustine says in the Enchiridion : "Since God is the highest good, He would not allow any evil to exist in His works, unless His omnipotence and goodness were such as to bring good even out of evil." This, therefore, belongs to the infinite goodness of God : that He permit evils to exist, and out of them draw goods.

Reply Objection 2. Since nature works for a determinate end under the direction of a higher agent, whatever is done by nature must be traced back to God as to its first cause. So too, whatever is done voluntarily must be traced back to a higher cause than human reason and will, since these can change and fail. For all things that are changeable and capable of defect must be traced back to an immutable and self-necessary primal source, as has been shown.

Medieval Student Life

A new energy shaped the political face of thirteenth-century Europe. Powerful kings in England and France were developing new instruments of political power to bring greater efficiency to royal governance and to weaken the power of their nobility. This revival of royal authority was paralled by a growth of population, a revival of cities, and the appearance of universities. The medieval university was an independent guild of masters and scholars with its own rules of membership and its own authority to grant degrees. Although these learned guilds of teachers and students existed in many parts of Europe before the thirteenth century, the University of Paris, organized early in the thirteenth century as an autonomous, chartered university, became the model for many other medieval universities. In the twelfth century, students focused their studies on the seven liberal arts — grammar, rhetoric, dialectic, music, geometry, arithmetic, and astronomy — but by the thirteenth century, the subjects of law, medicine, and theology had been added to the university curriculum. Theology was a most important subject at the French University of Toulouse, where the two students in the following selection studied, since this university was expressly founded by Pope Gregory IX in 1229 for students throughout Mediterranean Europe to combat the Albigensian heresy which was raging throughout southern France and northern Italy.[1]

Students went to medieval universities at about the age of 14 and because all the lectures were in Latin, would spend several months learning that language. Medieval universities did not have an extensive campus. Classes were frequently held outside in good weather; during inclement weather, the faculty would hire rooms for its lectures. Students did not live in university dormitories, but more often than not, they sought cheap lodgings with families or in special student hostels. Although these student lodgings were not owned by the university, students were expected to follow strict rules of conduct published in university handbooks. *Hic ludi prohibentur* (this pastime is forbidden) was the common phrase warning students not to gamble, brawl, drink strong spirits, or dress ostentatiously. One of the most popular guides regulating medieval student life advised students to always keep three things out their homes: "smoke, rain, and evil women." The following letter was written in 1315 by Peter Fagarola, master of arts and medicine, of Valencia (Spain) to his two sons studying at the University of Toulouse.

65

A Father's Letter to His Two Sons Studying at Toulouse

QUESTIONS TO CONSIDER

1. What does this letter tell us about the diet of medieval students, their lodgings, daily routine, and recreational pastimes? Are the conditions of student life today much different from those of the fourteenth century?
2. In his discussion of "Of accidents of the soul," was Peter Fagarola correct and complete in his list of the five faults students should avoid?
3. What does the letter suggest about medieval medical knowledge and practice?

1. The heresy takes its name from the French town of Albi. The Albigensians believed that all matter was created by the devil and that the soul was imprisoned in the body. By remaining chaste and by refusing to recognize the legitimacy of civil and church authority, the Albigensians believed they would attain perfection. The Popes were so fearful of this heresy that a crusade was declared against the Albigensians in 1208 and continued until 1229.

Of Foods, or How to Eat

Beware of eating too much and too often especially during the night. Avoid eating raw onions in the evening except rarely, because they dull the intellect and senses generally.

Avoid all very lacteal foods such as milk and fresh cheese except very rarely. Beware of eating milk and fish, or milk and wine, at the same meal, for milk and fish or milk and wine produce leprosy.

Don't have fresh pork too often. Salt pork is all right.

Don't eat many nuts except rarely and following fish. I say the same of meat and fruit, for they are bad and difficult to digest.

Thy drink be twice or thrice or four times during a meal. Between meals drink little, for it would be better once in a while to drink too much at table than to drink away from table. Don't take wine without water, and, if it is too cold, warm it in winter. For 'tis bad to grow used to strong wine without admixture of water.

Remember about the well water of Toulouse. Wherefore boil it, and the same with water of the Garonne, because such waters are bad.

Also, after you have risen from table wash out your mouth with wine. This done, take one spoonful of this powdered confection:

Of meat prepared with vinegar and dried coriander similarly prepared a modicum each; of roast meat, fennel seed, flowers of white eyebright, two ounces each; of candied coriander, candied anise, scraped licorice, each one ounce and a half; of cloves, mast, cubebs, each three drams; of galingale and cardamomum each two drams; of white ginger six drams; of white loaf sugar three drams; made into a powder and put in a paste. And keep this in your room in a secret [or, *dry*] place, for it will comfort your digestion, head, vision, intellect and memory, and protect from rheum.

As to Sleep

Sufficient and natural sleep is to sleep for a fourth part of a natural day or a trifle more or less. To do otherwise is to pervert nature. Too much is a sin, wherefore shun it, unless the case is urgent and necessary.

Avoid sleeping on your back except rarely, for it has many disadvantages, but sleep on your side or stomach, and first on the right side, then on the left.

Don't sleep in winter with cold feet, but first warm them at the fire or by walking about or some other method. And in summer don't sleep with bed slip-

British Museum MS Sloane 3124, fols 74r 77r in Lynn Thorndike, *University Records and Life in the Middle Ages* (New York : Columbia University Press, 1944), pp. 156–160. Reprinted by permission.

pers on your feet, because they generate vapors which are very bad for the brain and memory.

Don't go straight to bed on a full stomach but an hour after the meal. Also, unless some urgent necessity prevents, walk about for a bit after a meal, at least around the square, so that the food may settle in the stomach and not evaporate in the mouth of the stomach, since the vapors will rise to the head and fill it with rheum and steal away and cut short memory.

Also, avoid lying down in a rheumatic place, such as a basement or room underground.

Of Air or One's Surroundings

Choose lodgings removed from all foul smells as of ditches or latrines and the like, since in breathing we are continually drawing in air which, if it is infected, infects us more and more forcibly than tainted food and drink do.

Likewise in winter keep your room closed from all noxious wind and have straw on the pavement lest you suffer from cold.

Furthermore, if you can have coals or chopped wood in a clay receptacle of good clay, or if you have a chimneyplace and fire in your room, it is well.

Also, be well clad and well shod, and outdoors wear pattens to keep your feet warm.

Also, don't make yourself a cap "de salsamentis,"[1] as some do, for they are harmful.

And when you see other students wearing their caps, do you do likewise, and, if need be, put on one of fur.

And at night, when you study, you should wear a nightcap over the cap and about your cheeks (or throat?).

And when you go to bed at night, have a white nightcap on your head and beneath your cheeks, and another colored one over it, for at night the head should be kept warmer than during the day.

Moreover, at the time of the great rains it is well to wear outdoors over your cap a bonnet or helmet of undressed skin, that is, a covering to keep the head from getting wet. Indeed, some persons wear a bonnet over the cap in fair weather, more especially when it is cold, so that in the presence of the great they may remove the bonnet and be excused from doffing the cap.

Also, look after your stockings and don't permit your feet to become dirty.

Also, wash the head, if you are accustomed to wash it, at least once a fortnight with hot lye and in a place sheltered from draughts on the eve of a feast day towards nightfall. Then dry your hair with a brisk massage; afterwards do it up; then put on a bonnet or cap.

Also comb your hair daily, if you will morning and evening before eating or at least afterwards, if you cannot do otherwise.

---

1. Literally, of sauces or pickles or salt fish or sausages, which seems an impossible translation. Probably we have to do with a slang phrase for some current type of head-covering.

Also look out that a draught does not strike you from window or crack while you study or sleep, or indeed at any time, for it strikes men without their noticing.

Also, in summer, in order not to have fleas or to have no more of them, sweep your room daily with a broom and not sprinkle it with water, for they are generated from damp dust. But you may spray it occasionally with strong vinegar which comforts heart and brain.

If you will, walk daily somewhere morning and evening. And if the weather is cold, if you can run, run on empty stomach, or at least walk rapidly, that the natural heat may be revived. For a fire is soon extinguished unless the sticks are moved about or the bellows used. However, it is not advisable to run on a full stomach but to saunter slowly in order to settle the food in the stomach.

If you cannot go outside your lodgings, either because the weather does not permit or it is raining, climb the stairs rapidly three or four times, and have in your room a big heavy stick like a sword and wield it now with one hand, now with the other, as if in a scrimmage, until you are almost winded. This is splendid exercise to warm one up and expel noxious vapors through the pores and consume other superfluities. Jumping is a similar exercise. Singing, too, exercises the chest. And if you will do this, you will have healthy limbs, a sound intellect and memory, and you will avoid rheum. The same way with playing ball. All these were invented not for sport but for exercise. Moreover, too much labor is to be avoided as a continual practice.

Of Accidents of the Soul

Accidents of the soul have the greatest influence, such as anger, sadness, and love of women, fear, excessive anxiety : concerning all which I say nothing more than that you avoid all passions of the soul harmful to you and enjoy yourself happily with friends and good companions, and cultivate honesty and patience which bring the more delights to the soul, and especially if you love God with your whole heart.

For a Cough

If you are troubled with a cough, beware of all cold or sour things, or salt and fried. And if cold rheum is the cause of the cough, then make a bag of camamille, salt, and calamint in equal parts mixed together, and make a pepper poultice which should be placed on top of the head or over the commissure. And a small piece of licorice should be kept in the mouth and chewed between the teeth, or a candy should be made of licorice.

Equally good is sirup of Venus' hair, sirup of hyssop, sirup of bugloss, if they are taken with water of scabiosa, water of lily, elder water, water of betony, water of rosemary in equal parts, or wash the mouth with a tepid gargle.

Equally good are dyera yeris of Solomon, diapenidion, cold diagragant, preserved penidiarum, grains of pine, and the like.

And if the cough is accompanied by hot rheum, of which the signs are extreme heat, a burning sensation in the throat, saltiness, and great thirst, in this case take cold diagragant or diapenidion without spices with sirup of violets or sirup of pepper. And let this be taken in sips and not swallowed suddenly. And this is to be done without eating anything morning and evening. Immediately afterwards take a fine linen cloth and dip it in tepid oil of roses and apply it tepid to the commissure of the head, and this do twice daily.

And in cold rheum beware of all broth and meat puddings as much as is possible and of superfluous drink. And eat only roast meats not stewed in water, and eat any thick foodstuffs such as sweetbreads, split beans with their skins removed, and the like, cooked with meat.

Also in hot rheum one should eat barley-gruel, rice, oatmeal cooked with milk of almonds and sugar, pears and apples cooked with sugar, which are also good in case of cold rheum.

And one should drink yellow wine, clear and limpid.

Also equally beneficial in this case are cold diagragant, diapenidion without spices, sugar of violets, preserved penidiarum, and the like. And let this suffice so far as rheum is concerned.

Chinese Culture under the Tang and Sung [Song] Dynasties

After nearly four centuries of disruption and disunity following the end of the first great imperial period under the Ch'in [Qin][1] (221–206 B.C.) and Han (206 B.C.–A.D. 220) dynasties, China, reunified by the short-lived Sui dynasty (589–618), rejuvenated itself and entered into the second great imperial period under the Tang (618–907) and Sung (960–1279) dynasties. The Han and the Tang periods are often viewed as the two golden ages of the Chinese empire, but the Tang exceeded the Han in material splendor, cultural refinement, and international influence. Its empire was vast ; its military was powerful and feared ; its bureaucracy was elaborate and dependable ; its laws were codified ; its art and literature, especially its poetry, achieved new heights of sophistication. Changan, its capital, was large and cosmopolitan ; it attracted scholars, diplomats, missionaries, and merchants from surrounding lands and as far away as Persia and Arabia. The religious life of this period was rich in diversity. While Confucianism strengthened its hold on China, Buddhism and Taoism [Daoism] grew to maturity, and several foreign cults such as Zoroastrianism, Manichaeism, Judaism, Islam, and Nestorian Christianity entered China. Also, the Chinese invention of printing greatly stimulated intellectual life. The world's oldest extant printed book, a whole

---

1. Spellings in brackets are Pinyin transcriptions of Chinese terms (see footnote 1, p. 97 for further explanation).

Buddhist *sutra,* printed in 868, can be traced to this period. Thus Tang China furnished the models of advanced institutions and a way of life for neighboring countries to emulate. The foundation of this brilliant civilization was initially laid by the second ruler and co-founder of this dynasty, Emperor Tái-tsung [Taizong]. A heroic warrior and an ardent Confucianist, he was firm but willing to be guided by the counsel of his ministers on matters of state (see Reading 67).

The Sung dynasty came into existence in 960 after more than a half century of disruptions and fragmentation of the empire and remained in power until the Mongols overran the whole empire in 1279. By 1127, the Sung had lost the northern half of its empire to the Tungusic tribal people of Manchuria. Although it was militarily feeble, Sung China fostered great social and cultural development and economic prosperity. The advanced state of its material civilization was unmatched by any other civilization. Trade and industry flourished ; urbanization spread and the inventive genius of the Sung craftsmen was unexcelled in the technical perfection of their silk, lacquer, and porcelain. Gunpowder, an earlier Chinese invention, was now employed for the first time in warfare. Socially, the institution of concubinage grew, and the practice of foot-binding among the upper class women can be dated to the Sung period (see Reading 68). To run their large imperial bureaucracy efficiently, the Sung government relied heavily upon the imperial examination system, which had been reinaugurated by the Sui and reinvigorated by the Tang (see Reading 66). The widespread use of the imperial examination system contributed to a revival of interest in Confucianism (see Reading 32) and the development of a neo-Confucian movement during the Sung period.

66

Imperial Examination System

One of the unique features of the Imperial Government of China was the imperial examination system. Through it, the Chinese government recruited the members of its bureaucracy from the general populace, rather than leaving the imperial administration to the hereditary nobles. This system evolved gradually, starting in the second century B.C. during the Former Han dynasty (206 B.C.–A.D. 8), becoming more elaborate and institutionalized during the early part of the Sung [Song] dynasty (960–1279), and continuing with only slight modifications down to the early years of this century. The last imperial examinations were held in 1905.

Millions of young men in China during the imperial period invested their time, energy, money, and passion in an effort to pass the examination, since this was the road to power and wealth. Aspirants for imperial bureaucratic posts usually spent 10 or more years preparing for the examination, primarily by reading, analyzing, and memorizing the voluminous Confucian classics. During the Sung period, prospective candidates for imperial administrative posts were expected to pass three levels of highly competitive examinations — prefectural, metropolitan, and palace — and attain the Presented Scholar (Chin-shih [Jinshi]) degree, which was the most coveted degree, roughly comparable to a Ph.D. in the West. The candidates in the palace examination were ranked in order of their achievements in the examination. The higher the rank the candidates achieved, the better the chances were that they would receive more powerful and prestigious imperial appointments. The candidate for the Chin-shih degree was required to produce, among other things, poems in various styles, a rhyme prose piece, a policy essay, answers to five policy questions, and answers to 10 "written elucidation" questions on Confucian classics such as the *Spring and Autumn Annals* and the *Book of Rites*. The following selection is an example of an essay question on policy matters.

QUESTIONS TO CONSIDER

1. What do you think are the merits and demerits of the Chinese Imperial Examination System?
2. How does this system compare with the way the Ottoman or European governments recruited their officials (see Reading 80)?

It is stated in the Book of Kuan-tzu [Guan Zi][1] : "the method by which a sage rules the world is this : he does not let the four classes of people live together. Therefore, there are no complaints, and things run smoothly. As a result, scholars know how to spend their leisure, laborers abide with the orders of officials, merchants go to the marketplaces and farmers go to the fields. Everyone goes to his appropriate place and lives there satisfactorily. Young children are sent to study ; their wills are satisfied and they do not change their minds when they see strange things." The *Kuan-tzu* Book further states : "Children of scholars and farmers must always be scholars and farmers and children of merchants and laborers must also always be merchants and laborers, so that a scholar can give instructions and take care of his proper status, and a farmer can work attentively in cultivating his crops to feed the people. Every one is satisfied with his occupation and does not seek to change. This is truly good! Otherwise, hundreds of laborers might all go to the marketplaces and ten thousand merchants might all try to work in the same [most profitable] business ; they would all become cunning, deceitful, eager to play tricks, and they would also become capricious, greedy and seek only profits."

    Now, to fit people in their occupations is not to improve morals. To see something better and change — what harm is there in this ? Take the example of

Ou-yang Hsiu, *Ch'uan-chi*, Pt. IV, 40–41, in Thomas H. C. Lee, *Government Education and Examinations in Sung China* (New York : St. Martin's Press, 1985), pp. 150–151. Copyright © 1985 by St. Martin's Press. Reprinted by permission.

    1. Kuan-tzu or Master Kuan [Guan], who lived in the middle of the seventh century B.C., is regarded in Chinese history as one of the most innovative government reformers in ancient China. He was a great supporter of a centralized form of government.

Tuan-mu [Duanmu] who became a merchant [after being a disciple of Confucius], Chiao Li [Jiao Li] who became a fisherman [after being an important official] and Wang Meng who went to sell dust-baskets [after being a prime minister]; these men responded to their times and changed in a myriad ways, why should they have been restricted to their fixed occupations? Similarly, Huang Hsien [Huang Xian] was originally a lowly veterinarian, Sang Hung-yang [Sang Hongyang] a merchant, Sun Shu-ao a wood-cutter, and yet they all were able to preserve their intelligence and help strengthen their states. How can we accuse them of responding to their times and of going to take up responsibilities other than their own occupations! We now have a regulation keeping the descendants of those in despised occupations from taking the civil service examinations. Although this rule has been in force for some time, I consider that it still is a good time to examine this regulation. You candidates have excelled yourselves in knowledge of the past, and in debating various problems; I would like you to spend time considering the issue I have just outlined above.

67

Emperor T'ai-tsung [Taizong]: "On the Art of Government"

China under the T'ang [Tang] dynasty (618–907), which was contemporaneous with Charlemagne's empire in Western Europe, marked one of the most brilliant eras of Chinese history. At the height of its power, the empire stretched from Korea in the east to Central Asia in the west, and Siberia in the north to Annam (Vietnam) in the south. Its culture was sophisticated and cosmopolitan. Although Confucianism was the state cult, other religions were tolerated, and its art, architecture, and literature reached new levels of excellence. Changan, the capital of the empire, was one of the finest in the world, with two million people — including hundreds of foreign students who were eagerly seeking a model of civilized life.

The foundation of this great T'ang empire was largely laid by Emperor T'ai-tsung (also known as Li Shimin, 626–649) who had helped his father Kao—tsu [Gao Zu] (also known as Li Yuan) found the T'ang dynasty by overthrowing the Sui dynasty. Ambitious, energetic, and versatile, Emperor T'ai-tsung created an elaborate system of imperial bureaucracy, rebuilt palaces, constructed more canals, tolerated foreign religions, established publicly supported state colleges in provincial capitals and a university in Changan, and compiled extensive law codes. Externally, he pursued an aggressive foreign policy and expanded the empire. His extraordinary reign was thus the first high point of the three-century-long T'ang period. The following article by Emperor T'ai-tsung reflects his thoughts on the good ruler and good government.

QUESTIONS TO CONSIDER

1. How do you compare Emperor T'ai-tsung with Charlemagne? How similar and how different are these two rulers? (See Reading 57.)
2. What aspects of Emperor T'ai-tsung's essay reflect his being a great ruler? Why?

As a young man, I loved archery and prided myself as an expert in the evaluation of bows and arrows. Recently I came into possession of a dozen bows, the quality of which was the best I had ever observed. I showed them to the bow makers and was surprised to hear that they were not as good as they looked. "Why?" I asked.

"The center of the wood is not located at the center of the bow; consequently all the wood grain moves in a bizarre fashion," replied the bow makers. "Though the bow is strong and durable, an arrow released from it cannot travel straight for a long distance."

I used a countless number of bows and arrows in unifying the country; yet I still do not know enough about them. Now that I have the country for only a short time, how can I say that I know enough about it to govern it successfully, taking into consideration the fact that my knowledge of it is certainly inferior to my knowledge of bows which I have used throughout my life? . . .

Lately the draft decrees that originate from the First Secretariat are often contradictory and in some cases correct one another. To clarify this point, let me say that the purpose of having both the First and the Second Secretariats is for them to check and balance each other, so that the error of one will be corrected by the other and that an error, whoever commits it, will not remain undetected for a long time and thus cause irreparable damage.

Different people are bound to have different opinions; the important thing is that differences in opinion should not degenerate into personal antagonism. Sometimes to avoid the possibility of creating personal grievances or causing embarrassment to a colleague, an official might decide to go ahead with the implementation of a policy even though he knows that the policy is wrong. Let us remember that the preservation of a colleague's prestige, or the avoidance of embarrassment to him, cannot be compared with the welfare of the nation in importance, and to place personal consideration above the well-being of the multitude will lead to defeat for the government as a whole. I want all of you to understand this point and act accordingly.

During the Sui dynasty all officials, in the central as well as the local governments, adopted an attitude of conformity to the general trend in order to be amiable and agreeable with one another. The result was disaster as all of you well know. Most of them did not understand the importance of dissent and comforted themselves by saying that as long as they did not disagree, they could forestall harm to

"On the Art of Government" by T'ang T'ai-tsung, *Chen-kuan Cheng-yao* (Politics in Brief: The Chen-kuan Period, 627–49), ed. Wu Ching (669–749), in Dun J. Li, trans. and intro., *The Civilization of China, From the Formative Period to the Coming of the West* (New York: Charles Scribner's Sons, 1975), pp. 161–164. Reprinted by permission of Charles Scribner's Sons, an imprint of Macmillan Publishing Company. Copyright © by Dun J. Li.

themselves that might otherwise cross their path. When the government, as well as their families, finally collapsed in a massive upheaval, they were severely but justifiably criticized by their contemporaries for their complacency and inertia, even if they themselves may have been fortunate enough to escape death through a combination of circumstances. This is the reason that I want all of you to place public welfare above private interest and hold steadfastly the principle of righteousness, so that all problems, whatever they are, will be resolved in such a way as to bring about a most beneficial result. Under no circumstances are you allowed to agree with one another for the sake of agreement. . . .

As for Sui Wen-ti [Wendi], I would say that he was politically inquisitive but mentally closed. Being close-minded, he could not see truth even if it were spotlighted for him ; being overinquisitive, he was suspicious even when there was no valid reason for his suspicion. He rose to power by trampling on the rights of orphans and widows[1] and was consequently not so sure that he had the unanimous support of his own ministers. Being suspicious of his own ministers, he naturally did not trust them and had to make a decision on every matter himself. He became a hard worker out of necessity and, having overworked, could not make the right decision every time. Knowing the kind of man he was, all his ministers, including the prime minister, did not speak as candidly as they should have and unanimously uttered "Yes, sir" when they should have registered strong dissent.

I want all of you to know that I am different. The empire is large and its population enormous. There are thousands of matters to be taken care of, each of which has to be closely coordinated with the others in order to bring about maximum benefit. Each matter must be thoroughly investigated and thought out before a recommendation is submitted to the prime minister, who, having consulted all the men knowledgeable in this matter, will then present the recommendation, modified if necessary, to the emperor for approval and implementation. It is impossible for one person, however intelligent and capable, to be able to make wise decisions by himself. Acting alone, he may be able, if he is fortunate, to make five right decisions out of ten each day. While we congratulate him for the five right decisions he has made that bring benefit to the country, we tend to forget the enormous harm that results from the implementation of the other five decisions that prove to be wrong. How many wrong decisions will he accumulate in a period of days, months, and years if he makes five such decisions every day ? How, in that case, can he not lose his country or throne ? Instead he should delegate authority to the most able and virtuous men he can find and supervise their work from above most diligently. When he makes clear to them that he will not tolerate any violation of the law, it is doubtful that they will abuse the authority with which they have been entrusted.

I want all of you to know that whenever an imperial decree is handed down you should carefully study its content and decide for yourselves whether all or part of it is or is not wise or feasible. If you have any reservations, postpone the enforcement and petition me immediately. You can do no less as my loyal ministers. . . .

1. In 581 Sui Wen-ti forced Chou Ching-ti [Zhou Jingdi], aged seven, to abdicate the throne on his behalf. The boy's father had died only one year earlier ; his mother was a young widow at the time of the abdication. Four months after his abdication, the boy died under suspicious circumstances.

Governing a country is like taking care of a patient. The better the patient feels, the more he should be looked after, lest in a moment of complacency and neglect one irrevocably reverse the recovery process and send him to death. Likewise, when a country has only recently recovered from chaos and war, those responsible for running the country should be extremely diligent in their work, for false pride and self-indulgence will inevitably return the country to where it used to be and perhaps make it worse.

I realize that the safety of this nation relies to a great extent on what I can or may do and consequently I have not relaxed for a moment in doing the best I can. But I cannot do it alone. You gentlemen are my eyes and ears, legs and arms, and should do your best to assist me. If anything goes wrong anywhere in the empire, you should let me know immediately. If there is less than total trust between you and me and consequently you and I cannot do the best we can, the nation will suffer enormous damage. . . .

As the ancients say, a friend in need is a friend indeed. If mutual assistance governs the relations between two friends, how can it not do so between a king and his ministers? Whenever I read of Chieh's [Jie] execution of Kuan Lung-feng [Guan Lung feng] and Han Chingti's [Han Jingdi] execution of Ch'ao Ts'o [Chao Cuo][2], I cannot but feel deeply about the mistakes these monarchs made. Contrary to these monarchs, I am asking you gentlemen to speak candidly on matters that you believe are most important to the well-being of the nation, even though the opinion you express may not coincide with my own. Needless to say, there will be no penalty of any kind, let alone execution, for opinions honestly held.

Recently I have made several decisions that are clear violations of the law, even though such violations were not apparent to me at the time when the decisions were made. You gentlemen obviously thought that these violations were inconsequential and therefore abstained from speaking about them. The truth is that the most consequential acts are usually an accumulation of acts of less consequence and in order to prevent the greatest harm, one has to make sure that even the smallest harm does not occur. It will be too late to reverse the course after small disasters have coalesced to become a great one. Keep in mind that a government does not fall because of the occurrence of a major catastrophe; rather, its demise usually results from an accumulation of small misfortunes.

It enlightens one to note that not a single person expressed regret when Sui Yang-ti [Sui Yangdi], a brutal and merciless tyrant, met his death at the hands of a group of assassins. If you gentlemen keep in mind the reason why I have been able to overthrow the Sui regime, I, on my part, will constantly remind myself of the injustice suffered by Kuan Lung-feng and Ch'ao Ts'o. Only in this way can you and I be permanently secure.

---

2. Kuan Lung-feng was a loyal but outspoken minister under King Chieh (r. 1818–1765 B.C.), last ruler of the Hsia [Xia] dynasty. He was executed because of his criticism of the king's policies and personal behavior. Han Ching-ti (ca. 156–141 B.C.) ordered the execution of Ch'ao Ts'o (d. 154 B.C.) to appease some of the feudal lords who were then in rebellion. Previously Ch'ao Ts'o had recommended breaking up large feudal domains into smaller ones, a recommendation that angered the lords.

68

Chinese Footbinding

One of the most bizarre and painful customs of old China was the binding of women's feet. It is difficult to determine precisely when and how this custom came to be, but historical records seem to indicate that it began with the dancers of the imperial harem of the Southern T'ang [Tang] dynasty (937–975), sometime in the tenth century. In the beginning, the custom was practiced only by fashionable women of the upper classes, but footbinding gradually spread down to the rest of the female population and persisted well into the twentieth century. The custom persisted even after the end of the last imperial dynasty (1644–1912), despite a series of official efforts to end it, beginning with an anti-footbinding edict issued by Empress Dowager Tz'u-hsi [Ci Xi] in 1902. In the following selection, a middle-aged maidservant named Chang, probably born around the turn of the century, recalls her painful footbinding experience for her master. The story is told sometime in the early 1930s.

QUESTIONS TO CONSIDER

1. Compare the footbinding custom of old China with a comparable custom from another society in premodern times. How does it compare with the widow-burning custom of old India (see Reading 26)?
2. Why did such a painful custom continue for so long in China?

I was born in a certain district in western Honan Province, at the end of the Manchu dynasty. In accordance with custom, at the age of seven I began binding. I had witnessed the pain of my cousins, and in the year it was to begin was very much frightened. That autumn, distress befell me. One day prior my mother told me: "You are now seven, just at the right age for binding. If we wait, your foot will harden, increasing the pain. You should have started in the spring, but because you were weak we waited till now. Girls in other families have already completed the process. We start tomorrow. I will do this for you lightly and so that it won't hurt; what daughter doesn't go through this difficulty?" She then gave me fruit to eat, showed me a new pair of phoenix-tip shoes, and beguiled me with these words: "Only with bound feet can you wear such beautiful shoes. Otherwise, you'll become a large-footed barbarian and everyone will laugh at and feel

Howard S. Levy, *Chinese Footbinding : The History of a Curious Erotic Custom* (New York : Walton Rawls Publisher, 1966), pp. 224–227. Reprinted by permission.

ashamed of you." I felt moved by a desire to be beautiful and became steadfast in determination, staying awake all night.

I got up early the next morning. Everything had already been prepared. Mother had me sit on a stool by the bed. She threaded a needle and placed it in my hair, cut off a piece of alum and put it alongside the binding cloth and the flowered shoes. She then turned and closed the bedroom door. She first soaked my feet in a pan of hot water, then wiped them, and cut the toenails with a small scissors. She then took my right foot in her hands and repeatedly massaged it in the direction of the plantar.[1] She also sprinkled alum between my toes. She gave me a pen point to hold in my hands because of the belief that my feet might then become as pointed as it was. Later she took a cloth three feet long and two inches wide, grasped my right foot, and pressed down the four smaller toes in the direction of the plantar. She joined them together, bound them once, and passed the binding from the heel to the foot surface and then to the plantar. She did this five times and then sewed the binding together with thread. To prevent it from getting loosened, she tied a slender cotton thread from the tip of the foot to its center.

She did the same thing with the left foot and forced my feet into flowered shoes which were slightly smaller than the feet were. The tips of the shoes were adorned with threads in the shape of grain. There was a ribbon affixed to the mouth of the shoe and fastened on the heel. She ordered me to get down from the bed and walk, saying that if I didn't the crooked-shaped foot would be seriously injured. When I first touched the ground, I felt complete loss of movement; after a few trials, only the toes hurt greatly. Both feet became feverish at night and hurt from the swelling. Except for walking, I sat by the *k'ang* [Kang].[2] Mother rebound my feet weekly, each time more tightly than the last. I became more and more afraid. I tried to avoid the binding by hiding in a neighbor's house. If I loosened the bandage, mother would scold me for not wanting to look nice. After half a year, the tightly bound toes began to uniformly face the plantar. The foot became more pointed daily; after a year, the toes began to putrefy. Corns began to appear and thicken, and for a long time no improvement was visible. Mother would remove the bindings and lance the corns with a needle to get rid of the hard core. I feared this, but mother grasped my legs so that I couldn't move. Father betrothed me at the age of nine to a neighbor named Chao, and I went to their house to serve as a daughter-in-law in the home of my future husband. My mother-in-law bound my feet much more tightly than mother ever had, saying that I still hadn't achieved the standard. She beat me severely if I cried; if I unloosened the binding, I was beaten until my body was covered with bruises. Also, because my feet were somewhat fleshy, my mother-in-law insisted that the foot must become inflamed to get the proper results. Day and night, my feet were washed in a medicinal water; within a few washings I felt special pain. Looking down, I saw that every toe but the big one was inflamed and deteriorated. Mother-in-law said that this was all to the good. I had to be beaten with fists before I could bear to remove the bindings, which were congealed with pus and blood. To get them loose, such force had to be used that the skin often peeled off, causing further bleeding. The stench

1. Relating to the sole of the foot.
2. A brick-bed warmed by a fire.

was hard to bear, while I felt the pain in my very insides. My body trembled with agitation. Mother-in-law was not only unmoved but she placed tiles inside the binding in order to hasten the inflammation process. She was deaf to my childish cries. Every other day, the binding was made tighter and sewn up, and each time slightly smaller shoes had to be worn. The sides of the shoes were hard, and I could only get into them by using force. I was compelled to walk on them in the courtyard; they were called distance-walking shoes. I strove to cling to life, suffering indescribable pain. Being in an average family, I had to go to the well and pound the mortar unaided. Faulty blood circulation caused my feet to become insensible in winter. At night, I tried to warm them by the *k'ang*, but this caused extreme pain. The alternation between frost and thawing caused me to lose one toe on my right foot. Deterioration of the flesh was such that within a year my feet had become as pointed as new bamboo shoots, pointing upwards like a red chestnut. The foot surface was slightly convex, while the four bean-sized toes were deeply imbedded in the plantar like a string of cowry shells.[3] They were only a slight distance from the heel of the foot. The plantar was so deep that several coins could be placed in it without difficulty. The large toes faced upwards, while the place on the right foot where the little toe had deteriorated away pained at irregular intervals. It left an ineffacable scar.

My feet were only three inches long, at the most. Relatives and friends praised them, little realizing the cisterns of tears and blood which they had caused. My husband was delighted with them, but two years ago he departed this world. The family wealth was dissipated, and I had to wander about, looking for work. That was how I came down to my present circumstances. I envy the modern woman. If I too had been born just a decade or so later, all of this pain could have been avoided. The lot of the natural-footed woman and mine is like that of heaven and hell.

Mongols and the West

Until reports from Franciscan friars and Venetian merchant-travelers reached Europe in the thirteenth century, people in the West were only dimly aware of anything in the world east of India. The Romans became aware of the existence of China more by logic than knowledge. Silk was greatly prized by the Romans, so much so that in some periods ounces of silk were sold for the same weight in gold. The ancient Greeks had noted a people around eastern India called "the Seres," and the Romans picked up on the fact that *sericos* in both Greek and Latin meant "silk." Given the existence of *sericos* cloth, there must have been people out there in the furthest Orient whose lives revolved around making it: Ergo, "the Seres" were the Silk People. The natural assumption that the Silk People must have a land of their own led geographers to designate one for them, and so the land of

---

3. A type of shell somewhat resembling the female sex organ; it was used as a sort of primitive money in prehistoric times in China.

Serica or Sericum was born. Any country worthy of the name had to have a capital city, and so by the time we get to the great Greco-Roman geographer, Ptolemy (A.D. 127–151), the Seres had one, called ever so logically Sera Metropolis or Great Silk City. Ancient and medieval geographers ascribed both utopian and monstrous elements to the inhabitants of Asia east of India. The thought of total peace and harmony prevailing among some of the tribes there was a constant element in Western perceptions. On the other hand, several Greco-Roman sources described the Seres as towering 20 feet tall and having life expectancies of over 200 years; yet, even they were not thought to be the most unusual East Asians.

Contacts with the Mongols were to lead Westerners to China. Islamic *jihads* and Western crusades gave rise to a different sort of Western interest in East Asia. The notion of a great Christian kingdom to the East, headed by one Prester (Priest) John, secular and clerical ruler in one, spread rapidly throughout Western Europe after the mid-twelfth century. The accompanying hope was that Prester John's forces would make excellent allies against the Muslims. In the early thirteenth century, rumors reached the camps of crusaders in North Africa that Christian forces from the Far East were on the march, slaughtering Muslims left and right as they came to aid Western fighters in the liberation of the Holy Land. The reports of massive slaughter of Muslims turned out to be true in 1219, but the perpetrators were the armies of Jenghiz Khan [Chinghiz Khan], a distinctly non-Christian leader who did not resemble Prester John (or "King David," another hoped-for but fictional Christian king from the East). Jenghiz Khan's Mongol-led hordes soon acquired the name "Tartars," derived from Tartary, the infernal region below Hades in Greco-Roman mythology, for they killed off Slavic and Hungarian Christians with as much enthusiasm as they annihilated Muslims. By the 1240s, Matthew of Paris described the Mongols as "a monstrous and inhuman branch of mankind."

In spite of what we might call "a bad press," some Church leaders in the West still found the ongoing Mongol hostility to Turks, Persians, and Arabs an enduring and consoling fact. They were proven anti-Saracens, and if peace and friendship could be established with them, perhaps they could be converted to Christianity, after which they could be counted on as genuine allies against Islam. In 1245, Pope Innocent IV dispatched the first of a series of Franciscan missionary-explorers to negotiate with the great Khan of the Mongols. Friar John Pian del Carpini did, in fact, reach the court of Jenghiz's grandson, Kuyuk Khan, with a message from the Pope.

John wrote extensively of his travels and experiences at the Mongol court. It is not known how he entitled his work, which is often called the *History of the Mongols*, even though there is relatively little *history* in it. One of the surviving manuscripts has the simple title, *A Book about the Tartars*, which seems more accurate. The following excerpts from it are fairly typical in showing his admiration for the hardiness and capacity for cooperation the Mongols exhibited among themselves, coupled with his revulsion at their ferocity and lack of scruples in dealing with foreign peoples. John was less hopeful of converting the Mongols to Christianity than most of the explorer-missionaries who followed him; both his travel book and the letter he brought to the Pope from Kuyuk Khan indicate why. His Franciscan successors who visited China under Mongol conquest had better experiences, however; they and Venetian traders, particularly the very observant Marco Polo, who became a Mongol administrator in China, were beginning to acquaint Europe with some of the real East Asia.

69

John Pian del Carpini, *The Tartars*

QUESTIONS TO CONSIDER

1. Why does John consider the Mongol threat a real one?
2. What does John think Westerners could learn from the Mongols?

The Tartars have a very different appearance from other peoples. There is more space between their eyes and between their cheekbones than is true of other men. . . . They have flat noses and rather small eyes. . . . Almost all of them are of medium height. Their men have only sparce growths of beard, some letting their wispy moustaches droop long. . . .

I will tell something of their good characteristics and then of their bad ones. . . . They show greater respect to their superiors than any other people in the world. . . . They deceive their own masters rarely or never with words and never at all with deeds. . . . They do not fight among themselves: Internal warfare, brawls and assaults do not occur. . . . If a large animal strays, whoever finds it either lets it go or leads it to men of authority from whom the owner can get it back with no difficulty at all simply by asking for it. They respect each other quite well enough and . . . throw frequent banquets in spite of the scarcity of good things to eat among them. At the same time, they are so hardy that they can go a day or even two without eating and still sing and joke around as if they had had plenty to eat. . . . Tartar women are chaste: There are not even rumors of immodest female behavior among them, although the women do sometimes use filthy language. . . . Even though the Tartars get quite drunk often, this does not lead to hostile words or actions among them.

Having said this much about their good side, let me go on to their bad one. Their pride is terrible when they confront non-Tartars — nobles and commoners alike — whom they are apt to despise. . . . They show their angry and totally condescending natures to foreigners, to whom they habitually lie. When Tartars speak to non-Tartars the truth is seldom in them. When they start off, their conversation is nice enough, but they sting like scorpions before they are through

Historia Mongalorum, in *Studi Italiani di Filologia Indo-Iranica*, Vol. IX (Firenze: Carnesecchi e Figli, 1913), pp. 54–101, passim. Translated by Henry A. Myers.

talking. They are cunning, crafty, and very elusive with their falsehoods. When they have hostile plans toward foreigners, they are experts in concealing them so that the foreigners will not know to be on guard. . . . They are very greedy and shameless with their outrageous demands, while they hold fast to what is theirs and are unbelievably stingy givers. Killing off foreign peoples simply does not bother them.

Chinghiz Khan arranged their order of battle by putting ten men under the command of a squad leader, ten squad leaders under one centurion, ten centurions under a battalion commander, thus giving him a thousand men, ten battalion commanders under a colonel and the whole army under two or three generals, but with one of them clearly the theater commander. If in battle, one, two, or three — any number — of men flee from a squad, the whole squad is executed; if the whole squad flees, then the hundred soldiers with the centurion over them are all executed; and, to summarize this point briefly, units with men in them who flee are wiped out. . . . If members of a squad are captured and not rescued by the rest, the rest are executed. The minimum arms they are required to carry are: two bows . . . , three quivers full of arrows, one ax, and ropes to pull along machines of war. To be sure, their nobles carry . . . slightly curved swords with sharp points, and their horses wear armor of multiple thickness of leather shaped to fit their bodies. . . .

Some of them have a hook attached to the necks of their lances with which they will pull a rider off his saddle if they can. Their arrows are about two feet, eight inches long . . . and each man carries a file in his quiver to sharpen their heads. . . .

When they come to a river, they cross it with the higher-ups using large, lightweight leather bags with loops and drawstrings to seal up their clothes and necessary equipment for the crossing. The resulting pack floats. Tied to the tails of their horses, who swim over, the pack serves as a sort of boat. . . . Even the common soldiers have nearly waterproof leather bags, into which they stuff their things . . . and then hang them securely on the bases of their horses' tails before crossing.

You should know that the Tartar emperor told me in person that he wanted to send his armies into Livonia [on the Baltic Sea] and Prussia and that he intended to destroy the whole countryside or reduce it to servitude. They enslave people in a way which we find intolerable. . . . Their tactics include using captives from lands just conquered to fight against a province still holding out against them. They put these captives in the front ranks: If they fight poorly, they kill them; if they fight well, they encourage them with cheering words and promise to make them great lords so that they will not escape. However, once the dangers of battle are passed, they keep these people in line by making hapless serfs out of them, while taking the women they want for serving maids and concubines. Their use of men from one defeated country after another against the next country makes it impossible for any single country to resist them, unless God chooses to fight for them. . . .

Thus, if Christians wish to defend themselves, their countries, and Christianity, it will be necessary for kings, princes, barons, and other chiefs of the lands to cooperate as one and to send men under a consolidated command into battle against them before they have so drained the earth of men that there will be nowhere to draw aid from. . . . This army should be ordered as *they* do it, from officers commanding a thousand through officers commanding a hundred and overall commanders of the army. These generals should never enter the fighting themselves, just as Tartar commanders do not enter it, but they should be able to observe the army's action and direct it. Our people should make it a regulation that the soldiers advance into battle together or elsewhere in the order established.

70

Kuyuk Khan, Letter to Pope Innocent IV

QUESTION TO CONSIDER

1. How did Kuyuk Khan assess the relationship between Mongols and the Christian world?

Courage. Kuyuk Khan, Emperor of all men, whose courage is God-given, sends a letter of his own to the great Pope in reply to the message sent to us in which you express your desire to have peace and friendship with us, as we have understood from your emissary.

Your letter to us contains a number of things we must do : We must be baptized and must become Christians. To this we answer that we do not understand how you seek to require us to do anything. Then, as for what you have in your letter showing great surprise at such thorough slaughter of men, for the most part Hungarian Christians, as well as some Polish or Moravian ones, we have not heard of anything that would require us to answer you about that either ; however, so that you will not think that we wish to lull you through our silence [into feeling secure], we will answer you in this way :

No khan can heed more apt advice than comes from the command of God and the recorded words of Jenghiz Khan. Khans have been inspired to do some killing all right, because — once God has decided upon the destruction of men — what God does not do Himself He will enable man to do to man. Consequently, with our God-inspired courage we have wrought massive destruction on every land from the East to the West.

You Christians do worship God, but then — believing yourselves to be the only true ones — you despise nations other than those you consider worthy of having your grace bestowed upon them.

"Lettere del Gran Can al Sommo Pontefece," appended to Friar John's *Historia Mongalorum,* in *Studi Italiani di Filologia Indo-Iranica,* Vol. IX (Firenze : Carnesecchi e Figli, 1913), p. 125. Translated by Henry A. Myers.

You now, Pope : If you want to have peace and friendship with us, come with all the kings and potentates who serve you to our court. You should listen to this response of ours : Subject your will to us and bring us tribute, for if you do not obey our instructions and do not journey to us we are certain that you will have war with us. After that, to be sure, we do not know what the future holds. Only God knows that.

71

The Yuan Code : Homicide

In 1279, for the first time in Chinese history, all of China fell under an alien rule — that of the Mongols who invaded from across the Great Wall. The Mongol conquerors, who remained in control of the Chinese empire for less than a century (until 1368), adopted the dynastic name "Yuan," according to Chinese custom. Once in the seat of power, the Mongols, who were disdained by the Chinese as nomadic barbarians, sought to establish their supremacy as new masters by implementing systematic discriminatory policies against the Chinese, who constituted more than 90 percent of the Mongol empire's population. For instance, the Mongol rulers patronized Lamaism, a Buddhist sect which had originated in Tibet, in order to undercut the pervasive influence of Confucianism and Taoism. The Mongols stratified the population of the empire in such a way that the Chinese were placed at the very bottom of the social ladder, even below the foreigners. The Chinese suffered from administrative and judicial discrimination and were also forced to carry a heavy burden in taxes and forced labor. The following excerpts from the Yuan penal code show, for instance, that the murder of a Mongol by a Chinese invoked the death penalty, whereas the murder of a Chinese by a Mongol was punished by exile to an expeditionary army. Interestingly, the code also seems to reflect the Mongol's nomadic background in that it shows a preference for corporal punishment over imprisonment.

QUESTIONS TO CONSIDER

1. Compare the punishments for homicides provided in the Yuan Code with those in the Code of Hammurabi (see Reading 7).
2. How differently were the cases involving involuntary manslaughter and premeditated murders treated in the Yuan Code ? What seemed to be the criteria for the differences ?

1. A person who kills another person is punishable by death. The family of the victim is entitled to receive from the family of the killer fifty taels of silver for

funeral expenses. The amount could be reduced if the family of the killer is too poor, but under no circumstances should it be less than ten taels of silver in paper currency. If a general clemency is declared before the death sentence is carried out, the payment to the injured family will be doubled.

2. When more than one person conspire to kill an official and succeed in their attempt, all persons involved, the leader or leaders who plan the killing as well as their followers who execute the killing, are punishable by death. If injury rather than death is the result, all persons involved are to be punished by 107 blows and then be exiled to a distant region. The families of the guilty must pay funeral expenses for the dead official.

3. A person who, after having killed another person, chooses to commit suicide but fails in his attempt is punishable by death nevertheless.

4. A person who kills another person is eligible for clemency if he has accumulated good deeds after the killing, provided that the killing is accidental rather than intentional.

5. In a physical fight between two persons, the person who has no intention to kill at the beginning but acquires such intention during the process of fighting is regarded as having harbored the intention to kill, if the physical fight ends with the death of the other person.

6. In a physical fight between two or more persons, the person who has used a weapon, such as a knife, in the fight and thus caused the death of a person or persons against whom he has been fighting is regarded as having harbored the intention to kill. . . .

8. If a person wielding a knife intends to kill another person but is unsuccessful in his attempt after his intended victim has managed to escape and if, subsequent to this escape, he shifts his anger to those bystanders who have tried to stop him, he is regarded as having harbored the intention to kill, if he kills one or more of these bystanders.

9. A person who kills a tax collector is regarded as having harbored the intention to kill, even though the tax collector has used high-pressure methods to collect the taxes due and the taxpayer, out of desperation, decides to kill him.

10. If a man while intoxicated with liquor attempts to kill his wife and, having failed in his attempt, shifts his anger to those bystanders who have tried to stop him, the man is regarded as having harbored the intention to kill and will be sentenced to death if he kills one or more of these bystanders.

11. If a man kills a prostitute who has refused to elope with him, the man will be regarded as guilty as if he had killed a person other than a prostitute. . . .

13. A person who beats to death the person who has killed his father is regarded as guiltless. The family of the person who has killed his father is responsible for the payment of fifty taels of silver for his father's funeral expenses.

14. If a Mongol, in a physical fight or in a state of drunkenness, kills a Chinese, the Mongol will be punished by exile to an expeditionary army, in addition to the payment of funeral expenses for the dead person. . . .

Dun J. Li, trans., *The Civilization of China* (New York : Charles Scribner's Sons, 1975), pp. 259–269. Reprinted by permission of Charles Scribner's Sons, an imprint of Macmillan Publishing Company. Copyright © 1975 by Dun J. Li.

16. If a man beats to death another man who has been flirting with his wife, he will receive a punishment one degree lower than the death sentence. He will be responsible for the dead man's funeral expenses.

17. If a person beats to death a notorious outlaw who would have been sentenced to death if captured by governmental authorities, he is guiltless. He is not responsible for the dead man's funeral expenses.

18. If a person with an object other than a knife causes injury to another person who subsequently dies as a result of this injury, he will receive a punishment three degrees lower than the death sentence.

19. In a quarrel between two persons, if one person smashes his head into the chest of the other and, in the process of falling down, accidentally causes death by damaging the other person's heart with his elbow, the offending person will be punished by 107 blows, in addition to the payment of the dead person's funeral expenses. . . .

21. In a physical fight resulting from one person's violent response to another person's joke, the person who causes injury and subsequent death to the other person will be punished by 107 blows.

22. The man who marries a widow becomes the foster father of the widow's offspring by her first marriage. He will not be responsible, however, for any crime committed by any of his adopted sons if the latter has been evicted by him from his house and lives in a separate residence. In this case the son alone is responsible for any injury he causes to others.

23. A convicted criminal who kills another convicted criminal will be punished in the same manner as if he had killed any other person. A tax collector who beats a person to death in the process of exacting tax payment will be sentenced to death.

24. If an official beats to death a civilian who has accused him in the court of justice of having accepted bribery, the official will be regarded as having harbored the intention to kill and be punished accordingly. . . .

28. A father who inexcusably kills his son with a knife will be punished by 77 blows.

29. A father is guiltless if the son he kills has been undutiful toward him. However, any of his brothers or nephews who have collaborated in, or given assistance to, this killing will be punished by 107 blows.

30. If a father kills his married daughter after having discovered a serious offense committed by her, the father will be punished by 57 blows. The husband of his deceased daughter is entitled to receive from him the full amount of money which he paid for his daughter, so the husband can marry someone else.

31. If a father, with valid reason, beats a son or daughter of his and accidentally causes his or her death, the father is guiltless.

32. A man who kills the son of his wife by her first marriage is punishable by death.

33. A wife who kills a son of her husband's concubine will be punished by 97 blows. Her husband can either marry her off or sell her as a slave.

34. A man or woman who mistreats his or her daughter-in-law and causes her death will be punished by 107 blows, despite the fact that the woman, before her death, has not been a good daughter-in-law.

35. If a man kills not only his son who has been undutiful toward him but also his daughter-in-law, for no other reason than the fact that she happens to be his son's wife, the man will be punished by 77 blows. Her dowry and all of her other belongings shall be returned to her parents.

36. A man who, for flimsy reasons, kills his younger brother is punishable by death. . . .

38. If a man kills his younger brother who has struck him first, the man will be regarded as having killed a guilty person. He will not be punished in the same manner as a murderer would be.

39. If a man, in a quarrel, accidentally kills his younger brother who has lived in a separate residence, the man will be punished by 77 blows. He shall pay half of his younger brother's funeral expenses.

40. A man who kills his cousin in a quarrel will be punished in a manner as if he had killed an unrelated person.

41. If a man kills his younger sister who, though a nun, has had illicit sexual relations with some other man, the man is regarded as having killed a guilty person and will not be punished in the same manner as a murderer would be, provided that before the killing he has warned her about her improper conduct and that his sister, instead of heeding his advice, has verbally abused him in return and physically wrestled with him. . . .

47. A man who kills his wife for flimsy reasons will be punished by death.

48. If a man hates his wife and subsequently causes her death by poisoning, the man will be regarded as having killed an unrelated person.

49. If a man beats his wife and subsequently causes her death for her arrogant attitude toward his parents, the man will be punished by 77 blows.

50. If a man beats his wife and accidentally causes her death after his wife has refused to attend to his needs during his illness and if, in the meantime, she has been verbally abusing his parents and has caused him to lose all affection for her, the man is guiltless.

51. If a man who hates his wife and loves his concubine chooses to kill his wife by citing some minor faults of hers, the man will be punished by death.

52. If a man, having heard some rumor of a derogatory nature about his fiancée, kills her, the man will be regarded as having killed an unrelated person.

53. A woman who cruelly beats to death her husband's concubine will be punished by 107 blows. She shall be stripped before the beatings are inflicted upon her body. . . .

56. If a man beats to death his slave who has verbally and physically abused him, the man is guiltless.

57. If a person kills his or her slave who has been faultless, he or she will be punished by 87 blows. If he or she is in a state of drunkenness when the killing takes place, the punishment will be reduced by one degree [i.e., 77 blows].

58. If a person beats to death a slave who is about to gain his or her freedom, the offending person will be punished by 77 blows.

59. If a person plans and then carries out the killing of a former slave, he or she will be regarded as having killed a free person. . . .

71. A killer under the age of fourteen is guiltless if the killing is accidental rather than intentional. However, the killer and his family are responsible for the dead person's funeral expenses.

73. If a blind person beats another person who subsequently dies as a result of injury, the blind person will be punished by 107 blows. He is responsible for the dead person's funeral expenses.

74. If a person in a state of insanity beats another person who subsequently dies as a result of injury, the person is guiltless. He is responsible, however, for the dead person's funeral expenses.

75. If a physician, because of his insufficient knowledge, kills a patient with his needle or medicine, the physician will be punished by 107 blows. He shall pay for the dead person's funeral expenses.

72

Marco Polo in China

The creation of a huge Eurasian Empire by the Mongols in the thirteenth century again opened the overland routes — the roads once used by the ancient silk traders and Buddhist pilgrims — which had been blocked since the eleventh century by the expansion of Islam. Caravans of traders and pilgrims were again able to move to and from the East. Many European missionaries and merchants made overland journeys to the court of the Mongol Khans. Perhaps the best-known European traveler to the court of Kublai Khan in Cambaluc (Peking) was Marco Polo (1254–1324), the son of a Venetian merchant.

In about 1264, young Marco's adventurous father Nicolo and uncle Maffeo reached the Grand Khan's court after a long and difficult journey through southern Russia, Bukhara, and Chinese Turkestan. They aroused much curiosity in Kublai's mind about Europe and the Papacy. In 1266, they were sent back to Europe as Kublai's ambassadors to ask the Pope to send 100 well-schooled missionaries and scholars to China. The Holy See failed to take Kublai's request seriously and sent two priests who made it only as far east as Armenia. Had the Pope sent 100 dedicated and well-trained missionaries, the course of history might have been altered.

In 1271, Marco Polo joined his father and uncle in their second journey to the court of the Kublai Khan. After three and a half years of difficult, overland journey, they reached Shang-Tu (Xandu), the summer residence of Kublai Khan. The Grand Khan was delighted to see them and grew particularly fond of Marco, whom he appointed as his personal, roving administrator for important missions in several distant provinces. In 1292, after 17 years of service at Kublai Khan's court, the three Polos set out for Europe. This time they went by ship and took with them a young princess whom Kublai was sending as a bride to the Mongol Khan of Persia. In 1295, the Polos returned to Venice, where the Venetians lionized Marco with the nickname "Il milione" (the million).

Shortly after Marco Polo's return, a war broke out between Venice and Genoa. While serving as a Venetian naval commander in this war, Marco was captured and sent to a Genoese prison for three years. During this time Marco Polo dictated, to a fellow prisoner, the account of his adventures and travels in China. His book, printed in Italian, Latin, French, and other languages, introduced Asia to Renaissance Europe and also inspired the great explorers, such as Christopher Columbus, to begin the Age of Discovery in the fifteenth century.

The following excerpts are Marco Polo's eyewitness accounts of the Grand Khan and the capital city of Cambaluc.

QUESTIONS TO CONSIDER

1. Compare and contrast the Kublai Khan's power and palace with those of one of the powerful medieval kings of Europe (see Reading 57).
2. From a historical perspective, what do you think are the most important contributions made by Marco Polo?
3. How would you compare Marco Polo's views on China with Ibn Battuta's views on Africa (see Reading 76)?

Concerning the Person of the Great Kaan

The personal appearance of the Great Kaan [Khan], Lord of Lords, whose name is Cublay, is such as I shall now tell you. He is of a good stature, neither tall nor short, but of a middle height. He has a becoming amount of flesh, and is very shapely in all his limbs. His complexion is white and red, the eyes black and fine; the nose well formed and well set on. He has four wives, whom he retains permanently as his legitimate consorts; and the eldest of his sons by those four wives ought by rights to be emperor; — I mean when his father dies. Those four ladies are called empresses, but each is distinguished also by her proper name. And each of them has a special court of her own, very grand and ample; no one of them having fewer than 300 fair and charming damsels. They have also many pages and eunuchs, and a number of other attendants of both sexes; so that each of these ladies has not less than 10,000 persons attached to her court.

When the Emperor desires the society of one of these four consorts, he will sometimes send for the lady to his apartment and sometimes visit her at her own. He has also a great number of concubines, and I will tell you how he obtains them.

You must know that there is a tribe of Tartars called Ungrat, who are noted for their beauty. Now every year an hundred of the most beautiful maidens of this tribe are sent to the Great Kaan, who commits them to the charge of certain elderly ladies dwelling in his palace. And these old ladies make the girls sleep with them, in order to ascertain if they have sweet breath [and do not snore], and are

From Henry Yule, trans. and ed., *The Book of Ser Marco Polo*, vols. 1 and 2 (London: John Murray, 1903), pp. 356–358, 362–364, 374–375.

sound in all their limbs. Then such of them as are of approved beauty, and are good and sound in all respects, are appointed to attend on the Emperor by turns. Thus six of these damsels take their turn for three days and nights, and wait on him when he is in his chamber and when he is in his bed, to serve him in any way, and to be entirely at his orders. At the end of the three days and nights they are relieved by other six. And so throughout the year, there are reliefs of maidens by six and six, changing every three days and nights.

Concerning the Palace of the Great Kaan

You must know that for three months of the year, to wit December, January, and February, the Great Kaan resides in the capital city of Cathay, which is called Cambaluc [Peking]. . . . In that city stands his great Palace, and now I will tell you what it is like.

It is enclosed all round by a great wall forming a square, each side of which is a mile in length; that is to say, the whole compass thereof is four miles. This you may depend on; it is also very thick, and a good ten paces in height, whitewashed and loop-holed all around. At each angle of the wall there is a very fine and rich palace in which the war-harness of the Emperor is kept, such as bows and quivers, saddles and bridles, and bowstrings, and everything needful for an army. Also midway between every two of these Corner Palaces there is another of the like; so that taking the whole compass of the enclosure you find eight vast Palaces stored with the Great Lord's harness of war. And you must understand that each Palace is assigned to only one kind of article; thus one is stored with bows, a second with saddles, a third with bridles, and so on in succession right round.

The great wall has five gates on its southern face, the middle one being the great gate which is never opened on any occasion except when the Great Kaan himself goes forth or enters. Close on either side of this great gate is a smaller one by which all other people pass; and then towards each angle is another great gate; also open to people in general; so that on that side there are five gates in all.

Inside of this wall there is a second, enclosing a space that is somewhat greater in length than in breadth. This enclosure also has eight palaces corresponding to those of the outer wall, and stored like them with the Lord's harness of war. This wall also hath five gates on the southern face, corresponding to those in the outer wall, and hath one gate on each of the other faces, as the outer wall hath also. In the middle of the second enclosure is the Lord's Great Palace, and I will tell you what it is like.

You must know that it is the greatest Palace that ever was. [Towards the north it is in contact with the outer wall, whilst towards the south there is a vacant space which the Barons and the soldiers are constantly traversing. The Palace itself] hath no upper story, but is all on the ground floor, only the basement is raised some ten palms above the surrounding soil [and this elevation is retained by a wall of marble raised to the level of the pavement, two paces in width and projecting beyond the base of the Palace so as to form a kind of terrace-walk, by which people can pass round the building, and which is exposed to view, whilst on the outer edge of the wall there is a very fine pillared balustrade; and up to this the people are allowed to come]. The roof is very lofty, and the walls of the Palace are all covered with gold and silver. They are also adorned with representations of dragons [sculptured and gilt], beasts and birds, knights and idols, and sundry other subjects. And on the ceiling too you see nothing but gold and silver and painting. [On each of the four sides there is a great marble staircase leading to the top of the marble wall, and forming the approach to the Palace.]

The Hall of the Palace is so large that it could easily dine 6000 people ; and it is quite a marvel to see how many rooms there are besides. The building is altogether so vast, so rich, and so beautiful, that no man on earth could design anything superior to it. The outside of the roof also is all coloured with vermilion and yellow and green and blue and other hues, which are fixed with a varnish so fine and exquisite that they shine like crystal, and lend a resplendent lustre to the Palace as seen for a great way round. This roof is made too with such strength and solidity that it is fit to last for ever.

[On the interior side of the Palace are large buildings with halls and chambers, where the Emperor's private property is placed, such as his treasures of gold, silver, gems, pearls, and gold plate, and in which reside the ladies and concubines. There he occupies himself at his own convenience, and no one else has access.] . . .

Concerning the City of Cambaluc

Now there was on that spot in old times a great and noble city called Cambaluc, which is as much as to say in our tongue "The city of the Emperor." But the Great Kaan was informed by his Astrologers that this city would prove rebellious, and raise great disorders against his imperial authority. So he caused the present city to be built close beside the old one, with only a river between them. And he caused the people of the old city to be removed to the new town that he had founded ; and this is called Taidu. . . .

As regards the size of this (new) city you must know that it has a compass of 24 miles, for each side of it hath a length of 6 miles, and it is four-square. And it is all walled round with walls of earth which have a thickness of full ten paces at bottom, and a height of more than 10 paces ; but they are not so thick at top, for they diminish in thickness as they rise, so that at top they are only about 3 paces thick. And they are provided throughout with loop-holed battlements, which are all whitewashed.

There are 12 gates, and over each gate there is a great and handsome palace, so that there are on each side of the square three gates and five palaces ; for (I ought to mention) there is at each angle also a great and handsome palace. In those palaces are vast halls in which are kept the arms of the city garrison.

The streets are so straight and wide that you can see right along them from end to end and from one gate to the other. And up and down the city there are beautiful palaces, and many great and fine hostelries, and fine houses in great numbers. [All the plots of ground on which the houses of the city are built are four-square, and laid out with straight lines ; all the plots being occupied by great and spacious palaces, with courts and gardens of proportionate size. All these plots were assigned to different heads of families. Each square plot is encompassed by handsome streets for traffic ; and thus the whole city is arranged in squares just like a chess-board, and disposed in a manner so perfect and masterly that it is impossible to give a description that should do it justice.]

Moreover, in the middle of the city there is a great clock — that is to say, a bell — which is struck at night. And after it has struck three times no one must go out in the city, unless it be for the needs of a woman in labour, or of the sick. And those who go about on such errands are bound to carry lanterns with them. Moreover, the established guard at each gate of the city is 1000 armed men ; not that you are to imagine this guard is kept up for fear of any attack, but only as a guard of honour for the Sovereign, who resides there, and to prevent thieves from doing mischief in the town.

Samurai Culture in Japan

In the ninth century, as the aristocracy-dominated central government of Japan weakened and lost control of the provinces, the local gentry began to fortify its own armed constabulary forces. The leaders of these armed groups were called "the bushi" or "samurai," and they were largely descendants of the old provincial uji (clan) aristocracy. The bushi were mounted ; armored ; armed with bows, arrows, and curbed swords ; and accompanied by supporting foot soldiers. By the twelfth century, they had begun to emerge as a dominant social class, providing the key values that permeated life in medieval Japan. They became rulers and guardians of peace as well as fighters.

As clashes among the local armed groups became more frequent, the smaller ones were absorbed into larger and more powerful ones. These groups were eventually consolidated into two powerful rival military clans, one under Minamoto in eastern Japan and the other under Taira in the west. In 1156, a dispute over the imperial succession pitted them against each other in a series of struggles that continued until 1185. At this time, Minamoto Yoritomo (1147–1199) emerged as the unchallenged military master of Japan. In 1192, the court bestowed upon Minamoto Yoritomo the title of Seii-tai-shogun ("Barbarian-Subduing Generalissimo"). This title was once given to generals in charge of expeditions against the Ainu (old proto-Caucasoid inhabitants of Japan), but henceforth it was used in the shortened form of "Shogun" to denote supreme military commander. The country was governed from Minamoto's military headquarters at Kamakura. For the next 700 years, until the Meiji Restoration in 1868, Japan was ruled by the men of the sword. The samurai culture rooted in *Bushido* (meaning "the way of the warrior") flourished.

Bushido was roughly equivalent to medieval European chivalry or the noblesse oblige of the warrior class. Although it did not evolve into an articulated code of conduct for the ruling samurai class until the late seventeenth century, the incipient stage goes back to about the tenth century. The principles of *Bushido* were to be observed by the warrior in his daily life as well as in his vocation. An unwritten code consisting of a few maxims, *Bushido* was primarily transmitted orally or through the pen of some well-known warrior or savant. The principles of *Bushido* were drawn from Zen Buddhism, Shintoism, and the Confucian moral precepts. They stressed justice, honor, duty, loyalty, courage, self-control, and a transcendent fear of dying.

The following excerpt is from *Hagakure* (*In the Shadow of Leaves*), which is one of the best-known classics on *Bushido*. This book contains the teachings of Tsunetomo Yamamoto (1659–1719), who was a samurai turned Zen monk. Written and compiled in 1716 by Yamamoto's student Tsuramoto Tashiro, the *Hagakure* emphasizes the samurai philosophy of dying.

73

Tsunetomo Yamamoto, *Hagakure*

QUESTIONS TO CONSIDER

1. Compare and contrast *Bushido* with the medieval European chivalric code. How were they similar? How were they different? (See Reading 56.)
2. What aspects of *Bushido* were drawn from Confucianism and from Buddhism?

The Way of the Samurai is found in death. When it comes to either/or, there is only the quick choice of death. It is not particularly difficult. Be determined and advance. To say that dying without reaching one's aim is to die a dog's death is the frivolous way of sophisticates. When pressed with the choice of life or death, it is not necessary to gain one's aim.

We all want to live. And in large part we make our logic according to what we like. But not having attained our aim and continuing to live is cowardice. This is a thin dangerous line. To die without gaining one's aim *is* a dog's death and fanaticism. But there is no shame in this. This is the substance of the Way of the Samurai. If by setting one's heart right every morning and evening, one is able to live as though his body were already dead, he gains freedom in the Way. His whole life will be without blame, and he will succeed in his calling. . . .

Being a retainer is nothing other than being a supporter of one's lord, entrusting matters of good and evil to him, and renouncing self-interest. If there are but two or three men of this type, the fief will be secure.

If one looks at the world when affairs are going smoothly, there are many who go about putting in their appearance, being useful by their wisdom, discrimination and artfulness. However, if the lord should retire or go into seclusion, there are many who will quickly turn their backs on him and ingratiate themselves to the

From Tsunetomo Yamamoto, *Hagakure : The Book of the Samurai,* trans. William Scott Wilson (Tokyo and New York : Kodansha International, Ltd., 1979), pp. 17–18, 20–21, 33–34, 66–67. Reprinted with permission from Kodansha International ; © 1979. All rights reserved.

man of the day. Such a thing is unpleasant even to think about. Men of high position, low position, deep wisdom and artfulness all feel that *they* are the ones who are working righteously, but when it comes to the point of throwing away one's life for his lord, all get weak in the knees. This is rather disgraceful. The fact that a useless person often becomes a matchless warrior at such times is because he has already given up his life and has become one with his lord. At the time of Mitsushige's death there was an example of this. His one resolved attendant was I alone. The others followed in my wake. Always the pretentious, self-asserting notables turn their backs on the man just as his eyes are closing in death.

Loyalty is said to be important in the pledge between lord and retainer. Though it may seem unobtainable, it is right before your eyes. If you once set yourself to it, you will become a superb retainer at that very moment....

Every morning, the samurai of fifty or sixty years ago would bathe, shave their foreheads, put lotion in their hair, cut their fingernails and toenails rubbing them with pumice and then with wood sorrel, and without fail pay attention to their personal appearance. It goes without saying that their armor in general was kept free from rust, that it was dusted, shined, and arranged.

Although it seems that taking special care of one's appearance is similar to showiness, it is nothing akin to elegance. Even if you are aware that you may be struck down today and are firmly resolved to an inevitable death, if you are slain with an unseemly appearance, you will show your lack of previous resolve, will be despised by your enemy, and will appear unclean. For this reason it is said that both old and young should take care of their appearance.

Although you say that this is troublesome and time-consuming, a samurai's work is in such things. It is neither busy-work nor time-consuming. In constantly hardening one's resolution to die in battle, deliberately becoming as one already dead, and working at one's job and dealing with military affairs, there should be no shame. But when the time comes, a person will be shamed if he is not conscious of these things even in his dreams, and rather passes his days in self-interest and self-indulgence. And if he thinks that this is not shameful, and feels that nothing else matters as long as he is comfortable, then his dissipate and discourteous actions will be repeatedly regrettable.

The person without previous resolution to inevitable death makes certain that his death will be in bad form. But if one is resolved to death beforehand, in what way can he be despicable? One should be especially diligent in this concern.

Furthermore, during the last thirty years customs have changed; now when young samurai get together, if there is not just talk about money matters, loss and gain, secrets, clothing styles or matters of sex, there is no reason to gather together at all. Customs are going to pieces. One can say that formerly when a man reached the age of twenty or thirty, he did not carry despicable things in his heart, and thus neither did such words appear. If an elder unwittingly said something of that sort, he thought of it as a sort of injury. This new custom probably appears because people attach importance to being beautiful before society and to household finances. What things a person should be able to accomplish if he had no haughtiness concerning his place in society!

It is a wretched thing that the young men of today are so contriving and so proud of their material possessions. Men with contriving hearts are lacking in duty. Lacking in duty, they will have no self-respect....

If one were to say in a word what the condition of being a samurai is, its basis lies first in seriously devoting one's body and soul to his master. And if one is asked what to do beyond this, it would be to fit oneself inwardly with intelligence, humanity and courage. The combining of these three virtues may seem unobtainable to the ordinary person, but it is easy. Intelligence is nothing more than discussing things with others. Limitless wisdom comes from this. Humanity is something done for the sake of others, simply comparing oneself with them and putting them in the fore. Courage is gritting one's teeth; it is simply doing that and pushing ahead, paying no attention to the circumstances. Anything that seems above these three is not necessary to be known.

As for outward aspects, there are personal appearance, one's way of speaking and calligraphy. And as all of these are daily matters, they improve by constant practice. Basically, one should perceive their nature to be one of quiet strength. If one has accomplished all these things, then he should have a knowledge of our area's history and customs. After that he may study the various arts as recreation. If you think it over, being a retainer is simple. And these days, if you observe people who are even a bit useful, you will see that they have accomplished these three outward aspects.

74

The Forty-Seven Ronin

One of the most celebrated episodes in Japanese history is the vendetta of the 47 Ronin.[1] This story of the samurai ideals of loyalty and honor has been told innumerable times, on the stage and in literature, and has become an important part of the heritage of the Japanese people. Although its origins can be dated to the early eighteenth century, when the warrior class reigned supreme under the Tokugawa shogunate (1600–1867), the chivalric ideals it expresses were the very essence of the samurai culture of feudal Japan. In the spring of 1701, Asano Naganori, lord of the small fief of Ako in western Japan, was charged by the shogunal government with the reception of an imperial envoy from Kyoto. He was put under the guidance of Kira Yoshinaka, the shogun's chief of protocol, to prepare for this event. Lord Asano, who was inexperienced in the fine details of protocol, was ridiculed by Kira, who was reputed to be arrogant and corrupt. Pushed to the limits of his patience, Lord Asano drew his sword and wounded Kira in violation of the law prohibiting the drawing of a sword in the shogun's castle. For this offense, Lord Asano was ordered to commit suicide, and his domain was confiscated. His retainers suddenly found themselves masterless. Believing that Asano was a victim of Kira's arrogance and wrong-doing, 47 of Asano's most

---

1. Masterless samurai or warriors.

single-mindedly loyal retainers, led by the senior retainer Oishi Kuranosuke, vowed to avenge their lord's death. After long and careful planning, 46 conspirators[2] burst into Kira's mansion in Edo[3] and killed Kira Yoshinaka. They carried Kira's head to the Sengakuji temple outside Edo and offered it to their lord Asano's grave. Their vendetta was thus completed. In February 1703, after much controversy surrounding the case, the Ronin were finally punished by the shogunal government, not for the murder of Kira but for their contempt of authority, and were ordered to commit hara-kiri — ritual disembowelment. The bodies of the samurai, ranging in age from 15 to 77, were interred in the Sengakuji temple near their master's grave. The following two letters, the first of which was allegedly found on the person of each of the 47 men, and the second of which was laid upon the tomb of their master, together with the head of Kira, reflect the fanatical devotion of these samurai to the ideals of the feudal warrior in Japan.

QUESTIONS TO CONSIDER

1. If you were the judge assigned to this case, how would you rule? How would you reconcile the conflict between private morality and public law? Should the 47 Ronin have been acquitted? Why?
2. How would you compare the issues raised in this reading with the issues suggested in *Antigone* (see Reading 36)?

"Last year in the third month, Asano Takumi no Kami (Lord Asano), upon the occasion of the entertainment of the Imperial ambassador, was driven, by the force of the circumstances, to attack and wound my Lord Kotsuke no Suke (Kira Yoshinake) in the castle, in order to avenge an insult offered to him. Having done this without considering the dignity of the place, and having thus disregarded all rules of propriety, he was condemned to hara kiri, and his property and castle of Ako were forfeited to the State, and were delivered up by his retainers to the officers deputed by the Shogun to receive them. After this his followers were all dispersed. At the time of the quarrel, the high officials prevented [Lord Asano] from carrying out his intention of killing his enemy, my Lord Kotsuke no Suke [Kira]. So Asano Takumi no Kami [Lord Asano] died without having avenged himself, and this was more than his retainers could endure. It is impossible to remain under the same heaven with the enemy of lord or father; for this reason we have dared to declare enmity against a personage of so exalted rank. This day we shall attack Kira Kotsuke no Suke, in order to finish the deed of vengeance which was

From Donald Keene, trans., *Chushingura (The Treasury of Loyal Retainers)* (New York : Columbia University Press, 1971), pp. 2–3. Reprinted by permission of Columbia University Press.

2. One of the 47 did not participate in the final act of the vendetta but remains as an honorary member.
3. Present-day Tokyo.

begun by our dead lord. If any honorable person should find our bodies after death, he is respectfully requested to open and read this document."

15th year of Genroku, 12th month[1]

Signed, Oishi Kuranosuke, Retainer of Asano
Takumino no Kami, and forty-six others

"The 15th year of Genroku, the 12th month, and the 15th day. We have come this day to do homage here, forty-seven men in all, from Oishi Kuranosuke down to the foot-soldier Terasaka Kichiemon, all cheerfully about to lay down our lives on your behalf. We reverently announce this to the honored spirit of our dead master. On the 14th day of the third month of last year our honored master was pleased to attack Kira Kotsuke no Suke, for what reason we know not. Our honored master put an end to his own life, but Kira Kotsuke no Suke lived. Although we fear that after the decree issued by the Government this plot of ours will be displeasing to our honored master, still we, who have eaten of your food, could not without blushing repeat the verse, 'Thou shall not live under the same heaven, nor tread the same earth with the enemy of thy father or lord,' nor could we have dared to leave hell and present ourselves before you in paradise, unless we had carried out the vengeance which you began. Every day that we waited seemed as three autumns to us. Verily, we have trodden the snow for one day, nay, for two days, and have tasted food but once. The old and decrepit, the sick and ailing, have come forth gladly to lay down lives. Men might laugh at us, as at grasshoppers trusting in the strength of their arms, and thus shame our honored lord ; but we could not halt in our deed of vengeance. Having taken counsel together last night, we have escorted my Lord Kotsuke no Suke hither to your tomb. This dirk[2] by which our honored lord set great store last year, and entrusted to our care, we now bring back. If your noble spirit be now present before this tomb, we pray you, as a sign, to take the dirk, and, striking the head of your enemy with it a second time, to dispel your hatred for ever. This is the respectful statement of forty-seven men."

Ibn Battuta: World Traveler

Born in Algiers, Ibn Battuta (1304–1368) was the premier world traveler of the Middle Ages. Although Marco Polo's adventures are better known in the West, never did Polo travel as far or see as many different countries as this indefatigable Berber. In 1325, Ibn Battuta made the first of four visits to the Holy City of Mecca, thereby beginning an itinerary of 75,000 miles. Later in life, this devout Muslim would dictate to a Moroccan scribe an account of his journeys.

1. 1702.
2. A dirk is a dagger. The dirk with which Lord Asano disemboweled himself, and with which Oishi Kuranosuke cut off Kira's head.

For nearly 30 years, Ibn Battuta traveled continuously throughout Africa, the Middle East, Persia, Russia, India, China, and Spain. He made it a rule, if possible, never to travel the same road twice, and he frequently paid the price of taking the less-traveled road. He often was stranded or overcome by disease. His African editors note: "He seems to have experienced most travellers' diseases from Lahore sore to Dehli belly. Only the fact that the New World had not been discovered saved him from Montezuma's revenge."[1]

The two following selections illustrate the range of Ibn Battuta's travels and also suggest that, by the fourteenth century, Islamic civilization, spanning four continents, was truly the "world" civilization. In 1344, Ibn Battuta left the Malabar coast of India and sailed south to the Maldive Islands, where for 18 months he served as a judge of Islamic sacred law. His description of island customs not only reveals much of the islands' social structure but also underscores the importance of nautical technology for Indian Ocean seafarers. Later, after journeys to Ceylon, China, and Syria, he returned to Algiers. In 1352, on his last journey, he set off on foot across the Sahara to visit the African kingdoms of the Niger basin. His account of this experience — excerpted in the second selection below — is one of the primary records of the social customs in the Kingdom of Mali, particularly the city of Iwalatan (Walata).

75

Ibn Battuta in the Maldive Islands

QUESTIONS TO CONSIDER

1. What economic, geographic, and social conditions might account for the fact that the inhabitants of the Maldive Islands impressed Ibn Battuta as righteous and nonviolent?
2. Does this selection, and the next reading, suggest anything about Muslim attitudes toward the law, religious education, and treatment of foreigners?
3. What do Ibn Battuta's observations suggest about the position of women in the Maldive Islands?
4. How would you compare Ibn Battuta's account with that of Marco Polo (see Reading 72)?

1. Said Hamdun and Noel King, eds. and trans., *Ibn Battuta in Black Africa* (London: Rex Collings, 1975), p. 4.

... I decided to travel to Dhîbat Almahal [Maldive islands], about which I had heard a great deal. Ten days after leaving Calicut [India], we reached the Maldive Islands. There are about two thousand of these islands and surely they must be counted among the wonders of the world. About one hundred of these islands are grouped into a ring-like cluster; and each cluster has a channel of entry permitting ships to reach the islands. When a ship arrives near these islands, it is necessary that a native pilot from the islands bring the ship into port. The islands are so close to one another that only the tops of the palm trees are visible. If a ship loses its way, it will never penetrate these islands and could well be blown off course to the Coromandel Coast [East coast of India] or to Ceylon.

All the inhabitants of these islands are pious and honest Muslims. The islands are divided into twelve districts governed by a governor whom they call *Courdoûiy.* The Mahal district, which gives its name to the entire island group, is the residence of their sovereign. The Maldive islands do not produce cereal grains, except for a type of millet called *anly* which is grown in the Souweïd district and then shipped to Mahal. All the inhabitants live on a fish called *koulb almâs,* which has red meat, no grease, and smells like lamb. When they catch this fish, they cut it in four parts, cook it lightly, and then hang it in palm leaf baskets over smoke. When it is completely dry, they eat it. They export this smoked fish — which they call black fish — to India, China and Yemen.

Coconut trees are the most common trees on the islands, and these trees, along with the black fish described above, provide the food for the natives. Coconut trees are marvelous trees. Each of these trees produces twelve bunches a year, one each month. Some coconuts are small, others large, many are dry, and the rest are green. These coconuts give the natives milk, oil, and honey. They use the honey to make a pastry which they eat with dried coconuts. Their diet of fish and coconuts is not only very nourishing but also results in extraordinary sexual vigor, for these natives are without equal in their lovemaking. Truly, in this subject, the inhabitants of these islands are capable of astonishing feats. As for me, for the year and one half I was in the Maldives, I had four legitimate wives and several concubines. Each day I made a general tour of all, and at night I spent time with each of them in turn.

The inhabitants of the Maldives are upright, pious, of a sincere faith and righteous; their diet is pure and their prayers are answered. When greeting each other, they say "God is my Lord, Mohammed is my prophet; I am nothing." Their bodies are weak; they are not used to fighting, and their armor is in prayer. One day when in my court, I ordered the right hand of a thief to be cut off, several spectators in my courtroom fainted. Indian bandits do not attack or molest these people because they have learned that anyone who mistreats them suffers misfortune. Enemies who invade their lands abuse foreigners, but they do not attack the natives of these islands.

In each of these islands there are beautiful mosques and most of their buildings are made of wood. These islanders are very clean people; they avoid filth,

From Ibn Battuta, *Voyages D'Ibn Batoutah,* trans. from the Arabic by C. Defrémery and B. R. Sanguinétti (Paris : Imprimerie Impériale, 1858), IV, 110–125, passim. Translated by Philip F. Riley.

most of them bathe twice a day due to the extreme heat and constant perspiration. They use a great deal of perfumed oils such as the essence of sandalwood and musk oil from Macao. One of their customs is that when the men recite their morning prayers, their wives or mothers clean their eyes with salve and rub their skin with rose water and oil so that all traces of fatigue are banished. Their clothing consists of a loin cloth which they wear instead of trousers; on their backs they wear clothing resembling garments of Muslim pilgrims. Some wear a turban, others wear a small kerchief. Whenever any of them meets a Kâdi [a judge] or a preacher, he removes his clothing from his shoulders, uncovering his back and escorts him thus to his home. Another of their customs is that when a newly married husband wishes to be alone with his wife he leaves pieces of cotton from the door of his home to the bridal chamber; his wife places handfuls of cowrie shells [sea shells] to the right and left of the cotton trail, marking the road he should follow, while she stations herself at the door of the bridal chamber. When her husband arrives at the chamber, his wife throws her loin cloth at his feet. . . .

All the inhabitants of the Maldives, be they noble or plebeian, are barefooted. Their streets are swept very clean; shade trees protect pedestrians so that walking in the streets is like walking in an orchard. In spite of this, it is necessary that each person, upon entering a house wash his feet from a water jar kept near the entrance and wipe them with a towel placed there. This same procedure is followed upon entering a mosque.

It is the custom of the islands that when a foreign ship arrives, small boats, crewed by natives carrying betel nuts and green coconuts, go out to welcome the ship. The nuts are offered by the natives to the seafaring visitors in hopes of guiding the foreign ship to shore. The native captain who guides the ship to shore becomes the host for the foreigners and his home becomes their trading center. Any of the foreigners who wish to marry can do so, but when he leaves the island he must divorce his wife for these natives never leave their homeland. For those visitors who do not marry, the woman with whom he is lodging prepares all of his meals and also provides him with provisions for his return voyage. In return for this, she would expect to receive a small gift. . . .

The women of these islands do not cover their heads, not even their queen does so. They comb their hair and gather it to one side. Most of them are bare breasted and wear only a loin cloth when they are in public. When I was a judge there, I tried to change this custom and ordered the women to wear more clothing, but I was not successful. No woman was admitted to my court unless she was fully clothed, but this was the extent of my influence. I had some slave girls who wore the garments which were worn in Delhi and who covered their heads, but it was more of a disfigurement than an ornament, since they were not used to it. Women's jewelry consists of wearing silver bracelets which cover their arms between their wrists and their elbows. Only the Sultan's women wear bracelets of gold. One of the usual customs among these women was to work as domestic servants for a salary of five gold pieces. Their employer is responsible for their upkeep. They do not consider this dishonorable and most girls work in this capacity. You will find ten or twenty of them in a rich man's house. Every vase that a girl breaks is charged against her. When she wishes to transfer from one house to another, her new employers give her the sum which she owes her former employers.

She pays this to the latter and then is indebted to her new employer. The principal occupation of these female domestics is spinning *kanbar,* the fiber found in coconuts. It is easy to marry in these islands due to the small dowries and the pleasant disposition of the women.

76

Ibn Battuta in Black Africa

QUESTIONS TO CONSIDER

1. Why was Ibn Battuta so troubled by his African hosts' methods of tracing genealogy? Are there political implications of this genealogical system?
2. How would you compare Ibn Battuta's observations of Africa with those of Gomes Eannes de Azurara (see Reading 88)?

The condition of these people [of Iwalatan] is strange and their manners are bizarre. As for their men, there is no sexual jealousy about them. None of them is named after his father, but each traces his genealogy from his maternal uncle. A man's inheritance is not passed to his own sons but to the sons of his sister. I have never seen such a thing in any other part of the world except among the infidels who live on the Malabar coast of India. These people are Muslims who follow exactly the prescribed laws for prayer, study the laws of Islam, and know the Koran by heart. Their women are not modest in the presence of men; despite reciting their prayers punctually, they do not veil their faces. Any male who wishes to marry one of them can so very easily, but the women do not travel with their husbands for her family would not allow it. In this country, the women are permitted to have male friends and companions among men who are not members of her family. So too for men; they are permitted to have female companions among women who are not members of his family. It happens quite often that a man would enter his own house and find his wife with one of her own friends and would not rebuke her.

Anecdote

One day I entered the home of a judge in Iwalatan after he had given his permission, and I found him with a very young and beautiful woman. Immediately I thought it best to leave, but she laughed at me and was not at all embarrassed. The

From Ibn Battuta, *Voyages D'Ibn Batoutah,* trans. from the Arabic by C. Defrémery and B. R. Sanguinétti (Paris: Imprimerie Impériale, 1858), IV, 387–390, 421–424. Translated by Philip F. Riley.

judge asked me "Why would you want to leave? She is my friend." I was astonished at the conduct of these two. He was a judge and had made a pilgrimage to Mecca. Later I learned that he has asked permission of the sultan to go on a pilgrimage to Mecca that year with his female friend. Whether it was this one or another I do not know, but the Sultan refused to let him go.

A Similar Anecdote

One day I entered the home of Aboû Mohammed Yandecán, a man of the Mesoûfah tribe. He was sitting on a rug while in the middle of his house was a bed covered with a canopy. On it was his wife in conversation with another man sitting at her side. I said to Aboû Mohammed "Who is this woman?" — "She is my wife," he responded — "And who is the man with her?" I asked. "He is her friend," replied the judge. I asked how he, who knew the divine law on such matters, could permit such a thing. He replied that "The companionship of women with men in this country is proper and honorable: It does not inspire suspicion. Our women are not like the women of your country." I was shocked at his stupid answer and immediately left his home and never returned. . . .

Good and Bad Qualities

Among their good qualities we can cite the following:

1. There is a small amount of crime, for these people obey the law. Their sultan does not pardon criminals.
2. Travelers and natives alike are safe from brigands, robbers, and thieves.
3. The natives do not confiscate the property of white men who die in this country, even if they are very wealthy; instead they entrust it to another, respected white man to dispose of it properly.
4. The prayers are offered punctually and with fervor. Children who neglect their prayers are beaten. If you do not come to the mosque early on a Friday you cannot find a place to pray because the crowds are so large. Quite often they send their slaves to the mosque with a prayer rug to find and hold a place for their masters. These prayer rugs are made from the leaves of trees similar to palm trees, but one that bears no fruit.
5. White garments are worn on Fridays. If by chance one does not have a proper white garment, regular clothing is washed and cleaned to wear for public prayer.
6. They are committed to learn by heart the sublime Koran. Children who fail to learn the Koran by heart have their feet shackled and these shackles are not removed until they memorize the Koran. On a feast day I visited a judge who had his children in chains. I said to him "Why don't you release them?" He said "I will not do so until they know the Koran by heart." Another day I passed a handsome young black man dressed superbly, but shackled by a heavy chain on his feet. I asked my companion, "What has this young man done? Is he a mur-

derer?" The handsome young black man laughed and my companion told me, "He has been chained so that he will learn the Koran by heart."

Among their bad qualities we can cite the following:

1. Their female servants, slave women and small daughters appear before men completely naked, exposing their private parts. Even during the month of Ramadan [a period of fast], military commanders broke their fast in the palace of the Sultan. Twenty or more naked servant girls served them food.
2. Nude women without veils on their faces enter the palace of the Sultan. On the twenty-seventh night of Ramadan, I saw about a hundred naked female slaves coming out of the palace of the Sultan with food. Two of the Sultan's daughters, who have large breasts, were with them and they were naked.
3. These natives put dust and ashes on their head to show their education and as a sign of respect.
4. They laugh when poets recite their verse before the Sultan.
5. Finally, they eat impure meat such as dogs and donkeys.

The Black Death

The outbreak of the Black Death in fourteenth-century Europe is an example of how cross-cultural disease contacts can dramatically change the course of history for millions of people. The Black Death was a combination of three disease strains: a bubonic strain (so called because of buboes, or swelling of the victim's glands) that attacked the lymphatic system, a pneumonic strain that invaded the lungs, and a septicemic strain that was lethal upon entering the bloodstream. In all likelihood, Mongol horsemen carried these disease baccilli westward out of Asia so that by the 1340s, the disease had spread from the Gobi Desert to the Black Sea. In 1347, Genoese traders, returning from the Crimea, brought the disease to Italy. Because of a vigorous and hearty flea and rat population, it spread quickly throughout most of Europe, killing at least 20 million people by 1350. Once a victim was infected, death was certain, usually coming within four days. Certain groups of people, such as bakers, suffered particularly heavy losses because their warm ovens were the choice nests for infected rats. Monasteries, too, seemed to have suffered high mortality rates, as did virtually all the large urban areas.

What is certain is that after the first outbreak of plague, the Black Death recurred at regular intervals. Over time, the huge population losses were restored, not because Europe ever fully conquered the plague, but because the population slowly developed a greater tolerance for the disease. By the eighteenth century, the Black Death had lost much of its lethal effect on Europe.

Although these facts are clear, there is no way to determine the degree to which the disease contributed to political, religious, and social change in Europe after 1350. Post-plague European art showed a fascination with themes of death, decay, and suffering. Popular culture soon developed new rituals celebrating death, such as the dance of death (the word "macabre" describing this dance appeared first in 1376) and the processional liturgy of flagellants seeking deliverance while scourging themselves. High society's rituals changed as well. Post-plague nobility now often hired musicians to play at elaborate funerals. In Paris, polite society now sought the cemetery of the Holy Innocents for its Sunday promenades and amorous rendezvous.

The following account is by Jean de Venette (died c. 1368). A Carmelite who witnessed the ravages of death in France, he wrote this account in the late 1350s.

77

The Chronicle of Jean de Venette

QUESTIONS TO CONSIDER

1. How does Jean de Venette's account explain the origins of the Black Death?
2. What does the account reveal about the character and assumptions of fourteenth-century medicine?
3. What does the account suggest about medieval attitudes of anti-Semitism?
4. What were some of the plague's aftereffects in France?

In A.D. 1348, the people of France and of almost the whole world were struck by a blow other than war. For in addition to the famine . . . and to the wars . . . pestilence and its attendant tribulations appeared again in various parts of the world. In the month of August, 1348, after Vespers when the sun was beginning to set, a big and very bright star appeared above Paris, toward the west. It did not seem, as stars usually do, to be very high above our hemisphere but rather very near. As the sun set and night came on, this star did not seem to me or to many other friars who were watching it to move from one place. At length, when night had come, this big star, to the amazement of all of us who were watching, broke into many different rays and, as it shed these rays over Paris toward the east, totally disappeared and was completely annihilated. Whether it was a comet or not, whether it was composed of airy exhalations and was finally resolved into vapor, I leave to the decision of astronomers. It is, however, possible that it was a presage of the amazing pestilence to come, which, in fact, followed very shortly in Paris and throughout France and elsewhere, as I shall tell. All this year and the next, the mortality of men and women, of the young even more than of the old, in Paris and in the king-

From Richard A. Newhall, ed., *The Chronicle of Jean de Venette*, trans. Jean Birdsall, Records of Civilization, Sources and Studies, no. 50 (New York: Columbia University Press, 1953), pp. 48–52. Reprinted by permission of Columbia University Press.

dom of France, and also, it is said, in other parts of the world, was so great that it was almost impossible to bury the dead. People lay ill little more than two or three days and died suddenly, as it were in full health. He who was well one day was dead the next and being carried to his grave. Swellings appeared suddenly in the armpit or in the groin — in many cases both — and they were infallible signs of death. This sickness or pestilence was called an epidemic by the doctors. Nothing like the great numbers who died in the years 1348 and 1349 has been heard of or seen or read of in times past. This plague and disease came from *ymaginatione* or association and contagion, for if a well man visited the sick he only rarely evaded the risk of death. Wherefore in many towns timid priests withdrew, leaving the exercise of their ministry to such of the religious as were more daring. In many places not two out of twenty remained alive. So high was the mortality at the Hôtel-Dieu in Paris that for a long time, more than five hundred dead were carried daily with great devotion in carts to the cemetery of the Holy Innocents in Paris for burial. A very great number of the saintly sisters of the Hôtel-Dieu who, not fearing to die, nursed the sick in all sweetness and humility, with no thought of honor, a number too often renewed by death, rest in peace with Christ, as we may piously believe.

This plague, it is said, began among the unbelievers, came to Italy, and then crossing the Alps reached Avignon, where it attacked several cardinals and took from them their whole household. Then it spread, unforeseen, to France, through Gascony and Spain, little by little, from town to town, from village to village, from house to house, and finally from person to person. It even crossed over to Germany, though it was not so bad there as with us. During the epidemic, God of His accustomed goodness deigned to grant this grace, that however suddenly men died, almost all awaited death joyfully. Nor was there anyone who died without confessing his sins and receiving the holy viaticum. To the even greater benefit of the dying, Pope Clement VI through their confessors mercifully gave and granted absolution from penalty to the dying in many cities and fortified towns. Men died the more willingly for this and left many inheritances and temporal goods to churches and monastic orders, for in many cases they had seen their close heirs and children die before them.

Some said that this pestilence was caused by infection of the air and waters, since there was at this time no famine nor lack of food supplies, but on the contrary great abundance. As a result of this theory of infected water and air as the source of the plague the Jews were suddenly and violently charged with infecting wells and water and corrupting the air. The whole world rose up against them cruelly on this account. In Germany and other parts of the world where Jews lived, they were massacred and slaughtered by Christians, and many thousands were burned everywhere, indiscriminately. The unshaken, if fatuous, constancy of the men and their wives was remarkable. For mothers hurled their children first into the fire that they might not be baptized and then leaped in after them to burn with their husbands and children. It is said that many bad Christians were found who in a like manner put poison into wells. But in truth, such poisonings, granted that they actually were perpetrated, could not have caused so great a plague nor have infected so many people. There were other causes; for example, the will of God and the corrupt humors and evil inherent in air and earth. Perhaps the poisonings, if they actually took place in some localities, reenforced these causes. The plague lasted in France for the greater part of the years 1348 and 1349 and then ceased. Many country villages and many houses in good towns remained empty and deserted. Many houses, including some splendid dwellings, very soon fell into ruins. Even in Paris several houses were thus ruined, though fewer here than elsewhere.

After the cessation of the epidemic, pestilence, or plague, the men and women who survived married each other. There was no sterility among the women, but on the contrary fertility beyond the ordinary. Pregnant women were seen on every side. Many twins were born and even three children at once. But the most surprising fact is that children born after the plague, when they became of an age for teeth, had only twenty or twenty-two teeth, though before that time men commonly had thirty-two in their upper and lower jaws together. What this diminution in the number of teeth signified I wonder greatly, unless it be a new era resulting from the destruction of one human generation by the plague and its replacement by another. But woe is me! the world was not changed for the better but for the worse by this renewal of population. For men were more avaricious and grasping than before, even though they had far greater possessions. They were more covetous and disturbed each other more frequently with suits, brawls, disputes, and pleas. Nor by the mortality resulting from this terrible plague inflicted by God was peace between kings and lords established. On the contrary, the enemies of the king of France and of the Church were stronger and wickeder than before and stirred up wars on sea and on land. Greater evils than before pullulated everywhere in the world. And this fact was very remarkable. Although there was an abundance of all goods, yet everything was twice as dear, whether it were utensils, victuals, or merchandise, hired helpers or peasants and serfs, except for some hereditary domains which remained abundantly stocked with everything. Charity began to cool, and iniquity with ignorance and sin to abound, for few could be found in the good towns and castles who knew how or were willing to instruct children in the rudiments of grammar. . . .

In the year 1349, while the plague was still active and spreading from town to town, men in Germany, Flanders, Hainaut, and Lorraine uprose and began a new sect on their own authority. Stripped to the waist, they gathered in large groups and bands and marched in procession through the crossroads and squares of cities and good towns. There they formed circles and beat upon their backs with weighted scourges, rejoicing as they did so in loud voices and singing hymns suitable to their rite and newly composed for it. Thus for thirty-three days they marched through many towns doing their penance and affording a great spectacle to the wondering people. They flogged their shoulders and arms with scourges tipped with iron points so zealously as to draw blood. But they did not come to Paris nor to any part of France, for they were forbidden to do so by the king of France, who did not want them. He acted on the advice of the masters of theology of the University of Paris, who said that this new sect had been formed contrary to the will of God, to the rites of Holy Mother Church, and to the salvation of all their souls. That indeed this was and is true appeared shortly. For Pope Clement VI was fully informed concerning this fatuous new rite by the masters of Paris through emissaries reverently sent to him and, on the grounds that it had been damnably formed, contrary to law, he forbade the Flagellants under threat of anathema to practise in the future the public penance which they had so presumptuously undertaken. His prohibition was just, for the Flagellants, supported by certain fatuous priests and monks, were enunciating doctrines and opinions which were beyond measure evil, erroneous, and fallacious. For example, they said that their blood thus drawn by the scourge and poured out was mingled with the blood of Christ. Their many errors showed how little they knew of the Catholic faith. Wherefore, as they had begun fatuously of themselves and not of God, so in a short time they were reduced to nothing. On being warned, they desisted and humbly received absolution and penance at the hands of their prelates as the pope's representatives. Many honorable women and devout matrons, it must be added, had done this penance with scourges, marching and singing through towns and churches like the men, but after a little like the others they desisted.

A WORLD IN CHANGE

The Rise of the
Ottoman Empire

Osman, after whom the Ottomans were named, was the son of Ertogrul, who had led a small group of Turks out of Asia in advance of the Mongols during the second half of the thirteenth century. Ertogrul eventually received a small fief in northeastern Anatolia and became a frontier warrior against the Byzantines.

When Osman succeeded his father, the Ottomans had converted to Islam, which only served to reinforce their military ambitions. The territory expanded slowly until 1354, when a descendant of Osman crossed into Europe (Thrace) and began to attack Byzantine lands as well as other Balkan states.

In 1366, Sultan Murad I decided to move the Ottoman capital from Anatolia to Europe. The emphasis of Ottoman policy for the next century was to be on Christian Europe with the ultimate goal of Constantinople. This was achieved by Mehmed II in 1453, when he captured the former Byzantine capital and made it the center of Ottoman government.

78

Konstantin Mihailovic, *Memoirs of a Janissary*

After Mehmed II The Conqueror (1451–1481) had captured Constantinople in 1453 and made it the capital of the Ottoman Empire, he eliminated the last remnants of the Byzantine royal family in Trebizond, on the Black Sea, and in Greece. Thereafter, his Ottoman armies engaged in a series of battles to reduce Albania, Serbia (except for the city of Belgrade), Croatia, and Montenegro to complete subjection. Mehmed frequently sent his raiders across the Danube into the Christian provinces of Moldavia and Wallachia, ruled by the kings of Hungary, and forced a few of the local princes to become allies. His last action was to begin an invasion of Italy, which was stopped when it was learned by his troops that the Conqueror had died.

These military victories were gained by a very large and well-trained Ottoman army. At the core of the army was the Janissary Corps (*Yeni Cheri* or New Army), whose origins dated to the fourteenth century. The Ottoman sultans decided to create a loyal slave army from their Christian subjects who would have no ties to family or land. At irregular intervals, special commissioners traveled through Albania, Bosnia, and Bulgaria — though any area was subject — and collected a number of Christian boys between 10 and 15 years old. This practice was called *devshirme*. The boys were toughened, converted to Islam, and Turkified and then given out to high Ottoman officials who trained them in the art of war. A very small number were sent to the sultan's palace (Grand Seraglio) in Constantinople where they were trained to hold the highest governmental positions.

The following selections come from the *Memoirs* of a Serb named Konstantin Mihailovic (1430s?–?), who was captured in 1455 when Mehmed II tried to take the city of Belgrade. Without the necessary education or training, Konstantin acquired some function in the Janissary Corps as he was engaged in 1456 in Mehmed's siege of Belgrade. He later went with the sultan to fight against Trebizond and to participate in raids against Vlad Tsepes (Dracula) in Wallachia. He was finally put in charge of a Bosnian fortress in 1463. The Hungarian king, Matthew Corvinus, very quickly captured the fortress and Konstantin reconverted to Christianity. After these experiences, the author traveled through Bohemia, Hungary, and Poland where he settled to write his memoirs.

The first part of the selection relates how Mehmed II captured Konstantin and how the sultan later punished Serbian (Raskan) youths who had tried to assassinate him. The second describes the gathering, training, organization, and a typical military operation of the Janissaries.

QUESTIONS TO CONSIDER

1. Compare this selection with *The Palace School of Muhammad the Conqueror* (see Reading 80). What other positions in Ottoman service could Konstantin Mihailovic have had?
2. Why did the Ottoman sultans form the Janissary Corps from Christian tribute boys and not Muslim boys?
3. What were the rewards or punishments for these boys?

And from there the Emperor marched and surrounded a city which they called Novo Brdo, "Mountain of Silver and Gold," and having attacked it, conquered it [June, 1455], but by means of an agreement: he promised to let them keep their possessions and also not to enslave their young women and boys. And when the city of Novo Brdo had surrendered, the Emperor ordered that the gates be closed and that one small gate be left open. Having arrived in the city the Turks ordered all the householders with their families, both males and females, to go out of the

Konstantin Mihailovic, *Memoirs of a Janissary,* trans. Benjamin Stolz (Ann Arbor: Michigan Slavic Translations, no. 3, Michigan Slavic Publications, 1975), pp. 99–101, 157–159, 185–187. Published under the auspices of the Joint Committee on Eastern Europe, American Council of Learned Societies by the Department of Slavic Languages and Literatures. Reprinted by permission.

city through the small gate to a ditch, leaving their possessions in the houses. And so it happened that they went one after another, and the Emperor himself standing before the small gate sorted out the boys on one side and the females on the other, and the men along the ditch on one side and the women on the other side. All those among the men who were the most important and distinguished he ordered decapitated. The remainder he ordered released to the city. As for their possessions, nothing of theirs was harmed. The boys were 320 in number and the females 74. The females he distributed among the heathens, but he took the boys for himself into the Janissaries, and sent them beyond the sea to Anatolia, where their preserve is.

I was also taken in that city with my two brothers, and wherever the Turks to whom we were entrusted drove us in a band, and wherever we came to forests or mountains, there we always thought about killing the Turks and running away by ourselves among the mountains, but our youth did not permit us to do that ; for I myself with nineteen others ran away from them in the night from a village called Samokovo. Then the whole region pursued us, and having caught and bound us, they beat us and tortured us and dragged us behind horses. It is a wonder that our soul remained in us. Then others vouched for us, and my two brothers, that we would not permit this anymore, and so they peacefully led us across the sea.

Then the Emperor, having arrived at Adrianople, took eight youths of this same group among the chamberlains. These youths agreed to kill the Emperor on night watch, saying among themselves, "If we kill this Turkish dog, then all of Christendom will be freed ; but if we are caught, then we will become martyrs before God with the others."

And when the night watch came, they had made preparations, each having a knife on himself. And when the Emperor was to go to his bedchamber, then one of them named Dmitar Tomašić left them as an ignoble traitor and told the Emperor what was to happen. Then the Emperor ordered them seized and brought before him. The Emperor, having seen a knife on each one, asked them : "Who led you to this, that you dared attempt this ?" Their reply was in a word : "None other than our great sorrow for our fathers and dear friends."

Then the Emperor ordered that hens' eggs be brought and ordered that they be placed in hot ashes so that they would be baked as hard as possible. And having taken them from the ashes, he had a hot egg fastened under each one's knee so that their muscles would shrink and burn. Then he ordered that they be carried by wagon to Persia with the eggs [attached], not allowing them to be removed from them until they cooled off by themselves. And after a year he ordered that they be brought back ; and seeing that there was nothing to them, he ordered them beheaded, and several of us, having taken the bodies in the night, buried them beside an empty church called "Does Not See the Sun." And so it happened to those youths in Constantinople. And the one who had warned the Emperor he made a great lord at his court, but later such a serious illness — some sort of consumption — befell him, that he dried up to death. And his heathen name was Haydari. And so the Lord God deigned to visit that upon him for his ignobility and faithlessness.

Thereafter Emperor Machomet did not want to have any Raškan boys in his bedchamber. So he took six boys and had all their genital organs cut off to the very abdomen; and so one died and five remained alive. They are called in their language *hadomlar,* which means in our language "eunuchs." And these guard the Emperor's wives.

Whenever the Turks invade foreign lands and capture their people an imperial scribe follows immediately behind them, and whatever boys there are, he takes them all into the Janissaries and gives five gold pieces for each one and sends them across the sea. There are about two thousand of these boys. If, however, the number of them from enemy peoples does not suffice, then he takes from the Christians in every village in his land who have boys, having established what is the most every village can give so that the quota will always be full. And the boys whom he takes in his own land are called *cilik.* Each one of them can leave his property to whomever he wants after his death. And those whom he takes among the enemies are called *pendik.* These latter after their deaths can leave nothing; rather, it goes to the emperor, except that if someone comports himself well and is so deserving that he be freed, he may leave it to whomever he wants. And on the boys who are across the sea the emperor spends nothing; rather, those to whom they are entrusted must maintain them and send them where he orders. Then they take those who are suited for it on ships and there they study and train to skirmish in battle. There the emperor already provides for them and gives them a wage. From there he chooses for his own court those who are trained and then raises their wages. The younger must serve the older, and those who come of age and attain manhood he assigns to the fortress so that they will look after them. . . .

And at the court there are about four thousand Janissaries, and among them there is the following organization. They have over them a senior hetman [military commander] called an *aga,* a great lord. He receives ten gold pieces a day, and his steward, one gold piece a day. To each centurion they give a gold piece every two days, and to their stewards, a gold piece every four days. And all their sons who grow out of boyhood have a wage from the emperor. And no courtier who permits himself something will be punished by the honest ones by fine, but rather by death; they dare not, however, punish any courtier publicly, but secretly, because of the other courtiers, for they would revolt. And no Janissary nor any decurion [cavalry commander] of theirs dare ride a horse, save the hetman himself and the steward. And among them it is so arranged that some are archers who shoot bows, some are gunners who shoot mortars, others muskets, and still others, crossbows. And every day they must appear with their weapons before their hetmans. And he gives each one a gold piece per year for a bow, and in addition a tunic, a shirt, and large trousers made, as is their fashion, of three ells [27–45 inches in length] of cloth, and a shirt of eight ells. And this I myself distributed to them for two years from the imperial court.

Concerning the Organization of a Turkish Assault

The Turkish emperor storms and captures cities and also fortresses at great expense in order not to remain there long with the army. First having battered the city or fortress walls until it seems sufficient to him, and seeing that it is the moment to launch a general assault, he then orders it to be cried throughout the army first that horses and camels and all kinds of stock be brought from pasture to the army ; and when that is accomplished, he then orders it to be cried throughout the army second specifying the day of the assault. And they prefer to set the day on Friday. And they crying thus, they name the rewards in this fashion : to the one who carries a banner upon the wall they promise a voivodeship [governorship] ; . . . to others, money, naming the sum ; and in addition, distributing various garments. And whatever is mentioned then, without fail all of this if fulfilled and carried out whether the city is taken or not taken.

Then they cry in the evening throughout the army that lighted tallow candles be raised profusely throughout the army so that it looks as if the stars are shining profusely above the clouds. And that night and early in the morning the next day they prepare themselves for the assault, right up to evening.

And at night then they go toward the city from all sides silently, slowly approaching the fosse [ditch], carrying before them barricades woven of branches and also strongly-built ladders so that they can climb up and down both sides of the ladder. The Janissaries then in this fashion go to the place where the wall is breached, and having approached the breached place, they wait until day begins to appear. Then first the gunners fire from all the cannon and when they have fired off the cannon, the Janissaries quickly scale the wall, for at this moment the Christians are retreating before the cannon, and when they see that the Janissaries are on the walls, having turned about suddenly, they begin to fight bravely on both sides. And here the Janissaries, urging one another on, climb up. And in addition the shot from bows comes very thick, for they continually bring and replenish their shot, and besides [there is] a great tumult from drums and human outcry. Thus the battle lasts an hour or at most two, and if the Christians overcome the heathens in that time, then little by little the heathens weaken and slack off and the Christians grow stronger. And so this assault lasts until noon and can last no longer, for the ammunition is used up, some men are killed, some are wounded, and some are exhausted.

The emperor, seeing that he cannot take it, orders them to retreat from the city and to pull the cannon and other equipment away from the wall and to load them on wagons. And having picked up all the wounded he orders them sent ahead and himself stays at this place until nightfall, and only in the night departs from there with the whole army so that they will not cry out at them from the fortress. Therefore he always posts a rear guard in case some troops should come out of the fortress in order to seek vengeance upon them somehow. Therefore the men who are in the fortresses must take care not to ride or run out of the fortress haphazardly.

If, then, a certain fortress or city once defends itself against him, he will not make another attempt for a long time.

Now those heathens who are crippled in the arm or leg, each of them is provided by the emperor with a livelihood until he dies. And thus a Turkish general assault is accomplished.

79

Kritovoulos, *History of Mehmed the Conqueror*

Mehmed II (reigned 1451–1481) assumed the throne of the Ottoman Empire on the death of his father, Murad II. The new sultan began at once to plan his greatest achievement — the seizure of Constantinople from the last Byzantine Emperor, Constantine XI. This successful capture would earn Mehmed II the title of "The Conqueror."

In 1452, Mehmed gathered thousands of cavalry, Janissaries (Christian tribute slaves), irregular troops, naval personnel, and military engineers for the undertaking. For 54 days during the months of April and May 1453, the sultan's forces pounded on the 1100-year-old impenetrable land walls. Finally, on May 29 of that same year, his men, spying an inadvertently unlocked sally port, poured into the capital with a frenzy. That fateful day extinguished Greek independence for almost four centuries.

After taking the city, Sultan Mehmed's troops were not allowed to rest. For almost the next 30 years, they raided and captured land and inhabitants in the Balkans, Wallachia-Moldavia (Romania), and even in the hinterland of Venice.

The *History of Mehmed the Conqueror* is by a contemporary Greek historian named Kritovoulos. Little is known of this writer except that he was not at the fall of Constantinople but soon arrived at that city to record Mehmed's life. Kritovoulos eventually entered the sultan's service and became a governor on the island of Imbros.

QUESTIONS TO CONSIDER

1. Why was Mehmed II successful in his naval attack on the city?
2. Can you find an example that illustrates the superstitious nature of the Byzantines?
3. How would you compare the actions of the Ottoman warriors with those of the sultan when the city had been taken?
4. How did the fall of the Byzantine Empire affect the growth of the Russian monarchy (see Reading 82)?

He also resolved to carry into execution immediately the plan which he had long since studied out and elaborated in his mind and toward which he had bent every purpose from the start, and to wait no longer nor delay. This plan was to make war against the Romans [Byzantines or Greeks] and their Emperor Constantine and to

From Kritovoulos, *History of Mehmed the Conqueror,* trans. Charles T. Riggs (Princeton : Princeton University Press, 1954), pp. 22–23, 55–59, 66–67, 70–72, 76–77, 82–83. Copyright 1954, © renewed 1982 by Princeton University Press. Reprinted with permission of Princeton University Press.

besiege the city. For he thought, as was true, that if he could succeed in capturing it and becoming master of it, there was nothing to hinder him from sallying forth from it in a short time, as from a stronghold for all the environs, and overrunning all and subduing them to himself. For this reason he could no longer be restrained at all. He did not think he ought to stay quiet in his own parts any longer and maintain peace, but believed he should speedily make war and capture the city. . . .

Sultan Mehmed considered it necessary in preparation for his next move to get possession of the harbor and open the Horn for his own ships to sail in. So, since every effort and device of his had failed to force the entrance, he made a wise decision, and one worthy of his intellect and power. It succeeded in accomplishing his purpose and in putting an end to all uncertainties.

He ordered the commanders of the vessels to construct as quickly as possible glideways leading from the outer sea to the inner sea, that is, from the harbor to the Horn, near the place called Diplokion, and to cover them with beams. This road, measured from sea to sea, is just about eight stadia. It is very steep for more than half the way, until you reach the summit of the hill, and from there again it descends to the inner sea of the Horn. And as the glideways were completed sooner than expected, because of the large number of workers, he brought up the ships and placed large cradles under them, with stays against each of their sides to hold them up. And having undergirded them well with ropes, he fastened long cables to the corners and gave them to the soldiers to drag, some of them by hand, and others by certain machines and capstans. . . .

Thus, then, there was assembled in the bay called Cold Waters, a little beyond Galata, a respectable fleet of some sixty-seven vessels. They were moored there.

The Romans, when they saw such an unheard-of thing actually happen, and warships lying at anchor in the Horn — which they never would have suspected — were astounded at the impossibility of the spectacle, and were overcome by the greatest consternation and perplexity. They did not know what to do now, but were in despair. In fact they had left unguarded the walls along the Horn for a distance of about thirty stadia, and even so they did not have enough men for the rest of the walls, either for defense or for attack, whether citizens or men from elsewhere. Instead, two or even three battlements had but a single defender.

And now, when this sea-wall also became open to attack and had to be guarded, they were compelled to strip the other battlements and bring men there. This constituted a manifest danger, since the defenders were taken away from the rest of the wall while those remaining were not enough to guard it, being so few. . . .

During those same days there occurred the following divine signs and portents of the terrors that were very soon to come to the city. Three or four days before the battle, when all the people in the City were holding a religious procession, men and women together, and marching around with the Ikon of the Mother of God, this latter slipped suddenly from the hands of its bearers without any cause or power being apparent, and fell flat on the ground. And when everybody shouted immediately, and rushed to raise up the ikon, it sank down as if weighted with lead, and as if fastened to the ground, and became well-nigh impossible to raise. And so it continued for a considerable time, until, by a great effort and much shouting and prayers by all, the priests and its bearers barely managed to raise it up and place it on the shoulders of the men.

This strange occurrence filled everyone with much terror and very great agony and fear, for they thought this fall was no good omen — as was quite true. Later, when they had gone on but a short distance, immediately after that, at high noon, there was much thunder and lightning with clouds, and a violent rain with severe hail followed, so that they could neither stand against it nor make any progress. The priests and the bearers of the ikon and the crowds that followed were depressed and hindered by the force of the waters that flowed down and by the might of the hail. Many of the children following were in danger of being carried away and drowned by the violent and powerful rush of water, had not some men quickly seized them and with some difficulty dragged them out of the flood. Such was the unheard-of and unprecedented violence of that storm and hail which certainly foreshadowed the imminent loss of all, and that, like a torrent of fiercest waters, it would carry away and annihilate everything. . . .

The hour was already advanced, the day [May 28, 1453] was declining and near evening, and the sun was at the Ottomans' backs but shining in the faces of their enemies. This was just as the Sultan had wished ; accordingly he gave the order first for the trumpets to sound the battle-signal, and the other instruments, the pipes and flutes and cymbals too, as loud as they could. All the trumpets of the other divisions, with the other instruments in turn, sounded all together, a great and fearsome sound. Everything shook and quivered at the noise. After that, the standards were displayed.

To begin, the archers and slingers and those in charge of the cannon and the muskets, in accord with the commands given them, advanced against the wall slowly and gradually. When they got within bowshot, they halted to fight. And first they exchanged fire with the heavier weapons, with arrows from the archers, stones from the slingers, and iron and leaden balls from the cannon and muskets. Then, as they closed with battleaxes and javelins and spears, hurling them at each other and being hurled at pitilessly in rage and fierce anger. On both sides there was loud shouting and blasphemy and cursing. Many on each side were wounded, and not a few died. This kept up till sunset, a space of about two or three hours.

Then, with fine insight, the Sultan summoned the shield-bearers, heavy infantry and other troops and said : "Go to it, friends and children mine! It is time now to show yourselves good fighters!" They immediately crossed the moat, with shouts and fearful yells, and attacked the outer wall. All of it, however, had been demolished by the cannon. There were only stockades of great beams instead of a wall, and bundles of vine-branches, and jars full of earth. At that point a fierce battle ensued close in and with the weapons of hand-to-hand fighting. The heavy infantry and shield-bearers fought to overcome the defenders and get over the stockade, while the Romans and Italians tried to fight these off and to guard the stockade. At times the infantry did get over the wall and the stockade, pressing forward bravely and unhesitatingly. And at times they were stoutly forced back and driven off. . . .

Sultan Mehmed, who happened to be fighting quite near by, saw that the palisade and the other part of the wall that had been destroyed were now empty of men and deserted by the defenders. He noted that men were slipping away secretly and that those who remained were fighting feebly because they were so few. Realizing from this that the defenders had fled and that the wall was deserted, he shouted out : "Friends, we have the City! We have it! They are already fleeing from us! They can't stand it any longer! The wall is bare of defenders! It needs just a little more effort and the City is taken! Don't weaken, but on with the work with all your might, and be men and I am with you!"

Capture of the City

So saying, he led them himself. And they, with a shout on the run and with a fearsome yell, went on ahead of the Sultan, pressing on up to the palisade. After a long and bitter struggle they hurled back the Romans from there and climbed by force up the palisade. They dashed some of their foe down into the ditch between the great wall and the palisade, which was deep and hard to get out of, and they killed them there. The rest they drove back to the gate.

Death of Emperor Constantine

He had opened this gate in the great wall, so as to go easily over to the palisade. Now there was a great struggle there and great slaughter among those stationed there, for they were attacked by the heavy infantry and not a few others in irregular formation, who had been attracted from many points by the shouting. There the Emperor Constantine, with all who were with him, fell in gallant combat. . . .

Then a great slaughter occurred of those who happened to be there: some of them were on the streets, for they had already left the houses and were running toward the tumult when they fell unexpectedly on the swords of the soldiers; others were in their own homes and fell victims to the violence of the Janissaries and other soldiers, without any rhyme or reason; others were resisting, relying on their own courage; still others were fleeing to the churches and making supplication — men, women, and children, everyone, for there was no quarter given.

The soldiers fell on them with anger and great wrath. For one thing, they were actuated by the hardships of the siege. For another, some foolish people had hurled taunts and curses at them from the battlements all through the siege. Now, in general they killed so as to frighten all the City, and to terrorize and enslave all by the slaughter. . . .

Other women, sleeping in their beds, had to endure nightmares. Men with swords, their hands bloodstained with murder, breathing out rage, speaking out murder indiscriminate, flushed with all the worst things — this crowd, made up of men from every race and nation, brought together by chance, like wild and ferocious beasts, leaped into the houses, driving them out mercilessly, dragging, rending, forcing, hauling them disgracefully into the public highways, insulting them and doing every evil thing.

They say that many of the maidens, even at the mere unaccustomed sight and sound of these men, were terror-stricken and came near losing their very lives. And there were also honorable old men who were dragged by their white hair, and some of them beaten unmercifully. And well-born and beautiful young boys were carried off. . . .

After this the Sultan entered the City and looked about to see its great size, its situation, its grandeur and beauty, its teeming population, its loveliness, and the costliness of its churches and public buildings and of the private houses and community houses and of those of the officials. He also saw the setting of the harbor and of the arsenals, and how skilfully and ingeniously they had everything arranged in the City — in a word, all the construction and adornment of it. When he saw what a large number had been killed, and the ruin of the buildings, and the wholesale ruin and destruction of the City, he was filled with compassion and repented not a little at the destruction and plundering. Tears fell from his eyes as he groaned deeply and passionately : "What a city we have given over to plunder and destruction!" . . .

The Sultan Mehmed, when he had carefully viewed the City and all its contents, went back to the camp and divided the spoils. First he took the customary toll of the spoils for himself. Then also, as prizes from all the rest, he chose out beautiful virgins and those of the best families, and the handsomest boys, some of whom he even bought from the soldiers. He also chose some of the distinguished men who, he was informed, were above the rest in family and intelligence and valor. . . .

Then, with the notable men, and his courtiers, he went through the City. First he planned how to repopulate it, not merely as it formerly was but more completely, if possible, so that it should be a worthy capital for him, situated, as it was, most favorably by land and by sea. Then he donated to all the grandees, and to those of his household, the magnificent homes of the rich, with gardens and fields and vineyards inside of the City. And to some of them he even gave beautiful churches as their private residences.

For himself, he chose the most beautiful location in the center of the City for the erection of a royal palace. After this, he settled all the captives whom he had taken as his portion, together with their wives and children, along the shores of the city harbor, since they were sea-faring men whom they previously had called Stenites. He gave them houses and freed them from taxes for a specified time.

He also made a proclamation to all those who had paid their own ransom, or who promised to pay it to their masters within a limited time, that they might live in the City, and he granted them, also, freedom from taxes, and gave them houses, either their own or those of others.

He wanted those of the nobility whom he approved of to live there with their wives and children. Accordingly he gave them houses and lands and provisions for living, and tried in every way to help them. This was his intention and purpose, as has been stated.

80

Barnette Miller, *The Palace School of Muhammad the Conqueror*

Once Mehmed II had captured Constantinople, which was renamed Istanbul, he moved the center of his government from Adrianople to two new palaces. The first palace, Eski Sarai or Old Palace, is thought to have been built in 1454 ; but, because it was deemed too small, the sultan constructed a larger one, called Yeni Sarai or New Palace, about 1459. It is this second palace, better known to the West as the Grand Seraglio or the Sublime Porte, that became the center of government, education, and private life of the sultans until the downfall of the Ottoman Empire in the twentieth century.

The Grand Seraglio was divided into four courtyards. The first two could be visited by any Turkish subject who wished to approach the sultan or his ministers directly. Then came a gate, called the Gate of Felicity, that separated the public and private life of the sultan. Only members of his family and trusted slave officials could pass beyond this gate into the third and fourth courts.

It was to the third court that Christian tribute boys were brought. Here they were educated as slaves of the sultan. Once inside the Palace School, a boy did not leave until he was ready to graduate to high office, or unless he failed the rigorous mental and physical requirements.

The following selections deal with the procurement and education of the sultan's slaves, who eventually controlled most of the major decisions — as well as the sultans themselves. Also note who actually controlled the Palace School system.

QUESTIONS TO CONSIDER

1. Why do you suppose that the Ottoman sultans chose to govern their empire through a slave class? Compare this selection with Reading 78 on the life of a Janissary.
2. What was the basis for advancement in the ruling class?
3. How and why did the Ottomans use eunuchs in government? Do you know of any other civilizations that used eunuchs?
4. From your general knowledge, how did the institution of slavery in the Ottoman society differ from that of other civilizations?

Personnel and Organization

To understand the system of education evolved in the Palace School it must be kept constantly in mind that for more than three centuries the despotism of the Osmanli dynasty was based almost exclusively upon a deliberate policy of government by a slave class. This method of government would seem to have been developed by the Turkish rulers as a defensive mechanism designed to prevent, by the exclusion of native-born subjects from the government, the rise of an aristocracy of blood or of a hereditary official class.

It must be remembered also, in considering this system of government by a slave class, that slavery in Moslem lands not only was without the stigma that it bore throughout the West but often proved the most direct road to fortune and

From Barnette Miller, *The Palace School of Muhammad the Conqueror* (Cambridge, MA : Harvard University Press, 1941), pp. 70–72, 74–76, 81–82, 85–88, 94. Copyright 1941, © 1969 by the President and Fellows of Harvard College. Reprinted by permission.

honor. The teaching of the Prophet that slaves should be treated with kindness and with generosity, that they should be fed and clothed in the same manner as the members of the master's own family, had prevented the Moslem East from attributing to manual labor the degradation which attached to it in the West. This injunction, and the added provision that if for any reason it became impossible to deal with them justly they should be sold or otherwise disposed of in a beneficent manner, had in general greatly alleviated the condition of slaves in Islam. In Moslem lands also it was household slavery that was in general practiced, and not that of the field ; and the slave status was regarded not as a permanent one but as accidental and temporary. At the marriage or at the death of an owner or upon occasions of great rejoicing, it was the custom to manumit slaves on a large scale, and even to pension them, in accordance with which custom Muhammad II is said to have freed about forty thousand of his slaves at the conclusion of his campaign against Uzun Hasan of Persia. . . .

. . . Slaves for the palace service were supplied through capture, purchase, gift, and the Law of Tribute Children or the Law of Draft (*Devshirmeh*). Confronted with the problem of assimilating the hostile races of the Balkans and desirous, after a half century of continuous warfare, of releasing the population of Anatolia from conscription, Murad I . . . established this famous law. Henceforth recruits for the army were drafted from the conquered European provinces, later including Albania, Bosnia, Bulgaria, Servia, Greece (with the exceptions only of the cities of Constantinople and Athens, Rhodes, and the Mainotes), from the Armenians who resided in these provinces, and from the Christian subjects of the Caucasus. The law denied to the people of these countries the usual right accorded Christians of payment of the capitation tax in lieu of military service, and instead exacted as tribute a stipulated number of male children every three or four years. By the same law these youths were required to serve a novitiate of seven years in military schools provided for the purpose, or else in the royal palaces and upon royal domain, in the households of provincial governors and of high officials in the capital, or upon the cavalry fiefs of Anatolia. . . . It is, however, to be especially noted that although the number of tribute youths constituted something less than one-half of the sum total of slaves recruited by every means for all the various departments of the royal service, the majority of the pages for the palace service were almost invariably selected from the tribute children. So long as the Law of Tribute Children was in force, therefore, it was the Christian youths of the Balkans who gave the tone and color to the Palace School and, in the end, to the Turkish government itself. . . .

Upon their arrival in Constantinople the tribute children, who had been collected by the palace gatekeepers, were brought before a board of expert examiners presided over by the chief white eunuch in his capacity as director-in-chief of the system of palace education, a procedure that was applied also to purchased slaves and prisoners of war. By a kind of test which in its shrewdness seems curiously to anticipate the modern intelligence test, and by an examination of physical points similar to those applied at a horse, dog, or cattle show, the youths were separated into two classes. The *sine qua non* of the sultan's service being physical beauty and bodily perfection, the most physically perfect, the most intelligent, and the most promising in every respect were set aside for the palace service ; . . . The remainder, who were distinguished chiefly by reason of their physical strength and dexterity, were assigned to the Janizary corps. Those who had been set aside for the palace service were again separated into two classes. The comeliest and cleverest, . . . were designated as student pages. The remainder, who were classified as novices or apprentices . . . were put through a stiff course in manual training as gardeners or gatekeepers or halberdiers [guards] of the Grand Seraglio or other of the royal palaces, or less frequently, as artisans employed upon public works, preparatory to becoming members of the auxiliary corps, or irregulars, of the army. From the group set apart for student pages, the cream was for a third time skimmed for the Palace School of the Grand Seraglio. The remaining pages were then distributed among the three auxiliary schools, a certain portion being reserved for the high officials of the capital and provinces who maintained schools for pages along lines similar to those of the palace schools. When the process of examination and distribution had been duly completed, the pages were registered. The age, place of birth, name of parents, and new Turkish name of each page were entered in the school register, . . . which was thereafter sent to the chancellery of the treasury for safekeeping.

Following the policy inaugurated by Muhammad II, the sultans kept personal oversight of the progress and well-being of the pages of the Grand Seraglio by going constantly among them while they were studying and even . . . by occasional rounds of the halls in disguise at night. It was one of their favorite pastimes to watch the school games and practice of physical exercises. The three auxiliary schools they also inspected in person from time to time. They were accustomed to pass part of the night which precedes the festival of *Buyuk Bayram,* or Great Bayram, in the Hall of the Royal Bedchamber. On the eve of *Sheker Bayram,* or Bayram of Sweets, it was their custom to repair to the Great Hall, which was the general assembly hall of the school, and there to listen to the discourse of the pages upon philosophy and morals, and to review their sports — to hold what was in reality a kind of annual general examination. Above all else they made a point of recognizing merit by a system of rewards and of bestowing these rewards in person, in particular for excellence in the Arabic language and in penmanship. These rewards were usually in the form of money, or robes of cloth of gold and silver and of brocade, sometimes even of a banquet tendered an individual student. . . .

The general administration and surveillance of the palace schools was in charge of the white eunuchs who in their relation to the school were designated as literally trainers or drill masters ; . . . the teaching staff, as had already been said, were as a rule nonresident. As the practice of castration was forbidden by Moslem law, all eunuchs were imported, white eunuchs generally from the Caucasus region and, in the seventeenth century, also from certain states of India. The average cost in the slave market of a white eunuch, who as a class were only partially castrated, was from one hundred to one hundred and fifty crowns, or about one-fourth the cost of a completely castrated black eunuch, for whom the price demanded usually ranged from four hundred to six hundred crowns. Although the duties of the white eunuchs of the Grand Seraglio, who were also chamberlains of the Outer Palace and guardians of the Imperial Gate and later of the Gate of Felicity, were much more extensive than those of the black eunuchs, the relative value of the two at the time of purchase continued to hold in their wages.

Selected for admission to the palace at about the same age as the pages, the white eunuchs received precisely the same education as the pages, those in the

Grand Seraglio usually completing the entire course, including service in the Hall of the Royal Bedchamber.

After the introduction of black eunuchs as guards of the royal harem and the consequent restriction of the white eunuchs to the service of the royal *selamlik,* the number of the latter employed in the Grand Seraglio was usually in the ratio of one to about ten pages.

The organization of the white eunuchs constituted a rigid and elaborate hierarchy. The chief white eunuch, who was head gatekeeper of the Grand Seraglio, head of the Inner Service, grand master of ceremony, and confidential agent of the sultan, was also the director-in-chief of the system of palace schools. For a century and a half his was the most important post at the Turkish court and in consequence one of great political influence.

The Curriculum

The type of governing official which the Turkish sultans desired to produce through the medium of their palace system of education was the warrior-statesman and loyal Moslem. . . . To this end a student of the Palace School, from the day of his admission until he quitted the Grand Seraglio, was meticulously drilled in the ceremonies of the Moslem religion and Turkish etiquette . . . The pages received instruction also, in almost equal proportions, in the liberal arts, in the art of war and physical exercise, and in vocational training — a combination which seems to have been paralleled only by the samurai, the warrior-scholars of Japan. The liberal arts, in the Turkish, or Islamic, interpretation of the term, embraced the Turkish, Arabic, and Persian languages ; Turkish and Persian literatures ; Arabic grammar and syntax ; a study of the Koran and leading commentaries upon it ; Moslem theology, jurisprudence and law ; and Turkish history, music, and mathematics.

The Rise of Russia

The Byzantine Greeks converted the pagan Russians to Orthodox Christianity in the tenth century. With their conversion, the Russians obtained an alphabet, so they might copy religious texts ; they also adopted many aspects of Byzantine culture, which merged with their pagan Slavic and Viking culture.

In the thirteenth century, the close ties between Constantinople and Russia — still only a loose confederation of city-states — were broken by the Mongol conquest, which lasted over 200 years. It was not until the fifteenth century that the Moscovite Grand Princes succeeded in casting off the Mongol yoke and unifying Russia into a nation-state. Russian ties with Orthodox Christendom were then renewed ; but, by coincidence, Constantinople and the eastern Roman Empire fell in 1453 to the Ottoman Turks.

The Russian Orthodox Church was now the world's largest Orthodox church. In consequence, an elaborate ideology developed, portraying the Russian Grand Princes as the legitimate descendants of both the Roman Emperor Augustus Caesar and the Byzantine Emperor Constantine. These Princes were seen as leaders of the only true faith — Eastern Orthodoxy — and Moscow was the Third Rome. As the ruler of Orthodoxy and of Russia, the tsar (meaning caesar) had the religious, moral, and historical obligation to protect Russia from heresy, which in this case was Roman Catholicism. The tsar was portrayed as a saintly prince and pious Christ-like figure, suffering for his people. Although elements of this ideology were modified over the centuries, it nevertheless remained the basis for the close link between church and state during the later Russian imperial period. Furthermore, Western historians have suggested that the Soviet Communists, while attacking religion, have nonetheless retained certain aspects of the tsarist ideology in a modern guise — with the Communist Party and Marxism playing the secular role formerly played by church and religion.

81

The Russian Primary Chronicle

The Russian Primary Chronicle is the first written document for Russian history. It is a collection of different texts, written by monks in the twelfth century, about the period 852–1120. Modeled on Greek sources, the Chronicle offers a religious interpretation of past events, incorporating legendary and mythical stories about the early Russian princes and nobles (*boyars*).

QUESTIONS TO CONSIDER

1. Why did the Russians choose Greek Orthodoxy over other religions?
2. How did this choice affect Russia's relations with Western Europe?

Vladimir summoned together his boyars and the city-elders, and said to them, "Behold, the Bulgars came before me urging me to accept their religion. Then came the Germans and praised their own faith; and after them came the Jews. Finally the Greeks appeared, criticizing all other faiths but commending their own, and they spoke at length, telling the history of the whole world from its beginning. Their words were artful, and it was wondrous to listen and pleasant to hear them.

From *The Russian Primary Chronicle: Laurentian Text,* trans. and ed. Samuel Hazzard Cross and Olgerd P. Sherbowitz-Wetzor (Cambridge, MA.: The Medieval Academy of America, 1953), pp. 110–113. Reprinted by permission of The Medieval Academy of America. Footnotes omitted.

They preach the existence of another world. 'Whoever adopts our religion and then dies shall arise and live forever. But whosoever embraces another faith, shall be consumed with fire in the next world.' What is your opinion on this subject, and what do you answer?" The boyars and the elders replied, "You know, oh Prince, that no man condemns his own possessions, but praises them instead. If you desire to make certain, you have servants at your disposal. Send them to inquire about the ritual of each and how he worships God."

Their counsel pleased the prince and all the people, so that they chose good and wise men to the number of ten, and directed them to go first among the Bulgars and inspect their faith. The emissaries went their way, and when they arrived at their destination they beheld the disgraceful actions of the Bulgars and their worship in the mosque; then they returned to their country. Vladimir then instructed them to go likewise among the Germans, and examine their faith, and finally to visit the Greeks. They thus went into Germany, and after viewing the German ceremonial, they proceeded to Tsar'grad, where they appeared before the Emperor. He inquired on what mission they had come, and they reported to him all that had occurred. When the Emperor heard their words, he rejoiced, and did them great honor on that very day.

On the morrow, the Emperor sent a message to the Patriarch to inform him that a Russian delegation had arrived to examine the Greek faith, and directed him to prepare the church and the clergy, and to array himself in his sacerdotal robes, so that the Russes might behold the glory of the God of the Greeks. When the Patriarch received these commands, he bade the clergy assemble, and they performed the customary rites. They burned incense, and the choirs sang hymns. The Emperor accompanied the Russes to the church, and placed them in a wide space, calling their attention to the beauty of the edifice, the chanting, and the pontifical services and the ministry of the deacons, while he explained to them the worship of his God. The Russes were astonished, and in their wonder praised the Greek ceremonial. Then the Emperors Basil and Constantine invited the envoys to their presence, and said, "Go hence to your native country," and dismissed them with valuable presents and great honor.

Thus they returned to their own country, and the Prince called together his boyars and the elders. Vladimir then announced the return of the envoys who had been sent out, and suggested that their report be heard. He thus commanded them to speak out before his retinue. The envoys reported, "When we journeyed among the Bulgars, we beheld how they worship in their temple, called a mosque, while they stand ungirt. The Bulgar bows, sits down, looks hither and thither like one possessed, and there is no happiness among them, but instead only sorrow and a dreadful stench. Their religion is not good. Then we went among the Germans, and saw them performing many ceremonies in their temples; but we beheld no glory there. Then we went to Greece, and the Greeks led us to the edifices where they worship their God, and we knew not whether we were in heaven or on earth. For on earth there is no such splendor or such beauty, and we are at a loss how to describe it. We only know that God dwells there among men, and their service is fairer than the ceremonies of other nations. For we cannot forget that beauty. Every man, after tasting something sweet, is afterward unwilling to accept that which is bitter, and therefore we cannot dwell longer here." Then the boyars spoke and said, "If the Greek faith were evil, it would not have been adopted by your grandmother Olga who was wiser than all other men." Vladimir then inquired where they should all accept baptism, and they replied that the decision rested with him.

After a year had passed, in 6496 (988), Vladimir proceeded with an armed force against Kherson, a Greek city, and the people of Kherson barricaded themselves therein. Vladimir halted at the farther side of the city beside the harbor, a bowshot from the town, and the inhabitants resisted energetically while Vladimir besieged the town. Eventually, however, they became exhausted, and Vladimir warned them that if they did not surrender, he would remain on the spot for three years. When they failed to heed this threat, Vladimir marshalled his troops and ordered the construction of an earthwork in the direction of the city. While this work was under construction, the inhabitants dug a tunnel under the city-wall, stole the heaped-up earth, and carried it into the city, where they piled it up in the center of the town. But the soldiers kept on building, and Vladimir persisted. Then a man of Kherson, Anastasius by name, shot into the Russ camp an arrow on which he had written, "There are springs behind you to the east, from which water flows in pipes. Dig down and cut them off." When Vladimir received this information, he raised his eyes to heaven and vowed that if this hope was realized, he would be baptized. He gave orders straightway to dig down above the pipes, and the water-supply was thus cut off. The inhabitants were accordingly overcome by thirst, and surrendered.

Vladimir and his retinue entered the city, and he sent messages to the Emperors Basil and Constantine, saying, "Behold, I have captured your glorious city. I have also heard that you have an unwedded sister. Unless you give her to me to wife, I shall deal with your own city as I have with Kherson. When the Emperors heard this message they were troubled, and replied, "It is not meet for Christians to give in marriage to pagans. If you are baptized, you shall have her to wife, inherit the kingdom of God, and be our companion in the faith. Unless you do so, however, we cannot give you our sister in marriage." When Vladimir learned their response, he directed the envoys of the Emperors to report to the latter that he was willing to accept baptism, having already given some study to their religion, and that the Greek faith and ritual, as described by the emissaries sent to examine it, had pleased him well. When the Emperors heard this report, they rejoiced, and persuaded their sister Anna to consent to the match. They then requested Vladimir to submit to baptism before they should send their sister to him, but Vladimir desired that the Princess should herself bring priests to baptize him. The Emperors complied with his request, and sent forth their sister, accompanied by some dignitaries and priests. Anna, however, departed with reluctance. "It is as if I were setting out into captivity," she lamented; "better were it for me to die at home." But her brothers protested, "Through your agency God turns the land of Rus' to repentance, and you will relieve Greece from the danger of grievous war. Do you not see how much harm the Russes have already brought upon the Greeks? If you do not set out, they may bring on us the same misfortunes." It was thus that they overcame her hesitation only with great difficulty. The Princess embarked upon a ship, and after tearfully embracing her kinfolk, she set forth across the sea and arrived at Kherson. The natives came forth to greet her, and conducted her into the city, where they settled her in the palace.

By divine agency, Vladimir was suffering at that moment from a disease of the eyes, and could see nothing, being in great distress. The Princess declared to him that if he desired to be relieved of this disease, he should be baptized with all speed, otherwise it could not be cured. When Vladimir heard her message, he said, "If this proves true, then of a surety is the God of the Christians great," and gave order that he should be baptized. The Bishop of Kherson, together with the Princess's priests, after announcing the tidings, baptized Vladimir, and as the Bishop laid his hand upon him, he straightway received his sight. Upon experiencing this miraculous cure, Vladimir glorified God, saying, "I have now perceived the one true God." When his followers beheld this miracle, many of them were also baptized.

Vladimir was baptized in the Church of St. Basil, which stands at Kherson upon a square in the center of the city, where the Khersonians trade. The palace of Vladimir stands beside this church to this day, and the palace of the Princess is behind the altar. After his baptism, Vladimir took the Princess in marriage.

82

A Letter of Monk Philotheos to Grand Prince Vasily III

In this letter of Monk Philotheos to Grand Prince Vasily III (1505–1533), the theory of Moscow as the Third Rome was first elaborated. The Russian Grand Prince was now portrayed as the tsar (caesar), descendant of both Roman emperors and ruler of Orthodoxy. He personified the state and legitimized both state and church.

QUESTIONS TO CONSIDER

1. What were the political and religious implications of the theory of Moscow as the Third Rome?
2. What does this document suggest about the role of the church in Russian politics?

[I write] to you, the Most bright and most highly-throning Sovereign, Grand Prince, orthodox Christian tsar and lord of all, rein-holder of the Holy oecumenical and Apostolic Church of God of the Most Holy Virgin . . . which is shining gloriously instead of the Roman or Constantinopolitan [one]. For the Old

From a letter of Monk Philotheos to Grand Prince Vasily III, early sixteenth century, translated in Michael Cherniavsky, *Tsar and People : Studies in Russian Myths* (New York : Random House, 1969), p. 38. Reprinted by permission of Mrs. Lucy Cherniavsky.

Rome fell because of its church's lack of faith, the Apollinarian heresy; and of the second Rome, the city of Constantine, the pagans broke down the doors of the churches with their axes. . . . And now there is the Holy synodal Apostolic church of the reigning third Rome, of your tsardom, which shines like the sun in its orthodox Christian faith throughout the whole universe. And that is your realm, pious tsar, as all the empires [tsardoms] of the orthodox Christian faith have gathered into your single empire . . . you are the only tsar for Christians in the whole world. . . .

Do not break, O tsar, the commandments laid by your ancestors, the Great Constantine and the blessed Vladimir, and the God chosen Iaroslav, and the other blessed saints, of which root you are. . . .

Listen and attend, pious tsar, that all Christian empires are gathered in your single one, that two Romes have fallen, and the third one stands, and a fourth one there shall not be; your empire will not fall to others, according to the great Evangelist.

83

Correspondence between Prince Andrey Kurbsky and Tsar Ivan IV

In the following excerpts from the correspondence between Prince Andrey Kurbsky (1528–1583) and Ivan IV ("Ivan the Terrible," 1533–1584), Kurbsky justifies his defection from Russia to Lithuania, while Ivan IV defends his persecution of the *boyars* (nobles) by describing their mistreatment of him.

QUESTIONS TO CONSIDER

1. How does Ivan IV portray himself in his response to Prince Kurbsky?
2. How would you compare Ivan IV's arguments with those of Machiavelli (see Reading 84)?

First Epistle of Prince Andrey Kurbsky, Written to the Tsar and Grand Prince of Moscow in Consequence of His Fierce Persecution

To the tsar, exalted above all by God, who appeared [formerly] most illustrious, particularly in the Orthodox Faith, but who has now, in consequence of our sins, been found to be the contrary of this. If you have understanding, may you under-

From *The Correspondence Between Prince A. M. Kurbsky and Tsar Ivan IV of Russia 1564–1579*, trans. and ed. J.L.I. Fennell (Cambridge : Cambridge University Press, 1955), pp. 3, 5, 7, 13, 15, 69, 71, 73, 81, 83, 93, 95. Copyrighted by Cambridge University Press. Reprinted by permission of Cambridge University Press.

stand this with your leprous conscience — such a conscience as cannot be found even amongst the godless peoples. And I have not let my tongue say more than this on all these matters in turn ; but because of the bitterest persecution from your power, with much sorrow in my heart will I hasten to inform you of a little.

Wherefore, O tsar, have you destroyed the strong in Israel and subjected to various forms of death the *voevodas,* given to you by God ? And wherefore have you spilt their victorious, holy blood in the churches of God during sacerdotal ceremonies, and stained the thresholds of the churches with their blood of martyrs ? And why have you conceived against your well-wishers and against those who lay down their lives for you unheard-of torments and persecutions and death, falsely accusing the Orthodox of treachery and magic and other abuses, and endeavouring with zeal to turn light into darkness and to call sweet bitter ? What guilt did they commit before you, O tsar, and in what way did they, the champions of Christianity, anger you ? Have they not destroyed proud kingdoms and by their heroic bravery made subject to you in all things those in whose servitude our forefathers formerly were ? Was it not through the keenness of their understanding that the strong German towns were given to you by God ? Thus have you remunerated us, [your] poor [servants], destroying us by whole families ? Think you yourself immortal, O tsar ? Or have you been enticed into unheard-of heresy, as one no longer wishing to stand before the impartial judge, Jesus, begotten of God, who will judge according to justice the universe and especially the vainglorious tormentors, and who unhesitatingly will question them "right to the hairs [roots ?] of their sins," as the saying goes ? He is my Christ who sitteth on the throne of the Cherubims at the right hand of the power of the Almighty in the highest — the judge between you and me.

What evil and persecution have I not suffered from you! What ills and misfortunes have you not brought upon me! And what iniquitous tissues of lies have you not woven against me! But I cannot now recount the various misfortunes at your hands which have beset me owing to their multitude and since I am still filled with the grief of my soul. But, to conclude, I can summarize them all [thus]: of everything have I been deprived ; I have been driven from the land of God without guilt [*lit.* in vain], hounded by you. I did not ask [for aught] with humble words, nor did I beseech you with tearful plaint ; nor yet did I win from you any mercy through the intercession of the hierarchy. You have recompensed me with evil for good and for my love with implacable hatred. My blood, spilt like water for you, cries out against you to my Lord. God sees into [men's] hearts — in my mind have I ardently reflected and my conscience have I placed as a witness [against myself], and I have sought and pried within my thoughts, and, examining myself [*lit.* turning myself around], I know not now — nor have I ever found — my guilt in aught before you. In front of your army have I marched — and marched again ; and no dishonour have I brought upon you ; but only brilliant victories, with the help of the angel of the Lord, have I won for your glory, and never have I turned the back of your regiments to the foe. But far more, I have achieved most glorious conquests to increase your renown. And this, not in one year, nor yet in two — but throughout many years have I toiled with much sweat and patience ; and always have I been separated from my fatherland, and little have I seen my parents, and my wife have I not known ; but always in far-distant towns have I stood in arms against your foes and I have suffered many wants and natural illnesses, of which my Lord Jesus Christ is witness. Still more, I was visited with wounds inflicted by barbarian hands in various battles and all my body is already afflicted with sores. But to you, O tsar, was all this as nought ; rather do you show us your intolerable wrath and bitterest hatred, and, furthermore, burning stoves. . . .[1]

Epistle of the Tsar and Sovereign to All His Russian Kingdom against Those That Violate the Oath of Allegiance, against Prince Andrey Kurbsky and His Comrades, concerning Their Treacheries

Our God, Tripersonal, who was from everlasting and is now, Father, Son and Holy Ghost, who has neither beginning nor end, in whom we live and move, and by whom tsars rule and the mighty make laws, and the conquering banner, the Holy Cross of the only-begotten Word of God — nor is this banner ever conquerable — was given by Jesus Christ, Our Lord, to the first tsar in piety, Constantine, and to all Orthodox tsars and upholders of Orthodoxy, and to the divine servants, by whose vigilance the Word of God was fulfilled everywhere. And as the words of God encircled the whole world like an eagle in flight, so a spark of piety reached even the Russian kingdom. The autocracy of this Russian kingdom of veritable Orthodoxy, by the will of God, [has its] beginning from the great tsar Vladimir, who enlightened the whole Russian land with holy baptism, and [was maintained by] the great tsar Vladimir Monomach, who received the supreme honour from the Greeks, and the brave and great sovereign, Alexander Nevsky, who won a victory over the godless Germans, and the great and praiseworthy sovereign, Dimitry, who beyond the Don won a mighty victory over the godless sons of Hagar, [and autocracy was handed down] even to the avenger of evils, our grandfather, the Grand Prince Ivan, and to the acquirer of immemorially hereditary lands, our father of blessed memory, the great sovereign, Vasily — and [autocracy] has come down even to us, the humble sceptre-bearer of the Russian kingdom. And we praise [God] for his great mercy bestowed upon us, in that he has not hitherto allowed our right hand to become stained with the blood of our own race ; for we have not seized the kingdom from anyone, but, by the grace of God and with the blessing of our forefathers and fathers, as we were born to rule, so have we grown up and ascended the throne by the bidding of God, and with the blessing of our parents have we taken what is our own, and we have not seized what belongs to others. . . .

Why, O Prince, if you think that you have piety, have you cast out your very [*lit.* only-begotten] soul ? What will you give in exchange for it on the day of the last judgment ? Even if you gain the whole world, in the end death will in any case seize you ! . . .

As I have said above, I will prove in the greatest detail what evil I have suffered from my youth even unto the present day. For this is clear (even if you were young in those years, yet none the less this you can know) : when, by the decree(s) of God, our father, the great sovereign, Vasily, having exchanged the purple for the angel's form, had left all that was perishable and the fleeting earthly kingdom and come to the heavenly [realm], to that everlasting eternity, to stand before the

---

1. "Burning stoves" refers to Ivan's terror directed against the *boyars.*

Tsar of Tsars and the Lord of Lords, I remained with my only (-begotten) brother Georgiy, who has departed this life in sanctity. I was then three years old and my brother was one, and our mother, the pious Tsaritsa Elena, was left in such miserable widowhood — as though in the midst of flames, she suffered on all sides now unmitigated strife stirred up against her by all peoples — by the foreign peoples encircling [our realm], Lithuanians, Poles, Perikopians, Nadchitarkhan, and Nogais, and Kazan', — now manifold misfortune(s) and suffering(s) [inflicted by] you traitors; for, like unto you, you mad dog, Prince Semen Bel'sky and Ivan Lyatsky ran away to Lithuania; [from there] whither did they not run like men possessed? To Tsargrad and to Crimea and to the Nogai [Tatars] and on all sides they raised strife against the Orthodox. But they had no success. . . .

Thus by God's will did it come to pass that our mother, the pious Tsaritsa Elena, went from the earthly kingdom to the heavenly; and we and our brother Georgiy, who has departed this life in sanctity, remained as orphans, [having lost] our parents and receiving no human care from any quarter; and hoping only for the mercy of God, we put our trust in the mercy of the most pure Mother of God and the prayers of all the Saints and the blessing of our parents. But when I had entered upon my eighth year of life [*lit.* from birth] and when thus our subjects had achieved their desire, namely to have the kingdom without a ruler, then did they not deem us, their sovereigns, worthy of any loving care, but themselves ran after wealth and glory, and so leapt on one another [in conflict]. And what did they [not] do then! How many boyars and well-wishers of our father and *voevodas* did they massacre! And the courts and the villages and the possessions of our uncles did they seize and they set themselves up in them! And [the majority of] my mother's treasure did they transfer to the Great Treasury, furiously kicking out [at each other] and stabbing with sharp implements; but the remainder they shared amongst themselves. . . .

But when we reached the fifteenth year of our life, then did we take it upon ourselves to put our kingdom in order and thanks to the mercy of God our rule began favourably. But since human sin ever acerbates the Grace of God, it came to pass that — because of our sins and the intensification of God's wrath, — a fiery flame burned the ruling city of Moscow, and our treacherous boyars, who are called martyrs by you (their names will I intentionally pass over), seized the moment which appeared [*lit.* as it were] favourable to their treacherous wickedness [and] incited the feeblest-witted of the people [by saying] that the mother of our mother, Princess Anna Glinsky, together with her children and her retinue extracted human hearts and with such magic set fire to Moscow and that we had knowledge of this their counsel; and owing to the incitement of those traitors, the people, raising a cry and having seized in frenzied manner our boyar, Prince Yury Vasil'evitch Glinsky in the chapel of the holy martyr Dimitry of Salonica, and having dragged him out, inhumanly slew him in the apostolic cathedral of the Assumption of the most holy Mother of God opposite the throne of the metropolitan, and filled the church with his blood; and they dragged his dead body into the porch of the church and laid him, like one condemned [to death], in the market place. And this his murder in the church is known to all, and not as you lyingly assert, you cur! . . .

Likewise, when by God's will we set out against the godless people of Kazan' with the banner inscribed with the Cross, the banner of all the Orthodox Christian host, to defend Orthodox Christianity, and [when] thus by the inexpressible mercy of God, who gave [us] victory over that Mussulman people, we returned home safe and sound with all the host of Orthodox Christianity — what shall I say of the "well-wishing" towards me of those who are called martyrs by you? This then [will I say]: having placed me like a prisoner on a ship they conveyed me with very few people through the godless and most unbelieving land! Had not the all-powerful right hand of the Almighty protected my humility, then in any case would I have lost my life. Such is the "well-wishing" of those men in whose defence you speak, and thus do they "lay down their lives for us" by striving to deliver our soul into the hands of foreigners!

Likewise, when we had arrived in the ruling city of Moscow God increased his mercy towards us and gave us at that time an heir, our son Dimitry. But after a short time had passed [it fell to our lot] — as indeed it falls to the lot of [all] men — to be afflicted with sickness and to be sorely ill; and then did those who are called by you "well-wishers" rise up like drunken men with the priest Sylvester and with your chief Aleksey, thinking that we were no longer alive, having forgotten our good deeds and even their own souls too, and [having forgotten] that they had kissed the Cross [in allegiance] to our father and to us, [vowing] to seek no other sovereign but our children. Yet they desired to raise to the throne Prince Vladimir, who is far removed from us in the line of succession [*lit.* generation]; while our infant, given to us by God, did they, like Herod, desire to destroy (and how could they fail to destroy him!), having raised Prince Vladimir to the throne. For even though it was said in the ancient secular writings, yet none the less is [the following] fitting: "Tsar does not bow down to tsar; but when one dies, the other rules." [If] then we, while still alive, enjoyed such "well-wishing" from our subjects, what will it be like after our death! But again thanks to God's mercy we recovered, and thus was this counsel scattered. But the priest Sylvester and Aleksey ceased not from that time forth to counsel all that was evil and to inflict [on me] still harsher oppression, conceiving persecutions of various kinds against our [true] well-wishers, while indulging every whim of Prince Vladimir; and likewise they stirred up great hatred against our tsaritsa Anastasia and likened her to all the impious tsaritsas; as for our children, they were not able even to call them to mind.

The Renaissance and Reformation

By A.D. 1500, a sharp contrast had developed between Italy and northern Europe. Most northern European states, except the Holy Roman Empire, were evolving toward centralized political authority, while in Italy fragmentation became the norm. Italian rulers had none of the feudal loyalties with which they might have ruled their subjects. If rulers wished to succeed, they had to rely solely on what was termed *virtu*; they had only their own political, diplomatic, or military abilities to maintain their position. Constant maneuvering for supremacy among the states led to instability.

Economic prosperity of Italian cities was based on manufacturing and international trade. Individual cities and families were known for wool and silk weaving and for banking and the importation of luxury goods from the Near and Far East. The accumulated wealth was used to patronize artists and writers whose works enhanced the reputations of cities and patrons alike.

Italian scholars returned to a study of antiquity and sought to revive classical education in their own period. These studies or "liberal arts" included grammar, rhetoric, poetry, history, and moral philosophy and produced an educated elite called Renaissance humanists.

Perhaps the most famous Italian civic humanist and politician was Niccolò Machiavelli (1469–1527) who served as a secretary and diplomat to the Florentine Republic (1498–1512). Machiavelli's most famous works include *Discourses on the First Ten Books of Livy* (1518), *Mandragola* (1512–1520?), *The History of Florence* (1525) and *The Prince* (1513).

In northern Europe, feudal traditions and gothic art were the norm. Social change developed slowly, but with the growth of capitalism, scholars and princes came to admire the Italian humanist movement. Kings, princes, emperors, and high Church officials became patrons of humanists. Yet, there was a difference — northern scholars emphasized the need to purify the Christian church.

The greatest northern humanist was Desiderius Erasmus of Rotterdam (1469–1536). He was born and educated for the priesthood in Holland, studied in France, and traveled and taught in England and on the Continent. His Christian humanism was not based on a search for religious relics, buying indulgences, or doing good works, but rather on a desire to restore Christianity through true piety and a love of Christ. In this last respect, Erasmus hoped for an internal religious reform and refused to break with the Catholic church as Martin Luther did.

Among Erasmus's works were classical Latin quotations or the *Adages* (1500), *The Handbook of a Christian Knight* (1508), and a new translation of the New Testament (1516). Erasmus's most noted work was his satire on European morals, entitled *The Praise of Folly* (1511), whose Latin title was a pun on the name of his English fellow humanist, Sir Thomas More.

Although Christian humanists flourished in every country, those in the Germanies led the general revolt against the Catholic Church. Among the causes of the Reformation were a reaction against the gross abuses in the Church, lack of moral leadership of the popes, textual criticisms of the humanists, and the political disunity within the Holy Roman Empire.

Martin Luther (1483–1546) was to combine the demands for purification of the Church with a new theology. The son of a prosperous mine owner, Luther was educated for the law at Erfurt University until a crisis of conscience made him enter an Augustinian monastery and become a priest. Luther continued his studies and received a doctorate while teaching theology at Wittenberg University in Saxony. It was while lecturing on St. Paul's Letters to the Romans that Luther came to believe that God's salvation comes to each person through faith, not by personal actions or good works.

Luther might have remained a little noted priest had he not chosen to attack indulgence selling by posting his Ninety-Five Theses on the Castle

Church door in Wittenberg in 1517. Almost immediately, he became the center of a controversy that eventually led to his condemnation as a heretic. Luther took up the challenge and in a stream of pamphlets and treatises further elaborated his theology into what has become the Lutheran church.

84

Niccolò Machiavelli, *The Prince* and *The Discourses on Titus Livy*

Niccolò Machiavelli (1469–1527) remains one of the most articulate spokesmen for the Italian Renaissance, marking a shift toward secular or humanistic values, away from the church-oriented values of the Middle Ages. Like most men of the later Renaissance, Machiavelli looked back to the pagan Roman Republic for inspiration in addressing problems of his own times.

In defending a set of political, social, economic, and religious norms, Machiavelli writes as a philosopher in the sense of one who attempts to integrate knowledge from different fields into a coherent world outlook. He would probably not qualify as a philosopher under the more narrow twentieth-century meaning of that term. Machiavelli's Renaissance philosophy typically sets itself apart from that of the Middle Ages by its understanding of *virtu* as human excellence. Based on the Latin word *vir* (man), *virtu* in practice meant making the absolute most of human talents for human ends — as today a *virtuoso* violinist is one who gets the most out of a violin. In the first section of the reading, Pope Alexander VI (Rodrigo Borgia) and his son, Duke Valentine (Cesare Borgia) — who were too much tainted by intrigue and violent crime to qualify as "virtuous" by current standards — are both treated as virtuoso statesmen. Their grand designs may have been thwarted by fortune, but they made the most of their talents nonetheless.

The first two excerpts are from Machiavelli's most notorious work, *The Prince,* in which he appears to justify nearly any measures to gain and keep rulership. For example, he advises princes to break faith and treaties to keep themselves in power. One can interpret Machiavellianism as a cynical combination of the ideas that "Might makes right" and "The end justifies the means." Yet even in *The Prince,* as the second excerpt illustrates, there are limits. The best form of government for Machiavelli, as for most people of the later Renaissance, was a republic — rather than the monarchy (or "princely rule," as Machiavelli calls it) advocated by Dante. Consequently, someone who subverts a successful republic to establish selfish, personal rule is guilty of nothing less than "villainy."

Machiavelli wrote *The Prince* in a short period of time as he attempted to find employment in the service of the Medicis, one of the leading "princely families" of Italy. The Medicis had ruled Florence in the late fifteenth century and had recently come to power again after the overthrow of the republican government of Florence, which Machiavelli had served as an administrator and diplomat.

Machiavelli gives a better presentation of his world outlook in the much longer *Discourses on the First Ten Books of Titus Livy,* from which the second two excerpts are taken. Here, he describes the means for founding and preserving republics, using the early Roman method described by Livy as his primary model. Notice that in the section entitled "The Religion of the Romans," Machiavelli takes a totally humanistic view of religion. The truth or falsity of pagan Roman religion is irrelevant; he is merely interested in illustrating the type of religion that supports a healthy social and political order. In the final excerpts Machiavelli praises moderate poverty as a positive good, since he believes that small farmers are more likely than rich men to use their political talents for the public benefit.

QUESTIONS TO CONSIDER

1. Why were the activities of Pope Alexander VI contrary to his official position?
2. In modern textbooks, Pope Alexander VI generally gets bad reviews. Why does Machiavelli like him so much?
3. Why was Cesare Borgia an example of *virtu,* and not the villainous Agathocles the Sicilian?
4. Why was L. Quintius Cincinnatus an ideal Roman citizen according to Machiavelli?

Territories Acquired by Virtue or by Fortune

They who from private condition become princes, and, merely by the indulgence of fortune, arrive without much trouble at that dignity, though it costs them dear to maintain it, meet but little difficulty in their passage, being hurried as it were with wings, yet when they come to settle and establish then begins their misery.

... About the arrival at this authority, either by virtue or by good fortune, I shall instance two examples that are in our memory; one is Francesco Sforza, the other Caesar Borgia. Sforza, by just means and extraordinary virtue, made himself Duke of Milan, and enjoyed it in great peace, though it was gained with much trouble. Borgia, on the other hand, (called commonly Duke of Valentine), got several fair territories by the fortune of his father, Pope Alexander, and lost them all after his death, though he used all his industry, and employed all the arts that a wise and brave prince ought to use to fix himself in the sphere where the arms and fortune of other people had placed him....

First two excerpts from Niccolò Machiavelli, *The Prince,* trans. S. G. W. Benjamin (n.p.: The National Alumni, 1907), pp. 25–39, passim. Latter two excerpts from Niccolò Machiavelli, *The Discourses,* in *The Prince and The Discourses,* trans. Luigi Ricci, E. R. P. Vincent, and Christian E. Detmold (New York: Modern Library, 1950), pp. 145–148, 486–488, passim.

Pope Alexander VI had a desire to make his son Duke Valentine great, but he saw many impediments in the way, both for the present and for the future. First, he could not see any way to advance him to any territory that depended not upon the Church; and to those in his gift he was sure the Duke of Milan and the Venetians would never consent; for Faenza and Riminum had already put themselves under Venetian protection. He was likewise sensible that the forces of Italy, especially those that were capable of assisting him, were in the hands of those that ought to apprehend the greatness of the Pope . . . and therefore could not repose any great confidence in them; besides, the laws and alliances of all the states in Italy must of necessity be disturbed before he could make himself master of any part, which was no hard matter to do, finding the Venetians, upon some private interest of their own, inviting the French to another expedition into Italy, which his Holiness was so far from opposing that he promoted it by dissolution of King Louis's former marriage. Louis therefore passed the Alps by the assistance of the Venetians and Alexander's consent, and was no sooner in Milan than he sent forces to assist the Pope in his enterprise against Romagna, which was immediately surrendered upon the King's reputation. Romagna being in this manner reduced by the Duke, and the Colonnesi defeated, he was ambitious both to keep what he had got, and to advance in his conquests. . . .

When the Duke had possessed himself of Romagna, finding it had been governed by poor and inferior lords, who had rather robbed than corrected their subjects, and given them more occasion of discord than of unity, insomuch as that province was full of robberies, riots, and all manner of disturbances, to reduce them to unanimity and subjection to monarchy, he thought it necessary to provide them a good governor, and thereupon he conferred that office upon Remiro d'Orco, with absolute power, though he was a cruel and passionate man. Orco soon settled it in peace, with no small reputation to himself. Afterward the Duke, apprehending that so large a power might become odious to the people, erected a court of judicature in the center of the province, in which every city had its advocate, and an excellent person was appointed to preside. And as he discovered that his past severity had made him many enemies, to remove that ill opinion, and recover the affections of the people, he had a mind to show that, if any cruelty had been exercised, it proceeded not from him but from the arrogance of his minister; and for their further confirmation he caused the said governor to be apprehended, and his head chopped off one morning in the market-place at Cesena, with a wooden dagger on one side of him and a bloody knife on the other; the ferocity of which spectacle not only appeased but amazed the people for a while.

. . . The Duke, finding himself powerful enough, and secure against present danger, being as strong as he desired, and his neighbors in a manner reduced to an incapacity of hurting him, was willing to go on with his conquests. Nothing remained but jealousy of France, which was without cause, for he knew that King Louis had found his error at last, and would be sure to obstruct him. Hereupon he began to look abroad for new allies, and to hesitate and stagger toward France, as appeared when the French army advanced into the kingdom of Naples against the Spaniards, who had besieged Cajeta. His main design was to secure himself against the French, and he would doubtless have done it if Alexander had lived.

These were his provisions against the dangers that were imminent; but those that were remote were more doubtful and uncertain. The first thing he feared was, lest the next Pope should be his enemy and reassume all that Alexander had given him, to prevent which he considered four ways. The first was by destroying the whole line of those lords whom he had dispossessed, that his Holiness might have no occasion to restore them. The second was to cajole the nobility in Rome, and draw them over to his party, that thereby he might put an awe and restraint upon the Pope. The third was, if possible, to make the College his friends. The fourth was to make himself so strong before the death of his father as to be able to stand upon his own legs and repel the first violence that should be practised against him. Three of these four expedients he had tried before Alexander died, and he was in a fair way for the fourth. . . .

On serious examination, therefore, of the whole conduct of Duke Valentine, I see nothing to be reprehended ; it seems rather proper to me to present him, as I have done, as an example for the imitation of all such as by the favor of fortune, or the supplies of other princes, have got into power ; for, his mind being so large, and his intentions so high, he could not do otherwise, and nothing could have opposed the greatness and wisdom of his designs but his own infirmity and the death of his father. He, therefore, who thinks it necessary in the minority of his dominion to secure himself against his enemies, to gain himself friends ; to overcome, whether by force or by fraud ; to make himself beloved or feared by his people ; to be followed and reverenced by his soldiers ; to destroy and exterminate such as would do him injury ; to repeal and suppress old laws, and introduce new ; to be severe, grateful, magnanimous, liberal, cashier and disband such of his army as were unfaithful, and put new in their places ; manage himself so in his alliances with kings and princes that all should be either obliged to requite him or afraid to offend him — he, I say, cannot find a fresher or better model than the actions of this prince.

Of Such Who Have Arrived at Dominion by Wicked Means

Agathocles, the Sicilian, not only from a private but from a vile and abject condition was made King of Syracuse ; and being but the son of a potter, he continued the dissoluteness of his life through all the degrees of his fortune. Nevertheless, his vices were accompanied with such courage and activity that he applied himself to the wars, by which, and his great industry, he came at length to be the Pretor of Syracuse. Being settled in that dignity, and having determined to make himself prince, and hold by violence, without obligation to anybody, that which was conferred upon him by consent, he came to an understanding with Hamilcar the Carthaginian, who was then at the head of an army in Sicily ; and, calling the people and the Senate of Syracuse together one morning, as if he intended to consult them on some matter of importance to the state, on a signal appointed he caused his soldiers to kill all the senators and the most wealthy of the people ; after whose death he usurped the dominion of that city without any obstruction.

. . . Nevertheless it cannot be called virtue in him to kill his fellow-citizens, betray his friends, and be without faith, pity, or religion ; these are ways that may get a man empire, but no glory or reputation. Yet, if the wisdom of Agathocles be considered, his dexterity in encountering and overcoming of dangers, his courage in supporting and surmounting his misfortunes, I do not see why he should be held inferior to the best captains of his time. But his unbounded cruelty and barbarous inhumanity, added to numerous other vices, will not permit him to be numbered among the most excellent men. So, then, that which he performed cannot justly be attributed either to fortune or to virtue. . . .

It may seem wonderful to some that it should come to pass that Agathocles, and such as he, after so many treacheries and acts of inhumanity, should live quietly in their own country so long, defend themselves so well against foreign enemies, and none of their subjects conspire against them at home ; since several others, by reason of their cruelty, have not been able, even in time of peace, to maintain their government. I conceive it fell out according as their cruelty was well or ill applied. I say well applied (if that word may be applied to an ill action), and it may be called so when committed but once, and that of necessity for one's own preservation, but never repeated, and even then converted as much as possible to the benefit of the subjects. Ill applied are such cruelties as are but few in the beginning, but in time do rather multiply than decrease. . . .

Whence it is to be observed that he who usurps the government of any State is to execute and put in practice all the cruelties that he thinks material at once, that he may have no occasion to renew them often, but that by his discontinuance he may mollify the people, and by benefits bring them over to his side. He who does otherwise, whether from fear or from ill counsel, is obliged to be always ready with his knife in his hand ; for he never can repose any confidence in his subjects, while they, by reason of his fresh and continued inhumanities, cannot be secure against him.

So then injuries are to be committed all at once, that the last being the less, the distaste may be likewise the less ; but benefits should be distilled by drops, that the relish may be the greater.

The Religion of the Romans

Although the founder of Rome was Romulus, yet the gods did not judge the laws of this prince sufficient for so great an empire, and therefore inspired the Roman Senate to elect Numa Pompilius as his successor, so that he might regulate all those things that had been omitted by Romulus. Numa, finding a very savage people, and wishing to reduce them to civil obedience by the arts of peace, had recourse to religion as the most necessary and assured support of any civil society ; and he established it upon such foundations that for many centuries there was nowhere more fear of the gods than in that republic, which greatly facilitated all the enterprises which the Senate or its great men attempted. Whoever will examine the actions of the people of Rome as a body, or of many individual Romans, will see that these citizens feared much more to break an oath than the laws, like men who esteem the power of the gods more than that of men . . . , which can be ascribed to nothing else than the religious principles which Numa had instilled into the Romans. And whoever reads Roman history attentively will see in how great a degree religion served in the command of the armies, in uniting the people and keeping them well conducted, and in covering the wicked with shame. . . . In truth, there never was any remarkable lawgiver amongst any people who did not resort to divine authority, as otherwise his laws would not have been accepted by the people; for there are many good laws, the importance of which is known to the sagacious lawgiver, but the reasons for which are not sufficiently evident to enable him to persuade others to submit to them; and therefore do wise men, for the purpose of removing this difficulty, resort to divine authority. Thus did Lycurgus and Solon, and many others who aimed at the same thing.

The Roman people, then, admiring the wisdom and goodness of Numa, yielded in all things to his advice. It is true that those were very religious times, and the people with whom Numa had to deal were very untutored and superstitious, which made it easy for him to carry out his designs, being able to impress upon them any new form. And doubtless, if any one wanted to establish a republic at the present time, he would find it much easier with the simple mountaineers, who are almost without any civilization, than with such as are accustomed to live in cities, where civilization is already corrupt; as a sculptor finds it easier to make a fine statue out of a crude block of marble than out of a statue badly begun by another. Considering then, all these things, I conclude that the religion introduced by Numa into Rome was one of the chief causes of the prosperity of that city; for this religion gave rise to good laws, and good laws bring good fortune, and from good fortune results happy success in all enterprises. And as the observance of divine institutions is the cause of the greatness of republics, so the disregard of them produces their ruin; for where the fear of God is wanting, there the country will come to ruin.

Cincinnatus: Illustration of Poverty as Good for Republics

It is of the greatest advantage in a republic to have laws that keep her citizens poor. Although there does not appear to have been any special law to this effect in Rome . . . , yet experience shows that even so late as four hundred years after its foundation there was still great poverty in Rome. We cannot ascribe this fact to any other cause than that poverty never was allowed to stand in the way of the achievement of any rank or honor, and that virtue and merit were sought for under whatever roof they dwelt; it was this system that made riches naturally less desirable. We have a manifest proof of this on the occasion when the Consul Minutius and his army were surrounded by the Equeans, and all Rome was full of apprehensions lest the army should be lost, so that they resorted to the creation of a Dictator, their last remedy in times of difficulty. They appointed L. Quintius Cincinnatus, who at the time was on his little farm, which he cultivated with his own hands. This circumstance is celebrated by Titus Livius in the following golden words: "After this let men not listen to those who prefer riches to everything else in this world, and who think that there is neither honor nor virtue where wealth does not flow." Cincinnatus was engaged in ploughing his fields, which did not exceed four acres, when the messengers of the Senate arrived from Rome to announce his election to the dictatorship, and to point out to him the imminent danger of the Roman republic. He immediately put on his toga, gathered an army, and went to the relief of Minutius; and having crushed and despoiled the enemy, and freed the Consul and his army, he would not permit them to share the spoils, saying, "I will not allow you to participate in the spoils of those to whom you came so near falling a prey."

He deprived Minutius of the consulate, and reduced him to the rank of lieutenant, saying to him, "You will remain in this grade until you have learned to be Consul."

Cincinnatus had chosen for his master of cavalry L. Tarquinius whose poverty had obliged him to fight on foot. Let us note here how Rome honored poverty, (as has been said,) and how four acres of land sufficed for the support of so good and great a citizen as Cincinnatus. We find also that poverty was still honored in the times of Marcus Regulus, who when commanding an army in Africa asked permission of the Roman Senate to return to look after his farm, which was being spoiled by the laborers in whose charge it had been left by him. These instances suggest two reflections: the one, that these eminent citizens were content to remain in such poverty, and that they were satisfied merely to win honor by their military achievements, and to leave all the profits of them to the public treasury; for if they had thought of enriching themselves by their wars, they would have cared little whether their fields were being spoiled or not; and the other, as to the magnanimity of these citizens, who, when placed at the head of an army, rose above all princes solely by the grandeur of their souls. . . .

I might demonstrate here at length that poverty produces better fruit than riches, — that the first has conferred honor upon cities, countries, and religions, whilst the latter have only served to ruin them, — were it not that this subject has been so often illustrated by other writers.

85

Erasmus, *Julius II Excluded*

Popes generally supported the artistic and literary creativity of the Renaissance. At the same time, humanistic scholars north of Italy felt increasingly inclined to turn their learning and persuasive skills against the worldliness of the papacy as well as the backwardness of monastic orders.

Erasmus of Rotterdam (1469–1536) was a literary genius who thought that he had been unfairly coerced as a youth into taking monastic vows. Believing himself to be a defender of true Christianity while attacking monastic narrowness, he advocated both the study of Scripture and the study of classical, pre-Christian literature. In his words, the proper "weapons" for the struggle of life were "prayer and knowledge."

His major contribution to the Renaissance in Northern Europe was his edition of the Greek New Testament with a Latin translation and commentaries. Printed by a market-oriented publisher in Switzerland, it was a runaway best seller: 100,000 copies were sold in France alone. Erasmus's popular Latin translation and commentaries greatly heightened the debate on the nature of the Church and its function in society.

The following excerpts from a play by Erasmus illustrate sentiments of the coming Reformation. The play was first staged in 1514 for a sympathetic audience, largely composed of students and faculty members, in Paris. Julius

II, the pope from 1503 to 1514, had earned Machiavelli's admiration for his military and diplomatic skills. His excellent artistic taste led him to employ both Michelangelo and Raphael as he sought to adorn the Vatican. Yet for Christian humanists, Julius left something to be desired as the spiritual leader of Christendom. In an early version of an enduring story, the play presents Saint Peter dealing with someone with doubtful credentials for entering Heaven. Its serious theme — contrasting the headstrong success of Church leaders in accumulating worldly power with the totally different goals of the early fathers of the Church, or Christ himself — has resurfaced periodically in literary satire ; the best-known modern example is perhaps the "Grand Inquisitor" episode in Dostoyevsky's *Brothers Karamazov.*

When he wrote the play, Erasmus was looking to France as the country where leaders were most likely to further Church reform. The play's Julius II calls the French "barbarians," as did Machiavelli and other Italians of the time. But Erasmus sees a connection between the uncorrupted, natural, "barbarian" characteristics of the French and the hope of changing the Church for the better. Within a decade, Martin Luther would make a similar link in relating German national character to his program of reform.

Erasmus, who hated being caught up in the middle of controversies, despite a lifetime of helping to instigate them, disowned the authorship of the play. But the overwhelming similarities in sentiments, observations, and style between *Julius II Excluded* and other works he published make him the only likely candidate for consideration as its author.

QUESTIONS TO CONSIDER

1. Why was Pope Julius II not considered a reforming pope such as Gregory VII and Innocent III ?
2. Why would Machiavelli never have written this satire (see Reading 84) ?
3. Whom did Erasmus favor, the "barbarians" or the papacy ?
4. Why would the Protestant reformers have welcomed this satire ?

Scene — Gate of Heaven

Julius : What the devil is this ? The gates not opened ! Something is wrong with the lock. . . .

Peter : Well that the gates are adamant, or this fellow would have broken in. He must be some giant, or conqueror. Heaven, what a stench ! Who are you ? What do you want here ? . . .

Julius : Enough of this. I am Julius . . . , P.M., as you can see by the letters if you can read.

Peter : P.M. ! What is that ? Pestis Maxima ?

From Erasmus, *Julius II Exclusus : A Dialogue.* Translated and included by J. A. Froude in his *Life and Letters of Erasmus* (New York : Charles Scribner's Sons, 1894), pp. 149–168, passim.

Julius: Pontifex Maximus, you rascal. . . .

Peter: . . . Let me look at you a little closer. Hum! Signs of impiety in plenty . . . not precisely like an apostle. Priest's cassock and bloody armour below it, eyes savage, mouth insolent, forehead brazen, body scarred with sins all over, breath loaded with wine, health broken with debauchery. Ay, threaten as you will, I will tell you what you are for all your bold looks. You are Julius the Emperor come back from hell. . . .

Julius: Make an end, I say, or I will fling a thunderbolt at you. I will excommunicate you. I have done as much to kings before this. . . .

Peter: You must show your merits first; no admission without merits. . . .

Julius: The invincible Julius ought not to answer a beggarly fisherman. However, you shall know who and what I am. First, I am a Ligurian, and not a Jew like you. My mother was the sister of the great Pope Sextus IV. The Pope made me a rich man out of Church property. I became a cardinal. I had my misfortunes. I had the French pox. I was banished, hunted out of my country; but I knew all along that I should come to be pope myself in the end . . . I succeeded. I rose to the top, and I have done more for the Church and Christ than any pope before me.

Peter: What did you do?

Julius: I raised the revenue. I invented new offices and sold them. . . . Then I annexed Bologna to the Holy See. I have torn up treaties, kept great armies in the field. I have covered Rome with palaces, and I have left five millions in the Treasury behind me. . . .

Peter: Invincible warrior! All this is quite new to me. Pardon my simplicity, who are these fair curly-haired boys that you have with you?

Julius: Boys I took into training to improve their minds.

Peter: And those dark ones with the scars?

Julius: Those are my soldiers and generals who were killed fighting for me. They all deserve heaven. I promised it to them under hand and seal if they lost their lives in my service, no matter how wicked they might be. . . .

Peter: My orders are not to admit men who come with Bulls, but to admit those who have clothed the naked, fed the hungry, given the thirsty drink, visited the sick and those in prison. Men have cast out devils and worked miracles in Christ's name and yet have been shut out. . . .

Julius: If I had but known.

Peter: What would you have done? Declared war?

Julius: I would have excommunicated you.

Peter: . . . When I was pope the difficulty was to find men who would be priests or deacons.

Julius: Naturally, when bishops and priests had nothing for their reward but fasts, and vigils, and doctrines, and now and then death. Bishops nowadays are kings and lords, and such positions are worth struggling for. . . .

Peter: Why did you take Bologna . . . ?

Julius: Because I wanted the revenue for my own treasury, and because Bologna was otherwise convenient for me. So I used my thunderbolts, the French helped me, and now Bologna is mine, and every farthing of the taxes goes to Rome for the Church's use. If you had only seen my triumphal entry. . . .

Peter: He who represents Christ ought to try to be like Christ. But, tell me, is there no way of removing a wicked pope?

Julius: Absurd! Who can remove the highest authority of all?

Peter: That the Pope is the highest is a reason why he should be removed if he causes scandal. Bad princes can be removed. The Church is in a bad way if it must put up with a head who is ruining it.

Julius: A Pope can only be corrected by a general council, but no general council can be held without the Pope's consent; otherwise it is a synod, and not a council. Let the council sit, it can determine nothing unless the Pope agrees; and, again, a single pope having absolute power is superior to the council. Thus he cannot be deposed for any crime whatsoever. . . .

Peter: A novel privilege for my successors — to be the wickedest of men, yet be safe from punishment. So much the unhappier the Church which cannot shake such a monster off its shoulders.

Julius: Some say there is one cause for which a Pope can be deposed.

Peter: When he has done a good action, I suppose, since he is not to be punished for his bad actions.

Julius: If he can be convicted publicly of heresy. But this is impossible, too. For he can cancel any canon which he does not like. . . .

Peter: In the name of the papal majesty, who made these fine laws?

Julius: Who? Why, the source of all law, the Pope himself, and the power that makes a law can repeal it.

Peter: What else can you do?

Julius: What else? How do kings levy revenues? They persuade the people that they owe their fortunes to them, and then they ask, and the people give. So we make the people believe that they owe to us their knowledge of God, though we sleep all our lives. Besides, we sell them indulgences in small matters at a cheap rate, dispensations for not much more, and for blessings we charge nothing. . . .

Peter: This is all Greek to me. But why do you hate the barbarians, and move heaven and earth to get rid of them?

Julius: Because barbarians are superstitious, and the French worst of all.

Peter: Do the French worship other gods besides Christ?

Julius: No; but they have precise notions of what is due to Christ. They use hard words about certain things which we have left off.

Peter: Magical words, I presume?

Julius: No, not magical. They talk of simony and blasphemy, sodomy, poisoning, witchcraft, in language expressing abomination of such actions.

Peter: I do not wish to be personal, but can it be that such crimes are to be found among yourselves, professing Christians?

Julius: The barbarians have vices of their own. They censure ours and forget theirs. We tolerate ours and abominate theirs. Poverty, for instance, we look on as so wicked that anything is justifiable to escape from it, while the barbarians scarcely approve of wealth if innocently come by. . . . Barbarians forbid usury; we regard it as a necessary institution. They think looseness with women polluting and disgusting; we — well, we do not think so at all. They are shocked at simony; we never mention it. They stick to old laws and customs; we go for novelty and progress. While our views of life are so different, we don't like to have the barbarians too close to us. They have sharp eyes. They write letters about us to our friends. . . . Thus the Church suffers: we sell fewer dispensations, and get a worse price for them, and we receive less money for bishoprics and abbeys and colleges; worst of all, people are no longer frightened at our thunderbolts. Once let them think that a wicked Pope cannot hurt them, we shall be starved out. So we mean to keep the barbarian at a distance. . . .

Peter: The Church is a community of Christians with Christ's Spirit in them. You have been a subverter of the Church.

Julius: The Church consists of cathedrals, and priests, and the Court of Rome, and myself at the head of it.

Peter: Christ is our Head, and we are His ministers. Are there two Heads? How have you increased the Church?

Julius: I found it poor: I have made it splendid.

Peter: Splendid with what? With faith? . . .

Julius: I have filled Rome with palaces, trains of mules and horses, troops of servants, armies and officers.

Spirit: With scarlet women and the like.

Julius: With purple and gold, with revenues so vast that kings are poor beside the Roman Pontiff. Glory, luxury, hoards of treasure, these are splendours, and these all I have created.

Peter: Pray, inform me. The Church had nothing of all this when it was founded by Christ. Whence came all this splendour, as you call it? . . .

Julius: You are thinking of the old affair, when you starved as Pope, with a handful of poor hunted bishops about you. Time has changed all that, and much for the better. You had only the name of Pope. Look now at our gorgeous churches, our priests by thousands; bishops like kings, with retinues and palaces; cardinals in their purple gloriously attended, horses and mules decked with gold and jewels, and shod with gold and silver. Beyond all, myself, Supreme Pontiff, borne on soldiers' shoulders in a golden chair, and waving my hand majestically to adoring crowds. Hearken to the roar of the cannon, the bugle notes, the boom of the drums. Observe the military engines, the shouting populace, torches blazing in street and square, and the kings of the earth scarce admitted to kiss my Holiness's foot. Behold the Roman Bishop placing the crown on the head of the Emperor, who seems to be made king of kings, yet is but the shadow of a name. Look at all this, and tell me it is not magnificent!

Peter: I look at a very worldly tyrant, an enemy of Christ and a disgrace to the Church.

Julius: Mere envy! You perceive what a poor wretch of a bishop you were compared to me.

Peter: Insolent wretch! Dare you compare your glory with mine? — and mine was Christ's, and not my own. Christ gave to me the keys of the Kingdom of Heaven, trusted His sheep to my feeding and sealed my faith with His approval. Fraud, usury, and cunning made you Pope, if Pope you are to be called. I gained thousands of souls to Christ: you have destroyed as many thousands. I brought heathen Rome to acknowledge Christ: you have made it heathen again. I healed the sick, cast out devils, restored the dead to life, and brought a blessing with me where I went. What blessings have you and your triumphs brought? I used my power for the good of all: you have used yours to crush and vex mankind. . . .

Julius: Do you mean to say I am to give up money, dominion, revenues, pleasures, life? Will you leave me to misery?

Peter: Yes, if you count Christ as miserable. He who was Lord of all became the scorn of all, endured poverty, endured labour, fasting, and hunger, and ended with a death of shame.

Julius: Very admirable, no doubt. But He will not find many imitators in these times of ours.

Peter: To admire is to imitate. Christ takes nothing good from any man. He takes what is falsely called good, to give him instead eternal truth, as soon as he is purged from the taint of the world. Being Himself heavenly, He will have His Church like Him, estranged from the world's corruption, and those who are sunk in pollution can not resemble One who is sitting in heaven. Once for all, fling away your imagined wealth, and receive instead what is far better.

Julius: What, I beseech you?

Peter: The gift of prophecy, the gift of knowledge, the gift of miracles, Christ Himself. The more a man is afflicted in the world the greater his joy in Christ, the poorer in the world the richer in Christ, the more cast down in the world the more exalted in Christ. Christ will have His followers pure, and most of all His ministers, the bishops. The higher in rank they are the more like Christ they are bound to be, and the less entangled in earthly pleasures. Yet you, the bishop next to Christ, who make yourself equal with Christ, think only of money, and arms, and treaties, to say nothing of vicious pleasures, and you abuse His name to support your own vanities. You claim the honour due to Christ, while you are Christ's enemy. You bless others, you are yourself accursed. You pretend to have the keys of heaven, and you are yourself shut out from it. . . .

Julius: Then you won't open the gates?

Peter: Sooner to anyone than to such as you. We are not of your communion in this place. You have an army of sturdy rogues behind you, you have money, and you are a famous architect. Go build a paradise of your own, and fortify it, lest the devils break in on you.

86

Martin Luther at the Diet of Worms, 1521[1]

Although the Holy Roman Emperor Charles V (1500–1558) saw rebellion against the Church as leading to rebellion against the state, he could neither ignore the aroused German nationalism, nor Luther's powerful princely support. It is for these reasons that the emperor did not immediately publish the papal bull[2] "Exsurge domine" against Luther but, rather, granted Luther a safe conduct so that he could appear before the Diet of Princes at Worms in order to defend his religious views.

The following excerpt is from Luther's reply to the Diet at Worms on April 18, 1521.

QUESTIONS TO CONSIDER

1. What were Luther's criticisms of the Church?
2. What would have convinced Luther to change his opinions?
3. Why would the Catholic church not favor Luther's individual interpretation of the Scriptures?
4. From your general reading, how did the Protestant Reformation affect the political situation during the sixteenth century?

"Most serene emperor, most illustrious princes, concerning those questions proposed to me yesterday on behalf of your serene majesty, whether I acknowledged as mine the books enumerated and published in my name and whether I wished to persevere in their defense or to retract them, I have given to the first question my full and complete answer, in which I still persist and shall persist forever. These books are mine and they have been published in my name by me, unless in the meantime, either through the craft or the mistaken wisdom of my emulators, something in them has been changed or wrongly cut out. For plainly I cannot ac-

Martin Luther, *Luther's Works, Career of the Reformer II*, ed. George W. Forell (Philadelphia: Muhlenberg Press, 1958), pp. XXXII, 109–113.

1. The imperial Diet had been created in the fifteenth century; it included three houses: (1) the seven electors who chose the emperors, (2) the House of Princes, and (3) the House of Free Cities. The Diets always tried to stop the emperors from exercising any real authority over them. The emperors had to depend for any moneys or troops on voluntary contributions from the Diet. The imperial free city of Worms, located in Hesse on the Rhine, had been designated as the meeting place of the Emperor Charles V and the Diet in 1520. The emperor had promised the princes that no German should be branded an outlaw before a hearing in the empire; he, therefore, had to follow constitutional practices and give Martin Luther a safe-conduct pass to the meeting of the Diet.

2. A papal bull [*Bulla*] is the most solemn official pronouncement of a pope. It was sealed with lead or a *Bulla*.

knowledge anything except what is mine alone and what has been written by me alone, to the exclusion of all interpretations of anyone at all.

"In replying to the second question, I ask that your most serene majesty and your lordships may deign to note that my books are not all of the same kind.

"For there are some in which I have discussed religious faith and morals simply and evangelically, so that even my enemies themselves are compelled to admit that these are useful, harmless, and clearly worthy to be read by Christians. Even the bull, although harsh and cruel, admits that some of my books are inoffensive, and yet allows these also to be condemned with a judgment which is utterly monstrous. Thus, if I should begin to disavow them, I ask you, what would I be doing? Would not I, alone of all men, be condemning the very truth upon which friends and enemies equally agree, striving alone against the harmonious confession of all?

"Another group of my books attacks the papacy and the affairs of the papists as those who both by their doctrines and very wicked examples have laid waste the Christian world with evil that affects the spirit and the body. For no one can deny or conceal this fact, when the experience of all and the complaints of everyone witness that through the decrees of the pope and the doctrines of men the consciences of the faithful have been most miserably entangled, tortured, and torn to pieces. Also, property and possessions, especially in this illustrious nation of Germany, have been devoured by an unbelievable tyranny and are being devoured to this time without letup and by unworthy means. . . . If, therefore, I should have retracted these writings, I should have done nothing other than to have added strength to this [papal] tyranny and I should have opened not only windows but doors to such great godlessness. It would rage farther and more freely than ever it has dared up to this time. Yes, from the proof of such a revocation on my part, their wholly lawless and unrestrained kingdom of wickedness would become still more intolerable for the already wretched people; and their rule would be further strengthened and established, especially if it should be reported that this evil deed had been done by me by virtue of the authority of your most serene majesty and of the whole Roman Empire. Good God! What a cover for wickedness and tyranny I should have then become.

"I have written a third sort of book against some private and (as they say) distinguished individuals — those, namely, who strive to preserve the Roman tyranny and to destroy the godliness taught by me. Against these I confess I have been more violent than my religion or profession demands. But then, I do not set myself up as a saint; neither am I disputing about my life, but about the teaching of Christ. It is not proper for me to retract these works, because by this retraction it would again happen that tyranny and godlessness would, with my patronage, rule and rage among the people of God more violently than ever before.

"However, because I am a man and not God, I am not able to shield my books with any other protection than that which my Lord Jesus Christ himself offered for his teaching. When questioned before Annas about his teaching and struck by a servant, he said: 'If I have spoken wrongly, bear witness to the wrong'. . . . If the Lord himself, who knew that he could not err, did not refuse to hear testimony against his teaching, even from the lowliest servant, how much more ought I, who am the lowest scum and able to do nothing except err, desire and expect that somebody should want to offer testimony against my teaching! Therefore, I ask by the mercy of God, may your most serene majesty, most illustrious lordships, or anyone at all who is able, either high or low, bear witness, expose my errors, overthrowing them by the writings of the prophets and the evangelists. Once I have been taught I shall be quite ready to renounce every error, and I shall be the first to cast my books into the fire.

"From these remarks I think it is clear that I have sufficiently considered and weighed the hazards and dangers, as well as the excitement and dissensions aroused in the world as a result of my teachings, things about which I was gravely and forcefully warned yesterday. To see excitement and dissension arise because of the Word of God is to me clearly the most joyful aspect of all in these matters. For this is the way, the opportunity, and the result of the Word of God, just as He [Christ] said, I have not come to bring peace, but a sword. For I have come to set a man against his father, etc.'. . . Therefore, we ought to think how marvelous and terrible is our God in his counsels, lest by chance what is attempted for settling strife grows rather into an intolerable deluge of evils, if we begin by condemning the Word of God. And concern must be shown lest the reign of this most noble youth, Prince Charles (in whom after God is our great hope), become unhappy and inauspicious. I could illustrate this with abundant examples from Scripture — like Pharaoh, the king of Babylon, and the kings of Israel who, when they endeavored to pacify and strengthen their kingdoms by the wisest counsels, most surely destroyed themselves. For it is He who takes the wise in their own craftiness . . . and overturns mountains before they know it. . . . Therefore we must fear God. I do not say these things because there is a need of either my teachings or my warnings for such leaders as you, but because I must not withhold the allegiance which I owe my Germany. With these words I commend myself to your most serene majesty and to your lordships, humbly asking that I not be allowed through the agitation of my enemies, without cause, to be made hateful to you. I have finished."

When I had finished, the speaker for the emperor said, as if in reproach, that I had not answered the question, that I ought not call into question those things which had been condemned and defined in councils ; therefore what was sought from me was not a horned response, but a simple one, whether or not I wished to retract.

Here I answered :

"Since then your serene majesty and your lordships seek a simple answer, I will give it in this manner, neither horned nor toothed : Unless I am convinced by the testimony of the Scriptures or by clear reason (for I do not trust either in the pope or in councils alone, since it is well known that they have often erred and contradicted themselves), I am bound by the Scriptures I have quoted and my conscience is captive to the Word of God. I cannot and I will not retract anything, since it is neither safe nor right to go against conscience.

"I cannot do otherwise, here I stand, may God Help me, Amen."

Age of Exploration and Expansion

Almost a century before Portuguese captain Vasco da Gama successfully rounded the Cape of Good Hope and reached the Malabar coast of India in 1498, in 1405, Emperor Yung-lo (1403–1424) of the Ming dynasty (1308–1644) had launched the first of a series of grand-scale maritime expeditions. Over the next 28 years, the Chinese court dispatched six more large-scale naval expeditions to Southeast Asia, India, Persia, and the east coast of Africa. These gigantic expeditions involved more than 70,000 men and hundreds of vessels and covered thousands of nautical miles. In contrast with the goals of the European adventurers who came to Asia several decades later, the main purpose of these grand undertakings was neither conquest nor trade. The Ming government was mainly interested in spreading and enhancing its dynastic prestige and power as well as winning for China the nominal control of those distant regions. By 1415, 19 kingdoms had sent tributes to the Ming court; however, after nearly three decades of naval expeditions, not a single permanent overseas Ming colony was established.

Then, in 1433, the great Ming naval expeditions suddenly ceased, never to resume. Although scholars do not know the precise reasons why China refused to embark on her own Age of Exploration, possible explanations might include: the high cost of the naval expeditions; China's long-held tradition of anti-commercialism; and the ruling Confucian scholars' and officials' prejudice toward the seafaring people, who neglected to observe two important Confucian virtues — namely, filial piety and ancestor worship. Had those Chinese seafarers sustained support from a leader like Portugal's Prince Henry, the course of world history might have been quite different; certainly China would have "discovered" such distant lands as Spain, England, and France. A little more than six decades after the last Ming naval expedition of 1433, Vasco da Gama opened an era of European domination of the Asian waters. The compass and gunpowder, two important gifts of China to the West, permitted the Europeans to develop empires in Asia.

As the demand for Oriental products increased in Western Europe in the fifteenth century, merchants and monarchs, hoping to break the Italian monopoly of that trade, began their search for an all-water route to the East. Another powerful impetus was a strong sense of Christian duty to convert pagans and infidels. For centuries, Portuguese and Spaniards had struggled to expel the Muslims who occupied their land. That effort generated a religious fervor and missionary zeal and also helped establish a sense of national identity. By the early fifteenth century, Portugal had become a unified state, separate from the expanding Spanish kingdoms of Leon and Castile. The Iberians, with their strategic location facing the Atlantic and with new knowledge of navigation and shipbuilding gained from Italian seafarers on the Mediterranean, initiated the age of European exploration and expansion.

Prince Henry, the third son of King John I of Portugal (1385–1433), focused the small nation's attention on various maritime projects. Under his leadership, Portugal became a center of knowledge for shipbuilding, navigation, and the study of geography. Portugal also was the first European nation to embark on colonial expansion. Prince Henry took the initiative in settling Portuguese adventurers in the Azores, and in 1415 he crossed the Strait of Gibraltar to capture the North African port of Ceuta, the terminal of the caravan routes into Africa. In succeeding years, lured by the potential profits in trading gold, ivory, and slaves, Prince Henry directed Portuguese explorations down the West African coast and established trading centers there. He had also obtained from the Papacy a monopoly of missionary activities in the area. When he died in 1460, Prince Henry's economic and religious rights in West Africa passed to the Portuguese monarchs, who continued sending explorers to probe the African coast. They rounded the Cape of Good Hope by 1488 and a decade later arrived in the Indian Ocean, where Muslim states had a monopoly of the trade with India and the Far East. In the New World, Pedro Cabral landed on the east coast of South America in 1500, strengthening Portugal's claim to Brazil.

As a youth, Christopher Columbus (1451–1506) had served as a seaman on various ships in the Mediterranean. He eventually settled in Portugal, where he developed his idea of sailing west to Asia. He was unable to gain financial support from the Portuguese monarchs, who favored opening the sea route to India by way of Africa, but he continued his search for a sponsor in Spain. After the fall of the Muslim stronghold of Granada on January 2, 1492, Queen Isabella finally agreed to his terms. His four voyages established Spanish influence in the Caribbean.

It did not take long, however, for Spain and other European countries to begin conquering the New World that Columbus had stumbled upon. The final reading in this section describes the conquest of Mexico.

87

Cheng Ho [Zheng He]: Ming Maritime Expeditions

Most of the large naval expeditions of the Ming dynasty were led by a Muslim court eunuch named Cheng Ho (1371–1433). The following selection describes China's Columbus and the maritime explorations that he led.

QUESTIONS TO CONSIDER

1. What does the size, organization, and nature of the Ming maritime fleet indicate about China's capabilities in the early fifteenth century?

2. What do the Ming Emperor's bans on imperial naval explorations suggest about Chinese views of the world?
3. Compare and contrast the Ming maritime expeditions with the Age of Discovery in Western history. What motives inspired Cheng Ho, Columbus, and Magellan?
4. How might the course of world history been altered had the Chinese seafarers received sustained support from a leader like Prince Henry of Portugal?

Cheng Ho (1371–1433), eunuch and commander-in-chief of the Ming expeditionary fleets in the early years of the 15th century, was born into a family named Ma at K'un-yang [Kunyang] in central Yunnan. His great-grandfather was named Bayan, and his grandfather and father were both named Ḥājjī, which suggests that the two probably visited Mecca and that the family had a long tradition of Islamic faith and may have been of Mongol-Arab origin. At the beginning of the Ming dynasty, a number of generals who fought on the frontier were in charge of recruiting eunuchs for the court. In 1381, when Yunnan was pacified by an army under Fu Yu-de, Cheng Ho, at that time about ten years old, was one of the children selected to be castrated. As a trainee for eunuch service, he was assigned to the retinue of Chu Ti [Zhu Di] [Emperor Yung-lo]. In his early twenties, he accompanied Chu Ti on a series of military campaigns and in the course of them took up a career in the army. As his family records relate, "when he entered adulthood, he reportedly became seven feet tall and had a waist about five feet in circumference. His cheeks and forehead were high but his nose was small. He had glaring eyes and a voice as loud as a huge bell. He knew a great deal about warfare and was well accustomed to battle.". . .

Cheng Ho first achieved official prominence early in 1404 when he was promoted to the position of director of eunuch affairs and granted the surname of Cheng [Zheng]. Shortly afterward he received the appointment of commander-in-chief of the first expedition. Meanwhile local officials of the eastern coastal regions were ordered to build ocean-going vessels. By July, 1405, some 1,180 ships of various sizes and types had been constructed. The large or treasure ships were, according to measures of that time, as much as 440 feet long and 186.2 wide, and those of medium size, or horse ships, 370 feet long and 150 wide. There were supply ships which measured 280 feet in length and 120 in breadth, and billet ships measuring 240 feet by 94. The battleships equipped with cannon were much smaller, measuring only 180 feet by 68. Most of the treasure ships were the product of the Lung-chiang [Long Jiang] shipyard near Nanking [Nanjing]. None of these has survived, but near the site of the shipyard was recently discovered (1957) a large wooden rudder (length 11 meters) thought to have been fashioned for one of the bigger vessels. It is now preserved in the Kiangsu [Jiangsu] provincial museum.

The first voyage began in the summer of 1405 with a 27,800 man crew and 62 (or 63) large and 255 smaller vessels. . . . [In the second voyage, which was launched in late autumn of 1407, the expedition sailed into the Indian Ocean.]

From Carrington Goodrich, ed., *Dictionary of Ming Biography, 1368–1644*, vol. 1, A–L (New York: Columbia University Press, 1976), pp. 194–198, passim. Copyright © 1976 Columbia University Press. Reprinted by permission.

. . . In the summer of 1409 Cheng Ho returned to Nanking to report on his mission to the emperor. Here he built a temple in honor of T'ien-fei [Tianfei], the goddess of the sea, to whose virtue and power he attributed the safe voyages of his fleets. The inscription on the stele erected later (May 3, 1416) has been partly translated into French by Claudine Lombard-Salmon; the complete Chinese text may be found in the book by Louis Gaillard.

After a brief stay in the capital, Cheng Ho was again sent overseas, accompanied by Wang Ching-hung [Wang Jinghong] and Hou Hsien [Hou Xian]. His third voyage was comparable to the first and second in the number of men but with only 48 vessels; it lasted from September, 1409, to June, 1411. This expedition reached the same destination on the Malabar coast of India, but along the way several excursions were made, including brief visits to Siam, Malacca, Sumatra, and Ceylon. It also undertook lumbering operations and gathered fragrant herbs in the Sembilan Islands. . . .

It was the fourth voyage, which began in 1413 and ended in August, 1415, that took the expedition far beyond its earlier destinations. Under the same command but with a crew of 27,670 men and some 63 large vessels, the expedition touched at a number of new places, including the Maldives, Hormuz, the Hadramaut coast, and Aden. In Sumatra the expedition became involved in a local power struggle at Ch'iao-shan [Qiaoshan] (Samudra-Pasai). A usurper by the name of Su-wa-la, after murdering the king, directed his forces against the expedition, but was subsequently defeated and pursued as far as Lambri, where he and his family were captured. The prisoners were taken to Nanking on the return of the fleet. As a result of this voyage, nineteen countries sent envoys and tribute to the Ming court. Chu Ti was so pleased with the results that he rewarded all participants in the expedition according to their ranks.

In December, 1416, Cheng Ho was commissioned to escort home the envoys of the nineteen states, and embarked, possibly in the autumn of 1417, on his fifth voyage, which lasted up to August, 1419. The returning envoys, who had witnessed the delight of the Ming emperor at his first sight of a giraffe, spread the news to other countries. Hence an impressive collection of strange animals, among them lions, leopards, single-humped camels, ostriches, zebras, rhinoceroses, antelopes, and giraffes offered by rulers of several states highlighted this journey.

The spring of 1421 saw the launching of the sixth voyage, but Cheng may not have joined the fleet until later. It returned on September 3, 1422, accompanied by a large number of envoys from such states as Hormuz, Aden, Djofar, La-sa (Al-shsā?), Brawa, Mogadishu, Calicut, Cochin, Cail, Ceylon, the Maldive Islands, Lambri, Sumatra, Aru, Malacca, Kan-pa-li (Coyampadi?), Sulu, Bengal, Borneo, Ku-ma-la (-lang, Cabarruyan Islands?), and Ts'eng-pa (Zanzibar). The number of countries visited on this trip has not been listed, but the expedition reached at least as far as Aden, near the mouth of the Red Sea, and Mogadishu and Brawa on the coast of east Africa. . . .

In the meanwhile Chu Ti had died (August 12, 1424), and almost at once the idea of another maritime expedition came under attack. The emperor designate, Chu Kao-chih [Zhu Gaozhi], promptly (August 28) released from prison Hsia Yüan-chi [Xia Yuanji], perhaps the most outspoken critic of the treasure fleets, and on September 7, the very day of Chu's accession to the throne as the fourth

Ming emperor, other voices joined Hsia's in recommending their abolition. This protest seems to have settled the matter, for in the following February Cheng Ho received an appointment as garrison commander of the Nanking district, and was told to maintain order in his own expeditionary forces, and consult with Wang Ching-hung and two other eunuchs. . . .

Only a few months later the fourth emperor died and for several years the plan to launch another expedition lay dormant. Finally in June, 1430, his successor, the fifth emperor, Chu Chan-chi [Zhu Zhanji], issued an order for the seventh (and what proved to be the last) voyage, but it was not to leave the Fukien [Fujian] coast until a year and a half later. It returned in July, 1433. The mission was intended to regenerate the tributary relationships once maintained under Chu Ti, which had significantly weakened since his death. A score of states were revisited, including those along the coasts of the Arabian peninsula and eastern Africa. In this instance too ambassadors returned with the fleet, bringing such gifts as giraffes, elephants, and horses. Cheng Ho, who was already in his sixties, did not perhaps visit all of them in person, and some of the side missions were conducted by his aides. . . .

. . . What happened to Cheng Ho from this point is not clear. It has customarily been said that he died in 1435 or 1436 at the age of sixty-five, no specific date or site of burial being indicated in contemporary sources. A later source, the *T'ung-chih Shang Chiang liang-hsien chih* [*Tongzhi Shang Jiang liangxian Zhi*] (preface of 1874), 3 / 39a, however, maintains that Cheng Ho died at Calicut and was buried at Niushoushan outside Nanking. If this be true, he must have passed away early in 1433.

The Portuguese in Africa and Brazil

Portugal played a key role in initiating the age of discovery and exploration. A central figure in launching the new era was Prince Henry (1394–1460), who devoted much of his life to directing explorations along the west coast of Africa and advancing Portuguese commercial interests. As a transitional figure, he also exhibited medieval as well as more modern characteristics.

88

The Chronicle of Gomes Eannes de Azurara

The following excerpts are from the chronicle of Gomes Eannes de Azurara (1410–1474), who was a friend and contemporary of Prince Henry. The first portrays Henry's personal qualities and character; the second describes the birth of the African slave trade with Portugal.

QUESTIONS TO CONSIDER

1. In what ways did Prince Henry reflect traits of the medieval age combined with more modern characteristics? Do you think he would have understood and been receptive to Machiavelli's advice (see Reading 84)?
2. What physical qualities of the Africans led the writer to describe some of them as a "marvelous sight" and others as "images of a lower hemisphere"? What were the implications and consequences of these reactions?
3. How did the African natives respond to the Portuguese? According to Azurara, in addition to their enslavement, what caused African suffering to increase?
4. How does this selection reflect the importance of religion as a factor in the expansion of Europe?

Prince Henry

The prince was a man of great wisdom and authority, very discreet and of good memory, but in some matters a little tardy, whether it was from the influence of the phlegm in his nature, or from the choice of his will, directed to some certain end not known to men. His bearing was calm and dignified, his speech and address gentle. He was constant in adversity, humble in prosperity. Never was hatred known to him, nor ill-will toward any man, however great the wrong done him; and such was his benignity in this respect, that wiseacres reproached him as wanting in distributive justice. And this they said, because he left unpunished some of his servants who deserted him at the siege of Tangier, which was the most perilous affair in which he ever stood before or after, not only becoming reconciled to them, but even granting them honourable advancement over others who had served him well, which in the judgment of men was far from their deserts, and this is the only shortcoming of his I have to record. The Infant drank wine only for a very small part of his life and that in his youth, but afterwards he abstained entirely from it.

He ever showed great devotion to the public affairs of this kingdom, toiling greatly for their good advancement and he much delighted in the trial of new undertakings for the profit of all, though with great expense of his own substance, and he keenly enjoyed the labour of arms, especially against the enemies of the holy Faith, while he desired peace with all Christians. Thus he was loved by all alike, for he made himself useful to all and hindered no one. His answers were always gentle and he showed great honour to the standing of every one who came to him, without any lessening of his own estate. A base or unchaste word was never heard to issue from his mouth. He was very obedient to the commands of Holy Church and heard all its offices with great devotion; aye and caused the same to be celebrated in his chapel, with no less splendour and ceremony than they could have been in the college of any Cathedral Church.... Well-nigh one-half of the year he spent in fasting and the hands of the poor never went away empty from his presence.... His heart knew not fear, save the fear of sin....

From Gomes Eannes de Azurara, *The Chronicle of the Discovery and Conquest of Guinea*, vol. 1, trans. C. R. Beazley and Edgar Prestage (London: Hakluyt Society, 1896), pp. 12–15, 81–83, passim.

The African Slave Trade

On the next day, which was the 8th of the month of August, very early in the morning, by reason of the heat, the seamen began to make ready their boats, and to take out their captives and carry them on shore, as they were commanded. And these, placed altogether in that field, were a marvellous sight, for amongst them were some white enough, fair to look upon and well proportioned, others were less white like mulattoes; others again were as black as Ethiops, and so ugly, both in features and in body, as almost to appear the images of a lower hemisphere. But what heart could be so hard as not to be pierced with piteous feeling to see that company? For some kept their heads low and their faces bathed in tears, looking one upon another; others stood groaning very grievously, looking up to the height of heaven, fixing their eyes upon it, crying out loudly, as if asking help of the Father of Nature; others struck their faces with the palms of their hands, throwing themselves at full length upon the ground; others made their lamentations in the manner of a dirge, after the custom of their country. And though we could not understand the words of their language, the sound of it right well accorded with the measure of their sadness. But to increase their sufferings still more, there now arrived those who had charge of the division of the captives and who began to separate one from another in order to make an equal partition of the fifths; and then it was needful to part fathers from sons, husbands from wives, brothers from brothers. No respect was shewn either to friends or relations, but each fell where his lot took him.

And who could finish that partition without very great toil, for as often as they had placed them in one part, the sons, seeing their fathers in another, rose with great energy and rushed over to them; the mothers clasped their other children in their arms, and threw themselves flat on the ground with them, receiving blows with little pity for their own flesh, if only they might not be torn from them.

The Infant was there, mounted upon a powerful steed, and accompanied by his retinue, making distribution of his favours, as a man who sought to gain but small treasure from his share; for he made a very speedy partition of the forty-six souls that fell to him as his fifth. His chief riches lay in his purpose, and he reflected with great pleasure upon the salvation of those souls that before were lost. And certainly his expectation was not in vain, since, as we said before, as soon as they understood our language, they turned Christians with very little ado; and I who put together this history into the present volume, saw in the town of Lagos boys and girls (the children and grandchildren of those first captives) born in this land, as good and true Christians as if they had directly descended, from the beginning of the dispensation of Christ, from those who were first baptised.

89

Pero Vaz de Caminha and the Brazilian Indians

The following selection comes from a letter written by Pero Vaz de Caminha who was with Pedro Cabral's expedition to Brazil in 1500. It describes the first encounter between the Portuguese and the Brazilian Indians.

QUESTIONS TO CONSIDER

1. What was the Portuguese reaction to the Brazilian Indians? Does the writer appear disturbed by any of the native customs? Which ones? Explain why or why not.
2. Compare Portuguese reactions with those of other world travelers such as Ibn Fadlan (see Reading 58) and Ibn Battuta (see Readings 75 and 76).
3. Why did the Brazilian Indians react adversely to the animals, foods, and beverages the Portuguese showed them?
4. What were the immediate and long-range consequences for the Portuguese of these initial encounters? For the Africans and Brazilian Indians?

At the Captain's order Afonso Lopez, our pilot in one of the smaller boats, being a fit and skillful man for such a task, boarded a skiff to enter and sound the harbor. And he seized from a canoe two of the young and huskier natives, one of whom was carrying a bow with six or seven arrows. And many more were standing on the beach with their bows and arrows but did not make use of them. That very night the same two were brought before the captain, where they were received with great pleasure and festivity.

They are darkish red in appearance with good-looking faces and well-shaped noses. They go naked without the slightest covering and pay no special attention to showing or not showing their shameful parts — and in this respect with as much innocence as they have in showing their faces. The lower lips of both natives were punctured and through each puncture a white bone was inserted: the length of the width of one hand and the thickness of a cotton spindle and pointed like a bodkin. They insert it from the inside of the lip, and the part of the bone which remains between lip and teeth is fashioned much like a chess rook. And they seem to place it somehow so that it never annoys them in any way or prevents their speaking or eating or drinking. Their hair is straight and they go with heads shaven nearly to the crown, where the hair grows quite long, and their faces are shaven clean to above the ears. And one of the two was wearing a kind of headdress, which extended from both temples around the back of the head and the ears. He had feather after feather stuck to his hair by means of a kind of smooth concoction, like wax but not; so that he had a very round and very full and very even

From *The Borzoi Anthology of Latin American Literature*, ed. Emir Rodríguez Monegal with the assistance of Thomas Colchie (New York: Alfred A. Knopf, 1987), Vol. I, pp. 12–13.

headdress which was by no means small and was in fact a difficult thing to carry upright.

When the two came before the Captain, he was seated in a chair with a carpet at his feet for a dais and was well dressed with a great gold collar around his neck. And Sancho de Toar, Simão de Miranda, Nicolao Coelho, Aires Correa, and the rest of us there in the boat with the Captain were seated upon the carpet on the floor. We lit the torches and the two entered the cabin, but showed none of the usual courtesies nor spoke to the Captain or to anyone; but one of them noticed the Captain's collar and began to point with his hand to land and then to the collar, as if to say to us that there was gold on the land. And he also noticed a silver candleholder and, in the same way as before, pointed to land and then to the holder, as if there were silver there also. We showed them a gray parrot which belonged to the captain; they took it easily in hand and pointed to land, as if they had parrots there. We showed them a ram, but they made no mention of its being there also. We showed them a chicken; they were somewhat afraid of it and did not want to put a hand out for it, and they touched it, fearfully, only after a while. At that point we gave them bread and cooked fish, sweets, cakes, honey, and dried figs; they did not want to eat most of the foods and tried only one or two things and threw these down at once. We brought them wine in a cup; they barely touched it to their lips and did not like what they tasted or want any more of it. We brought them water in a waterskin; they each took a taste without swallowing any, only to wash their mouths and spit it out. One of them saw some white rosary beads, made signs for us to give them to him, and with these amused himself for quite a while, putting them around his neck and throwing them up in the air, getting them tangled around his arm. And he pointed to land and then to the beads and the Captain's collar, as if to give gold for the beads. Or rather we took this to be his meaning because we wished it to be so, while he really meant to say that he would take the beads and the collar together for himself; this we did not wish to understand because we did not have it to give. And after that he returned the rosary to the one who had given it, and then he and the other stretched out on their backs to sleep on the carpet without showing the least concern for covering their shameful parts, which were not circumcised and were shaven clean of any hair. The Captain ordered us to place pillows for each one beneath their heads and to be careful with the one's headdress, not to break it, and to throw blankets over both of them. And they consented to this and lay there and fell asleep.

90

Antonio Pigafetta, *Magellan's Voyage*

Ferdinand Magellan (1480–1521), a native of Portugal, believed that a passage to the East existed somewhere south of Brazil. Although the King of Portugal refused to support his project, the King of Spain gave him five ships for the voyage. On September 20, 1519, Magellan left Seville to reconnoiter the eastern coast of South America. By the end of November 1520, after suppressing a mutiny, he turned west and sailed through the straits now bearing his name. Sailing northwest, Magellan succeeded in reaching the Philippines but was killed in an encounter with the natives on April 27, 1521. Only one of his ships returned to Spain in 1522, but that ship, by sailing west, completed the first circumnavigation of the earth. Magellan's secretary, Antonio Pigafetta, kept careful records of the long voyage and, in the following excerpts, describes the Pacific crossing and the events surrounding Magellan's death.

QUESTIONS TO CONSIDER

1. How did Magellan's crew survive the sailing across the Pacific Ocean for over three months without fresh food and supplies?
2. What is the significance of Magellan's death and burial on Matan?
3. Compare and contrast the Spanish encounters with natives in the Caribbean and the Philippines with that of the Portuguese in Brazil. How might you account for the differences?

Wednesday, November 28, 1520, we debouched from that strait, engulfing ourselves in the Pacific Sea. We were three months and twenty days without getting any kind of fresh food. We ate biscuit, which was no longer biscuit, but powder of biscuits swarming with worms, for they had eaten the good. It stank strongly of the urine of rats. We drank yellow water that had been putrid for many days. We also ate some ox hides that covered the top of the mainyard to prevent the yard from chafing the shrouds, and which had become exceedingly hard because of the sun, rain, and wind. We left them in the sea for four or five days, and then placed them for a few moments on top of the embers, and so ate them ; and often we ate sawdust from boards. Rats were sold for one-half ducado[1] apiece, and even then we could not get them. But above all the other misfortunes the following was the worst. The gums of both the lower and upper teeth of some of our men swelled, so that they could not eat under any circumstances and therefore died. Nineteen men died from that sickness, and the giant together with an Indian from the country of Verzin. Twenty-five or thirty men fell sick [during that time], in the arms, legs, or in another place, so that but few remained well. However, I, by the grace of God, suffered no sickness. We sailed about four thousand leguas[2] during those three months and twenty days through an open stretch in that Pacific Sea. In truth it is very pacific, for during that time we did not suffer any storm. We saw no land except two desert islets, where we found nothing but birds and trees, for which we called them the Ysolle Infortunate [i.e., the Unfortunate Isles]. They are two hundred leguas apart. We found no anchorage, [but] near them saw many sharks. The first islet lies fifteen degrees of south latitude, and the other nine. Daily we made

From Antonio Pigafetta, *Magellan's Voyage around the World,* vol. 1, trans. and ed. James A. Robertson (Cleveland : Arthur M. Clark Company, 1902), pp. 91–93, 171–179.

1. From *ducat,* an ancient monetary unit of low value.
2. Leagues.

runs of fifty, sixty, or seventy leguas at the catena or at the stern. Had not God and His blessed mother given us so good weather we would all have died of hunger in that exceeding vast sea. Of a verity I believe no such voyage will ever be made [again].

When we left that strait, if we had sailed continuously westward we would have circumnavigated the world without finding other land than the cape of the xi thousand Virgins. The latter is a cape of that strait at the Ocean Sea, straight east and west with Cape Deseado of the Pacific Sea. Both of these capes lie in a latitude of exactly fifty-two degrees toward the Antarctic Pole.

On Friday, April twenty-six, Zula, a chief of the island of Matan,[3] sent one of his sons to present two goats to the captain-general, and to say that he would send him all that he had promised, but that he had not been able to send it to him because of the other chief Cilalulapu, who refused to obey the king of Spagnia.[4] He requested the captain to send him only one boatload of men on the next night, so that they might help him and fight against the other chief. The captain-general decided to go thither with three boatloads. We begged him repeatedly not to go, but he, like a good shepherd, refused to abandon his flock. At midnight, sixty men of us set out armed with corselets[5] and helmets, together with the Christian king, the prince, some of the chief men, and twenty or thirty balanguais. We reached Matan three hours before dawn. The captain did not wish to fight them, but sent a message to the natives by the Moro to the effect that if they would obey the king of Spagnia, recognize the Christian king as their sovereign, and pay us our tribute, he would be their friend; but that if they wished otherwise, they should wait to see how our lances sounded. They replied that if we had lances they had lances of bamboo and stakes hardened with fire. [They asked us] not to proceed to attack them at once, but to wait until morning, so that they might have more men. They said that in order to induce us to go in search of them; for they had dug certain pitholes between the houses in order that we might fall into them. When morning came forty-nine of us leaped into the water up to our thighs, and walked through water for more than two crossbow flights before we could reach the shore. The boats could not approach nearer because of certain rocks in the water. The other eleven men remained behind to guard the boats. When we reached land, those men had formed in three divisions to the number of more than one thousand five hundred persons. When they saw us, they charged down upon us with exceeding loud cries, two divisions on our flanks and the other on our front. When the captain saw that, he formed us into two divisions, and thus did we begin to fight. The musketeers and crossbowmen shot from a distance for about a half-hour, but uselessly; for the shots only passed through the shields which were made of thin wood and the arms [of the bearers]. The captain cried to them, "Cease firing! Cease firing!" but his order was not at all heeded. When the natives saw that we were shooting our muskets to no purpose, crying out they determined to stand firm, but they redoubled their shouts. When our muskets were discharged, the natives would never stand still, but leaped hither and thither, covering themselves with their

3. Spanish name for one of the islands in the Philippines.
4. Spain.
5. A type of chest guard.

shields. They shot so many arrows at us and hurled so many bamboo spears (some of them tipped with iron) at the captain-general, besides pointed stakes hardened with fire, stones, and mud, that we could scarcely defend ourselves. Seeing that, the captain-general sent some men to burn their houses in order to terrify them. When they saw their houses burning, they were roused to greater fury. Two of the men were killed near the houses, while we burned twenty or thirty houses. So many of them charged down upon us that they shot the captain through the right leg with a poisoned arrow. On that account, he ordered us to retire slowly, but the men took to flight, except six or eight of us who remained with the captain. The natives shot only at our legs, for the latter were bare ; and so many were the spears and stones that they hurled at us, that we could offer no resistance. The mortars in the boats could not aid us as they were too far away. So we continued to retire for more than a good crossbow flight from the shore always fighting up to our knees in the water. The natives continued to pursue us, and picking up the same spear four or six times, hurled it at us again and again. Recognizing the captain, so many turned upon him that they knocked his helmet off his head twice, but he stood firmly like a good knight, together with some others. Thus did we fight for more than one hour, refusing to retire farther. An Indian hurled a bamboo spear into the captain's face, but the latter immediately killed him with his lance, which he left in the Indian's body. Then, trying to lay hand on sword, he could draw it out but halfway, because he had been wounded in the arm with a bamboo spear. When the natives saw that, they all hurled themselves upon him. One of them wounded him on the left leg with a large cutlass, which resembles a scimitar, only being larger. That caused the captain to fall face downward, when immediately they rushed upon him with iron and bamboo spears and with their cutlasses, until they killed our mirror, our light, our comfort, and our true guide. When they wounded him, he turned back many times to see whether we were all in the boats. Thereupon, beholding him dead, we, wounded, retreated, as best we could, to the boats, which were already pulling off. The Christian king would have aided us, but the captain charged him before we landed, not to leave his balanghai, but to stay to see how we fought. When the king learned that the captain was dead, he wept. Had it not been for that unfortunate captain, not a single one of us would have been saved in the boats, for while he was fighting the others retired to the boats. I hope through [the efforts of] your most illustrious Lordship that the fame of so noble a captain will not become effaced in our times. Among the many virtues which he possessed, he was more constant than ever any one else in the greatest of adversity. He endured hunger better than all the others, and more accurately than any man in the world did he understand sea charts and navigation. And that this was the truth was seen openly, for no other had had so much natural talent nor the boldness to learn how to circumnavigate the world, as he had almost done. That battle was fought on Saturday, April twenty-seven, 1521. The captain desired to fight on Saturday, because it was the day especially holy to him. Eight of our men were killed with him in that battle, and four Indians, who had become Christians and who had come afterward to aid us were killed by the mortars of the boats. Of the enemy, only fifteen were killed, while many of us were wounded.

In the afternoon the Christian king sent a message with our consent to the people of Matan, to the effect that if they would give us the captain and the other men that had been killed, we would give them as much merchandise as they wished. They answered that they would not give up such a man, as we imagined [they would do], and that they would not give him up for all the riches in the world, but that they intended to keep him as a memorial.

Spain in America

In his eagerness to discover a western sea route to Asia, Christopher Columbus did not anticipate the extent of the Atlantic Ocean when he and his crew set sail from Spain. The following excerpt from Columbus's *Journal* includes an account of the effect on the men of sailing two months without sighting land. After this initial voyage, the Admiral led three additional expeditions which established Spain's base for expansion in the Indies and the Western hemisphere. In February 1519, the Governor of Cuba sent an expedition of some 600 men led by Hernán Cortés to the mainland of Mexico, where the conquistadors encountered Indian resistance. Bernal Díaz del Castillo, a participant in the battle that ensued, describes the historic confrontation in the second selection.

91

Christopher Columbus, *Journal of First Voyage to America*

Columbus and his crew of 90 sailed from Spain on August 3, 1492, arriving at San Salvador in the Bahamas in October. After three additional voyages exploring the Yucatan peninsula and Central America, he died in poverty and neglect, still believing he had discovered the coast of Asia.

QUESTIONS TO CONSIDER

1. What did Columbus tell his crew in order to pacify and encourage them when they complained and became impatient with the length of the voyage?
2. What was the nature of this initial encounter between Spaniards and the natives? What were the reactions of each?
3. In what ways do these journal notes reveal some of Spain's motives for exploration, conquest, and colonization?
4. Consider how the Age of Exploration and Expansion changed the course of world history.

Monday, Oct. 8th. Steered W.S.W. and sailed day and night eleven or twelve leagues ; at times during the night, fifteen miles an hour, if the account can be depended upon. Found the sea like the river at Seville, *"thanks to God,"* says the Admiral. The air soft as that of Seville in April, and so fragrant that it was delicious to breathe it. The weeds appeared very fresh. Many land birds, one of which they took, flying towards the S.W. ; also *grajaos,* ducks, and a pelican were seen.

Tuesday, Oct. 9th. Sailed S.W. five leagues, when the wind changed, and they stood W. by N. four leagues. Sailed in the whole day and night, twenty leagues and a half ; reckoned to the crew seventeen. All night heard birds passing.

Wednesday, Oct. 10th. Steered W.S.W. and sailed at time ten miles an hour, at others twelve, and at others, seven ; day and night made fifty-nine leagues' progress ; reckoned to the crew but forty-four. Here the men lost all patience, and complained of the length of the voyage, but the Admiral encouraged them in the best manner he could, representing the profits they were about to acquire, and adding that it was to no purpose to complain, having come so far, they had nothing to do but continue on to the Indies, till with the help of our Lord, they should arrive there.

Thursday, Oct. 11th. Steered W.S.W. ; and encountered a heavier sea than they had met with before in the whole voyage. Saw pardelas and a green rush near the vessel. The crew of the Pinta saw a cane and a log ; they also picked up a stick which appeared to have been carved with an iron tool, a piece of cane, a plant which grows on land, and a board. The crew of the Niña saw other signs of land, and a stalk loaded with roseberries. These signs encouraged them, and they all grew cheerful. Sailed this day till sunset, twenty-seven leagues.

After sunset steered their original course W. and sailed twelve miles an hour till two hours after midnight, going ninety miles, which are twenty-two leagues and a half ; and as the Pinta was the swiftest sailer, and kept ahead of the Admiral, she discovered land and made the signals which had been ordered.... At two o'clock in the morning the land was discovered, at two leagues' distance ; they took in sail and remained under the squaresail lying to till day, which was Friday, when they found themselves near a small island, one of the Lucayos, called in the Indian language Guanahani. Presently they descried people, naked, and the Admiral landed in the boat, which was armed, along with Martin Alonzo Pinzon, and Vincent Yañez his brother, captain of the Niña. The Admiral bore the royal standard, and the two captains each a banner of the Green Cross, which all the ships had carried ; this contained the initials of the names of the King and Queen each side of the cross, and a crown over each letter. Arrived on shore, they saw trees very green, many streams of water, and divers sorts of fruits. The Admiral called upon the two Captains, and the rest of the crew who landed, as also to Rodrigo de Escovedo, notary of the fleet, and Rodrigo Sánchez, of Segovia, to bear witness that he before all others took possession (as in fact he did) of that island for the King and Queen his sovereigns, making the requisite declarations, which are

From Christopher Columbus, *Journal of First Voyage to America* (New York : A. & C. Boni, 1924), pp. 20–26, passim.

more at large set down here in writing. Numbers of the people of the island straightway collected together. Here follow the precise words of the Admiral : "As I saw that they were very friendly to us, and perceived that they could be much more easily converted to our holy faith by gentle means than by force, I presented them with some red caps, and strings of beads to wear upon the neck, and many other trifles of small value, wherewith they were much delighted, and became wonderfully attached to us. Afterwards they came swimming to the boats, bringing parrots, balls of cotton thread, javelins and many other things which they exchanged for articles we gave them, such as glass beads, and hawk's bells ; which trade was carried on with the utmost good will. But they seemed on the whole to me, to be a very poor people. They all go completely naked, even the women, though I saw but one girl. All whom I saw were young, not above thirty years of age, well made, with fine shapes and faces ; their hair short, and coarse like that of a horse's tail, combed toward the forehead, except a small portion which they suffer to hang down behind, and never cut. . . . It appears to me, that the people are ingenious, and would be good servants ; and I am of opinion that they would very readily become Christians, as they appear to have no religion.

They very quickly learn such words as are spoken to them. If it please our Lord, I intend at my return to carry home six of them to your Highnesses, that they may learn our language. I saw no beasts in the island, nor any sort of animals except parrots." These are the words of the Admiral.

92

Bernal Díaz del Castillo, The Conquest of Mexico

Bernal Díaz del Castillo, one of the soldiers who fought with Cortés in the conquest of Mexico, wrote a vivid account of that event. In the selection that follows, he describes the battle with the Tlascalan Indians who were traditional enemies of the Aztecs and who, after their defeat by the Spaniards, became their allies after witnessing the superiority of their weapons and fighting ability. This alliance was a major factor in the success of the Spanish conquest.

QUESTIONS TO CONSIDER

1. Why were so few conquistadors able to defeat considerably larger numbers of Indians?
2. How did the Spaniards treat their wounded?
3. Compare this battle with the Ottoman conquest of Constantinople (see Reading 79).

The next morning, the 5th September, 1519, we mustered the horses. There was not one of the wounded men who did not come forward to join the ranks and give as much help as he could. The crossbowmen were warned to use the store of darts very cautiously, some of them loading while the others were shooting, and the musketeers were to act in the same way, and the men with sword and shield were instructed to aim their cuts and thrusts at the bowels [of their enemies] so that they would not dare to come as close to us as they did before. With our banner unfurled, and four of our comrades guarding the standard-bearer, Corral, we set out from our camp. We had not marched half a quarter of a league before we began to see the fields crowded with warriors with great feather crests and distinguishing devices, and to hear the blare of horns and trumpets.

All the plain was swarming with warriors and we stood four hundred men in number, and of those many sick and wounded. And we knew for certain that this time our foe came with the determination to leave none of us alive excepting those who would be sacrificed to their idols.

How they began to charge on us! What a hail of stones sped from their slings! As for their bowmen, the javelins lay like corn on the threshing floor; all of them barbed and fire-hardened, which would pierce any armour and would reach the vitals where there is no protection; the men with swords and shields and other arms larger than swords, such as broadswords, and lances, how they pressed on us and with what mighty shouts and yells they charged upon us! The steady bearing of our artillery, musketeers, and crossbowmen, was indeed a help to us, and we did the enemy much damage, and those of them who came close to us with their swords and broadswords met with such sword play from us that they were forced back and they did not close in on us so often as in the last battle. The horsemen were so skillful and bore themselves so valiantly that, after God who protected us, they were our bulwark. However, I saw that our troops were in considerable confusion, so that neither the shouts of Cortés nor the other captains availed to make them close up their ranks, and so many Indians charged down on us that it was only by a miracle of sword play that we could make them give way so that our ranks could be reformed. One thing only saved our lives, and that was that the enemy were so numerous and so crowded one on another that the shots wrought havoc among them, and in addition to this they were not well commanded, for all the captains with their forces could not come into action and from what we knew, since the last battle had been fought, there had been disputes and quarrels between the Captain Xicotenga and another captain the son of Chichimecatecle, over what the one had said to the other, that he had not fought well in the previous battle; to this the son of Chichimecatecle replied that he had fought better than Xicotenga, and was ready to prove it by personal combat. So in this battle Chichimecatecle and his men would not help Xicotenga, and we knew for a certainty that he had also called on the company of Huexotzinco to abstain from fighting. Besides this, ever since the last battle they were afraid of the horses and the musketry, and the swords and crossbows, and our hard fighting; above all was the mercy of God which gave us strength to endure. So Xicotenga was not obeyed by two of the commanders, and we were doing great damage to his men, for we

Bernal Díaz del Castillo, *The True History of the Conquest of New Spain*, trans. and ed. A. P. Maudslay (London : The Hakluyt Society, 1908–1916), 5 vols., I, pp. 237–240, passim.

were killing many of them, and this they tried to conceal ; for as they were so numerous, whenever one of their men was wounded, they immediately bound him up and carried him off on their shoulders, so that in this battle, as in the last, we never saw a dead man.

The enemy was already losing heart, and knowing that the followers of the other two captains whom I have already named, would not come to their assistance, they began to give way. It seems that in that battle we had killed one very important captain, and the enemy began to retreat in good order, our horsemen following them at a hard gallop for a short distance, for they could not sit their horses for fatigue, and when we found ourselves free from that multitude of warriors, we gave thanks to God.

In this engagement, one soldier was killed, and sixty were wounded, and all the horses were wounded as well. They gave me two wounds, one in the head with a stone, and one in the thigh with an arrow ; but this did not prevent me from fighting, and keeping watch, and helping our soldiers, and all the soldiers who were wounded did the same ; for if the wounds were not very dangerous, we had to fight and keep guard, wounded as we were, for few of us remained unwounded.

Then we returned to our camp, well contented, and giving thanks to God. We buried the dead in one of those houses which the Indians had built underground, so that the enemy should not see that we were mortals, but should believe that, as they said, we were Teules. We threw much earth over the top of the house, so that they should not smell the bodies, then we doctored all the wounded with the fat of an Indian. It was cold comfort to be even without salt or oil with which to cure the wounded. There was another want from which we suffered, and it was a severe one — and that was clothes with which to cover ourselves, for such a cold wind came from the snow mountains, that it made us shiver, for our lances and muskets and crossbows made a poor covering.